North America
Vol. II

by

Anthony Trollope

North America
Vol. II
by Anthony Trollope

Copyright © 2024

All Rights reserved.

ISBN: 978-93-64287-55-5

Published by

DOUBLE 9 BOOKS

2/13-B, Ansari Road
Daryaganj, New Delhi – 110002
info@double9books.com
www.double9books.com
Tel. 011-40042856

ABOUT THE AUTHOR

Anthony Trollope (1815-1882) was a renowned English novelist of the Victorian era, best known for his insightful and richly detailed portrayals of 19th-century English society. His prolific writing career produced a vast array of novels, many of which have become classics of English literature. First Novels: Trollope's debut novel, "The Macdermots of Ballycloran", was published in 1847. However, it was not until the publication of "The Warden" in 1855 that he gained significant recognition. Trollope's writing is known for its realism, detailed character development, and exploration of social issues. His characters are often complex and multifaceted, reflecting the diverse nature of human experiences. He employed a straightforward narrative style, often interjecting his own commentary and opinions, which adds a distinctive voice to his works. Trollope's works remain significant in the study of Victorian literature. His keen observations of society, human relationships, and institutional behaviors continue to be appreciated for their depth and insight. Many of his novels have been adapted for television, radio, and stage, keeping his stories and characters alive for new generations. Anthony Trollope's contribution to literature is marked by his ability to combine detailed social critique with engaging storytelling, making him one of the enduring figures of English literature.

CONTENTS

CHAPTER I
WASHINGTON

The site of the present city of Washington was chosen with three special views; firstly, that being on the Potomac it might have the full advantage of water-carriage and a sea-port; secondly, that it might be so far removed from the seaboard as to be safe from invasion; and, thirdly, that it might be central alike to all the States. It was presumed when Washington was founded that these three advantages would be secured by the selected position. As regards the first, the Potomac affords to the city but few of the advantages of a sea-port. Ships can come up, but not ships of large burthen. The river seems to have dwindled since the site was chosen; and at present it is, I think, evident that Washington can never be great in its shipping. *Statio benefida carinis* can never be its motto. As regards the second point, singularly enough Washington is the only city of the Union that has been in an enemy's possession since the United States became a nation. In the war of 1812 it fell into our hands, and we burnt it. As regards the third point, Washington, from the lie of the land, can hardly have been said to be centrical at any time. Owing to the irregularities of the coast it is not easy of access by railways from different sides. Baltimore would have been far better. But as far as we can now see, and as well as we can now judge, Washington will soon be on the borders of the nation to which it belongs, instead of at its centre. I fear, therefore, that we must acknowledge that the site chosen for his country's capital by George Washington has not been fortunate.

I have a strong idea, which I expressed before in speaking of the capital of the Canadas, that no man can ordain that on such a spot shall be built a great and thriving city. No man can so ordain even though he leave behind him, as was the case with Washington, a prestige sufficient to bind his successors to his wishes. The political leaders of the country have done what they could for Washington. The pride of the nation has endeavoured to sustain the character of its chosen metropolis. There has been no rival, soliciting favour on the strength of other charms. The country has all been agreed on the point since the father of the country first commenced the work. Florence and Rome in Italy have each their pretensions; but in the States no other city has put itself forward for the honour of entertaining Congress. And yet Washington has been a failure. It is commerce that makes great cities, and commerce has refused to back the General's choice. New York and Philadelphia, without any political power, have become great among the cities of the earth. They are beaten by none except by London and Paris. But Washington is but a ragged, unfinished collection of unbuilt broad streets, as to the completion of which there can now, I imagine, be but little hope.

Of all places that I know it is the most ungainly and most unsatisfactory; — I fear I must also say the most presumptuous in its pretensions. There is a map of Washington accurately laid down; and taking that map with him in his journeyings a man may lose himself in the streets, not as one loses oneself in London between Shoreditch and Russell Square, but as one does so in the deserts of the Holy Land, between Emmaus and Arimathea. In the first place no one knows where the places are, or is sure of their existence, and then between their presumed localities the country is wild, trackless, unbridged, uninhabited, and desolate. Massachusetts Avenue runs the whole length of the city, and is inserted on the maps as a full-blown street, about four miles in length. Go there, and you will find yourself not only out of town, away among the fields, but you will find yourself beyond the fields, in an uncultivated, undrained wilderness. Tucking your trousers up to your knees you will wade through the bogs, you will lose yourself among rude hillocks, you will be out of the reach of humanity. The unfinished dome of the Capitol will loom before you in the distance, and you will think that you approach the ruins of some western Palmyra. If you are a sportsman, you will desire to shoot snipe within sight of the President's house. There is much unsettled land within the States of America, but I think none so desolate in its state of nature as three-fourths of the ground on which is supposed to stand the city of Washington.

The city of Washington is something more than four miles long, and is something more than two miles broad. The land apportioned to it is nearly as compact as may be, and it exceeds in area the size of a parallelogram four miles long by two broad. These dimensions are adequate for a noble city, for a city to contain a million of inhabitants. It is impossible to state with accuracy the actual population of Washington, for it fluctuates exceedingly. The place is very full during Congress, and very empty during the recess. By which I mean it to be understood that those streets, which are blessed with houses, are full when Congress meets. I do not think that Congress makes much difference to Massachusetts Avenue. I believe that the city never contains as many as eighty thousand, and that its permanent residents are less than sixty thousand.

But, it will be said, — was it not well to prepare for a growing city? Is it not true that London is choked by its own fatness, not having been endowed at its birth or during its growth, with proper means for accommodating its own increasing proportions? Was it not well to lay down fine avenues and broad streets, so that future citizens might find a city well prepared to their hand?

There is no doubt much in such an argument, but its correctness must be tested by its success. When a man marries it is well that he should make provision for a coming family. But a Benedict, who early in his career shall have carried his friends with considerable self-applause through half-a-dozen nurseries and at the end of twelve years shall still be the father of one rickety baby, will incur a certain amount of ridicule. It is very well to be prepared for good fortune, but one should limit one's preparation within a reasonable scope. Two miles by one might perhaps have done for the skeleton sketch of a new city. Less than half that would contain much more than the present population of Washington; and there are, I fear, few towns in the Union so little likely to enjoy any speedy increase.

Three avenues sweep the whole length of Washington;—Virginia Avenue, Pennsylvania Avenue, and Massachusetts Avenue. But Pennsylvania Avenue is the only one known to ordinary men, and the half of that only is so known. This avenue is the backbone of the city, and those streets which are really inhabited cluster round that half of it which runs westward from the Capitol. The eastern end, running from the front of the Capitol, is again a desert. The plan of the city is somewhat complicated. It may truly be called "a mighty maze, but not without a plan." The Capitol was intended to be the centre of the city. It faces eastward, away from the Potomac,—or rather from the main branch of the Potomac, and also unfortunately from the main body of the town. It turns its back upon the chief thoroughfare, upon the Treasury buildings, and upon the President's house; and indeed upon the whole place. It was, I suppose, intended that the streets to the eastward should be noble and populous, but hitherto they have come to nothing. The building therefore is wrong side foremost, and all mankind who enter it, senators, representatives, and judges included, go in at the back-door. Of course it is generally known that in the Capitol is the Chamber of the Senate, that of the House of Representatives, and the Supreme Judicial Court of the Union. It may be said that there are two centres in Washington, this being one and the President's house the other. At these centres the main avenues are supposed to cross each other, which avenues are called by the names of the respective States. At the Capitol, Pennsylvania Avenue, New Jersey Avenue, Delaware Avenue, and Maryland Avenue converge. They come from one extremity of the city to the square of the Capitol on one side, and run out from the other side of it to the other extremity of the city. Pennsylvania Avenue, New York Avenue, Vermont Avenue, and Connecticut Avenue do the same at what is generally called President's Square. In theory, or on paper, this seems to be a clear and intelligible arrangement; but it does not work well. These centre depots are large spaces, and consequently one portion of a street is removed a considerable distance from the other. It is as though the same name should be given to two streets, one of which entered St. James's Park at Buckingham Gate, while the other started from the Park at Marlborough House. To inhabitants the matter probably is not of much moment, as it is well known that this portion of such an avenue and that portion of such another avenue are merely myths,—unknown lands away in the wilds. But a stranger finds himself in the position of being sent across the country knee-deep into the mud, wading through snipe grounds, looking for civilization where none exists.

All these avenues have a slanting direction. They are so arranged that none of them run north and south or east and west; but the streets, so called, all run in accordance with the points of the compass. Those from east to west are A Street, B Street, C Street, and so on,—counting them away from the Capitol on each side, so that there are two A streets and two B streets. On the map these streets run up to V Street, both right and left,—V Street North and V Street South. Those really known to mankind are E, F, G, H, I, and K Streets North. Then those streets which run from north to south are numbered First Street, Second Street, Third Street, and so on, on each front of the Capitol, running to Twenty-fourth or Twenty-fifth Street on each side. Not very many of these have any existence, or I might perhaps more properly say, any vitality in their existence.

Such is the plan of the city, that being the arrangement and those the dimensions intended by the original architects and founders of Washington; but the inhabitants have hitherto confined themselves to Pennsylvania Avenue West, and to the streets abutting from it or near to it. Whatever address a stranger may receive, however perplexing it may seem to him, he may be sure that the house indicated is near Pennsylvania Avenue. If it be not, I should recommend him to pay no attention to the summons. Even in those streets with which he will become best acquainted, the houses are not continuous. There will be a house, and then a blank; then two houses, and then a double blank. After that a hut or two, and then probably an excellent, roomy, handsome family mansion. Taken altogether, Washington as a city is most unsatisfactory, and falls more grievously short of the thing attempted than any other of the great undertakings of which I have seen anything in the States. San Jose, the capital of the republic of Costa Rica, in Central America, has been prepared and arranged as a new city in the same way. But even San Jose comes nearer to what was intended than does Washington.

For myself, I do not believe in cities made after this fashion. Commerce, I think, must select the site of all large congregations of mankind. In some mysterious way she ascertains what she wants, and having acquired that, draws men in thousands round her properties. Liverpool, New York, Lyons, Glasgow, Venice, Marseilles, Hamburg, Calcutta, Chicago, and Leghorn, have all become populous, and are or have been great, because trade found them to be convenient for its purposes. Trade seems to have ignored Washington altogether. Such being the case, the Legislature and the Executive of the country together have been unable to make of Washington anything better than a straggling congregation of buildings in a wilderness. We are now trying the same experiment at Ottawa, in Canada, having turned our back upon Montreal in dudgeon. The site of Ottawa is more interesting than that of Washington, but I doubt whether the experiment will be more successful. A new town for art, fashion, and politics has been built at Munich, and there it seems to answer the expectation of the builders; but at Munich there is an old city as well, and commerce had already got some considerable hold on the spot before the new town was added to it.

The streets of Washington, such as exist, are all broad. Throughout the town there are open spaces,—spaces, I mean, intended to be open by the plan laid down for the city. At the present moment it is almost all open space. There is also a certain nobility about the proposed dimensions of the avenues and squares. Desirous of praising it in some degree, I can say that the design is grand. The thing done, however, falls so infinitely short of that design, that nothing but disappointment is felt. And I fear that there is no look-out into the future which can justify a hope that the design will be fulfilled. It is therefore a melancholy place. The society into which one falls there consists mostly of persons who are not permanently resident in the capital; but of those who were permanent residents I found none who spoke of their city with affection. The men and women of Boston think that the sun shines nowhere else;—and Boston Common is very pleasant. The New Yorkers believe in Fifth Avenue with an unswerving faith; and Fifth Avenue is calculated to inspire a faith. Philadelphia to a Philadelphian is the centre of the universe, and the progress of Philadelphia, perhaps, justifies the partiality. The same thing may be said of Chicago, of Buffalo, and of Baltimore. But the same thing cannot be said in any degree of Washington. They who belong to it turn up their noses at it. They feel that they live surrounded by a failure. Its grand names are as yet false, and none of the efforts made have hitherto been successful. Even in winter, when Congress is sitting, Washington is melancholy;—but Washington in summer must surely be the saddest spot on earth.

There are six principal public buildings in Washington, as to which no expense seems to have been spared, and in the construction of which a certain amount of success has been obtained. In most of these this success has been more or less marred by an independent deviation from recognized rules of architectural taste. These are the Capitol, the Post-office, the Patent-office, the Treasury, the President's house, and the Smithsonian Institute. The five first are Grecian, and the last in Washington is called—Romanesque. Had I been left to classify it by my own unaided lights, I should have called it bastard Gothic.

The Capitol is by far the most imposing; and though there is much about it with which I cannot but find fault, it certainly is imposing. The present building was, I think, commenced in 1815, the former Capitol having been destroyed by the English in the war of 1812-13. It was then finished according to the original plan, with a fine portico and well-proportioned pediment above it,—looking to the east. The outer flight of steps, leading up to this from the eastern approach, is good and in excellent taste. The expanse of the building to the right and left, as then arranged, was well proportioned, and, as far as we can now judge, the then existing dome was well proportioned also. As seen from the east the original building must have been in itself very fine. The stone is beautiful, being bright almost as marble, and I do not know that there was any great architectural defect to offend the eye. The figures in the pediment are mean. There is now in the Capitol a group apparently prepared for a pediment, which is by no means mean. I was informed that they were intended for this position; but they, on the other hand, are too good for such a place, and are also too numerous. This set of statues is by Crawford. Most of them are well known, and they are very fine. They now stand within the old chamber of the Representative House, and the pity is, that if elevated to such a position as that indicated, they can never be really seen. There are models of them all at West Point, and some of them I have seen at other places in marble. The Historical Society at New York has one or two of them. In and about the front of the Capitol there are other efforts of sculpture,—imposing in their size, and assuming, if not affecting, much in the attitudes chosen. Statuary at Washington runs too much on two subjects, which are repeated perhaps almost ad nauseam; one is that of a stiff, steady-looking, healthy, but ugly individual, with a square jaw and big jowl, which represents the great General; he does not prepossess the beholder, because he appears to be thoroughly ill-natured. And the other represents a melancholy, weak figure without any hair, but often covered with feathers, and is intended to typify the red Indian. The red Indian is generally supposed to be receiving comfort; but it is manifest that he never enjoys the comfort ministered to him. There is a gigantic statue of Washington, by Greenough, out in the grounds in front of the building. The figure is seated and holding up one of its arms towards the city. There is about it a kind of weighty magnificence; but it is stiff, ungainly, and altogether without life.

But the front of the original building is certainly grand. The architect who designed it must have had skill, taste, and nobility of conception; but even this was spoilt, or rather wasted, by the fact that the front is made to look upon nothing, and is turned from the city. It is as though the *façade* of the London Post-office had been made to face the Goldsmiths' Hall. The Capitol stands upon the side of a hill, the front occupying a much higher position than the back; consequently they who enter it from the back—and everybody does so enter it—are first called on to rise to the level of the lower floor by a stiff ascent of exterior steps, which are in no way grand or imposing, and then, having entered by a mean back-door, are instantly obliged to ascend again by another flight,—by stairs sufficiently appropriate to a back entrance, but altogether unfitted for the chief approach to such a building. It may, of course, be said that persons who are particular in such matters should go in at the front door and not at the back; but one must take these things as one finds them. The entrance by which the Capitol is approached is such as I have described. There are mean little brick chimneys at the left hand as one walks in, attached to modern bakeries which have been constructed in the basement for the use of the soldiers; and there is on the other hand the road by which waggons find their way to the underground region with fuel, stationery, and other matters desired by senators and representatives,—and at present by bakers also.

In speaking of the front I have spoken of it as it was originally designed and built. Since that period very heavy wings have been added to the pile;—wings so heavy that they are or seem to be much larger than the original structure itself. This, to my thinking, has destroyed the symmetry of the whole. The wings, which in themselves are by no means devoid of beauty, are joined to the centre by passages so narrow that from exterior points of view the light can be seen through them. This robs the mass of all oneness, of all entirety as a whole, and gives a scattered straggling appearance where there should be a look of massiveness and integrity. The dome also has been raised, a double drum having been given to it. This is unfinished and should not therefore yet be judged; but I cannot think that the increased height will be an improvement. This again, to my eyes, appears to be straggling rather than massive. At a distance it commands attention, and to one journeying through the desert places of the city gives that idea of Palmyra which I have before mentioned.

Nevertheless, and in spite of all that I have said, I have had pleasure in walking backwards and forwards, and through the grounds which lie before the eastern front of the Capitol. The space for the view is ample, and the thing to be seen has points which are very grand. If the Capitol were finished and all Washington were built around it, no man would say that the house in which Congress sat disgraced the city.

Going west, but not due west, from the Capitol, Pennsylvania Avenue stretches in a right line to the Treasury Chambers. The distance is beyond a mile, and men say, scornfully, that the two buildings have been put so far apart in order to save the Secretaries who sit in the bureaux from a too rapid influx of members of Congress. This statement I by no means indorse; but it is undoubtedly the fact that both senators and representatives are very diligent in their calls upon gentlemen high in office. I have been present on some such occasions, and it has always seemed to me that questions of patronage have been paramount. This reach of Pennsylvania Avenue is the quarter for the best shops of Washington,—that is to say, the frequented side of it is so,—that side which is on your right as you leave the Capitol. Of the other side the world knows nothing. And very bad shops they are. I doubt whether there be any town in the world at all equal in importance to Washington, which is in such respects so ill provided. The shops are bad and dear. In saying this I am guided by the opinions of all whom I heard speak on the subject. The same thing was told me of the hotels. Hearing that the city was very full at the time of my visit—full to overflowing—I had obtained private rooms through a friend before I went there. Had I not done so, I might have lain in the streets, or have made one with three or four others in a small room at some third-rate inn. There had never been so great a throng in the town. I am bound to say that my friend did well for me. I found myself put up at the house of one Wormley, a coloured man, in I Street, to whose attention I can recommend any Englishman who may chance to want quarters in Washington. He has an hotel on one side of the street, and private lodging-houses on the other in which I found myself located. From what I heard of the hotels I conceived myself to be greatly in luck. Willard's is the chief of these, and the everlasting crowd and throng of men with which the halls and passages of the house were always full, certainly did not seem to promise either privacy or comfort. But then there are places in which privacy and comfort are not expected,—are hardly even desired,—and Washington is one of them.

The Post-office and the Patent-office lie a little away from Pennsylvania Avenue in F Street, and are opposite to each other. The Post-office is certainly a very graceful building. It is square, and hardly can be said to have any settled front or any grand entrance. It is not approached by steps, but stands flush on the ground, alike on each of the four sides. It is ornamented with Corinthian pilasters, but is not over ornamented. It is certainly a structure creditable to any city. The streets around it are all unfinished, and it is approached through seas of mud and sloughs of despond, which have been contrived, as I imagine, to lessen, if possible, the crowd of callers, and lighten in this way the overtasked officials within. That side by which the public in general were supposed to approach was, during my sojourn, always guarded by vast mountains of flour-barrels. Looking up at the windows of the building I perceived also that barrels were piled within, and then I knew that the Post-office had become a provision depot for the army. The official arrangements here for the public were so bad as to be absolutely barbarous. I feel some remorse in saying this, for I was myself treated with the utmost courtesy by gentlemen holding high positions in the office,—to which I was specially attracted by my own connection with the Post-office in England. But I do not think that such courtesy should hinder me from telling what I saw that was bad,—seeing that it would not hinder me from telling what I saw that was good. In Washington there is but one Post-office. There are no iron pillars or wayside letter-boxes, as are to be found in other towns of the Union;—no subsidiary offices at which stamps can be bought and letters posted. The distances of the city are very great, the means of transit through the city very limited, the dirt of the city ways unrivalled in depth and tenacity; and yet there is but one Post-office. Nor is there any established system of letter-carriers. To those who desire it, letters are brought out and delivered by carriers who charge a separate porterage for that service; but the rule is that letters shall be delivered from the window. For strangers this is of course a necessity of their position; and I found that when once I had left instructions that my letters should be delivered, those instructions were carefully followed. Indeed nothing could exceed the civility of the officials within;—but so also nothing can exceed the barbarity of the arrangements without. The purchase of stamps I found to be utterly impracticable. They were sold at a window in a corner, at which newspapers were also delivered, to which there was no regular ingress, and from which there was no egress. It would generally be deeply surrounded by a crowd of muddy soldiers, who would wait there patiently till time should enable them to approach the window. The delivery of letters was almost more tedious, though in that there was a method. The aspirants stood in a long line, *en cue*, as we are told by Carlyle that the bread-seekers used to approach the bakers' shops at Paris during the Revolution. This "cue" would sometimes project out into the street. The work inside was done very slowly. The clerk had no facility, by use of a desk or otherwise, for running through the letters under the initials denominated, but turned letter by letter through his hand. To one questioner out of ten would a letter be given. It no doubt may be said in excuse for this that the presence of the army round Washington caused at that period special inconvenience; and that plea should of course be taken, were it not that a very trifling alteration in the management within would have remedied all the inconvenience. As a building the Washington Post-office is very good; as the centre of a most complicated and difficult department, I believe it to be well managed: but as regards the special accommodation given by it to the city in which it stands, much cannot, I think, be said in its favour.

Opposite to that which is, I presume, the back of the Post-office, stands the Patent-office. This also is a grand building, with a fine portico of Doric pillars at each of its three fronts. These are approached by flights of steps, more gratifying to the eye than to the legs. The whole structure is massive and grand, and, if the streets round it were finished, would be imposing. The utilitarian spirit of the nation has, however, done much toward marring the appearance of the building, by piercing it with windows altogether unsuited to it, both in number and size. The walls, even under the porticoes, have been so pierced, in order that the whole space might be utilized without loss of light; and the effect is very mean. The windows are small and without ornament, — something like a London window of the time of George III. The effect produced by a dozen such at the back of a noble Doric porch, looking down among the pillars, may be imagined.

In the interior of this building the Minister of the Interior holds his court, and of course also the Commissioners of Patents. Here is, in accordance with the name of the building, a museum of models of all patents taken out. I wandered through it, gazing with listless eye, now upon this, and now upon that; but to me, in my ignorance, it was no better than a large toy-shop. When I saw an ancient dusty white hat, with some peculiar appendage to it which was unintelligible, it was no more to me than any other old white hat. But had I been a man of science, what a tale it might have told! Wandering about through the Patent-office I also found a hospital for soldiers. A British officer was with me who pronounced it to be, in its kind, very good. At any rate it was sweet, airy, and large. In these days the soldiers had got hold of everything.

The Treasury Chambers is as yet an unfinished building. The front to the south has been completed; but that to the north has not been built. Here at the north stands as yet the old Secretary of State's office. This is to come down, and the Secretary of State is to be located in the new building, which will be added to the Treasury. This edifice will probably strike strangers more forcibly than any other in the town, both from its position and from its own character. It stands with its side to Pennsylvania Avenue, but the avenue here has turned round, and runs due north and south, having taken a twist, so as to make way for the Treasury and for the President's house, through both of which it must run had it been carried straight on throughout. These public offices stand with their side to the street, and the whole length is ornamented with an exterior row of Ionic columns raised high above the footway. This is perhaps the prettiest thing in the city, and when the front to the north has been completed, the effect will be still better. The granite monoliths which have been used, and which are to be used, in this building are very massive. As one enters by the steps to the south there are two flat stones, one on each side of the ascent, the surface of each of which is about 20 feet by 18. The columns are, I think, all monoliths. Of those which are still to be erected, and which now lie about in the neighbouring streets, I measured one or two—one which was still in the rough I found to be 32 feet long by 5 feet broad, and 4½ deep. These granite blocks have been brought to Washington from the State of Maine. The finished front of this building, looking down to the Potomac, is very good; but to my eyes this also has been much injured by the rows of windows which look out from the building into the space of the portico.

The President's house—or the White House as it is now called all the world over—is a handsome mansion fitted for the chief officer of a great Republic, and nothing more. I think I may say that we have private houses in London considerably larger. It is neat and pretty, and with all its immediate outside belongings calls down no adverse criticism. It faces on to a small garden, which seems to be always accessible to the public, and opens out upon that everlasting Pennsylvania Avenue, which has now made another turn. Here in front of the White House is President's Square, as it is generally called. The technical name is, I believe, La Fayette Square. The houses round it are few in number,—not exceeding three or four on each side, but they are among the best in Washington, and the whole place is neat and well kept. President's Square is certainly the most attractive part of the city. The garden of the square is always open, and does not seem to suffer from any public ill-usage; by which circumstance I am again led to suggest that the gardens of our London squares might be thrown open in the same way. In the centre of this one at Washington, immediately facing the President's house, is an equestrian statue of General Jackson. It is very bad; but that it is not nearly as bad as it might be is proved by another equestrian statue,—of General Washington,—erected in the centre of a small garden-plat at the end of Pennsylvania Avenue, near the bridge leading to Georgetown. Of all the statues on horseback which I ever saw, either in marble or bronze, this is by far the worst and most ridiculous. The horse is most absurd, but the man sitting on the horse is manifestly drunk. I should think the time must come when this figure at any rate will be removed.

I did not go inside the President's house, not having had while at Washington an opportunity of paying my personal respects to Mr. Lincoln. I had been told that this was to be done without trouble, but when I inquired on the subject I found that this was not exactly the case. I believe there are times when anybody may walk into the President's house without an introduction; but that, I take it, is not considered to be the proper way of doing the work. I found that something like a favour would be incurred, or that some disagreeable trouble would be given, if I made a request to be presented, —and therefore I left Washington without seeing the great man.

The President's house is nice to look at, but it is built on marshy ground, not much above the level of the Potomac, and is very unhealthy. I was told that all who live there become subject to fever and ague, and that few who now live there have escaped it altogether. This comes of choosing the site of a new city, and decreeing that it shall be built on this or on that spot. Large cities, especially in these latter days, do not collect themselves in unhealthy places. Men desert such localities, —or at least do not congregate at them when their character is once known. But the poor President cannot desert the White House. He must make the most of the residence which the nation has prepared for him.

Of the other considerable public building of Washington, called the Smithsonian Institution, I have said that its style was bastard Gothic; by this I mean that its main attributes are Gothic, but that liberties have been taken with it, which, whether they may injure its beauty or no, certainly are subversive of architectural purity. It is built of red stone, and is not ugly in itself. There is a very nice Norman porch to it, and little bits of Lombard Gothic have been well copied from Cologne. But windows have been fitted in with stilted arches, of which the stilts seem to crack and bend, so narrow are they and so high. And then the towers with high pinnacled roofs are a mistake, —unless indeed they be needed to give to the whole structure that name of Romanesque which it has assumed. The building is used for museums and lectures, and was given to the city by one James Smithson, an Englishman. I cannot say that the city of Washington seems to be grateful, for all to whom I spoke on the subject hinted that the Institution was a failure. It is to be remarked that nobody in Washington is proud of Washington, or of anything in it. If the Smithsonian Institution were at New York or at Boston, one would have a different story to tell.

There has been an attempt made to raise at Washington a vast obelisk to the memory of Washington, —the first in war and first in peace, as the country is proud to call him. This obelisk is a fair type of the city. It is unfinished, —not a third of it having as yet been erected, —and in all human probability ever will remain so. If finished it would be the highest monument of its kind standing on the face of the globe,—and yet, after all, what would it be even then as compared with one of the great pyramids? Modern attempts cannot bear comparison with those of the old world in simple vastness. But in lieu of simple vastness, the modern world aims to achieve either beauty or utility. By the Washington monument, if completed, neither would be achieved. An obelisk with the proportions of a needle may be very graceful; but an obelisk which requires an expanse of flat-roofed, sprawling buildings for its base, and of which the shaft shall be as big as a cathedral tower, cannot be graceful. At present some third portion of the shaft has been built, and there it stands. No one has a word to say for it. No one thinks that money will ever again be subscribed for its completion. I saw somewhere a box of plate-glass kept for contributions for this purpose, and looking in perceived that two half-dollar pieces had been given;—but both of them were bad. I was told also that the absolute foundation of the edifice is bad;—that the ground, which is near the river and swampy, would not bear the weight intended to be imposed on it.

A sad and saddening spot was that marsh, as I wandered down on it all alone one Sunday afternoon. The ground was frozen and I could walk dry-shod, but there was not a blade of grass. Around me on all sides were cattle in great numbers—steers and big oxen—lowing in their hunger for a meal. They were beef for the army, and never again I suppose would it be allowed to them to fill their big maws and chew the patient cud. There, on the brown, ugly, undrained field, within easy sight of the President's house, stood the useless, shapeless, graceless pile of stones. It was as though I were looking on the genius of the city. It was vast, pretentious, bold, boastful with a loud voice, already taller by many heads than other obelisks, but nevertheless still in its infancy,—ugly, unpromising, and false. The founder of the monument had said, Here shall be the obelisk of the world! and the founder of the city had thought of his child somewhat in the same strain. It is still possible that both city and monument shall be completed; but at the present moment nobody seems to believe in the one or in the other. For myself I have much faith in the American character, but I cannot believe either in Washington city or in the Washington monument. The boast made has been too loud, and the fulfilment yet accomplished has been too small!

Have I as yet said that Washington was dirty in that winter of 1861-1862? Or, I should rather ask, have I made it understood that in walking about Washington one waded as deep in mud as one does in floundering through an ordinary ploughed field in November? There were parts of Pennsylvania Avenue which would have been considered heavy ground by most hunting-men, and through some of the remoter streets none but light weights could have lived long. This was the state of the town when I left it in the middle of January. On my arrival in the middle of December, everything was in a cloud of dust. One walked through an atmosphere of floating mud; for the dirt was ponderous and thick, and very palpable in its atoms. Then came a severe frost and a little snow; and if one did not fall while walking, it was very well. After that we had the thaw; and Washington assumed its normal winter condition. I must say that, during the whole of this time, the atmosphere was to me exhilarating; but I was hardly out of the doctor's hands while I was there, and he did not support my theory as to the goodness of the air. "It is poisoned by the soldiers," he said, "and everybody is ill." But then my doctor was perhaps a little tinged with southern proclivities.

On the Virginian side of the Potomac stands a country-house called Arlington Heights, from which there is a fine view down upon the city. Arlington Heights is a beautiful spot,—having all the attractions of a fine park in our country. It is covered with grand timber. The ground is varied and broken, and the private roads about sweep here into a dell and then up a brae-side, as roads should do in such a domain. Below it was the Potomac, and immediately on the other side stands the city of Washington. Any city seen thus is graceful; and the white stones of the big buildings when the sun gleams on them, showing the distant rows of columns, seem to tell something of great endeavour and of achieved success. It is the place from whence Washington should be seen by those who wish to think well of the present city and of its future prosperity. But is it not the case that every city is beautiful from a distance?

The house at Arlington Heights is picturesque, but neither large nor good. It has before it a high Greek colonnade, which seems to be almost bigger than the house itself. Had such been built in a city,—and many such a portico does stand in cities through the States,—it would be neither picturesque nor graceful; but here it is surrounded by timber, and as the columns are seen through the trees, they gratify the eye rather than offend it. The place did belong, and as I think does still belong, to the family of the Lees,—if not already confiscated. General Lee, who is or would be the present owner, bears high command in the army of the Confederalists, and knows well by what tenure he holds, or is likely to hold, his family property. The family were friends of General Washington, whose seat, Mount Vernon, stands about twelve miles lower down the river; and here, no doubt, Washington often stood, looking on the site he had chosen. If his spirit could stand there now and look around upon the masses of soldiers by which his capital is surrounded, how would it address the city of his hopes? When he saw that every foot of the neighbouring soil was desecrated by a camp, or torn into loathsome furrows of mud by cannon and army waggons,—that agriculture was gone, and that every effort both of North and South was concentrated on the art of killing; when he saw that this was done on the very spot chosen by himself for the centre temple of an everlasting union, what would he then say as to that boast made on his behalf by his countrymen that he was first in war and first in peace? Washington was a great man, and I believe a good man. I, at any rate, will not belittle him. I think that he had the firmness and audacity necessary for a revolutionary leader, that he had honesty to preserve him from the temptations of ambition and ostentation, and that he had the good sense to be guided in civil matters by men who had studied the laws of social life and the theories of free government. He was *justus et tenax propositi*; and in periods that might well have dismayed a smaller man, he feared neither the throne to which he opposed himself, nor the changing voices of the fellow-citizens for whose welfare he had fought. But sixty or seventy years will not suffice to give to a man the fame of having been first among all men. Washington did much, and I for one do not believe that his work will perish. But I have always found it difficult,—I may say impossible,—to sound his praises in his own land. Let us suppose that a courteous Frenchman ventures an opinion among Englishmen that Wellington was a great general, would he feel disposed to go on with his eulogium when encountered on two or three sides at once with such observations as the following:—"I should rather calculate he was; about the first that ever did live or ever will live. Why, he whipped your Napoleon everlasting whenever he met him. He whipped everybody out of the field. There warn't anybody ever lived was able to stand nigh him, and there won't come any like him again. Sir, I guess our Wellington never had his likes on your side of the water. Such men can't grow in a down-trodden country of slaves and paupers." Under such circumstances the Frenchman would probably be shut up. And when I strove to speak of Washington I generally found myself shut up also.

Arlington Heights, when I was at Washington, was the head-quarters of General M'Dowell, the General to whom is attributed—I believe most wrongfully—the loss of the battle of Bull's Run. The whole place was then one camp. The fences had disappeared. The gardens were trodden into mud. The roads had been cut to pieces, and new tracks made everywhere through the grounds. But the timber still remained. Some no doubt had fallen, but enough stood for the ample ornamentation of the place. I saw placards up, prohibiting the destruction of the trees, and it is to be hoped that they have been spared. Very little in this way has been spared in the country all around.

Mount Vernon, Washington's own residence, stands close over the Potomac, above six miles below Alexandria. It will be understood that the capital is on the eastern, or Maryland side of the river, and that Arlington

Heights, Alexandria, and Mount Vernon are in Virginia. The river Potomac divided the two old colonies, or States as they afterwards became; but when Washington was to be built, a territory, said to be ten miles square, was cut out of the two States and was called the district of Columbia. The greater portion of this district was taken from Maryland, and on that the city was built. It comprised the pleasant town of Georgetown, which is now a suburb—and the only suburb—of Washington. The portion of the district on the Virginian side included Arlington Heights, and went so far down the river as to take in the Virginian city of Alexandria. This was the extreme western point of the district; but since that arrangement was made, the State of Virginia petitioned to have their portion of Columbia back again, and this petition was granted. Now it is felt that the land on both sides of the river should belong to the city, and the Government is anxious to get back the Virginian section. The city and the immediate vicinity are freed from all State allegiance, and are under the immediate rule of the United States Government,—having of course its own municipality; but the inhabitants have no political power, as power is counted in the States. They vote for no political officer, not even for the President, and return no member to Congress, either as a senator or as a representative. Mount Vernon was never within the district of Columbia.

When I first made inquiry on the subject I was told that Mount Vernon at that time was not to be reached;—that though it was not in the hands of the rebels, neither was it in the hands of Northerners, and that therefore strangers could not go there; but this, though it was told to me and others by those who should have known the facts, was not the case. I had gone down the river with a party of ladies, and we were opposite to Mount Vernon; but on that occasion we were assured we could not land. The rebels, we were told, would certainly seize the ladies, and carry them off into Secessia. On hearing which the ladies were of course doubly anxious to be landed. But our stern commander, for we were on a Government boat, would not listen to their prayers, but carried us instead on board the "Pensacola," a sloop-of-war which was now lying in the river, ready to go to sea, and ready also to run the gauntlet of the rebel batteries which lined the Virginian shore of the river for many miles down below Alexandria and Mount Vernon. A sloop-of-war in these days means a large man-of-war, the guns of which are so big that they only stand on one deck, whereas a frigate would have them on two decks, and a line-of-battle ship on three. Of line-of-battle ships there will, I suppose, soon be none, as the "Warrior" is only a frigate. We went over the "Pensacola," and I must say she was very nice, pretty, and clean. I have always found American sailors on their men-of-war to be clean and nice-looking,—as much so I should say as our own; but nothing can be dirtier, more untidy, or apparently more ill-preserved than all the appurtenances of their soldiers.

We landed also on this occasion at Alexandria, and saw as melancholy and miserable a town as the mind of man can conceive. Its ordinary male population, counting by the voters, is 1500, and of these 700 were in the southern army. The place had been made a hospital for northern soldiers, and no doubt the site for that purpose had been well chosen. But let any woman imagine what would be the feelings of her life while living in a town used as a hospital for the enemies against whom her absent husband was then fighting! Her own man would be away ill,—wounded, dying, for what she knew, without the comfort of any hospital attendance, without physic, with no one to comfort him; but those she hated, with a hatred much keener than his, were close to her hand, using some friend's house that had been forcibly taken, crawling out into the sun under her eyes, taking the bread from her mouth! Life in Alexandria at this time must have been sad enough. The people were all secessionists, but the town was held by the northern party. Through the lines, into Virginia, they could not go at all. Up to Washington they could not go without a military pass, not to be obtained without some cause given. All trade was at an end. In no town at that time was trade very flourishing; but here it was killed altogether,—except that absolutely necessary trade of bread. Who would buy boots or coats, or want new saddles, or waste money on books, in such days as these, in such a town as Alexandria? And then out of 1500 men, one-half had gone to fight the southern battles! Among the women of Alexandria secession would have found but few opponents.

It was here that a hot-brained young man, named Ellsworth, was killed in the early days of the rebellion. He was a colonel in the northern volunteer army, and on entering Alexandria found a secession flag flying at the chief hotel. Instead of sending up a corporal's guard to remove it, he rushed up and pulled it down with his own hand. As he descended, the landlord shot him dead, and one of his soldiers shot the landlord dead. It was a pity that so brave a lad, who had risen so high, should fall so vainly; but they have made a hero of him in America;—have inscribed his name on marble monuments, and counted him up among their great men. In all this their mistake is very great. It is bad for a country to have no names worthy of monumental brass; but it is worse for a country to have monumental brasses covered with names which have never been made worthy of such honour. Ellsworth had shown himself to be brave and foolish. Let his folly be pardoned on the score of his courage, and there, I think, should have been an end of it.

I found afterwards that Mount Vernon was accessible, and I rode thither with some officers from the staff of General Heintzleman, whose outside pickets were stationed beyond the old place. I certainly should not have been well pleased had I been forced to leave the country without seeing the house in which Washington had lived and died. Till lately this place was owned and inhabited by one of the family, a Washington, descended from a brother of the General's; but it has now become the property of the country, under the auspices of Mr. Everett, by whose exertions was raised the money with which it was purchased. It is a long house, of two stories, built, I think, chiefly of wood, with a verandah, or rather long portico, attached to the front, which looks upon the river. There are two wings, or sets of outhouses, containing the kitchen and servants' rooms, which were joined by open wooden verandahs to the main building; but one of these verandahs has gone, under the influence of years. By these a semicircular sweep is formed before the front door, which opens away from the river, and towards the old prim gardens, in which, we were told, General Washington used to take much delight. There is nothing very special about the house. Indeed, as a house, it would now be found comfortless and inconvenient. But the ground falls well down to the river, and the timber, if not fine, is plentiful and picturesque. The chief interest of the place, however, is in the tomb of Washington and his wife. It must be understood that it was a common practice throughout the States to make a family burying-ground in any secluded spot on the family property. I have not unfrequently come across these in my rambles, and in Virginia I have encountered small, unpretending gravestones under a shady elm, dated as lately as eight or ten years back. At Mount Vernon there is now a cemetery of the Washington family; and there, in an open vault—a vault open, but guarded by iron grating—is the great man's tomb, and by his side the tomb of Martha his wife. As I stood there alone, with no one by to irritate me by assertions of the man's absolute supremacy, I acknowledged that I had come to the final resting-place of a great and good man,—of a man whose patriotism was, I believe, an honest feeling, untinged by any personal ambition of a selfish nature. That he was pre-eminently a successful man may have been due chiefly to the excellence of his cause, and the blood and character of the people who put him forward as their right arm in their contest; but that he did not mar that success by arrogance, or destroy the brightness of his own name by personal aggrandisement, is due to a noble nature and to the calm individual excellence of the man.

Considering the circumstances and history of the place, the position of Mount Vernon, as I saw it, was very remarkable. It lay exactly between the lines of the two armies. The pickets of the Northern army had been extended beyond it, not improbably with the express intention of keeping a spot so hallowed within the power of the northern Government. But since the war began it had been in the hands of the seceders. In fact, it stood there in the middle of the battle-field, on the very line of division between loyalism and secession. And this was the spot which Washington had selected as the heart and centre, and safest rallying homestead of the united nation which he left behind him. But Washington, when he resolved to found his capital on the banks of the Potomac, knew nothing of the glories of the Mississippi. He did not dream of the speedy addition to his already gathered constellations of those Western stars, of Wisconsin, Illinois, Minnesota, and Iowa; nor did he dream of Texas conquered, Louisiana purchased, and Missouri and Kansas rescued from the wilderness.

I have said that Washington was at that time,—the Christmas of 1861-1862,—a melancholy place. This was partly owing to the despondent tone in which so many Americans then spoke of their own affairs. It was not that the northern men thought that they were to be beaten, or that the southern men feared that things were going bad with their party across the river; but that nobody seemed to have any faith in anybody. Maclellan had been put up as the true man—exalted perhaps too quickly, considering the limited opportunities for distinguishing himself which fortune had thrown in his way; but now belief in Maclellan seemed to be slipping away. One felt that it was so from day to day, though it was impossible to define how or whence the feeling came. And then the character of the ministry fared still worse in public estimation. That Lincoln, the President, was honest, and that Chase, the Secretary of the Treasury, was able, was the only good that one heard spoken. At this time two Jonahs were specially pointed out as necessary sacrifices, by whose immersion into the comfortless ocean of private life the ship might perhaps be saved. These were Mr. Cameron, the Secretary of War, and Mr. Welles, the Secretary of the Navy. It was said that Lincoln, when pressed to rid his Cabinet of Cameron, had replied, that when a man was crossing a stream the moment was hardly convenient for changing his horse; but it came to that at last, that he found he must change his horse, even in the very sharpest run of the river. Better that than sit an animal on whose exertions he knew that he could not trust. So Mr. Cameron went, and Mr. Stanton became Secretary at War in his place. But Mr. Cameron, though put out of the Cabinet, was to be saved from absolute disgrace by being sent as Minister to Russia. I do not know that it would become me here to repeat the accusations made against Mr. Cameron, but it had long seemed to me that the maintenance in such a position, at such a time, of a gentleman who had to sustain such a universal absence of public confidence, must have been most detrimental to the army and to the Government.

Men whom one met in Washington were not unhappy about the state of things, as I had seen men unhappy in the North and in the West. They were mainly indifferent, but with that sort of indifference which arises from a break down of faith in anything. "There was the army! Yes, the army! But what an army! Nobody obeyed anybody. Nobody did anything! Nobody thought of advancing! There were, perhaps, two hundred thousand men assembled round Washington; and now the effort of supplying them with food and clothing was as much as could be accomplished! But the contractors, in the meantime, were becoming rich. And then as to the Government! Who trusted it? Who would put their faith in Seward and Cameron? Cameron was now gone, it was true; and in that way the whole of the Cabinet would soon be broken up. As to Congress, what could Congress do? Ask questions which no one would care to answer, and finally get itself packed up and sent home." The President and the constitution fared no better in men's mouths. The former did nothing,—neither harm nor good; and as for the latter, it had broken down and shown itself to be inefficient. So men ate, and drank, and laughed, waiting till chaos should come, secure in the belief that the atoms into which their world would resolve itself, would connect themselves again in some other form without trouble on their part.

And at Washington I found no strong feeling against England and English conduct towards America. "We men of the world," a Washington man might have said, "know very well that everybody must take care of himself first. We are very good friends with you,—of course, and are very glad to see you at our table whenever you come across the water; but as for rejoicing at your joys, or expecting you to sympathize with our sorrows, we know the world too well for that. We are splitting into pieces, and of course that is gain to you. Take another cigar." This polite, fashionable, and certainly comfortable way of looking at the matter had never been attained at New York or Philadelphia, at Boston or Chicago. The northern provincial world of the States had declared to itself that those who were not with it were against it; that its neighbours should be either friends or foes; that it would understand nothing of neutrality. This was often mortifying to me, but I think I liked it better on the whole than the *laisser-aller* indifference of Washington.

Everybody acknowledged that society in Washington had been almost destroyed by the loss of the southern half of the usual sojourners in the city. The senators and members of Government, who heretofore had come from the southern States, had no doubt spent more money in the capital than their northern brethren. They and their families had been more addicted to social pleasures. They are the descendants of the old English Cavaliers, whereas the northern men have come from the old English Roundheads. Or if, as may be the case, the blood of the races has now been too well mixed to allow of this being said with absolute truth, yet something of the manners of the old forefathers has been left. The southern gentleman is more genial, less dry,—I will not say more hospitable, but more given to enjoy hospitality than his northern brother; and this difference is quite as strong with the women as with the men. It may therefore be understood that secession would be very fatal to the society of Washington. It was not only that the members of Congress were not there. As to very many of the representatives, it may be said that they do not belong sufficiently to Washington to make a part of its society. It is not every representative that is, perhaps, qualified to do so. But secession had taken away from Washington those who held property in the South—who were bound to the South by any ties, whether political or other; who belonged to the South by blood, education, and old habits. In very many cases—nay, in most such cases—it had been necessary that a man should select whether he would be a friend to the South, and therefore a rebel; or else an enemy to the South, and therefore untrue to all the predilections and sympathies of his life. Here has been the hardship. For such people there has been no neutrality possible. Ladies even have not been able to profess themselves simply anxious for peace and goodwill, and so to remain tranquil. They who are not for me are against me, has been spoken by one side and by the other. And I suppose that in all civil war it is necessary that it should be so. I heard of various cases in which father and son had espoused different sides in order that property might be retained both in the North and in the South. Under such circumstances it may be supposed that society in Washington would be considerably cut up. All this made the place somewhat melancholy.

CHAPTER II
CONGRESS

In the interior of the Capitol much space is at present wasted, but this arises from the fact of great additions to the original plan having been made. The two chambers,—that of the Senate and of the Representatives, are in the two new wings, on the middle, or what we call the first-floor. The entrance is made under a dome, to a large circular hall, which is hung around with surely the worst pictures by which a nation ever sought to glorify its own deeds. There are yards of paintings at Versailles which are bad enough; but there is nothing at Versailles comparable in villany to the huge daubs which are preserved in this hall at the Capitol. It is strange that even self-laudatory patriotism should desire the perpetuation of such rubbish. When I was there the new dome was still in progress, and an ugly column of woodwork, required for internal support and affording a staircase to the top, stood in this hall. This of course was a temporary and necessary evil; but even this was hung around with the vilest of portraits.

From the hall, turning to the left, if the entrance be made at the front door, one goes to the new Chamber of Representatives, passing through that which was the old chamber. This is now dedicated to the exposition of various new figures by Crawford, and to the sale of tarts and gingerbread,— of very bad tarts and gingerbread. Let that old woman look to it, or let the House dismiss her. In fact this chamber is now but a vestibule to a passage, a second hall as it were, and thus thrown away. Changes probably will be made which will bring it into some use, or some scheme of ornamentation. From this a passage runs to the Representative Chamber, passing between those tell-tale windows, which, looking to the right and left, proclaim the tenuity of the building. The windows on one side, that looking to the east or front, should, I think, be closed. The appearance, both from the inside and from the outside, would be thus improved.

The Representative Chamber itself—which of course answers to our House of Commons—is a handsome, commodious room, admirably fitted for the purposes required. It strikes one as rather low, but I doubt if it were higher whether it would be better adapted for hearing. Even at present it is not perfect in this respect as regards the listeners in the gallery. It is a handsome, long chamber, lighted by skylights from the roof, and is amply large enough for the number to be accommodated. The Speaker sits opposite to the chief entrance, his desk being fixed against the opposite wall. He is thus brought nearer to the body of the men before him than is the case with our Speaker. He sits at a marble table, and the clerks below him are also accommodated with marble. Every representative has his own arm-chair, and his own desk before it. This may be done for a house consisting of about 240 members, but could hardly be contrived with us. These desks are arranged in a semicircular form, or in a broad horseshoe, and every member as he sits faces the Speaker. A score or so of little boys are always running about the floor, ministering to the members' wishes, carrying up petitions to the chair, bringing water to long-winded legislators, delivering and carrying out letters, and running with general messages. They do not seem to interrupt the course of business, and yet they are the liveliest little boys I ever saw. When a member claps his hands, indicating a desire for attendance, three or four will jockey for the honour. On the whole, I thought the little boys had a good time of it.

But not so the Speaker. It seemed to me that the amount of work falling upon the Speaker's shoulders was cruelly heavy. His voice was always ringing in my ears, exactly as does the voice of the croupier at a gambling-table who goes on declaring and explaining the results of the game, and who generally does so in sharp, loud, ringing tones, from which all interest in the proceeding itself seems to be excluded. It was just so with the Speaker in the House of Representatives. The debate was always full of interruptions; but on every interruption the Speaker asked the gentleman interrupted whether he would consent to be so treated. "The gentleman from Indiana has the floor." "The gentleman from Ohio wishes to ask the gentleman from Indiana a question." "The gentleman from Indiana gives permission." "The gentleman from Ohio!"—these last words being a summons to him of Ohio to get up and ask his question. "The gentleman from Pennsylvania rises to order." "The gentleman from Pennsylvania is in order." And then the House seems always to be voting, and the Speaker is always putting the question. "The gentlemen who agree to the amendment will say, Ay." Not a sound is heard. "The gentlemen who oppose the amendment will say, No." Again not a sound. "The Ayes have it," says the Speaker, and then he goes on again. All this he does with amazing rapidity, and is always at it with the same hard, quick, ringing, uninterested voice. The gentleman whom I saw in the chair was very clever, and quite up to the task. But as for dignity—! Perhaps it might be found that any great accession of dignity would impede the celerity of the work to be done, and that a closer copy of the British model might not on the whole increase the efficiency of the American machine.

When any matter of real interest occasioned a vote, the ayes and noes would be given aloud; and then, if there were a doubt arising from the volume of sound, the Speaker would declare that the "ayes" or the "noes" would seem to have it! And upon this a poll would be demanded. In such cases the Speaker calls on two members, who come forth and stand fronting each other before the chair, making a gangway. Through this the ayes walk like sheep, the tellers giving them an accelerating poke when they fail to go on with rapidity. Thus they are counted, and the noes are counted in the same way. It seemed to me that it would be very possible in a dishonest legislator to vote twice on any subject of great interest; but it may perhaps be the case that there are no dishonest legislators in the House of Representatives.

According to a list which I obtained, the present number of members is 173, and there are 63 vacancies occasioned by secession. New York returns 33 members, Pennsylvania 25, Ohio 21, Virginia 13, Massachusetts and Indiana 11, Tennessee and Kentucky 10, South Carolina 6, and so on, till Delaware, Kansas, and Florida return only 1 each. When the constitution was framed, Pennsylvania returned 8, and New York only 6; whereas Virginia returned 10, and South Carolina 5. From which may be gathered the relative rate of increase in population of the Free-soil States and the Slave States. All these States return two senators each to the other House, Kansas sending as many as New York. The work in the House begins at 12 noon, and is not often carried on late into the evening. Indeed this, I think, is never done till towards the end of the session.

The Senate House is in the opposite wing of the building, the position of the one house answering exactly to that of the other. It is somewhat smaller, but is, as a matter of course, much less crowded. There are 34 States, and therefore 68 seats and 68 desks only are required. These also are arranged in a horse-shoe form, and face the President; but there was a sad array of empty chairs when I was in Washington, nineteen or twenty seats being vacant in consequence of secession. In this house the Vice-President of the United States acts as President, but has by no means so hard a job of work as his brother on the other side of the way. Mr. Hannibal Hamlin, from Maine, now fills this chair. I was driven, while in Washington, to observe something amounting almost to a peculiarity in the Christian names of the gentlemen who were then administrating the Government of the country. Mr. Abraham Lincoln was the President, Mr. Hannibal Hamlin the Vice-President, Mr. Galusha Grow the Speaker of the Representatives, Mr. Salmon Chase the Secretary of the Treasury, Mr. Caleb Smith the Attorney-General, Mr. Simon Cameron the Secretary at War, and Mr. Gideon Welles the Secretary of the Navy.

In the Senate House, as in the other house, there are very commodious galleries for strangers, running round the entire chambers, and these galleries are open to all the world. As with all such places in the States, a large portion of them is appropriated to ladies. But I came at last to find that the word lady signified a female or a decently dressed man. Any arrangement for classes is in America impossible; the seats intended for gentlemen must as a matter of course be open to all men; but by giving up to the rougher sex half the amount of accommodation nominally devoted to ladies, the desirable division is to a certain extent made. I generally found that I could obtain admittance to the ladies' gallery if my coat were decent and I had gloves with me.

All the adjuncts of both these chambers are rich and in good keeping. The staircases are of marble, and the outside passages and lobbies are noble in size and in every way convenient. One knows well the trouble of getting into the House of Lords and House of Commons, and the want of comfort which attends one there; and an Englishman cannot fail to make comparisons injurious to his own country. It would not, perhaps, be possible to welcome all the world in London as is done in Washington, but there can be no good reason why the space given to the public with us should not equal that given in Washington. But, so far are we from sheltering the public, that we have made our House of Commons so small, that it will not even hold all its own members.

I had an opportunity of being present at one of their field-days in the Senate. Slidell and Mason had just then been sent from Fort Warren across to England in the Rinaldo. And here I may as well say what further there is for me to say about those two heroes. I was in Boston when they were taken, and all Boston was then full of them. I was at Washington when they were surrendered, and at Washington for a time their names were the only household words in vogue. To me it had, from the first, been a matter of certainty that England would demand the restitution of the men. I had never attempted to argue the matter on the legal points, but I felt, as though by instinct, that it would be so. First of all there reached us, by telegram, from Cape Race, rumours of what the press in England was saying;—rumours of a meeting in Liverpool, and rumours of the feeling in London. And then the papers followed, and we got our private letters. It was some days before we knew what was actually the demand made by Lord Palmerston's cabinet; and during this time, through the five or six days which were thus passed, it was clear to be seen that the American feeling was undergoing a great change—or if not the feeling, at any rate the purpose. Men now talked of surrendering these Commissioners as though it were a line of conduct which Mr. Seward might find convenient; and then men went further, and said that Mr. Seward would find any other line of conduct very inconvenient. The newspapers, one after another, came round. That, under all the circumstances, the States Government behaved well in the matter no one, I think, can deny; but the newspapers, taken as a whole, were not very consistent and, I think, not very dignified. They had declared with throats of brass that these men should never be surrendered to perfidious Albion; but when it came to be understood that in all probability they would be so surrendered, they veered round without an excuse, and spoke of their surrender as of a thing of course. And thus, in the course of about a week, the whole current of men's minds was turned. For myself, on my first arrival at Washington, I felt certain that there would be war, and was preparing myself for a quick return to England; but from the moment that the first whisper of England's message reached us, and that I began to hear how it was received and what men said about it, I knew that I need not hurry myself. One met a minister here, and a senator there, and anon some wise diplomatic functionary. By none of these grave men would any secret be divulged; none of them had any secret ready for divulging. But it was to be read in every look of the eye, in every touch of the hand, and in every fall of the foot of each of them, that Mason and Slidell would go to England.

Then we had, in all the fulness of diplomatic language, Lord Russell's demand and Mr. Seward's answer. Lord Russell's demand was worded in language so mild, was so devoid of threat, was so free from anger, that at the first reading it seemed to ask for nothing. It almost disappointed by its mildness. Mr. Seward's reply, on the other hand, by its length of argumentation, by a certain sharpness of diction to which that gentleman is addicted in his State papers, and by a tone of satisfaction inherent through it all, seemed to demand more than he conceded. But, in truth, Lord Russell had demanded everything, and the United States Government had conceded everything.

I have said that the American Government behaved well in its mode of giving the men up, and I think that so much should be allowed to them on a review of the whole affair. That Captain Wilkes had no instructions to seize the two men is a known fact. He did seize them and brought them into Boston harbour, to the great delight of his countrymen. This delight I could understand, though of course I did not share it. One of these men had been the parent of the Fugitive Slave Law; the other had been great in fostering the success of filibustering. Both of them were hot secessionists, and undoubtedly rebels. No two men on the continent were more grievous by their antecedents and present characters to all northern feeling. It is impossible to deny that they were rebels against the Government of their country. That Captain Wilkes was not on this account justified in seizing them is now a matter of history, but that the people of the loyal States should rejoice in their seizure was a matter of course. Wilkes was received with an ovation, which as regarded him was ill-judged and undeserved, but which in its spirit was natural. Had the President's Government at that moment disowned the deed done by Wilkes, and declared its intention of giving up the men unasked, the clamour raised would have been very great, and perhaps successful. We were told that the American lawyers were against their doing so; and indeed there was such a shout of triumph that no ministry in a country so democratic could have ventured to go at once against it, and to do so without any external pressure.

Then came the one ministerial blunder. The President put forth his message, in which he was cunningly silent on the Slidell and Mason affair; but to his message was appended, according to custom, the report from Mr. Welles, the Secretary of the Navy. In this report approval was expressed of the deed done by Captain Wilkes. Captain Wilkes was thus in all respects indemnified, and the blame, if any, was taken from his shoulders and put on to the shoulders of that officer who was responsible for the Secretary's letter. It is true that in that letter the Secretary declared that in case of any future seizure the vessel seized must be taken into port, and so declared in animadverting on the fact that Captain Wilkes had not brought the "Trent" into port. But, nevertheless, Secretary Welles approved of Captain Wilkes's conduct. He allowed the reasons to be good which Wilkes had put forward for leaving the ship, and in all respects indemnified the captain. Then the responsibility shifted itself to Secretary Welles; but I think it must be clear that the President, in sending forward that report, took that responsibility upon himself. That he is not bound to send forward the reports of his Secretaries as he receives them;—that he can disapprove them and require alteration, was proved at the very time by the fact that he had in this way condemned Secretary Cameron's report, and caused a portion of it to be omitted. Secretary Cameron had unfortunately allowed his entire report to be printed, and it appeared in a New York paper. It contained a recommendation with reference to the slave question most offensive to a part of the Cabinet, and to the majority of Mr. Lincoln's party. This, by order of the President, was omitted in the official way. It was certainly a pity that Mr. Welles's paragraph respecting the "Trent" was not omitted also. The President was dumb on the matter, and that being so the Secretary should have been dumb also.

But when the demand was made the States Government yielded at once, and yielded without bluster. I cannot say I much admired Mr. Seward's long letter. It was full of smart special pleading, and savoured strongly, as Mr. Seward's productions always do, of the personal author. Mr. Seward was making an effort to place a great State paper on record, but the *ars celare artem* was altogether wanting; and, if I am not mistaken, he was without the art itself. I think he left the matter very much where he found it. The men however were to be surrendered, and the good policy consisted in this, — that no delay was sought, no diplomatic ambiguities were put into request. It was the opinion of very many that some two or three months might be gained by correspondence, and that at the end of that time things might stand on a different footing. If during that time the North should gain any great success over the South, the States might be in a position to disregard England's threats. No such game was played. The illegality of the arrest was at once acknowledged, and the men were given up, — with a tranquillity that certainly appeared marvellous after all that had so lately occurred.

Then came Mr. Sumner's field day. Mr. Charles Sumner is a senator from Massachusetts, known as a very hot abolitionist and as having been the victim of an attack made upon him in the Senate House by Senator Brookes. He was also at the time of which I am writing Chairman of the Committee on Foreign Affairs, which position is as near akin to that of a British minister in Parliament as can be attained under the existing constitution of the States. It is not similar, because such chairman is by no means bound to the Government; but he has ministerial relations, and is supposed to be specially conversant with all questions relating to foreign affairs. It was understood that Mr. Sumner did not intend to find fault either with England or with the Government of his own country as to its management of this matter; or that, at least, such fault-finding was not his special object, but that he was desirous to put forth views which might lead to a final settlement of all difficulties with reference to the right of international search.

On such an occasion, a speaker gives himself very little chance of making a favourable impression on his immediate hearers if he reads his speech from a written manuscript. Mr. Sumner did so on this occasion, and I must confess that I was not edified. It seemed to me that he merely repeated, at greater length, the arguments which I had heard fifty times during the last thirty or forty days. I am told that the discourse is considered to be logical, and that it "reads" well. As regards the gist of it, or that result which Mr. Sumner thinks to be desirable, I fully agree with him, as I think will all the civilized world before many years have passed. If international law be what the lawyers say it is, international law must be altered to suit the requirements of modern civilization. By those laws, as they are construed, everything is to be done for two nations at war with each other; but nothing is to be done for all the nations of the world that can manage to maintain the peace. The belligerents are to be treated with every delicacy, as we treat our heinous criminals; but the poor neutrals are to be handled with unjust rigour, as we handle our unfortunate witnesses in order that the murderer may, if possible, be allowed to escape. Two men living in the same street choose to pelt each other across the way with brickbats, and the other inhabitants are denied the privileges of the footpath lest they should interfere with the due prosecution of the quarrel! It is, I suppose, the truth, that we English have insisted on this right of search with more pertinacity than any other nation. Now in this case of Slidell and Mason we have felt ourselves aggrieved, and have resisted. Luckily for us there was no doubt of the illegality of the mode of seizure in this instance; but who will say that if Captain Wilkes had taken the "Trent" into the harbour of New York, in order that the matter might have been adjudged there, England would have been satisfied? Our grievance was, that our mail-packet was stopped on the seas while doing its ordinary beneficent work. And our resolve is, that our mail-packets shall not be so stopped with impunity. As we were high-handed in old days in insisting on this right of search, and as we are high-handed now in resisting a right of search, it certainly behoves us to see that we be just in our modes of proceeding. Would Captain Wilkes have been right according to the existing law if he had carried the "Trent" away to New York? If so, we ought not to be content with having escaped from such a trouble merely through a mistake on his part. Lord Russell says that the "Trent's" voyage was an innocent voyage. That is the fact that should be established;—not only that the voyage was, in truth, innocent, but that it should not be made out to be guilty by any international law. Of its real innocency all thinking men must feel themselves assured. But it is not only of the seizure that we complain, but of the search also. An honest man is not to be handled by a policeman while on his daily work, lest by chance a stolen watch should be in his pocket. If international law did give such power to all belligerents, international law must give it no longer. In the beginning of these matters, as I take it, the object was when two powerful nations were at war to allow the smaller fry of nations to enjoy peace and quiet, and to avoid if possible the general scuffle. Thence arose the position of a neutral. But it was clearly not fair that any such nation, having proclaimed its neutrality, should, after that, fetch and carry for either of the combatants to the prejudice of the other. Hence came the right of search, in order that unjust falsehood might be prevented. But the seas were not then bridged with ships as they are now bridged, and the laws as written were, perhaps, then practical and capable of execution. Now they are impracticable and not capable of execution. It will not, however, do for us to ignore them if they exist; and therefore they should be changed. It is, I think, manifest that our own pretensions as to the right of search must be modified after this. And now I trust I may finish my book without again naming Messrs. Slidell and Mason.

The working of the Senate bears little or no analogy to that of our House of Lords. In the first place, the senator's tenure there is not hereditary, nor is it for life. They are elected, and sit for six years. Their election is not made by the people of their States, but by the State legislature. The two Houses, for instance, of the State of Massachusetts meet together and elect by their joint vote to the vacant seat for their State. It is so arranged that an entirely new senate is not elected every sixth year. Instead of this a third of the number is elected every second year. It is a common thing for senators to be re-elected, and thus to remain in the House for twelve and eighteen years. In our Parliament the House of Commons has greater political strength and wider political action than the House of Lords; but in Congress the Senate counts for more than the House of Representatives in general opinion. Money bills must originate in the House of Representatives, but that is, I think, the only special privilege attaching to the public purse which the lower House enjoys over the upper. Amendments to such bills can be moved in the Senate; and all such bills must pass the Senate before they become law. I am inclined to think that individual members of the Senate work harder than individual representatives. More is expected of them, and any prolonged absence from duty would be more remarked in the Senate than in the other House. In our Parliament this is reversed. The payment made to members of the Senate is 3000 dollars, or £600, per annum, and to a representative, £500 per annum. To this is added certain mileage allowance for travelling backwards and forwards, between their own State and the Capitol. A senator, therefore, from California or Oregon has not altogether a bad place; but the halcyon days of mileage allowances are, I believe, soon to be brought to an end. It is quite within rule that the senator of to-day should be the representative of to-morrow. Mr. Crittenden, who was senator from Kentucky, is now a member of the Lower House from an electoral district in that State. John Quincy Adams went into the House of Representatives after he had been President of the United States.

Divisions in the Senate do not take place as in the House of Representatives. The ayes and noes are called for in the same way; but if a poll be demanded, the clerk of the House calls out the names of the different senators, and makes out lists of the votes according to the separate answers given by the members. The mode is certainly more dignified than that pursued in the other House, where during the ceremony of voting the members look very much like sheep being passed into their pens.

I heard two or three debates in the House of Representatives, and that one especially in which, as I have said before, a chapter was read out of the book of Joshua. The manner in which the Creator's name and the authority of His Word was bandied about the house on that occasion, did not strike me favourably. The question originally under debate was the relative power of the civil and military authority. Congress had desired to declare its ascendancy over military matters; but the army and the Executive generally had demurred to this,—not with an absolute denial of the rights of Congress, but with those civil and almost silent generalities with which a really existing Power so well knows how to treat a nominal Power. The ascendant wife seldom tells her husband in so many words that his opinion in the house is to go for nothing; she merely resolves that such shall be the case, and acts accordingly. An observer could not but perceive that in those days Congress was taking upon itself the part, not exactly of an obedient husband, but of a husband vainly attempting to assert his supremacy. "I have got to learn," said one gentleman after another, rising indignantly on the floor, "that the military authority of our generals is above that of this House." And then one gentleman relieved the difficulty of the position by branching off into an eloquent discourse against slavery, and by causing a chapter to be read out of the book of Joshua.

On that occasion the gentleman's diversion seemed to have the effect of relieving the House altogether from the embarrassment of the original question; but it was becoming manifest, day by day, that Congress was losing its ground, and that the army was becoming indifferent to its thunders:—that the army was doing so, and also that ministers were doing so. In the States, the President and his ministers are not in fact subject to any parliamentary responsibility. The President may be impeached, but the member of an opposition does not always wish to have recourse to such an extreme measure as impeachment. The ministers are not in the houses, and cannot therefore personally answer questions. Different large subjects, such as Foreign affairs, Financial affairs, and Army matters, are referred to Standing Committees in both houses; and these Committees have relations with the ministers. But they have no constitutional power over the ministers; nor have they the much more valuable privilege of badgering a minister hither and thither by *vivâ voce* questions on every point of his administration. The minister sits safe in his office—safe there for the term of the existing Presidency if he can keep well with the President; and therefore, even under ordinary circumstances, does not care much for the printed or written messages of Congress. But under circumstances so little ordinary as those of 1861-62, while Washington was surrounded by hundreds of thousands of soldiers, Congress was absolutely impotent. Mr. Seward could snap his fingers at Congress, and he did so. He could not snap his fingers at the army; but then he could go with the army,—could keep the army on his side by remaining on the same side with the army; and this, as it seemed, he resolved to do. It must be understood that Mr. Seward was not

Prime Minister. The President of the United States has no Prime Minister, — or hitherto has had none. The Minister for Foreign Affairs has usually stood highest in the Cabinet, and Mr. Seward, as holding that position, was not inclined to lessen its authority. He was gradually assuming for that position the prerogatives of a Premier, and men were beginning to talk of Mr. Seward's ministry. It may easily be understood that at such a time the powers of Congress would be undefined, and that ambitious members of Congress would rise and assert on the floor, with that peculiar voice of indignation so common in parliamentary debate, "that they had got to learn," &c., &c., &c. It seemed to me that the lesson which they had yet to learn was then in the process of being taught to them. They were anxious to be told all about the mischance at Ball's Bluff, but nobody would tell them anything about it. They wanted to know something of that blockade on the Potomac; but such knowledge was not good for them. "Pack them up in boxes, and send them home," one military gentleman said to me. And I began to think that something of the kind would be done, if they made themselves troublesome. I quote here the manner in which their questions, respecting the affair at Ball's Bluff, were answered by the Secretary of War. "The Speaker laid before the House a letter from the Secretary at War, in which he says that he has the honour to acknowledge the receipt of the resolution adopted on the 6th instant, to the effect that the answer of the department to the resolution passed on the second day of the session, is not responsive and satisfactory to the House, and requesting a further answer. The Secretary has now to state that measures have been taken to ascertain who is responsible for the disastrous movement at Ball's Bluff, but that it is not compatible with the public interest to make known those measures at the present time."

In truth the days are evil for any Congress of debaters, when a great army is in camp on every side of them. The people had called for the army, and there it was. It was of younger birth than Congress, and had thrown its elder brother considerably out of favour, as has been done before by many a new-born baby. If Congress could amuse itself with a few set speeches, and a field-day or two, such as those afforded by Mr. Sumner, it might all be very well, —provided that such speeches did not attack the army. Over and beyond this, let them vote the supplies and have done with it. Was it probable that General Maclellan should have time to answer questions about Ball's Bluff, —and he with such a job of work on his hands? Congress could of course vote what committees of military inquiry it might please, and might ask questions without end; but we all know to what such questions lead, when the questioner has no power to force an answer by a penalty. If it might be possible to maintain the semblance of respect for

Congress, without too much embarrassment to military secretaries, such semblance should be maintained; but if Congress chose to make itself really disagreeable, then no semblance could be kept up any longer. That, as far as I could judge, was the position of Congress in the early months of 1862; and that, under existing circumstances, was perhaps the only possible position that it could fill.

All this to me was very melancholy. The streets of Washington were always full of soldiers. Mounted sentries stood at the corners of all the streets with drawn sabres,—shivering in the cold and besmeared with mud. A military law came out that civilians might not ride quickly through the street. Military riders galloped over one at every turn, splashing about through the mud, and reminding one not unfrequently of John Gilpin. Why they always went so fast, destroying their horses' feet on the rough stones, I could never learn. But I, as a civilian, given, as Englishmen are, to trotting, and furnished for the time with a nimble trotter, found myself harried from time to time by muddy men with sabres, who would dash after me, rattling their trappings, and bid me go at a slower pace. There is a building in Washington, built by private munificence and devoted, according to an inscription which it bears, "To the Arts." It has been turned into an army clothing establishment. The streets of Washington, night and day, were thronged with army waggons. All through the city military huts and military tents were to be seen, pitched out among the mud and in the desert places. Then there was the chosen locality of the teamsters and their mules and horses—a wonderful world in itself; and all within the city! Here horses and mules lived,—or died,—*sub dio*, with no slightest apology for a stable over them, eating their provender from off the waggons to which they were fastened. Here, there, and everywhere large houses were occupied as the head-quarters of some officer, or the bureau of some military official. At Washington and round Washington the army was everything. While this was so, is it to be conceived that Congress should ask questions about military matters with success?

All this, as I say, filled me with sorrow. I hate military belongings, and am disgusted at seeing the great affairs of a nation put out of their regular course. Congress to me is respectable. Parliamentary debates, be they ever so prosy,—as with us, or even so rowdy, as sometimes they have been with our cousins across the water,—engage my sympathies. I bow inwardly before a Speaker's chair, and look upon the elected representatives of any nation as the choice men of the age. Those muddy, clattering dragoons, sitting at the corners of the streets with dirty woollen comforters round their ears, were to me hideous in the extreme. But there at Washington, at the period of which I am writing, I was forced to acknowledge that Congress was at a discount, and that the rough-shod generals were the men of the day. "Pack them up and send them in boxes to their several States." It would come to that, I thought, or to something like that unless Congress would consent to be submissive. "I have yet to learn—!" said indignant members, stamping with their feet on the floor of the house. One would have said that by that time the lesson might almost have been understood.

Up to the period of this civil war Congress has certainly worked well for the United States. It might be easy to pick holes in it;—to show that some members have been corrupt, others quarrelsome, and others again impracticable. But when we look at the circumstances under which it has been from year to year elected,—when we remember the position of the newly-populated States from which the members have been sent, and the absence throughout the country of that old traditional class of Parliament men on whom we depend in England; when we think how recent has been the elevation in life of the majority of those who are and must be elected,— it is impossible to deny them praise for intellect, patriotism, good sense, and diligence. They began but sixty years ago, and for sixty years Congress has fully answered the purpose for which it was established. With no antecedents of grandeur, the nation, with its Congress, has made itself one of the five great nations of the world. And what living English politician will say even now, with all its troubles thick upon it, that it is the smallest of the five? When I think of this, and remember the position in Europe which an American has been able to claim for himself, I cannot but acknowledge that Congress on the whole has been conducted with prudence, wisdom, and patriotism.

The question now to be asked is this,—Have the powers of Congress been sufficient, or are they sufficient, for the continued maintenance of free government in the States under the constitution? I think that the powers given by the existing constitution to Congress can no longer be held to be sufficient; and that if the Union be maintained at all, it must be done by a closer assimilation of its congressional system to that of our Parliament. But to that matter I must allude again, when speaking of the existing constitution of the States.

CHAPTER III
THE CAUSES OF THE WAR

I have seen various essays purporting to describe the causes of this civil war between the North and South; but they have generally been written with the view of vindicating either one side or the other, and have spoken rather of causes which should, according to the ideas of their writers, have produced peace, than of those which did, in the course of events, actually produce war. This has been essentially the case with Mr. Everett, who in his lecture at New York, on the 4th of July, 1860, recapitulated all the good things which the North has done for the South, and who proved—if he has proved anything—that the South should have cherished the North instead of hating it. And this was very much the case also with Mr. Motley in his letter to the "London Times." That letter is good in its way, as is everything that comes from Mr. Motley, but it does not tell us why the war has existed. Why is it that eight millions of people have desired to separate themselves from a rich and mighty empire,—from an empire which was apparently on its road to unprecedented success, and which had already achieved wealth, consideration, power, and internal well-being?

One would be led to imagine from the essays of Mr. Everett and of Mr. Motley, that slavery has had little or nothing to do with it. I must acknowledge it to be my opinion that slavery in its various bearings has been the single and necessary cause of the war;—that slavery being there in the South, this war was only to be avoided by a voluntary division,—secession voluntary both on the part of North and South;—that in the event of such voluntary secession being not asked for, or if asked for not conceded, revolution and civil war became necessary,—were not to be avoided by any wisdom or care on the part of the North.

The arguments used by both the gentlemen I have named prove very clearly that South Carolina and her sister States had no right to secede under the constitution; that is to say, that it was not open to them peaceably to take their departure, and to refuse further allegiance to the President and Congress without a breach of the laws by which they were bound. For a certain term of years, namely, from 1781 to 1787, the different States endeavoured to make their way in the world, simply leagued together by certain articles of confederation. It was declared that each State retained its sovereignty, freedom, and independence; and that the said States then entered severally into a firm league of friendship with each other for their common defence. There was no President, no Congress taking the place of our Parliament, but simply a congress of delegates or ambassadors, two or three from each State, who were to act in accordance with the policy of their own individual States. It is well that this should be thoroughly understood, not as bearing on the question of the present war, but as showing that a loose confederation, not subversive of the separate independence of the States, and capable of being partially dissolved at the will of each separate State, was tried, and was found to fail. South Carolina took upon herself to act as she might have acted had that confederation remained in force; but that confederation was an acknowledged failure. National greatness could not be achieved under it, and individual enterprise could not succeed under it. Then in lieu of that, by the united consent of the thirteen States the present constitution was drawn up and sanctioned, and to that every State bound itself in allegiance. In that constitution no power of secession is either named or presumed to exist. The individual sovereignty of the States had, in the first instance, been thought desirable. The young republicans hankered after the separate power and separate name which each might then have achieved; but that dream had been found vain,—and therefore the States, at the cost of some fond wishes, agreed to seek together for national power, rather than run the risks entailed upon separate existence. I append to this volume the articles of confederation and the constitution of the United States, as they who desire to look into this matter may be anxious to examine them without reference to other volumes. The latter alone is clear enough on the subject, but is strengthened by the former in proving that under the latter no State could possess the legal power of seceding.

But they who created the constitution, who framed the clauses, and gave to this terribly important work what wisdom they possessed, did not presume to think that it could be final. The mode of altering the constitution is arranged in the constitution. Such alterations must be proposed either by two-thirds of both the houses of the general Congress, or by the legislatures of two-thirds of the States; and must, when so proposed, be ratified by the legislatures of three-fourths of the States.—(Article V.) There can, I think, be no doubt that any alteration so carried would be valid; even though that alteration should go to the extent of excluding one or any number of States from the Union. Any division so made would be made in accordance with the constitution.

South Carolina and the southern States no doubt felt that they would not succeed in obtaining secession in this way, and therefore they sought to obtain the separation which they wanted by revolution, —by revolution and rebellion, as Naples has lately succeeded in her attempt to change her political status; as Hungary is looking to do; as Poland has been seeking to do any time since her subjection; as the revolted colonies of Great Britain succeeded in doing in 1776, whereby they created this great nation which is now undergoing all the sorrows of a civil war. The name of secession claimed by the South for this movement is a misnomer. If any part of a nationality or empire ever rebelled against the government established on behalf of the whole, South Carolina so rebelled when, on the 20th November, 1860, she put forth her ordinance of so-called secession; and the other southern States joined in that rebellion when they followed her lead. As to that fact, there cannot, I think, much longer be any doubt in any mind. I insist on this especially, repeating perhaps unnecessarily, opinions expressed in my first volume, because I still see it stated by English writers that the secession ordinance of South Carolina should have been accepted as a political act by the government of the United States. It seems to me that no government can in this way accept an act of rebellion without declaring its own functions to be beyond its own power.

But what if such rebellion be justifiable, or even reasonable? what if the rebels have cause for their rebellion? For no one will now deny that rebellion may be both reasonable and justifiable; or that every subject in the land may be bound in duty to rebel. In such case the government will be held to have brought about its own punishment by its own fault. But as government is a wide affair, spreading itself gradually, and growing in virtue or in vice from small beginnings, —from seeds slow to produce their fruits, —it is much easier to discern the incidence of the punishment than the perpetration of the fault. Government goes astray by degrees, or sins by the absence of that wisdom which should teach rulers how to make progress, as progress is made by those whom they rule. The fault may be absolutely negative and have spread itself over centuries; may be, and generally has been, attributable to dull good men; —but not the less does the punishment come at a blow. The rebellion exists and cannot be put down, —will put down all that opposes it; but the government is not the less bound to make its fight. That is the punishment that comes on governing men or on a governing people, that govern not well or not wisely.

As Mr. Motley says in the paper to which I have alluded, "No man, on either side of the Atlantic, with Anglo-Saxon blood in his veins, will dispute the right of a people, or of any portion of a people, to rise against oppression, to demand redress of grievances, and in case of denial of justice to take up arms to vindicate the sacred principle of liberty. Few Englishmen or Americans will deny that the source of government is the consent of the governed, or that every nation has the right to govern itself according to its will. When the silent consent is changed to fierce remonstrance, revolution is impending. The right of revolution is indisputable. It is written on the whole record of our race. British and American history is made up of rebellion and revolution. Hampden, Pym, and Oliver Cromwell; Washington, Adams, and Jefferson, all were rebels." Then comes the question whether South Carolina and the Gulf States had so suffered as to make rebellion on their behalf justifiable or reasonable; or if not, what cause had been strong enough to produce in them so strong a desire for secession,—a desire which has existed for fully half the term through which the United States has existed as a nation, and so firm a resolve to rush into rebellion with the object of accomplishing that which they deemed not to be accomplished on other terms.

It must, I think, be conceded that the Gulf States have not suffered at all by their connection with the northern States; that in lieu of any such suffering, they owe all their national greatness to the northern States; that they have been lifted up by the commercial energy of the Atlantic States and by the agricultural prosperity of the western States, to a degree of national consideration and respect through the world at large, which never could have belonged to them standing alone. I will not trouble my readers with statistics which few would care to follow, but let any man of ordinary every-day knowledge turn over in his own mind his present existing ideas of the wealth and commerce of New York, Boston, Philadelphia, Chicago, Pittsburg, and Cincinnati, and compare them with his ideas as to New Orleans, Charleston, Savannah, Mobile, Richmond, and Memphis. I do not name such towns as Baltimore and St. Louis, which stand in slave States, but which have raised themselves to prosperity by northern habits. If this be not sufficient, let him refer to population tables and tables of shipping and tonnage. And of those southern towns which I have named the commercial wealth is of northern creation. The success of New Orleans as a city can be no more attributed to Louisianians than can that of the Havana to the men of Cuba, or of Calcutta to the natives of India. It has been a repetition of the old story, told over and over again through every century since commerce has flourished in the world; the tropics can produce,—but the men from the North shall sow and reap, and garner and enjoy. As the Creator's work has progressed, this privilege has extended itself to regions further removed and still further from southern influences. If we look to Europe, we see that this has been so in Greece, Italy, Spain, France, and the Netherlands; in England and Scotland; in Prussia and in Russia; and the Western world shows us the same story. Where is now the glory of the Antilles? where the riches of Mexico, and the power of Peru? They still produce sugar, guano, gold, cotton, coffee, almost whatever we may ask them,—and will continue to do so while held to labour under sufficient restraint; but where are their men, where are their books, where are their learning, their art, their enterprise? I say it with sad regret at the decadence of so vast a population; but I do say that the southern States of America have not been able to keep pace with their northern brethren;—that they have fallen behind in the race, and feeling that the struggle is too much for them, have therefore resolved to part.

The reasons put forward by the South for secession have been trifling almost beyond conception. Northern tariffs have been the first, and perhaps foremost. Then there has been a plea that the national exchequer has paid certain bounties to New England fishermen, of which the South has paid its share,—getting no part of such bounty in return. There is also a complaint as to the navigation laws,—meaning, I believe, that the laws of the States increase the cost of coast traffic by forbidding foreign vessels to engage in the trade, thereby increasing also the price of goods and confining the benefit to the North, which carries on the coasting trade of the country, and doing only injury to the South, which has none of it. Then last, but not least, comes that grievance as to the Fugitive Slave Law. The law of the land as a whole,—the law of the nation,—requires the rendition from free States of all fugitive slaves. But the free States will not obey this law. They even pass State laws in opposition to it. "Catch your own slaves," they say, "and we will not hinder you; at any rate we will not hinder you officially. Of non-official hindrance you must take your chance. But we absolutely decline to employ our officers to catch your slaves." That list comprises, as I take it, the amount of southern official grievances. Southern people will tell you privately of others. They will say that they cannot sleep happy in their beds, fearing lest insurrection should be roused among their slaves. They will tell you of domestic comfort invaded by northern falsehood. They will explain to you how false has been Mrs. Beecher Stowe. Ladies will fill your ears and your hearts too with tales of the daily efforts they make for the comfort of their "people," and of the ruin to those efforts which arises from the malice of the abolitionists. To all this you make some answer with your tongue that is hardly true,—for in such a matter courtesy forbids the plain truth. But your heart within answers truly, "Madam,—dear madam, your sorrow is great; but that sorrow is the necessary result of your position."

As to those official reasons, in what fewest words I can use I will endeavour to show that they come to nothing. The tariff—and a monstrous tariff it then was—was the ground put forward by South Carolina for secession, when General Jackson was President, and Mr. Calhoun was the hero of the South. Calhoun bound himself and his State to take certain steps towards secession at a certain day if that tariff were not abolished. The tariff was so absurd that Jackson and his Government were forced to abandon it,—would have abandoned it without any threat from Calhoun; but under that threat it was necessary that Calhoun should be defied. General Jackson proposed a compromise tariff, which was odious to Calhoun,—not on its own behalf, for it yielded nearly all that was asked, but as being subversive of his desire for secession. The President, however, not only insisted on his compromise, but declared his purpose of preventing its passage into law unless Calhoun himself, as senator, would vote for it. And he also declared his purpose, not, we may presume, officially, of hanging Calhoun if he took that step towards secession which he had bound himself to take in the event of the tariff not being repealed. As a result of all this Calhoun voted for the compromise, and secession for the time was beaten down. That was in 1832, and may be regarded as the commencement of the secession movement. The tariff was then a convenient reason, a ground to be assigned with a colour of justice, because it was a tariff admitted to be bad. But the tariff has been modified again and again since that; and the tariff existing when South Carolina seceded in 1860 had been carried by votes from South Carolina. The absurd Morrill tariff could not have caused secession, for it was passed without a struggle in the collapse of Congress occasioned by secession.

The bounty to fishermen was given to create sailors, so that a marine might be provided for the nation. I need hardly show that the national benefit would accrue to the whole nation for whose protection such sailors were needed. Such a system of bounties may be bad, but if so it was bad for the whole nation. It did not affect South Carolina otherwise than it affected Illinois, Pennsylvania, or even New York.

The navigation laws may also have been bad. According to my thinking such protective laws are bad; but they created no special hardship on the South. By any such a theory of complaint all sections of all nations have ground of complaint against any other section which receives special protection under any law. The drinkers of beer in England should secede because they pay a tax, whereas the consumers of paper pay none. The navigation laws of the States are no doubt injurious to the mercantile interests of the States. I at least have no doubt on the subject. But no one will think that secession is justified by the existence of a law of questionable expediency. Bad laws will go by the board if properly handled by those whom they pinch, as the navigation laws went by the board with us in England.

As to that Fugitive Slave Law, it should be explained that the grievance has not arisen from the loss of slaves. I have heard it stated that South Carolina, up to the time of the secession, had never lost a slave in this way—that is, by northern opposition to the Fugitive Slave Law; and that the total number of slaves escaping successfully into the northern States, and there remaining through the non-operation of this law, did not amount to five in the year. It has not been a question of property but of feeling. It has been a political point, and the South has conceived—and probably conceived truly—that this resolution on the part of northern States to defy the law with reference to slaves, even though in itself it might not be immediately injurious to southern property, was an insertion of the narrow end of the wedge. It was an action taken against slavery,—an action taken by men of the North against their fellow-countrymen in the South. Under such circumstances the sooner such countrymen should cease to be their fellows the better it would be for them. That, I take it, was the argument of the South; or at any rate that was its feeling.

I have said that the reasons given for secession have been trifling, and among them have so estimated this matter of the Fugitive Slave Law. I mean to assert that the ground actually put forward is trifling;—the loss, namely, of slaves to which the South has been subjected. But the true reason pointed at in this—the conviction, namely, that the North would not leave slavery alone, and would not allow it to remain as a settled institution—was by no means trifling. It has been this conviction on the part of the South, that the North would not live in amity with slavery, would continue to fight it under this banner or under that, would still condemn it as disgraceful to man and rebuke it as impious before God, which has produced rebellion and civil war—and will ultimately produce that division for which the South is fighting, and against which the North is fighting; and which, when accomplished, will give the North new wings, and will leave the South without political greatness or commercial success.

Under such circumstances I cannot think that rebellion on the part of the South was justified by wrongs endured or made reasonable by the prospect of wrongs to be inflicted. It is disagreeable, that having to live with a wife who is always rebuking one for some special fault; but the outside world will not grant a divorce on that account, especially if the outside world is well aware that the fault so rebuked is of daily occurrence. "If you do not choose to be called a drunkard by your wife," the outside world will say, "it will be well that you should cease to drink." Ah! but that habit of drinking when once acquired cannot easily be laid aside. The brain will not work, the organs of the body will not perform their functions, the blood will not run. The drunkard must drink till he dies. All that may be a good ground for divorce, the outside world will say; but the plea should be put in by the sober wife, not by the intemperate husband. But what if the husband takes himself off without any divorce and takes with him also his wife's property, her earnings, that on which he has lived and his children? It may be a good bargain still for her, the outside world will say; but she, if she be a woman of spirit, will not willingly put up with such wrongs. The South has been the husband drunk with slavery, and the North has been the ill-used wife.

Rebellion, as I have said, is often justifiable, but it is, I think, never justifiable on the part of a paid servant of that Government against which it is raised. We must at any rate feel that this is true of men in high places,—as regards those men to whom by reason of their offices it should specially belong to put down rebellion. Had Washington been the Governor of Virginia, had Cromwell been a minister of Charles, had Garibaldi held a marshal's baton under the Emperor of Austria or the King of Naples, those men would have been traitors as well as rebels. Treason and rebellion may be made one under the law, but the mind will always draw the distinction. I, if I rebel against the Crown, am not on that account necessarily a traitor. A betrayal of trust is, I take it, necessary to treason. I am not aware that Jefferson Davis is a traitor; but that Buchanan was a traitor admits, I think, of no doubt. Under him and with his connivance, the rebellion was allowed to make its way. Under him and by his officers arms and ships, and men and money, were sent away from those points at which it was known that they would be needed if it were intended to put down the coming rebellion, and to those points at which it was known that they would be needed if it were intended to foster the coming rebellion. But Mr. Buchanan had no eager feeling in favour of secession. He was not of that stuff of which are made Davis and Toombs and Slidell. But treason was easier to him than loyalty. Remonstrance was made to him, pointing out the misfortunes which his action, or want of action, would bring upon the country. "Not in my time," he answered. "It will not be in my time." So that he might escape unscathed out of the fire, this chief ruler of a nation of thirty millions of men was content to allow treason and rebellion to work their way! I venture to say so much here as showing how impossible it was that Mr. Lincoln's government, on its coming into office, should have given to the South,—not what the South had asked, for the South had not asked,—but what the South had taken; what the South had tried to filch. Had the South waited for secession till Mr. Lincoln had been in his chair, I could understand that England should sympathize with her. For myself I cannot agree to that scuttling of the ship by the captain on the day which was to see the transfer of his command to another officer.

The southern States were driven into rebellion by no wrongs inflicted on them; but their desire for secession is not on that account matter for astonishment. It would have been surprising had they not desired secession. Secession of one kind, a very practical secession, had already been forced upon them by circumstances. They had become a separate people, dissevered from the North by habits, morals, institutions, pursuits, and every conceivable difference in their modes of thought and action. They still spoke the same language, as do Austria and Prussia; but beyond that tie of language they had no bond but that of a meagre political union in their Congress at Washington. Slavery, as it had been expelled from the North, and as it had come to be welcomed in the South, had raised such a wall of difference, that true political union was out of the question. It would be juster, perhaps, to say that those physical characteristics of the South which had induced this welcoming of slavery, and those other characteristics of the North which had induced its expulsion, were the true causes of the difference. For years and years this has been felt by both, and the fight has been going on. It has been continued for thirty years, and almost always to the detriment of the South. In 1845 Florida and Texas were admitted into the Union as slave States. I think that no State had then been admitted, as a free State, since Michigan, in 1836. In 1846 Iowa was admitted as a free State, and from that day to this Wisconsin, California, Minnesota, Oregon, and Kansas have been brought into the Union; all as free States. The annexation of another slave State to the existing Union had become, I imagine, impossible—unless such object were gained by the admission of Texas. We all remember that fight about Kansas, and what sort of a fight it was! Kansas lies alongside of Missouri, a slave State, and is contiguous to no other State. If the free-soil party could, in the days of Pierce and Buchanan, carry the day in Kansas, it is not likely that they would be beaten on any new ground under such a President as Lincoln. We have all heard in Europe how southern men have ruled in the White House, nearly from the days of Washington downwards; or if not southern men, northern men, such as Pierce and Buchanan, with southern politics; and therefore we have been taught to think that the South has been politically the winning party. They have, in truth, been the losing party as regards national power. But what they have so lost they have hitherto recovered by political address and individual statecraft. The leading men of the South have seen their position, and have gone to their work with the exercise of all their energies. They organized the Democrat party so as to include the leaders among the northern politicians. They never begrudged to these assistants a full share of the good things of official life. They have been aided by the fanatical abolitionism of the North by which the Republican party has been divided into two sections. It has been fashionable to be a Democrat, that is, to hold southern politics, and unfashionable to be a Republican, or to hold anti-southern politics. In that way the South has lived and struggled on against the growing will of the population; but at last that will became too strong, and when Mr. Lincoln was elected, the South knew that its day was over.

It is not surprising that the South should have desired secession. It is not surprising that it should have prepared for it. Since the days of Mr. Calhoun its leaders have always understood its position with a fair amount of political accuracy. Its only chance of political life lay in prolonged ascendancy at Washington. The swelling crowds of Germans, by whom the western States were being filled, enlisted themselves to a man in the ranks of abolition. What was the acquisition of Texas against such hosts as these? An evil day was coming on the southern politicians, and it behoved them to be prepared. As a separate nation,—a nation trusting to cotton, having in their hands, as they imagined, a monopoly of the staple of English manufacture, with a tariff of their own, and those rabid curses on the source of all their wealth no longer ringing in their ears, what might they not do as a separate nation? But as a part of the Union, they were too weak to hold their own if once their political finesse should fail them. That day came upon them, not unexpected, in 1860, and therefore they cut the cable.

And all this has come from slavery. It is hard enough, for how could the South have escaped slavery? How, at least, could the South have escaped slavery any time during these last thirty years? And is it, moreover, so certain that slavery is an unmitigated evil, opposed to God's will, and producing all the sorrows which have ever been produced by tyranny and wrong? It is here, after all, that one comes to the difficult question. Here is the knot which the fingers of men cannot open, and which admits of no sudden cutting with the knife. I have likened the slave-holding States to the drunken husband, and in so doing have pronounced judgment against them. As regards the state of the drunken man, his unfitness for partnership with any decent, diligent, well-to-do wife, his ruined condition, and shattered prospects, the simile, I think, holds good. But I refrain from saying, that as the fault was originally with the drunkard in that he became such, so also has the fault been with the slave States. At any rate I refrain from so saying here, on this page. That the position of a slave-owner is terribly prejudicial, not to the slave of whom I do not here speak, but to the owner;—of so much at any rate I feel assured. That the position is therefore criminal and damnable, I am not now disposed to take upon myself to assert.

The question of slavery in America cannot be handled fully and fairly by any one who is afraid to go back upon the subject, and take its whole history since one man first claimed and exercised the right of forcing labour from another man. I certainly am afraid of any such task; but I believe that there has been no period yet, since the world's work began, when such a practice has not prevailed in a large portion, probably in the largest portion, of the world's work-fields. As civilization has made its progress, it has been the duty and delight, as it has also been the interest of the men at the top of affairs, not to lighten the work of the men below, but so to teach them that they should recognize the necessity of working without coercion. Emancipation of serfs and thralls, of bondsmen and slaves, has always meant this,—that men having been so taught, should then work without coercion. As men become educated and aware of the nature of the tenure on which they hold their life, they learn the fact that work is a necessity for them, and that it is better to work without coercion than with it. When men have learned this they are fit for emancipation, but they are hardly fit till they have learned so much.

In talking or writing of slaves, we always now think of the negro slave. Of us Englishmen it must at any rate be acknowledged that we have done what in us lay to induce him to recognize this necessity for labour. At any rate we acted on the presumption that he would do so, and gave him his liberty throughout all our lands at a cost which has never yet been reckoned up in pounds, shillings, and pence. The cost never can be reckoned up, nor can the gain which we achieved in purging ourselves from the degradation and demoralization of such employment. We come into court with clean hands, having done all that lay with us to do to put down slavery both at home and abroad. But when we enfranchised the negroes, we did so with the intention, at least, that they should work as free men. Their share of the bargain in that respect they have declined to keep, wherever starvation has not been the result of such resolve on their part; and from the date of our emancipation, seeing the position which the negroes now hold with us, the southern States of America have learned to regard slavery as a permanent institution, and have taught themselves to regard it as a blessing, and not as a curse.

Negroes were first taken over to America because the white man could not work under the tropical heats, and because the native Indian would not work. The latter people has been, or soon will be, exterminated,—polished off the face of creation, as the Americans say,—which fate must, I should say, in the long run attend all non-working people. As the soil of the world is required for increasing population, the non-working people must go. And so the Indians have gone. The negroes under compulsion did work, and work well; and under their hands vast regions of the western tropics became fertile gardens. The fact that they were carried up into northern regions which from their nature did not require such aid, that slavery prevailed in New York and Massachusetts, does not militate against my argument. The exact limits of any great movement will not be bounded by its purpose. The heated wax which you drop on your letter spreads itself beyond the necessities of your seal. That these negroes would not have come to the western world without compulsion, or having come, would not have worked without compulsion, is, I imagine, acknowledged by all. That they have multiplied in the western world and have there become a race happier, at any rate in all the circumstances of their life, than their still untamed kinsmen in Africa, must also be acknowledged. Who, then, can dare to wish that all that has been done by the negro immigration should have remained undone?

The name of slave is odious to me. If I know myself I would not own a negro though he could sweat gold on my behoof. I glory in that bold leap in the dark which England took with regard to her own West Indian slaves. But I do not see the less clearly the difficulty of that position in which the southern States have been placed; and I will not call them wicked, impious, and abominable, because they now hold by slavery, as other nations have held by it at some period of their career. It is their misfortune that they must do so now,—now, when so large a portion of the world has thrown off the system, spurning as base and profitless all labour that is not free. It is their misfortune, for henceforth they must stand alone, with small rank among the nations, whereas their brethren of the North will still "flame in the forehead of the morning sky."

When the present constitution of the United States was written,—the merit of which must probably be given mainly to Madison and Hamilton, Madison finding the French democratic element, and Hamilton the English conservative element,—this question of slavery was doubtless a great trouble. The word itself is not mentioned in the constitution. It speaks not of a slave, but of a "person held to service or labour." It neither sanctions nor forbids slavery. It assumes no power in the matter of slavery; and under it, at the present moment, all Congress voting together, with the full consent of the legislatures of thirty-three States, could not constitutionally put down slavery in the remaining thirty-fourth State. In fact the constitution ignored the subject.

But nevertheless Washington, and Jefferson from whom Madison received his inspiration, were opposed to slavery. I do not know that Washington ever took much action in the matter, but his expressed opinion is on record. But Jefferson did so throughout his life. Before the declaration of independence he endeavoured to make slavery illegal in Virginia. In this he failed, but long afterwards, when the United States was a nation, he succeeded in carrying a law by which the further importation of slaves into any of the States was prohibited after a certain year—1820. When this law was passed, the framers of it considered that the gradual abolition of slavery would be secured. Up to that period the negro population in the States had not been self-maintained. As now in Cuba, the numbers had been kept up by new importations, and it was calculated that the race, when not recruited from Africa, would die out. That this calculation was wrong we now know, and the breeding-grounds of Virginia have been the result.

At that time there were no cotton-fields. Alabama and Mississippi were outlying territories. Louisiana had been recently purchased, but was not yet incorporated as a State. Florida still belonged to Spain, and was all but unpopulated. Of Texas no man had yet heard. Of the slave States, Virginia, the two Carolinas, and Georgia were alone wedded to slavery. Then the matter might have been managed. But under the constitution as it had been framed, and with the existing powers of the separate States, there was not even then open any way by which slavery could be abolished other than by the separate action of the States; nor has there been any such way opened since. With slavery these southern States have grown and become fertile. The planters have thriven, and the cotton-fields have spread themselves. And then came emancipation in the British islands. Under such circumstances and with such a lesson, could it be expected that the southern States should learn to love abolition?

It is vain to say that slavery has not caused secession, and that slavery has not caused the war. That, and that only, has been the real cause of this conflict, though other small collateral issues may now be put forward to bear the blame. Those other issues have arisen from this question of slavery, and are incidental to it and a part of it. Massachusetts, as we all know, is democratic in its tendencies, but South Carolina is essentially aristocratic. This difference has come of slavery. A slave country, which has progressed far in slavery, must be aristocratic in its nature,—aristocratic and patriarchal. A large slave-owner from Georgia may call himself a democrat,—may think that he reveres republican institutions, and may talk with American horror of the thrones of Europe; but he must in his heart be an aristocrat. We, in England, are apt to speak of republican institutions, and of universal suffrage which is perhaps the chief of them, as belonging equally to all the States. In South Carolina there is not and has not been any such thing. The electors for the President there are chosen not by the people, but by the legislature; and the votes for the legislature are limited by a high property qualification. A high property qualification is required for a member of the House of Representatives in South Carolina;—four hundred freehold acres of land and ten negroes is one qualification. Five hundred pounds clear of debt is another qualification;—for, where a sum of money is thus named, it is given in English money. Russia and England are not more unlike in their political and social feelings than are the real slave States and the real free-soil States. The gentlemen from one and from the other side of the line have met together on neutral ground, and have discussed political matters without flying frequently at each other's throats, while the great question on which they differed was allowed to slumber. But the awakening has been coming by degrees, and now the South had felt that it was come. Old John Brown, who did his best to create a servile insurrection at Harper's Ferry, has been canonized through the North and West, to the amazement and horror of the South. The decision in the "Dred Scott" case, given by the Chief Justice of the Supreme Court of the United States, has been received with shouts of execration through the North and West. The southern gentry have been Uncle-Tommed into madness. It is no light thing to be told daily by your fellow-citizens, by your fellow-representatives, by your fellow-senators, that you are guilty of the one damning sin that cannot be forgiven. All this they could partly moderate, partly rebuke, and partly bear as long as political power remained in their hands; but they have gradually felt that that was going, and were prepared to cut the rope and run as soon as it was gone.

Such, according to my ideas, have been the causes of the war. But I cannot defend the South. As long as they could be successful in their schemes for holding the political power of the nation, they were prepared to hold by the nation. Immediately those schemes failed, they were prepared to throw the nation overboard. In this there has undoubtedly been treachery as well as rebellion. Had these politicians been honest, — though the political growth of Washington has hardly admitted of political honesty, — but had these politicians been even ordinarily respectable in their dishonesty, they would have claimed secession openly before Congress, while yet their own President was at the White House. Congress would not have acceded. Congress itself could not have acceded under the constitution; but a way would have been found, had the southern States been persistent in their demand. A way, indeed, has been found; but it has lain through fire and water, through blood and ruin, through treason and theft, and the downfall of national greatness. Secession will, I think, be accomplished, and the southern Confederation of States will stand something higher in the world than Mexico and the republics of Central America. Her cotton monopoly will have vanished, and her wealth will have been wasted.

I think that history will agree with me in saying that the northern States had no alternative but war. What concession could they make? Could they promise to hold their peace about slavery? And had they so promised, would the South have believed them? They might have conceded secession; that is, they might have given all that would have been demanded. But what individual chooses to yield to such demands; and if not an individual,—then what people will do so? But in truth they could not have yielded all that was demanded. Had secession been granted to South Carolina and Georgia, Virginia would have been coerced to join those States by the nature of her property, and with Virginia Maryland would have gone, and Washington, the capital. What may be the future line of division between the North and the South I will not pretend to say; but that line will probably be dictated by the North. It may still be hoped that Missouri, Kentucky, Virginia, and Maryland will go with the North, and be rescued from slavery. But had secession been yielded, had the prestige of success fallen to the lot of the South, those States must have become southern.

While on this subject of slavery—for in discussing the cause of the war, slavery is the subject that must be discussed—I cannot forbear to say a few words about the negroes of the North American States. The republican party of the North is divided into two sections, of which one may be called abolitionist, and the other non-abolitionist. Mr. Lincoln's government presumes itself to belong to the latter, though its tendencies towards abolition are very strong. The abolition party is growing in strength daily. It is but a short time since Wendell Phillips could not lecture in Boston without a guard of police. Now, at this moment of my writing, he is a popular hero. The very men who, five years since, were accustomed to make speeches, strong as words could frame them, against abolition, are now turning round, and if not preaching abolition, are patting the backs of those who do so. I heard one of Mr. Lincoln's cabinet declare old John Brown to be a hero and a martyr. All the Protestant Germans are abolitionists,—and they have become so strong a political element in the country that many now declare that no future President can be elected without their aid. The object is declared boldly. No long political scheme is asked for, but instant abolition is wanted; abolition to be declared while yet the war is raging. Let the slaves of all rebels be declared free; and all slave-owners in the seceding States are rebels!

One cannot but ask what abolition means, and to what it would lead. Any ordinance of abolition now pronounced would not effect the emancipation of the slaves, but might probably effect a servile insurrection. I will not accuse those who are preaching this crusade of any desire for so fearful a scourge on the land. They probably calculate that an edict of abolition once given would be so much done towards the ultimate winning of the battle. They are making their hay while their sun shines. But if they could emancipate those four million slaves, in what way would they then treat them? How would they feed them? In what way would they treat the ruined owners of the slaves, and the acres of land which would lie uncultivated? Of all subjects with which a man can be called on to deal, it is the most difficult. But a New England abolitionist talks of it as though no more were required than an open path for his humanitarian energies. "I could arrange it all to-morrow morning," a gentleman şaid to me, who is well known for his zeal in this cause!

Arrange it all to-morrow morning,—abolition of slavery having become a fact during the night! I should not envy that gentleman his morning's work. It was bad enough with us, but what were our numbers compared with those of the southern States? We paid a price for the slaves, but no price is to be paid in this case. The value of the property would probably be lowly estimated at £100 a piece for men, women, and children, or four hundred million pounds for the whole population. They form the wealth of the South; and if they were bought, what should be done with them? They are like children. Every slave-owner in the country,—every man who has had ought to do with slaves,—will tell the same story. In Maryland and Delaware are men who hate slavery, who would be only too happy to enfranchise their slaves; but the negroes who have been slaves are not fit for freedom. In many cases, practically, they cannot be enfranchised. Give them their liberty, starting them well in the world at what expense you please, and at the end of six months they will come back upon your hands for the means of support. Everything must be done for them. They expect food and clothes, and instruction as to every simple act of life, as do children. The negro domestic servant is handy at his own work; no servant more so; but he cannot go beyond that. He does not comprehend the object and purport of continued industry. If he have money he will play with it,—will amuse himself with it. If he have none, he will amuse himself without it. His work is like a schoolboy's task; he knows it must be done, but never comprehends that the doing of it is the very end and essence of his life. He is a child in all things, and the extent of prudential wisdom to which he ever attains is to disdain emancipation, and cling to the security of his bondage. It is true enough that slavery has been a curse. Whatever may have been its effect on the negroes, it has been a deadly curse upon the white masters.

The preaching of abolition during the war is to me either the deadliest of sins or the vainest of follies. Its only immediate result possible would be servile insurrection. That is so manifestly atrocious,—a wish for it would be so hellish, that I do not presume the preachers of abolition to entertain it. But if that be not meant, it must be intended that an act of emancipation should be carried throughout the slave States,—either in their separation from the North, or after their subjection and consequent reunion with the North. As regards the States while in secession, the North cannot operate upon their slaves any more than England can operate on the slaves of Cuba. But if a reunion is to be a precursor of emancipation, surely that reunion should be first effected. A decision in the northern and western mind on such a subject cannot assist in obtaining that reunion,—but must militate against the practicability of such an object. This is so well understood, that Mr. Lincoln and his Government do not dare to call themselves abolitionists. *

> *President Lincoln has proposed a plan for the emancipation of slaves in the border States, and for compensation to the owners. His doing so proves that he regards present emancipation in the Gulf States as quite out of the question. It also proves that he looks forward to the recovery of the border States for the North, but that he does not look forward to the recovery of the Gulf States.

Abolition, in truth, is a political cry. It is the banner of defiance opposed to secession. As the differences between the North and South have grown with years, and have swelled to the proportions of national antipathy, southern nullification has amplified itself into secession, and northern free-soil principles have burst into this growth of abolition. Men have not calculated the results. Charming pictures are drawn for you of the negro in a state of Utopian bliss, owning his own hoe and eating his own hog; in a paradise, where everything is bought and sold, except his wife, his little ones, and himself. But the enfranchised negro has always thrown away his hoe, has eaten any man's hog but his own,—and has too often sold his daughter for a dollar when any such market has been open to him.

I confess that this cry of abolition has been made peculiarly displeasing to me by the fact that the northern abolitionist is by no means willing to give even to the negro who is already free that position in the world which alone might tend to raise him in the scale of human beings,—if anything can so raise him and make him fit for freedom. The abolitionists hold that the negro is the white man's equal. I do not. I see, or think that I see, that the negro is the white man's inferior through laws of nature. That he is not mentally fit to cope with white men,—I speak of the full-blooded negro,— and that he must fill a position simply servile. But the abolitionist declares him to be the white man's equal. But yet, when he has him at his elbow, he treats him with a scorn which even the negro can hardly endure. I will give him political equality, but not social equality, says the abolitionist. But even in this he is untrue. A black man may vote in New York, but he cannot vote under the same circumstances as a white man. He is subjected to qualifications which in truth debar him from the poll. A white man votes by manhood suffrage, providing he has been for one year an inhabitant of his State; but a man of colour must have been for three years a citizen of the State, and must own a property qualification of £50 free of debt. But political equality is not what such men want, nor indeed is it social equality. It is social tolerance and social sympathy; and these are denied to the negro. An American abolitionist would not sit at table with a negro. He might do so in England at the house of an English duchess; but in his own country the proposal of such a companion would be an insult to him. He will not sit with him in a public carriage if he can avoid it. In New York I have seen special street-cars for coloured people. The abolitionist is struck with horror when he thinks that a man and a brother should be a slave; but when the man and the brother has been made free, he is regarded with loathing and contempt. All this I cannot see with equanimity. There is falsehood in it from the beginning to the end. The slave as a rule is well treated,—gets all he wants and almost all he desires. The free negro as a rule is ill treated, and does not get that consideration which alone might put him in the worldly position for which his advocate declares him to be fit. It is false throughout,—this preaching. The negro is not the white man's equal by nature. But to the free negro in the northern States this inequality is increased by the white man's hardness to him.

In a former book which I wrote some few years since, I expressed an opinion as to the probable destiny of this race in the West Indies. I will not now go over that question again. I then divided the inhabitants of those islands into three classes,—the white, the black, and the coloured, taking a nomenclature which I found there prevailing. By coloured men I alluded to mulattoes, and all those of mixed European and African blood. The word "coloured," in the States, seems to apply to the whole negro race, whether full-blooded or half-blooded. I allude to this now because I wish to explain that, in speaking of what I conceive to be the intellectual inferiority of the negro race, I allude to those of pure negro descent,—or of descent so nearly pure as to make the negro element manifestly predominant. In the West Indies, where I had more opportunity of studying the subject, I always believed myself able to tell a negro from a coloured man. Indeed the classes are to a great degree distinct there, the greater portion of the retail trade of the country being in the hands of the coloured people. But in the States I have been able to make no such distinction. One sees generally neither the rich yellow of the West Indian mulatto, nor the deep oily black of the West Indian negro. The prevailing hue is a dry, dingy brown,—almost dusty in its dryness. I have observed but little difference made between the negro and the half-caste,—and no difference in the actual treatment. I have never met in American society any man or woman in whose veins there can have been presumed to be any taint of African blood. In Jamaica they are daily to be found in society.

Every Englishman probably looks forward to the accomplishment of abolition of slavery at some future day. I feel as sure of it as I do of the final judgment. When or how it shall come I will not attempt to foretell. The mode which seems to promise the surest success and the least present or future inconvenience, would be an edict enfranchising all female children born after a certain date, and all their children. Under such an arrangement the negro population would probably die out slowly,—very slowly. What might then be the fate of the cotton-fields of the Gulf States, who shall dare to say? It may be that coolies from India and from China will then have taken the place of the negro there, as they probably will have done also in Guiana and the West Indies.

CHAPTER IV
WASHINGTON TO ST. LOUIS

Though I had felt Washington to be disagreeable as a city, yet I was almost sorry to leave it when the day of my departure came. I had allowed myself a month for my sojourn in the capital, and I had stayed a month to the day. Then came the trouble of packing up, the necessity of calling on a long list of acquaintances one after another, the feeling that bad as Washington might be, I might be going to places that were worse, a conviction that I should get beyond the reach of my letters, and a sort of affection which I had acquired for my rooms. My landlord, being a coloured man, told me that he was sorry I was going. Would I not remain? Would I come back to him? Had I been comfortable? Only for so and so or so and so, he would have done better for me. No white American citizen, occupying the position of landlord, would have condescended to such comfortable words. I knew the man did not in truth want me to stay, as a lady and gentleman were waiting to go in the moment I went out; but I did not the less value the assurance. One hungers and thirsts after such civil words among American citizens of this class. The clerks and managers at hotels, the officials at railway stations, the cashiers at banks, the women in the shops;—ah! they are the worst of all. An American woman who is bound by her position to serve you,—who is paid in some shape to supply your wants, whether to sell you a bit of soap or bring you a towel in your bedroom at an hotel,—is, I think, of all human creatures, the most insolent. I certainly had a feeling of regret at parting with my coloured friend,—and some regret also as regards a few that were white.

As I drove down Pennsylvania Avenue, through the slush and mud, and saw, perhaps for the last time, those wretchedly dirty horse sentries who had refused to allow me to trot through the streets, I almost wished that I could see more of them. How absurd they looked, with a whole kit of rattletraps strapped on their horses' backs behind them,—blankets, coats, canteens, coils of rope, and, always at the top of everything else, a tin pot! No doubt these things are all necessary to a mounted sentry, or they would not have been there; but it always seemed as though the horse had been loaded gipsy-fashion, in a manner that I may perhaps best describe as higgledy-piggledy, and that there was a want of military precision in the packing. The man would have looked more graceful, and the soldier more warlike, had the pannikin been made to assume some rigidly fixed position instead of dangling among the ropes. The drawn sabre, too, never consorted well with the dirty outside woollen wrapper which generally hung loose from the man's neck. Heaven knows, I did not begrudge him his comforter in that cold weather, or even his long, uncombed shock of hair; but I think he might have been made more spruce, and I am sure that he could not have looked more uncomfortable. As I went, however, I felt for him a sort of affection, and wished in my heart of hearts that he might soon be enabled to return to some more congenial employment.

I went out by the Capitol, and saw that also, as I then believed, for the last time. With all its faults it is a great building, and, though unfinished, is effective; its very size and pretension give it a certain majesty. What will be the fate of that vast pile, and of those other costly public edifices at Washington, should the South succeed wholly in their present enterprise? If Virginia should ever become a part of the southern republic, Washington cannot remain the capital of the northern republic. In such case it would be almost better to let Maryland go also, so that the future destiny of that unfortunate city may not be a source of trouble, and a stumbling block of opprobrium. Even if Virginia be saved, its position will be most unfortunate.

I fancy that the railroads in those days must have been doing a very prosperous business. From New York to Philadelphia, thence on to Baltimore, and again to Washington, I had found the cars full; so full that sundry passengers could not find seats. Now, on my return to Baltimore, they were again crowded. The stations were all crowded. Luggage-trains were going in and out as fast as the rails could carry them. Among the passengers almost half were soldiers. I presume that these were men going on furlough, or on special occasions; for the regiments were of course not received by ordinary passenger trains. About this time a return was called for by Congress of all the moneys paid by the government, on account of the army, to the lines between New York and Washington. Whether or no it was ever furnished I did not hear; but it was openly stated that the colonels of regiments received large gratuities from certain railway companies for the regiments passing over their lines. Charges of a similar nature were made against officers, contractors, quartermasters, paymasters, generals, and cabinet ministers. I am not prepared to say that any of these men had dirty hands. It was not for me to make inquiries on such matters. But the continuance and universality of the accusations were dreadful. When everybody is suspected of being dishonest, dishonesty almost ceases to be regarded as disgraceful.

I will allude to a charge made against one member of the Cabinet, because the circumstances of the case were all acknowledged and proved. This gentleman employed his wife's brother-in-law to buy ships, and the agent so employed pocketed about £20,000 by the transaction in six months. The excuse made was that this profit was in accordance with the usual practice of the ship-dealing trade, and that it was paid by the owners who sold, and not by the Government which bought. But in so vast an agency the ordinary rate of profit on such business became an enormous sum; and the gentleman who made the plea must surely have understood that that £20,000 was in fact paid by the government. It is the purchaser, and not the seller, who in fact pays all such fees. The question is this,—Should the government have paid so vast a sum for one man's work for six months? And if so, was it well that that sum should go into the pocket of a near relative of the Minister whose special business it was to protect the government?

American private soldiers are not pleasant fellow-travellers. They are loud and noisy, and swear quite as much as the army could possibly have sworn in Flanders. They are, moreover, very dirty; and each man, with his long, thick great-coat, takes up more space than is intended to be allotted to him. Of course I felt that if I chose to travel in a country while it had such a piece of business on its hands, I could not expect that everything should be found in exact order. The matter for wonder, perhaps, was that the ordinary affairs of life were so little disarranged, and that any travelling at all was practicable. Nevertheless the fact remains that American private soldiers are not agreeable fellow-travellers.

It was my present intention to go due west across the country into Missouri, skirting, as it were, the line of the war which had now extended itself from the Atlantic across into Kansas. There were at this time three main armies,—that of the Potomac, as the army of Virginia was called, of which Maclellan held the command; that of Kentucky, under General Buell, who was stationed at Louisville on the Ohio; and the army on the Mississippi, which had been under Fremont, and of which General Halleck now held the command. To these were opposed the three rebel armies of Beauregard, in Virginia; of Johnston, on the borders of Kentucky and Tennessee; and of Price, in Missouri. There was also a fourth army in Kansas, west of Missouri, under General Hunter; and while I was in Washington another general, supposed by some to be the "coming man," was sent down to Kansas to participate in General Hunter's command. This was General Jim Lane, who resigned a seat in the Senate in order that he might undertake this military duty. When he reached Kansas, having on his route made sundry violent abolition speeches, and proclaimed his intention of sweeping slavery out of the south-western States, he came to loggerheads with his superior officer respecting their relative positions.

On my arrival at Baltimore, I found the place knee-deep in mud and slush and half-melted snow. It was then raining hard,—raining dirt, not water, as it sometimes does. Worse weather for soldiers out in tents could not be imagined,—nor for men who were not soldiers, but who nevertheless were compelled to leave their houses. I only remained at Baltimore one day, and then started again, leaving there the greater part of my baggage. I had a vague hope,—a hope which I hardly hoped to realize,—that I might be able to get through to the South. At any rate I made myself ready for the chance by making my travelling impediments as light as possible, and started from Baltimore, prepared to endure all the discomfort which lightness of baggage entails. My route lay over the Alleghanies by Pittsburg and Cincinnati, and my first stopping-place was at Harrisburg, the political capital of Pennsylvania. There is nothing special at Harrisburg to arrest any traveller; but the local legislature of the State was then sitting, and I was desirous of seeing the Senate and Representatives of at any rate one State, during its period of vitality.

In Pennsylvania the General Assembly, as the joint legislature is called, sits every year, commencing their work early in January, and continuing till it be finished. The usual period of sitting seems to be about ten weeks. In the majority of States, the legislature only sits every other year. In this State it sits every year, and the representatives are elected annually. The senators are elected for three years, a third of the body being chosen each year. The two chambers were ugly, convenient rooms, arranged very much after the fashion of the halls of Congress at Washington. Each member had his own desk, and his own chair. They were placed in the shape of a horse-shoe, facing the chairman, before whom sat three clerks. In neither house did I hear any set speech. The voices of the Speaker and of the clerks of the houses were heard more frequently than those of the members; and the business seemed to be done in a dull, serviceable, methodical manner, likely to be useful to the country, and very uninteresting to the gentlemen engaged. Indeed at Washington also, in Congress, it seemed to me that there was much less of set speeches than in our House of Commons. With us there are certain men whom it seems impossible to put down, and by whom the time of Parliament is occupied from night to night, with advantage to no one and with satisfaction to none but themselves. I do not think that the evil prevails to the same extent in America, either in Congress or in the State legislatures. As regards Washington, this good result may be assisted by a salutary practice which, as I was assured, prevails there. A member gets his speech printed at the Government cost, and sends it down free by post to his constituents, without troubling either the house with hearing it, or himself with speaking it. I cannot but think that the practice might be copied with success on our side of the water.

The appearance of the members of the legislature of Pennsylvania did not impress me very favourably. I do not know why we should wish a legislator to be neat in his dress, and comely, in some degree, in his personal appearance. There is no good reason, perhaps, why they should have cleaner shirts than their outside brethren, or have been more particular in the use of soap and water, and brush and comb. But I have an idea that if ever our own Parliament becomes dirty, it will lose its prestige; and I cannot but think that the Parliament of Pennsylvania would gain an accession of dignity by some slightly increased devotion to the Graces. I saw in the two houses but one gentleman, a senator, who looked like a Quaker; but even he was a very untidy Quaker.

I paid my respects to the Governor, and found him briskly employed in arranging the appointments of officers. All the regimental appointments to the volunteer regiments,—and that is practically to the whole body of the army, * —are made by the State in which the regiments are mustered. When the affair commenced, the captains and lieutenants were chosen by the men; but it was found that this would not do. When the skeleton of a State militia only was required, such an arrangement was popular and not essentially injurious; but now that war had become a reality, and that volunteers were required to obey discipline, some other mode of promotion was found necessary. As far as I could understand, the appointments were in the hands of the State Governor, who however was expected in the selection of the superior officers to be guided by the expressed wishes of the regiment, when no objection existed to such a choice. In the present instance the Governor's course was very thorny. Certain unfinished regiments were in the act of being amalgamated;—two perfect regiments being made up from perhaps five imperfect regiments, and so on. But though the privates had not been forthcoming to the full number for each expected regiment, there had been no such dearth of officers, and consequently the present operation consisted in reducing their number.

*The army at this time consisted nominally of 660,000 men, of whom only 20,000 were regulars.

Nothing can be much uglier than the State House at Harrisburg, but it commands a magnificent view of one of the valleys into which the Alleghany mountains is broken. Harrisburg is immediately under the range, probably at its finest point, and the railway running west from the town to Pittsburg, Cincinnati, and Chicago passes right over the chain. The line has been magnificently engineered, and the scenery is very grand. I went over the Alleghanies in mid-winter when they were covered with snow, but even when so seen they were very fine. The view down the valley from Altoona, a point near the summit, must in summer be excessively lovely. I stopped at Altoona one night with the object of getting about among the hills, and making the best of the winter view; but I found it impossible to walk. The snow had become frozen and was like glass. I could not progress a mile in any way. With infinite labour I climbed to the top of one little hill, and when there became aware that the descent would be very much more difficult. I did get down, but should not choose to describe the manner in which I accomplished the descent.

In running down the mountains to Pittsburg an accident occurred which in any other country would have thrown the engine off the line, and have reduced the carriages behind the engine to a heap of ruins. But here it had no other effect than that of delaying us for three or four hours. The tire of one of the heavy driving wheels flew off, and in the shock the body of the wheel itself was broken, one spoke and a portion of the circumference of the wheel was carried away, and the steam-chamber was ripped open. Nevertheless the train was pulled up, neither the engine nor any of the carriages got off the line, and the men in charge of the train seemed to think very lightly of the matter. I was amused to see how little was made of the affair by any of the passengers. In England a delay of three hours would in itself produce a great amount of grumbling, or at least many signs of discomfort and temporary unhappiness. But here no one said a word. Some of the younger men got out and looked at the ruined wheel; but most of the passengers kept their seats, chewed their tobacco, and went to sleep. In all such matters an American is much more patient than an Englishman. To sit quiet, without speech, and ruminate in some contorted position of body comes to him by nature. On this occasion I did not hear a word of complaint—nor yet a word of surprise or thankfulness that the accident had been attended with no serious result. "I have got a furlough for ten days," one soldier said to me. "And I have missed every connection all through from Washington here. I shall have just time to turn round and go back when I get home." But he did not seem to be in any way dissatisfied. He had not referred to his relatives when he spoke of "missing his connections," but to his want of good fortune as regarded railway travelling. He had reached Baltimore too late for the train on to Harrisburg, and Harrisburg too late for the train on to Pittsburg. Now he must again reach Pittsburg too late for his further journey. But nevertheless he seemed to be well pleased with his position.

Pittsburg is the Merthyr-Tydvil of Pennsylvania,—or perhaps I should better describe it as an amalgamation of Swansea, Merthyr-Tydvil, and South Shields. It is without exception the blackest place which I ever saw. The three English towns which I have named are very dirty, but all their combined soot and grease and dinginess do not equal that of Pittsburg. As regards scenery it is beautifully situated, being at the foot of the Alleghany mountains, and at the juncture of the two rivers Monongahela and Alleghany. Here, at the town, they come together and form the river Ohio. Nothing can be more picturesque than the site; for the spurs of the mountains come down close round the town, and the rivers are broad and swift, and can be seen for miles from heights which may be reached in a short walk. Even the filth and wondrous blackness of the place are picturesque when looked down upon from above. The tops of the churches are visible, and some of the larger buildings may be partially traced through the thick, brown, settled smoke. But the city itself is buried in a dense cloud. The atmosphere was especially heavy when I was there, and the effect was probably increased by the general darkness of the weather. The Monongahela is crossed by a fine bridge, and on the other side the ground rises at once, almost with the rapidity of a precipice; so that a commanding view is obtained down upon the town and the two rivers and the different bridges, from a height immediately above them. I was never more in love with smoke and dirt than when I stood here and watched the darkness of night close in upon the floating soot which hovered over the housetops of the city. I cannot say that I saw the sun set, for there was no sun. I should say that the sun never shone at Pittsburg,—as foreigners who visit London in November declare that the sun never shines there.

Walking along the river-side I counted thirty-two steamers, all beached upon the shore with their bows towards the land,—large boats, capable probably of carrying from one to two hundred passengers each, and about 300 tons of merchandise. On inquiry I found that many of these were not now at work. They were resting idle, the trade down the Mississippi below St. Louis having been cut off by the war. Many of them, however, were still running, the passage down the river being open to Wheeling in Virginia, to Portsmouth, Cincinnati and the whole of South Ohio, to Louisville in Kentucky, and to Cairo in Illinois, where the Ohio joins the Mississippi. The amount of traffic carried on by these boats while the country was at peace within itself was very great, and conclusive as to the increasing prosperity of the people. It seems that everybody travels in America, and that nothing is thought of distance. A young man will step into a car and sit beside you, with that easy, careless air which is common to a railway passenger in England who is passing from one station to the next; and on conversing with him you will find that he is going seven or eight hundred miles. He is supplied with fresh newspapers three or four times a day as he passes by the towns at which they are published; he eats a large assortment of gum-drops and apples, and is quite as much at home as in his own house. On board the river boats it is the same with him, with this exception, that when there he can get whisky when he wants it. He knows nothing of the ennui of travelling, and never seems to long for the end of his journey, as travellers do with us. Should his boat come to grief upon the river, and lie by for a day or a night, it does not in the least disconcert him. He seats himself upon three chairs, takes a bite of tobacco, thrusts his hands into his trousers pockets and revels in an elysium of his own.

I was told that the stockholders in these boats were in a bad way at the present time. There were no dividends going. The same story was repeated as to many and many an investment. Where the war created business, as it had done on some of the main lines of railroad and in some special towns, money was passing very freely; but away from this, ruin seemed to have fallen on the enterprise of the country. Men were not broken-hearted, nor were they even melancholy; but they were simply ruined. That is nothing in the States, so long as the ruined man has the means left to him of supplying his daily wants till he can start himself again in life. It is almost the normal condition of the American man in business; and therefore I am inclined to think that when this war is over, and things begin to settle themselves into new grooves, commerce will recover herself more quickly there than she would do among any other people. It is so common a thing to hear of an enterprise that has never paid a dollar of interest on the original outlay,—of hotels, canals, railroads, banks, blocks of houses, &c., that never paid even in the happy days of peace,—that one is tempted to disregard the absence of dividends, and to believe that such a trifling accident will not act as any check on future speculation. In no country has pecuniary ruin been so common as in the States; but then in no country is pecuniary ruin so little ruinous. "We are a recuperative people," a west-country gentleman once said to me. I doubted the propriety of his word, but I acknowledged the truth of his assertion.

Pittsburg and Alleghany, which latter is a town similar in its nature to Pittsburg on the other side of the river of the same name, regard themselves as places apart; but they are in effect one and the same city. They live under the same blanket of soot, which is woven by the joint efforts of the two places. Their united population is 135,000, of which Alleghany owns about 50,000. The industry of the towns is of that sort which arises from a union of coal and iron in the vicinity. The Pennsylvanian coalfields are the most prolific in the Union; and Pittsburg is therefore great, exactly as Merthyr-Tydvil and Birmingham are great. But the foundry-work at Pittsburg is more nearly allied to the heavy, rough works of the Welsh coal metropolis than to the finish and polish of Birmingham.

"Why cannot you consume your own smoke?" I asked a gentleman there. "Fuel is so cheap that it would not pay," he answered. His idea of the advantage of consuming smoke was confined to the question of its paying as a simple operation in itself. The consequent cleanliness and improvement in the atmosphere had not entered into his calculations. Any such result might be a fortuitous benefit, but was not of sufficient importance to make any effort in that direction expedient on its own account. "Coal was burned," he said, "in the foundries at something less than two dollars a ton; while that was the case, it could not answer the purpose of any iron-founder to put up an apparatus for the consumption of smoke." I did not pursue the argument any further, as I perceived that we were looking at the matter from two different points of view.

Everything in the hotel was black; not black to the eye, for the eye teaches itself to discriminate colours even when loaded with dirt, but black to the touch. On coming out of a tub of water my foot took an impress from the carpet exactly as it would have done had I trod barefooted on a path laid with soot. I thought that I was turning negro upwards, till I put my wet hand upon the carpet, and found that the result was the same. And yet the carpet was green to the eye,—a dull, dingy green, but still green. "You shouldn't damp your feet," a man said to me, to whom I mentioned the catastrophe. Certainly Pittsburg is the dirtiest place I ever saw, but it is, as I said before, very picturesque in its dirt when looked at from above the blanket.

From Pittsburg I went on by train to Cincinnati, and was soon in the State of Ohio. I confess that I have never felt any great regard for Pennsylvania. It has always had in my estimation a low character for commercial honesty, and a certain flavour of pretentious hypocrisy. This probably has been much owing to the acerbity and pungency of Sydney Smith's witty denunciations against the drab-coloured State. It is noted for repudiation of its own debts, and for sharpness in exaction of its own bargains. It has been always smart in banking. It has given Buchanan as a President to the country, and Cameron as a Secretary at War to the Government! When the battle of Bull's Run was to be fought, Pennsylvanian soldiers were the men who, on that day, threw down their arms because the three months' term for which they had been enlisted was then expired! Pennsylvania does not in my mind stand on a par with Massachusetts, Connecticut, New York, Illinois, or Virginia. We are apt to connect the name of Benjamin Franklin with Pennsylvania, but Franklin was a Boston man. Nevertheless, Pennsylvania is rich and prosperous. Indeed it bears all those marks which Quakers generally leave behind them.

I had some little personal feeling in visiting Cincinnati, because my mother had lived there for some time, and had there been concerned in a commercial enterprise, by which no one, I believe, made any great sum of money. Between thirty and forty years ago she built a bazaar in Cincinnati, which I was assured by the present owner of the house, was at the time of its erection considered to be the great building of the town. It has been sadly eclipsed now, and by no means rears its head proudly among the great blocks around it. It had become a "Physico-medical Institute" when I was there, and was under the dominion of a quack doctor on one side, and of a college of rights-of-women female medical professors on the other. "I believe, sir, no man or woman ever yet made a dollar in that building; and as for rent, I don't even expect it." Such was the account given of the unfortunate bazaar by the present proprietor.

Cincinnati has long been known as a great town,—conspicuous among all towns for the number of hogs which are there killed, salted, and packed. It is the great hog metropolis of the western States; but Cincinnati has not grown with the rapidity of other towns. It has now 170,000 inhabitants, but then it got an early start. St. Louis, which is west of it again, near the confluence of the Missouri and Mississippi, has gone ahead of it. Cincinnati stands on the Ohio river, separated by a ferry from Kentucky, which is a slave State. Ohio itself is a free-soil State. When the time comes for arranging the line of division, if such time shall ever come, it will be very hard to say where northern feeling ends and where southern wishes commence. Newport and Covington, which are in Kentucky, are suburbs of Cincinnati; and yet in these places slavery is rife. The domestic servants are mostly slaves, though it is essential that those so kept should be known as slaves who will not run away. It is understood that a slave who escapes into Ohio will not be caught and given up by the intervention of the Ohio police; and from Covington or Newport any slave can escape into Ohio with ease. But when that division takes place, no river like the Ohio can form the boundary between the divided nations. Such rivers are the highways, round which in this country people have clustered themselves. A river here is not a natural barrier, but a connecting street. It would be as well to make a railway a division, or the centre line of a city a national boundary. Kentucky and Ohio States are joined together by the Ohio river, with Cincinnati on one side and Louisville on the other; and I do not think that man's act can upset these ties of nature. But between Kentucky and Tennessee there is no such bond of union. There a mathematical line has been simply drawn, a continuation of that line which divides Virginia from North Carolina, to which two latter States Kentucky and Tennessee belonged when the thirteen original States first formed themselves into a union. But that mathematical line has offered no peculiar advantages to population. No great towns cluster there, and no strong social interests would be disseevered should Kentucky throw in her lot with the North, and Tennessee with the South; but Kentucky owns a quarter of a million of slaves, and those slaves must either be emancipated or removed before such a junction can be firmly settled.

The great business of Cincinnati is hog-killing now, as it used to be in the old days of which I have so often heard. It seems to be an established fact, that in this portion of the world the porcine genus are all hogs. One never hears of a pig. With us a trade in hogs and pigs is subject to some little contumely. There is a feeling, which has perhaps never been expressed in words, but which certainly exists, that these animals are not so honourable in their bearings as sheep and oxen. It is a prejudice which by no means exists in Cincinnati. There hog killing and salting and packing are very honourable, and the great men in the trade are the merchant princes of the city. I went to see the performance, feeling it to be a duty to inspect everywhere that which I found to be of most importance; but I will not describe it. There were a crowd of men operating, and I was told that the point of honour was to "put through" a hog a minute. It must be understood that the animal enters upon the ceremony alive, and comes out in that cleanly, disembowelled guise in which it may sometimes be seen hanging up previous to the operation of the pork-butcher's knife. To one special man was appointed a performance which seemed to be specially disagreeable, so that he appeared despicable in my eyes; but when on inquiry I learned that he earned five dollars, or a pound sterling, a day, my judgment as to his position was reversed. And after all what matters the ugly nature of such an occupation when a man is used to it?

Cincinnati is like all other American towns, with second, third, and fourth streets, seventh, eighth, and ninth streets, and so on. Then the cross-streets are named chiefly from trees. Chesnut, walnut, locust, &c. I do not know whence has come this fancy for naming streets after trees in the States, but it is very general. The town is well built, with good fronts to many of the houses, with large shops and larger stores;—of course also with an enormous hotel, which has never paid anything like a proper dividend to the speculator who built it. It is always the same story. But these towns shame our provincial towns by their breadth and grandeur. I am afraid that speculators with us are trammelled by an "ignorant impatience of ruin." I should not myself like to live in Cincinnati or in any of these towns. They are slow, dingy, and uninteresting; but they all possess an air of substantial, civic dignity. It must however be remembered that the Americans live much more in towns than we do. All with us that are rich and aristocratic and luxurious live in the country, frequenting the metropolis for only a portion of the year. But all that are rich and aristocratic and luxurious in the States live in the towns. Our provincial towns are not generally chosen as the residences of our higher classes.

Cincinnati has 170,000 inhabitants, and there are 14,000 children at the free schools,—which is about one in twelve of the whole population. This number gives the average of scholars throughout the year ended 30th June, 1861. But there are other schools in Cincinnati,—parish schools and private schools, and it is stated to me that there were in all 32,000 children attending school in the city throughout the year. The education at the State schools is very good. Thirty-four teachers are employed, at an average salary of £92 each, ranging from £260 to £60 per annum. It is in this matter of education that the cities of the free States of America have done so much for the civilization and welfare of their population. This fact cannot be repeated in their praise too often. Those who have the management of affairs, who are at the top of the tree, are desirous of giving to all an opportunity of raising themselves in the scale of human beings. I dislike universal suffrage; I dislike vote by ballot; I dislike above all things the tyranny of democracy. But I do like the political feeling—for it is a political feeling—which induces every educated American to lend a hand to the education of his fellow-citizens. It shows, if nothing else does so, a germ of truth in that doctrine of equality. It is a doctrine to be forgiven when he who preaches it is in truth striving to raise others to his own level;—though utterly unpardonable when the preacher would pull down others to his level.

Leaving Cincinnati I again entered a slave State, namely, Kentucky. When the war broke out Kentucky took upon itself to say that it would be neutral, as if neutrality in such a position could by any means have been possible! Neutrality on the borders of secession, on the battle-field of the coming contest, was of course impossible. Tennessee, to the south, had joined the South by a regular secession ordinance. Ohio, Illinois, and Indiana to the north were of course true to the Union. Under these circumstances it became necessary that Kentucky should choose her side. With the exception of the little State of Delaware, in which from her position secesssion would have been impossible, Kentucky was, I think, less inclined to rebellion, more desirous of standing by the North, than any other of the slave States. She did all she could, however, to put off the evil day of so evil a choice. Abolition within her borders was held to be abominable as strongly as it was so held in Georgia. She had no sympathy and could have none with the teachings and preachings of Massachusetts. But she did not wish to belong to a Confederacy of which the northern States were to be the declared enemy, and be the border State of the South under such circumstances. She did all she could for personal neutrality. She made that effort for general reconciliation of which I have spoken as the Crittenden compromise. But compromises and reconciliation were not as yet possible, and therefore it was necessary that she should choose her part. Her Governor declared for secession; and at first also her legislature was inclined to follow the Governor. But no overt act of secession by the State was committed, and at last it was decided that

Kentucky should be declared to be loyal. It was in fact divided. Those on the southern border joined the secessionists, whereas the greater portion of the State, containing Frankfort the capital and the would-be secessionist Governor who lived there, joined the North. Men in fact became unionists or secessionists, not by their own conviction, but through the necessity of their positions; and Kentucky, through the necessity of her position, became one of the scenes of civil war.

I must confess that the difficulty of the position of the whole country seems to me to have been under-estimated in England. In common life it is not easy to arrange the circumstances of a divorce between man and wife, all whose belongings and associations have for many years been in common. Their children, their money, their house, their friends, their secrets, have been joint property and have formed bonds of union. But yet such quarrels may arise, such mutual antipathy, such acerbity and even ill-usage, that all who know them admit that a separation is needed. So it is here in the States. Free-soil and slave-soil could, while both were young and unused to power, go on together,—not without many jars and unhappy bickerings; but they did go on together. But now they must part; and how shall the parting be made? With which side shall go this child, and who shall remain in possession of that pleasant homestead? Putting secession aside, there were in the United States two distinct political doctrines, of which the extremes were opposed to each other as pole is opposed to pole. We have no such variance of creed, no such radical difference as to the essential rules of life between parties in our country. We have no such cause for personal rancour in our Parliament as has existed for some years past in both Houses of Congress. These two extreme parties were the slave-owners of the South and the abolitionists of the North and West. Fifty years ago the former regarded the institution of slavery as a necessity of their position,—generally as an evil necessity,—and generally also as a custom to be removed in the course of years. Gradually they have learned to look upon slavery as good in itself, and to believe that it has been the source of their wealth and the strength of their position. They have declared it to be a blessing inalienable,—that should remain among them for ever,—as an inheritance not to be touched, and not to be spoken of with hard words. Fifty years ago the abolitionists of the North differed only in opinion from the slave-owners of the South in hoping for a speedier end to this stain upon the nation; and in thinking that some action should be taken towards the final emancipation of the bondsmen. But they also have progressed; and as the southern masters have called the institution blessed, they have called it accursed. Their numbers have increased, and with their numbers their power and their violence. In this way two parties have been formed who could not look on each other without hatred. An intermediate doctrine has been held by men who were nearer in their sympathies to the slave-owners than to the abolitionists; but who were not disposed to justify slavery as a thing apart. These men have been aware that slavery has existed in accordance with the constitution of their country, and have been willing to attach the stain which accompanies the institution to the individual State which entertains it, and not to the national Government, by which the question has been constitutionally ignored. The men who have participated in the Government have naturally been inclined towards the middle doctrine; but as the two extremes have retreated further from each other, the power of this middle-class of politicians has decreased. Mr. Lincoln, though he does not now declare himself an abolitionist, was elected by the abolitionists; and when, as a consequence of that election, secession was threatened, no step which he could have taken would have satisfied the South which had opposed him, and been at the same time true to the North which had chosen him. But it was possible that his Government might save Maryland, Virginia, Kentucky, and Missouri. As Radicals in England become simple Whigs when they are admitted into public offices, so did Mr. Lincoln with his government become anti-abolitionist when he entered on his functions. Had he combated secession with emancipation of the slaves, no slave State would or could have held by the Union. Abolition for a lecturer may be a telling subject. It is easy to bring down rounds of applause by tales of the wrongs of bondage. But to men in office, abolition was too stern a reality. It signified servile insurrection, absolute ruin to all southern slave-owners, and the absolute enmity of every slave State.

But that task of steering between the two has been very difficult. I fear that the task of so steering with success is almost impossible. In England it is thought that Mr. Lincoln might have maintained the Union by compromising matters with the South,—or if not so, that he might have maintained peace by yielding to the South. But no such power was in his hands. While we were blaming him for opposition to all southern terms, his own friends in the North were saying that all principle and truth was abandoned for the sake of such States as Kentucky and Missouri. "Virginia is gone; Maryland cannot go. And slavery is endured and the new virtue of Washington is made to tamper with the evil one, in order that a show of loyalty may be preserved in one or two States which after all are not truly loyal!" That is the accusation made against the government by the abolitionists; and that made by us on the other side is the reverse. I believe that Mr. Lincoln had no alternative but to fight, and that he was right also not to fight with abolition as his battle-cry. That he may be forced by his own friends into that cry, is, I fear, still possible. Kentucky at any rate did not secede in bulk. She still sent her senators to Congress, and allowed herself to be reckoned among the stars in the American firmament. But she could not escape the presence of the war. Did she remain loyal or did she secede, that was equally her fate.

The day before I entered Kentucky a battle was fought in that State, which gave to the northern arms their first actual victory. It was at a place called Mill Spring, near Somerset, towards the south of the State. General Zollicoffer, with a Confederate army, numbering, it was supposed, some eight thousand men, had advanced upon a smaller Federal force, commanded by General Thomas, and had been himself killed, while his army was cut to pieces and dispersed; the cannon of the Confederates were taken, and their camp seized and destroyed. Their rout was complete; but in this instance again the advancing party had been beaten, as had, I believe, been the case in all the actions hitherto fought throughout the war. Here, however, had been an actual victory, and it was not surprising that in Kentucky loyal men should rejoice greatly, and begin to hope that the Confederates would be beaten out of the State. Unfortunately, however, General Zollicoffer's army had only been an offshoot from the main rebel army in Kentucky. Buell, commanding the Federal troops at Louisville, and Sydney Johnston, the Confederate General, at Bowling Green, as yet remained opposite to each other, and the work was still to be done.

I visited the little towns of Lexington and Frankfort, in Kentucky. At the former I found in the hotel to which I went seventy-five teamsters belonging to the army. They were hanging about the great hall when I entered, and clustering round the stove in the middle of the chamber;—a dirty, rough, quaint set of men, clothed in a wonderful variety of garbs, but not disorderly or loud. The landlord apologized for their presence, alleging that other accommodation could not be found for them in the town. He received, he said, a dollar a day for feeding them, and for supplying them with a place in which they could lie down. It did not pay him,—but what could he do? Such an apology from an American landlord was in itself a surprising fact. Such high functionaries are, as a rule, men inclined to tell a traveller that if he does not like the guests among whom he finds himself, he may go elsewhere. But this landlord had as yet filled the place for not more than two or three weeks, and was unused to the dignity of his position. While I was at supper, the seventy-five teamsters were summoned into the common eating-room by a loud gong, and sat down to their meal at the public table. They were very dirty; I doubt whether I ever saw dirtier men; but they were orderly and well-behaved, and but for their extreme dirt might have passed as the ordinary occupants of a well-filled hotel in the West. Such men, in the States, are less clumsy with their knives and forks, less astray in an unused position, more intelligent in adapting themselves to a new life than are Englishmen of the same rank. It is always the same story. With us there is no level of society. Men stand on a long staircase, but the crowd congregates near the bottom, and the lower steps are very broad. In America men stand upon a common platform, but the platform is raised above the ground, though it does not approach in height the top of our staircase. If we take the average altitude in the two countries, we shall find that the American heads are the more elevated of the two. I conceived rather an affection for those dirty teamsters; they answered me civilly when I spoke to them, and sat in quietness, smoking their pipes, with a dull and dirty, but orderly demeanour.

The country about Lexington is called the Blue Grass Region, and boasts itself as of peculiar fecundity in the matter of pasturage. Why the grass is called blue, and or in what way or at what period it becomes blue, I did not learn; but the country is very lovely and very fertile. Between Lexington and Frankfort a large stock farm, extending over three thousand acres, is kept by a gentleman, who is very well known as a breeder of horses, cattle, and sheep. He has spent much money on it, and is making for himself a Kentucky elysium. He was kind enough to entertain me for a while, and showed me something of country life in Kentucky. A farm in that part of the State depends, and must depend, chiefly on slave-labour. The slaves are a material part of the estate, and as they are regarded by the law as real property—being actually adstricti glebæ—an inheritor of land has no alternative but to keep them. A gentleman in Kentucky does not sell his slaves. To do so is considered to be low and mean, and is opposed to the aristocratic traditions of the country. A man who does so willingly, puts himself beyond the pale of good-fellowship with his neighbours. A sale of slaves is regarded as a sign almost of bankruptcy. If a man cannot pay his debts, his creditors can step in and sell his slaves; but he does not himself make the sale. When a man owns more slaves than he needs, he hires them out by the year; and when he requires more than he owns, he takes them on hire by the year. Care is taken in such hirings not to remove a married man away from his home. The price paid for a negro's labour at the time of my visit was about a hundred dollars, or twenty pounds, for the year; but this price was then extremely low in consequence of the war disturbances. The usual price had been about fifty or sixty per cent. above this. The man who takes the negro on hire feeds him, clothes him, provides him with a bed, and supplies him with medical attendance. I went into some of their cottages on the estate which I visited, and was not in the least surprised to find them preferable in size, furniture, and all material comforts to the dwellings of most of our own agricultural labourers. Any comparison between the material comfort of a Kentucky slave and an English ditcher and delver would be preposterous. The Kentucky slave never wants for clothing fitted to the weather. He eats meat twice a day, and has three good meals; he knows no limit but his own appetite; his work is light; he has many varieties of amusement; he has instant medical assistance at all periods of necessity for himself, his wife, and his children. Of course he pays no rent, fears no baker, and knows no hunger. I would not have it supposed that I conceive slavery with all these comforts to be equal to freedom without them; nor do I conceive that the negro can be made equal to the white man. But in discussing the condition of the negro, it is necessary that we should understand what are the advantages of which abolition would deprive him, and in what condition he has been placed by the daily receipt of such advantages. If a negro slave wants new shoes, he asks for them, and receives them, with the undoubting simplicity of a child. Such a state of things has its picturesquely patriarchal side; but what would be the state of such a man if he were emancipated to-morrow?

The natural beauty of the place which I was visiting was very great. The trees were fine and well-scattered over the large, park-like pastures, and the ground was broken on every side into hills. There was perhaps too much timber, but my friend seemed to think that that fault would find a natural remedy only too quickly. "I do not like to cut down trees if I can help it," he said. After that I need not say that my host was quite as much an Englishman as an American. To the purely American farmer a tree is simply an enemy to be trodden under foot, and buried underground, or reduced to ashes and thrown to the winds with what most economical despatch may be possible. If water had been added to the landscape here it would have been perfect, regarding it as ordinary English park-scenery. But the little rivers at this place have a dirty trick of burying themselves under the ground. They go down suddenly into holes, disappearing from the upper air, and then come up again at the distance of perhaps half a mile. Unfortunately their periods of seclusion are more prolonged than those of their upper-air distance. There were three or four such ascents and descents about the place.

My host was a breeder of race-horses, and had imported sires from England; of sheep also, and had imported famous rams; of cattle too, and was great in bulls. He was very loud in praise of Kentucky and its attractions, if only this war could be brought to an end. But I could not obtain from him an assurance that the speculation in which he was engaged had been profitable. Ornamental farming in England is a very pretty amusement for a wealthy man, but I fancy,—without intending any slight on Mr. Mechi,—that the amusement is expensive. I believe that the same thing may be said of it in a slave State.

Frankfort is the capital of Kentucky, and is as quietly dull a little town as I ever entered. It is on the river Kentucky, and as the grounds about it on every side rise in wooded hills, it is a very pretty place. In January it was very pretty, but in summer it must be lovely. I was taken up to the cemetery there by a path along the river, and am inclined to say that it is the sweetest resting-place for the dead that I have ever visited. Daniel Boone lies there. He was the first white man who settled in Kentucky; or rather, perhaps, the first who entered Kentucky with a view to a white man's settlement. Such frontier men as was Daniel Boone never remained long contented with the spots they opened. As soon as he had left his mark in that territory he went again further west over the big rivers into Missouri, and there he died. But the men of Kentucky are proud of Daniel Boone, and so they have buried him in the loveliest spot they could select, immediately over the river. Frankfort is worth a visit, if only that this grave and graveyard may be seen. The legislature of the State was not sitting when I was there, and the grass was growing in the streets.

Louisville is the commercial city of the State, and stands on the Ohio. It is another great town, like all the others, built with high stores, and great houses and stone-faced blocks. I have no doubt that all the building speculations have been failures, and that the men engaged in them were all ruined. But there, as the result of their labour, stands a fair great city on the southern banks of the Ohio. Here General Buell held his head-quarters, but his army lay at a distance. On my return from the West I visited one of the camps of this army, and will speak of it as I speak of my backward journey. I had already at this time begun to conceive an opinion that the armies in Kentucky and in Missouri would do at any rate as much for the northern cause as that of the Potomac, of which so much more had been heard in England.

While I was at Louisville the Ohio was flooded. It had begun to rise when I was at Cincinnati, and since then had gone on increasing hourly, rising inch by inch up into the towns upon its bank. I visited two suburbs of Louisville, both of which were submerged, as to the streets and ground-floors of the houses. At Shipping Port, one of these suburbs, I saw the women and children clustering in the up-stairs room, while the men were going about in punts and wherries, collecting drift wood from the river for their winter's firing. In some places bedding and furniture had been brought over to the high ground, and the women were sitting, guarding their little property. That village, amidst the waters, was a sad sight to see; but I heard no complaints. There was no tearing of hair and no gnashing of teeth; no bitter tears or moans of sorrow. The men who were not at work in the boats stood loafing about in clusters, looking at the still rising river;

but each seemed to be personally indifferent to the matter. When the house of an American is carried down the river, he builds himself another;—as he would get himself a new coat when his old coat became unserviceable. But he never laments or moans for such a loss. Surely there is no other people so passive under personal misfortune!

Going from Louisville up to St. Louis, I crossed the Ohio river and passed through parts of Indiana and of Illinois, and striking the Mississippi opposite St. Louis, crossed that river also, and then entered the State of Missouri. The Ohio was, as I have said, flooded, and we went over it at night. The boat had been moored at some unaccustomed place. There was no light. The road was deep in mud up to the axle-tree, and was crowded with waggons and carts, which in the darkness of the night seemed to have stuck there. But the man drove his four horses through it all, and into the ferry-boat, over its side. There were three or four such omnibuses, and as many waggons, as to each of which I predicted in my own mind some fatal catastrophe. But they were all driven on to the boat in the dark, the horses mixing in through each other in a chaos which would have altogether incapacitated any English coachman. And then the vessel laboured across the flood, going sideways, and hardly keeping her own against the stream. But we did get over, and were all driven out again, up to the railway station in safety. On reaching the Mississippi about the middle of the next day, we found it frozen over, or rather covered from side to side with blocks of ice which had forced its way down the river, so that the steam ferry could not reach its proper landing. I do not think that we in England would have attempted the feat of carrying over horses and carriages under stress of such circumstances. But it was done here. Huge plankings were laid down over the ice, and omnibuses and waggons were driven on. In getting out again, these vehicles, each with four horses, had to be twisted about, and driven in and across the vessel, and turned in spaces to look at which would have broken the heart of an English coachman. And then with a spring they were driven up a bank as steep as a ladder! Ah me! under what mistaken illusions have I not laboured all the days of my youth, in supposing that no man could drive four horses well but an English stage-coachman? I have seen performances in America,—and in Italy and France also, but above all in America,—which would have made the hair of any English professional driver stand on end.

And in this way I entered St. Louis.

CHAPTER V
MISSOURI

Missouri is a slave State lying to the west of the Mississippi and to the north of Arkansas. It forms a portion of the territory ceded by France to the United States in 1803. Indeed, it is difficult to say how large a portion of the continent of North America is supposed to be included in that territory. It contains the States of Louisiana, Arkansas, Missouri, and Kansas, as also the present Indian territory; but it also is said to have contained all the land lying back from them to the Rocky Mountains, Utah, Nebraska, and Dacotah, and forms no doubt the widest dominion ever ceded by one nationality to another.

Missouri lies exactly north of the old Missouri compromise line, that is, 36·30 north. When the Missouri compromise was made it was arranged that Missouri should be a slave State, but that no other State north of the 36·30 line should ever become slave soil. Kentucky and Virginia, as also of course Maryland and Delaware, four of the old slave States, were already north of that line; but the compromise was intended to prevent the advance of slavery in the north-west. The compromise has been since annulled, on the ground, I believe, that Congress had not constitutionally the power to declare that any soil should be free, or that any should be slave soil. That is a question to be decided by the States themselves, as each individual State may please. So the compromise was repealed. But slavery has not on that account advanced. The battle has been fought in Kansas, and after a long and terrible struggle, Kansas has come out of the fight as a free State. Kansas is in the same parallel of latitude as Virginia, and stretches west as far as the Rocky Mountains.

When the census of the population of Missouri was taken in 1860, the slaves amounted to 10 per cent. of the whole number. In the Gulf States the slave population is about 45 per cent. of the whole. In the three border States of Kentucky, Virginia, and Maryland, the slaves amount to 30 per cent. of the whole population. From these figures it will be seen that Missouri, which is comparatively a new slave State, has not gone a-head with slavery as the old slave States have done, although from its position and climate, lying as far south as Virginia, it might seem to have had the same reasons for doing so. I think there is every reason to believe that slavery will die out in Missouri. The institution is not popular with the people generally; and as white labour becomes abundant,—and before the war it was becoming abundant,—men recognize the fact that the white man's labour is the more profitable. The heat in this State, in midsummer, is very great, especially in the valleys of the rivers. At St. Louis, on the Mississippi, it reaches commonly to 90 degrees, and very frequently goes above that. The nights moreover are nearly as hot as the days; but this great heat does not last for any very long period, and it seems that white men are able to work throughout the year. If correspondingly severe weather in winter affords any compensation to the white man for what of heat he endures during the summer, I can testify that such compensation is to be found in Missouri. When I was there we were afflicted with a combination of snow, sleet, frost, and wind, with a mixture of ice and mud, that makes me regard Missouri as the most inclement land into which I ever penetrated.

St. Louis, on the Mississippi, is the great town of Missouri, and is considered by the Missourians to be the star of the West. It is not to be beaten in population, wealth, or natural advantages by any other city so far west; but it has not increased with such rapidity as Chicago, which is considerably to the north of it on Lake Michigan. Of the great western cities I regard Chicago as the most remarkable, seeing that St. Louis was a large town before Chicago had been founded.

The population of St. Louis is 170,000. Of this number only 2000 are slaves. I was told that a large proportion of the slaves of Missouri are employed near the Missouri river in breaking hemp. The growth of hemp is very profitably carried on in that valley, and the labour attached to it is one which white men do not like to encounter. Slaves are not generally employed in St. Louis for domestic service, as is done almost universally in the towns of Kentucky. This work is chiefly in the hands of Irish and Germans. Considerably above one-third of the population of the whole city is made up of these two nationalities. So much is confessed; but if I were to form an opinion from the language I heard in the streets of the town, I should say that nearly every man was either an Irishman or a German.

St. Louis has none of the aspects of a slave city. I cannot say that I found it an attractive place, but then I did not visit it at an attractive time. The war had disturbed everything, given a special colour of its own to men's thoughts and words, and destroyed all interest except that which might proceed from itself. The town is well built, with good shops, straight streets, never-ending rows of excellent houses, and every sign of commercial wealth and domestic comfort,—of commercial wealth and domestic comfort in the past, for there was no present appearance either of comfort or of wealth.

The new hotel here was to be bigger than all the hotels of all other towns. It is built, and is an enormous pile, and would be handsome but for a terribly ambitious Grecian doorway. It is built, as far as the walls and roof are concerned, but in all other respects is unfinished. I was told that the shares of the original stockholders were now worth nothing. A shareholder, who so told me, seemed to regard this as the ordinary course of business.

The great glory of the town is the "levée," as it is called, or the long river beach up to which the steamers are brought with their bows to the shore. It is an esplanade looking on to the river, not built with quays or wharves, as would be the case with us, but with a sloping bank running down to the water. In the good days of peace a hundred vessels were to be seen here, each with its double funnels. The line of them seemed to be never ending even when I was there, but then a very large proportion of them were lying idle. They resemble huge wooden houses, apparently of frail architecture, floating upon the water. Each has its double row of balconies running round it, and the lower or ground floor is open throughout. The upper stories are propped and supported on ugly sticks and ricketty-looking beams; so that the first appearance does not convey any great idea of security to a stranger. They are always painted white and the paint is always very dirty. When they begin to move, they moan and groan in melancholy tones which are subversive of all comfort; and as they continue on their courses they puff and bluster, and are for ever threatening to burst and shatter themselves to pieces. There they lie in a continuous line nearly a mile in length along the levée of St. Louis, dirty, dingy, and now, alas, mute. They have ceased to groan and puff, and if this war be continued for six months longer, will become rotten and useless as they lie.

They boast at St. Louis that they command 46,000 miles of navigable river water, counting the great rivers up and down from that place. These rivers are chiefly the Mississippi, the Missouri and Ohio which fall into the Mississippi near St. Louis, the Platte and Kansas rivers—tributaries of the Missouri, the Illinois, and the Wisconsin. All these are open to steamers, and all of them traverse regions rich in corn, in coal, in metals, or in timber. These ready-made highways of the world centre, as it were, at St. Louis, and make it the depôt of the carrying trade of all that vast country. Minnesota is 1500 miles above New Orleans, but the wheat of Minnesota can be brought down the whole distance without change of the vessel in which it is first deposited. It would seem to be impossible that a country so blessed should not become rich. It must be remembered that these rivers flow through lands that have never yet been surpassed in natural fertility. Of all countries in the world one would say that the States of America should have been the last to curse themselves with a war; but now the curse has fallen upon them with a double vengeance. It would seem that they could never be great in war: their very institutions forbid it; their enormous distances forbid it; the price of labour forbids it; and it is forbidden also by the career of industry and expansion which has been given to them. But the curse of fighting has come upon them, and they are showing themselves to be as eager in the works of war as they have shown themselves capable in the works of peace. Men and angels must weep as they behold the things that are being done, as they watch the ruin that has come and is still coming, as they look on commerce killed and agriculture suspended. No sight so sad has come upon the earth in our days. They were a great people; feeding the world, adding daily to the mechanical appliances of mankind, increasing in population beyond all measures of such increase hitherto known, and extending education as fast as they extended their numbers. Poverty had as yet found no place among them, and hunger was an evil of which they had read, but were themselves ignorant. Each man among their crowds had a right to be proud of his manhood. To read and write,—I am speaking here of the North,—was as common as to eat and drink. To work was no disgrace, and the wages of work were plentiful. To live without work was the lot of none. What blessing above these blessings was needed to make a people great and happy? And now a stranger visiting them would declare that they are wallowing in a very slough of despond. The only trade open is the trade of war. The axe of the woodsman is at rest; the plough is idle; the artificer has closed his shop. The roar of the foundry is still heard because cannon are needed, and the river of molten iron comes out as an implement of death. The stone-cutter's hammer and the mason's trowel are never heard. The gold of the country is hiding itself as though it had returned to its mother-earth, and the infancy of a paper currency has been commenced. Sick soldiers, who have never seen a battlefield, are dying by hundreds in the squalid dirt of their unaccustomed camps. Men and women talk of war, and of war only. Newspapers full of the war are alone read. A contract for war stores,—too often a dishonest contract,—is the one path open for commercial enterprise. The young man must go to the war or he is disgraced. The war swallows everything, and as yet has failed to produce even such bitter fruits as victory or glory. Must it not be said that a curse has fallen upon the land?

And yet I still hope that it may ultimately be for good. Through water and fire must a nation be cleansed of its faults. It has been so with all nations, though the phases of their trials have been different. It did not seem to be well with us in Cromwell's early days; nor was it well with us afterwards in those disgraceful years of the later Stuarts. We know how France was bathed in blood in her effort to rid herself of her painted sepulchre of an ancient throne; how Germany was made desolate, in order that Prussia might become a nation. Ireland was poor and wretched, till her famine came. Men said it was a curse, but that curse has been her greatest blessing. And so will it be here in the West. I could not but weep in spirit as I saw the wretchedness around me,—the squalid misery of the soldiers, the inefficiency of their officers, the bickerings of their rulers, the noise and threats, the dirt and ruin, the terrible dishonesty of those who were trusted! These are things which made a man wish that he were anywhere but there. But I do believe that God is still over all, and that everything is working for good. These things are the fire and water through which this nation must pass. The course of this people had been too straight, and their ways had been too pleasant. That which to others had been ever difficult had been made easy for them. Bread and meat had come to them as things of course, and they hardly remembered to be thankful. "We ourselves have done it," they declared aloud. "We are not as other men. We are gods upon the earth. Whose arm shall be long enough to stay us, or whose bolt shall be strong enough to strike us?"

Now they are stricken sore, and the bolt is from their own bow. Their own hands have raised the barrier that has stayed them. They have stumbled in their running, and are lying hurt upon the ground; while they who have heard their boastings turn upon them with ridicule, and laugh at them in their discomfiture. They are rolling in the mire, and cannot take the hand of any man to help them. Though the hand of the bystander may be stretched to them, his face is scornful and his voice full of reproaches. Who has not known that hour of misery when in the sullenness of the heart all help has been refused, and misfortune has been made welcome to do her worst? So is it now with those once United States. The man who can see without inward tears the self-inflicted wounds of that American people can hardly have within his bosom the tenderness of an Englishman's heart.

But the strong runner will rise again to his feet, even though he be stunned by his fall. He will rise again, and will have learned something by his sorrow. His anger will pass away, and he will again brace himself for his work. What great race has ever been won by any man, or by any nation, without some such fall during its course? Have we not all declared that some check to that career was necessary? Men in their pursuit of intelligence had forgotten to be honest; in struggling for greatness they had discarded purity. The nation has been great, but the statesmen of the nation have been little. Men have hardly been ambitious to govern, but they have coveted the wages of governors. Corruption has crept into high places,—into places that should have been high,—till of all holes and corners in the land they have become the lowest. No public man has been trusted for ordinary honesty. It is not by foreign voices, by English newspapers or in French pamphlets, that the corruption of American politicians has been exposed, but by American voices and by the American press. It is to be heard on every side. Ministers of the cabinet, senators, representatives, State legislatures, officers of the army, officials of the navy, contractors of every grade,—all who are presumed to touch, or to have the power of touching public money, are thus accused. For years it has been so. The word politician has stunk in men's nostrils. When I first visited New York, some three years since, I was warned not to know a man, because he was a "politician." We in England define a man of a certain class as a black-leg. How has it come about that in American ears the word politician has come to bear a similar signification?

The material growth of the States has been so quick, that the political growth has not been able to keep pace with it. In commerce, in education, in all municipal arrangements, in mechanical skill, and also in professional ability, the country has stalked on with amazing rapidity; but in the art of governing, in all political management and detail, it has made no advance. The merchants of our country and of that country have for many years met on terms of perfect equality, but it has never been so with their statesmen and our statesmen, with their diplomatists and our diplomatists. Lombard Street and Wall Street can do business with each other on equal footing, but it is not so between Downing Street and the State-office at Washington. The science of statesmanship has yet to be learned in the States,—and certainly the highest lesson of that science, which teaches that honesty is the best policy.

I trust that the war will have left such a lesson behind it. If it do so, let the cost in money be what it may, that money will not have been wasted. If the American people can learn the necessity of employing their best men for their highest work,—if they can recognize these honest men and trust them when they are so recognized,—then they may become as great in politics as they have become great in commerce and in social institutions.

St. Louis, and indeed the whole State of Missouri, was at the time of my visit under martial law. General Halleck was in command, holding his head-quarters at St. Louis, and carrying out, at any rate as far as the city was concerned, what orders he chose to issue. I am disposed to think that, situated as Missouri then was, martial law was the best law. No other law could have had force in a town surrounded by soldiers, and in which half of the inhabitants were loyal to the existing Government, and half of them were in favour of rebellion. The necessity for such power is terrible, and the power itself in the hands of one man must be full of danger; but even that is better than anarchy. I will not accuse General Halleck of abusing his power, seeing that it is hard to determine what is the abuse of such power and what its proper use. When we were at St. Louis a tax was being gathered of £100 a head from certain men presumed to be secessionists, and as the money was not of course very readily paid, the furniture of these suspected secessionists was being sold by auction. No doubt such a measure was by them regarded as a great abuse. One gentleman informed me that, in addition to this, certain houses of his had been taken by the Government at a fixed rent, and that the payment of the rent was now refused unless he would take the oath of allegiance. He no doubt thought that an abuse of power! But the worst abuse of such power comes not at first, but with long usage.

Up to the time however at which I was at St. Louis, martial law had chiefly been used in closing grog-shops and administering the oath of allegiance to suspected secessionists. Something also had been done in the way of raising money by selling the property of convicted secessionists; and while I was there eight men were condemned to be shot for destroying railway bridges. "But will they be shot?" I asked of one of the officers. "Oh, yes. It will be done quietly, and no one will know anything about it. We shall get used to that kind of thing presently." And the inhabitants of Missouri were becoming used to martial law. It is surprising how quickly a people can reconcile themselves to altered circumstances, when the change comes upon them without the necessity of any expressed opinion on their own part. Personal freedom has been considered as necessary to the American of the States as the air he breathes. Had any suggestion been made to him of a suspension of the privilege of habeas corpus, of a censorship of the press, or of martial law, the American would have declared his willingness to die on the floor of the House of Representatives, and have proclaimed with ten million voices his inability to live under circumstances so subversive of his rights as a man. And he would have thoroughly believed the truth of his own assertions. Had a chance been given of an argument on the matter, of stump speeches, and caucus meetings, these things could never have been done. But as it is, Americans are, I think, rather proud of the suspension of the habeas corpus. They point with gratification to the uniformly loyal tone of the newspapers, remarking that any editor who should dare to give even a secession squeak, would immediately find himself shut up. And now nothing but good is spoken of martial law. I thought it a nuisance when I was prevented by soldiers from trotting my horse down Pennsylvania Avenue in Washington, but I was assured by Americans that such restrictions were very serviceable in a community. At St. Louis martial law was quite popular. Why should not General Halleck be as well able to say what was good for the people as any law or any lawyer? He had no interest in the injury of the State, but every interest in its preservation. "But what," I asked, "would be the effect were he to tell you to put out all your fires at eight o'clock?" "If he were so to order, we should do it; but we know that he will not." But who does know to what General Halleck or other generals may come; or how soon a curfew-bell may be ringing in American towns? The winning of liberty is long and tedious, but the losing it is a downhill easy journey.

It was here, in St. Louis, that General Fremont had held his military court. He was a great man here during those hundred days through which his command lasted. He lived in a great house, had a bodyguard, was inaccessible as a great man should be, and fared sumptuously every day. He fortified the city,—or rather, he began to do so. He constructed barracks here, and instituted military prisons. The fortifications have been discontinued as useless, but the barracks and the prisons remain. In the latter there were 1200 secessionist soldiers who had been taken in the State of Missouri. "Why are they not exchanged?" I asked. "Because they are not exactly soldiers," I was informed. "The secessionists do not acknowledge them." "Then would it not be cheaper to let them go?" "No," said my informant; "because in that case we should have to catch them again." And so the 1200 remain in their wretched prison,—thinned from week to week and from day to day by prison disease and prison death.

I went out twice to Benton barracks, as the camp of wooden huts was called, which General Fremont had erected near the fair-ground of the city. This fair-ground, I was told, had been a pleasant place. It had been constructed for the recreation of the city, and for the purpose of periodical agricultural exhibitions. There is still in it a pretty ornamented cottage, and in the little garden a solitary Cupid stood dismayed by the dirt and ruin around him. In the fair-green are the round buildings intended for show cattle and agricultural implements, but now given up to cavalry horses and Parrott guns. But Benton barracks are outside the fair-green. Here on an open space, some half-mile in length, two long rows of wooden sheds have been built, opposite to each other, and behind them are other sheds used for stabling and cooking-places. Those in front are divided, not into separate huts, but into chambers capable of containing nearly two hundred men each. They were surrounded on the inside by great wooden trays, in three tiers,—and on each tray four men were supposed to sleep. I went into one or two while the crowd of soldiers was in them, but found it inexpedient to stay there long. The stench of those places was foul beyond description. Never in my life before had I been in a place so horrid to the eyes and nose as Benton barracks. The path along the front outside was deep in mud. The whole space between the two rows of sheds was one field of mud, so slippery that the foot could not stand. Inside and outside every spot was deep in mud. The soldiers were mud-stained from foot to sole. These volunteer soldiers are in their nature dirty, as must be all men brought together in numerous bodies without special appliances for cleanliness, or control and discipline as to their personal habits. But the dirt of the men in the Benton barracks surpassed any dirt that I had hitherto seen. Nor could it have been otherwise with them. They were surrounded by a sea of mud, and the foul hovels in which they were made to sleep and live were fetid with stench and reeking with filth. I had at this time been joined by another Englishman, and we went through this place together. When we inquired as to the health of the men, we heard the saddest tales,—of three hundred men gone out of one regiment, of whole companies that had perished, of hospitals crowded with fevered patients. Measles had been the great scourge of the soldiers here,—as it had also been in the army of the Potomac. I shall not soon forget my visits to Benton barracks. It may be that our own soldiers were as badly treated in the Crimea; or that French soldiers were treated worse on their march into Russia. It may be that dirt, and wretchedness, disease and listless idleness, a descent from manhood to habits lower than those of the beasts, are necessary in warfare. I have sometimes thought that it is so; but I am no military critic and will not say. This I say,—that the degradation of men to the state in which I saw the American soldiers in Benton barracks, is disgraceful to humanity.

General Halleck was at this time commanding in Missouri, and was himself stationed at St. Louis; but his active measures against the rebels were going on to the right and to the left. On the left shore of the Mississippi, at Cairo, in Illinois, a fleet of gun-boats was being prepared to go down the river, and on the right an army was advancing against Springfield, in the south-western district of Missouri, with the object of dislodging Price, the rebel guerilla leader there, and, if possible, of catching him. Price had been the opponent of poor General Lyon who was killed at Wilson's Creek, near Springfield, and of General Fremont, who during his hundred days had failed to drive him out of the State. This duty had now been intrusted to General Curtis, who had for some time been holding his head-quarters at Rolla, halfway between St. Louis and Springfield. Fremont had built a fort at Rolla, and it had become a military station. Over 10,000 men had been there at one time, and now General Curtis was to advance from Rolla against Price with something above that number of men. Many of them, however, had already gone on, and others were daily being sent up from St. Louis. Under these circumstances my friend and I, fortified with a letter of introduction to General Curtis, resolved to go and see the army at Rolla.

On our way down by the railway we encountered a young German officer, an aide-de-camp of the Federals, and under his auspices we saw Rolla to advantage. Our companions in the railway were chiefly soldiers and teamsters. The car was crowded and filled with tobacco smoke, apple peel, and foul air. In these cars during the winter there is always a large lighted stove, a stove that might cook all the dinners for a French hotel, and no window is ever opened. Among our fellow-travellers there was here and there a west-country Missouri farmer going down, under the protection of the advancing army, to look after the remains of his chattels,—wild, dark, uncouth, savage-looking men. One such hero I specially remember, as to whom the only natural remark would be that one would not like to meet him alone on a dark night. He was burly and big, unwashed and rough, with a black beard, shorn some two months since. He had sharp, angry eyes, and sat silent, picking his teeth with a bowie knife. I met him afterwards at the Rolla hotel, and found that he was a gentleman of property near Springfield. He was mild and meek as a sucking dove, asked my advice as to the state of his affairs, and merely guessed that things had been pretty rough with him. Things had been pretty rough with him. The rebels had come upon his land. House, fences, stock, and crop were all gone. His homestead had been made a ruin, and his farm had been turned into a wilderness. Everything was gone. He had carried his wife and children off to Illinois, and had now returned, hoping that he might get on in the wake of the army till he could see the debris of his property. But even he did not seem disturbed. He did not bemoan himself or curse his fate. "Things were pretty rough," he said; and that was all that he did say.

It was dark when we got into Rolla. Everything had been covered with snow, and everywhere the snow was frozen. We had heard that there was an hotel, and that possibly we might get a bedroom there. We were first taken to a wooden building, which we were told was the head-quarters of the army, and in one room we found a colonel with a lot of soldiers loafing about, and in another a provost-marshal attended by a newspaper correspondent. We were received with open arms, and a suggestion was at once made that we were no doubt picking up news for European newspapers. "Air you a son of the Mrs. Trollope?" said the correspondent. "Then, sir, you are an accession to Rolla." Upon which I was made to sit down, and invited to "loaf about" at the head-quarters as long as I might remain at Rolla. Shortly, however, there came on a violent discussion about waggons. A general had come in and wanted all the colonel's waggons, but the colonel swore that he had none, declared how bitterly he was impeded with sick men, and became indignant and reproachful. It was Brutus and Cassius again; and as we felt ourselves in the way, and anxious moreover to ascertain what might be the nature of the Rolla hotel, we took up our heavy portmanteaux—for they were heavy—and with a guide to show us the way, started off through the dark and over the hill up to our inn. I shall never forget that walk. It was up hill and down hill, with an occasional half-frozen stream across it. My friend was impeded with an enormous cloak lined with fur, which in itself was a burden for a coalheaver. Our guide, who was a clerk out of the colonel's office, carried an umbrella and a small dressing-bag, but we ourselves manfully shouldered our portmanteaux. Sydney Smith declared that an Englishman only wasted his time in training himself for gymnastic aptitudes, seeing that for a shilling he could always hire a porter. Had Sydney Smith ever been at Rolla he would have written differently. I could tell at great length how I fell on my face in the icy snow, how my friend stuck in the frozen mud when he essayed to jump the stream, and how our guide walked on easily in advance, encouraging us with his voice from a distance. Why is it that a stout Englishman bordering on fifty finds himself in such a predicament as that? No Frenchman, no Italian, no German, would so place himself, unless under the stress of insurmountable circumstances. No American would do so under any circumstances. As I slipped about on the ice and groaned with that terrible fardle on my back, burdened with a dozen shirts, and a suit of dress clothes, and three pair of boots, and four or five thick volumes, and a set of maps, and a box of cigars, and a washing-tub, I confessed to myself that I was a fool. What was I doing in such a galley as that? Why had I brought all that useless lumber down to Rolla? Why had I come to Rolla, with no certain hope even of shelter for a night? But we did reach the hotel; we did get a room between us with two bedsteads. And, pondering over the matter in my mind, since that evening, I have been inclined to think that the stout Englishman is in the right of it. No American of my age and weight will ever go through what I went through then; but I am not sure that he does not in his accustomed career go through worse things even than that. However, if I go to Rolla again during the war, I will at any rate leave the books behind me.

What a night we spent in that inn! They who know America will be aware that in all hotels there is a free admixture of different classes. The traveller in Europe may sit down to dinner with his tailor and shoemaker; but if so, his tailor and shoemaker have dressed themselves as he dresses, and are prepared to carry themselves according to a certain standard, which in exterior does not differ from his own. In the large Eastern cities of the States, such as Boston, New York, and Washington, a similar practice of life is gradually becoming prevalent. There are various hotels for various classes, and the ordinary traveller does not find himself at the same table with a butcher fresh from the shambles. But in the West there are no distinctions whatever. "A man's a man for a' that" in the West, let the "a' that" comprise what it may of coarse attire and unsophisticated manners. One soon gets used to it. In that inn at Rolla was a public room, heated in the middle by a stove, and round that we soon found ourselves seated in a company of soldiers, farmers, labourers, and teamsters. But there was among them a general;—not a fighting, or would-be fighting general of the present time, but one of the old-fashioned local generals,—men who held, or had once held, some fabulous generalship in the State militia. There we sat, cheek by jowl with our new friends, till nearly twelve o'clock, talking politics and discussing the war. The General was a stanch Unionist, having, according to his own showing, suffered dreadful things from secessionist persecutors since the rebellion commenced. As a matter of course everybody present was for the Union. In such a place one rarely encounters any difference of opinion. The General was very eager about the war, advocating the immediate abolition of slavery, not as a means of improving the condition of the southern slaves, but on the ground that it would ruin the southern masters. We all sat by, edging in a word now and then, but the General was the talker of the evening. He was very wrathy, and swore at every other word. "It was pretty well time," he said, "to crush out this rebellion, and by —— it must and should be crushed out; General Jim Lane was the man to do it, and by —— General Jim Lane would do it!" and so on. In all such conversations the time for action has always just come, and also the expected man. But the time passes by as other weeks and months have passed before it, and the new General is found to be no more successful than his brethren. Our friend was very angry against England. "When we've polished off these accursed rebels, I guess we'll take a turn at you. You had your turn when you made us give up Mason and Slidell, and we'll have our turn by-and-by." But in spite of his dislike to our nation he invited us warmly to come and see him at his home on the Missouri river. It was, according to his showing, a new Eden,—a Paradise upon earth. He seemed to think that we might perhaps desire to buy a location, and explained to us how readily we could make our fortunes. But he admitted in the course of his eulogiums that it would be as much as his life was worth for him to ride out five miles from his own house. In the meantime the teamsters greased their boots, the soldiers snored, those who were wet took off their shoes and stockings, hanging them to dry round the stove, and the western farmers chewed tobacco in silence and ruminated. At such a house all the guests go in to their meals together. A gong is sounded on a sudden, close behind your ears; accustomed as you may probably be to the sound you jump up from your chair in the agony of the crash, and by the time that you have collected your thoughts the whole crowd is off in a general stampede into the eating room. You may as well join them; if you hesitate as to feeding with so rough a lot of men, you will have to sit down afterwards with the women and children of the family, and your lot will then be worse. Among such classes in the western States the men are always better than the women. The men are dirty and civil, the women are dirty and uncivil.

On the following day we visited the camp, going out in an ambulance and returning on horseback. We were accompanied by the General's aide-de-camp, and also, to our great gratification, by the General's daughter. There had been a hard frost for some nights, but though the cold was very great there was always heat enough in the middle of the day to turn the surface of the ground into glutinous mud; consequently we had all the roughness induced by frost, but none of the usually attendant cleanliness. Indeed, it seemed that in these parts nothing was so dirty as frost. The mud stuck like paste and encompassed everything. We heard that morning that from sixty to seventy baggage-waggons had "broken through," as they called it, and stuck fast near a river in their endeavour to make their way on to Lebanon. We encountered two generals of brigade, General Siegel, a German, and General Ashboth, an Hungarian, both of whom were waiting till the weather should allow them to advance. They were extremely courteous, and warmly invited us to go on with them to Lebanon and Springfield, promising to us such accommodation as they might be able to obtain for themselves. I was much tempted to accept the offer; but I found that day after day might pass before any forward movement was commenced, and that it might be weeks before Springfield or even Lebanon could be reached. It was my wish, moreover, to see what I could of the people, rather than to scrutinize the ways of the army. We dined at the tent of General Ashboth, and afterwards rode his horses through the camp back to Rolla. I was greatly taken with this Hungarian gentleman. He was a tall, thin, gaunt man of fifty, a pure-blooded Magyar as I was told, who had come from his own country with Kossuth to America. His camp circumstances were not very luxurious, nor was his table very richly spread; but he received us with the ease and courtesy of a gentleman. He showed us his sword, his rifle, his pistols, his chargers, and daguerreotype of a friend he had loved in his own country. They were all the treasures that he carried with him,—over and above a chess-board and a set of chessmen which sorely tempted me to accompany him in his march.

In my next chapter, which will, I trust, be very short, I purport to say a few words as to what I saw of the American army, and therefore I will not now describe the regiments which we visited. The tents were all encompassed by snow, and the ground on which they stood was a bed of mud; but yet the soldiers out here were not so wretchedly forlorn, or apparently so miserably uncomfortable, as those at Benton barracks. I did not encounter that horrid sickly stench, nor were the men so pale and wobegone. On the following day we returned to St. Louis, bringing back with us our friend the German aide-de-camp. I stayed two days longer in that city, and then I thought that I had seen enough of Missouri;—enough of Missouri at any rate under the present circumstances of frost and secession. As regards the people of the

West, I must say that they were not such as I expected to find them. With the Northerns we are all more or less intimately acquainted. Those Americans whom we meet in our own country, or on the Continent, are generally from the North, or if not so they have that type of American manners which has become familiar to us. They are talkative, intelligent, inclined to be social, though frequently not sympathetically social with ourselves; somewhat *soi-disant*, but almost invariably companionable. As the traveller goes southward into Maryland and Washington, the type is not altered to any great extent. The hard intelligence of the Yankee gives place gradually to the softer, and perhaps more polished manner of the Southern. But the change thus experienced is not so great as is that between the American of the western and the American of the Atlantic States. In the West I found the men gloomy and silent,—I might almost say sullen. A dozen of them will sit for hours round a stove, speechless. They chew tobacco and ruminate. They are not offended if you speak to them, but they are not pleased. They answer with monosyllables, or, if it be practicable, with a gesture of the head. They care nothing for the graces,—or shall I say, for the decencies of life? They are essentially a dirty people. Dirt, untidiness, and noise, seem in nowise to afflict them. Things are constantly done before your eyes, which should be done and might be done behind your back. No doubt we daily come into the closest contact with matters which, if we saw all that appertains to them, would cause us to shake and shudder. In other countries we do not see all this, but in the western States we do. I have eaten in Bedouin tents, and have been ministered to by Turks and Arabs. I have sojourned in the hotels of old Spain and of Spanish America. I have lived in Connaught, and have taken up my quarters with monks of different nations. I have, as it were, been educated to dirt, and taken out my degree in outward abominations. But my education had not reached a point which would enable me to live at my ease in the western States. A man or woman who can do that may be said to have graduated in the highest honours, and to have become absolutely invulnerable, either through the sense of touch, or by the eye, or by the nose. Indifference to appearances is there a matter of pride. A foul shirt is a flag of triumph. A craving for soap and water is as the wail of the weak and the confession of cowardice. This indifference is carried into all their affairs, or rather this manifestation of indifference. A few pages back, I spoke of a man whose furniture had been sold to pay a heavy tax raised on him specially as a secessionist; the same man had also been refused the payment of rent due to him by the Government, unless he would take a false oath. I may presume that he was ruined in his circumstances by the strong hand of the northern army. But he seemed in nowise to be unhappy about his ruin. He spoke with some scorn of the martial law in Missouri, but I felt that it was esteemed a small matter by him that his furniture was seized and sold. No men love money with more eager love than these western men, but they bear the loss of it as an Indian bears his torture at the stake. They are energetic in trade, speculating deeply whenever speculation is possible; but nevertheless they are slow in motion, loving to loaf about. They are slow in speech, preferring to sit in silence, with the tobacco between their teeth. They drink, but are seldom drunk to the eye; they begin at it early in the morning, and take it in a solemn, sullen, ugly manner, standing always at a bar; swallowing their spirits, and saying nothing as they swallow it. They drink often, and to great excess; but they carry it off without noise, sitting down and ruminating over it with the everlasting cud within their jaws. I believe that a stranger might go into the West, and passing from hotel to hotel through a dozen of them, might sit for hours at each in the large everlasting public hall, and never have a word addressed to him. No stranger should travel in the western States, or indeed in any of the States, without letters of introduction. It is the custom of the country, and they are easily procured. Without them everything is barren; for men do not travel in the States of America as they do in Europe, to see scenery and visit the marvels of old cities which are open to all the world. The social and political life of the Americans must constitute the interest of the traveller, and to these he can hardly make his way without introductions.

I cannot part with the West without saying in its favour that there is a certain manliness about its men, which gives them a dignity of their own. It is shown in that very indifference of which I have spoken. Whatever turns up the man is still there,—still unsophisticated and still unbroken. It has seemed to me that no race of men requires less outward assistance than these pioneers of civilization. They rarely amuse themselves. Food, newspapers, and brandy-smashes suffice for life; and while these last, whatever may occur, the man is still there in his manhood. The fury of the mob does not shake him, nor the stern countenance of his present martial tyrant. Alas! I cannot stick to my text by calling him a just man. Intelligence, energy, and endurance are his virtues. Dirt, dishonesty, and morning drinks are his vices.

All native American women are intelligent. It seems to be their birthright. In the eastern cities they have, in their upper classes, superadded womanly grace to this intelligence, and consequently they are charming as companions. They are beautiful also, and, as I believe, lack nothing that a lover can desire in his love. But I cannot fancy myself much in love with a western lady, or rather with a lady in the West. They are as sharp as nails, but then they are also as hard. They know, doubtless, all that they ought to know, but then they know so much more than they ought to know. They are tyrants to their parents, and never practise the virtue of obedience till they have half-grown-up daughters of their own. They have faith in the destiny of their country, if in nothing else; but they believe that that destiny is to be worked out by the spirit and talent of the young women. I confess that for me Eve would have had no charms had she not recognized Adam as her lord. I can forgive her in that she tempted him to eat the apple. Had she come from the West country she would have ordered him to make his meal, and then I could not have forgiven her.

St. Louis should be, and still will be, a town of great wealth. To no city can have been given more means of riches. I have spoken of the enormous mileage of water-communication of which she is the centre. The country around her produces Indian corn, wheat, grasses, hemp, and tobacco. Coal is dug even within the boundaries of the city, and iron-mines are worked at a distance from it of a hundred miles. The iron is so pure, that it is broken off in solid blocks, almost free from alloy; and as the metal stands up on the earth's surface in the guise almost of a gigantic metal pillar, instead of lying low within its bowels, it is worked at a cheap rate, and with great certainty. Nevertheless, at the present moment, the iron-works of Pilot Knob, as the place is called, do not pay. As far as I could learn, nothing did pay, except government contracts.

CHAPTER VI
CAIRO AND CAMP WOOD

To whatever period of life my days may be prolonged, I do not think that I shall ever forget Cairo. I do not mean Grand Cairo, which is also memorable in its way, and a place not to be forgotten,—but Cairo in the State of Illinois, which by native Americans is always called Caaro. An idea is prevalent in the States, and I think I have heard the same broached in England, that a popular British author had Cairo, State of Illinois, in his eye when under the name of Eden he depicted a chosen, happy spot on the Mississippi river, and told us how certain English emigrants fixed themselves in that locality, and there made light of those little ills of life which are incident to humanity even in the garden of the valley of the Mississippi. But I doubt whether that author ever visited Cairo in mid-winter, and I am sure that he never visited Cairo when Cairo was the seat of an American army. Had he done so, his love of truth would have forbidden him to presume that even Mark Tapley could have enjoyed himself in such an Eden.

I had no wish myself to go to Cairo, having heard it but indifferently spoken of by all men; but my friend with whom I was travelling was peremptory in the matter. He had heard of gun-boats and mortar-boats, of forts built upon the river, of Columbiads, Dahlgrens, and Parrotts, of all the pomps and circumstance of glorious war, and entertained an idea that Cairo was the nucleus or pivot of all really strategetic movements in this terrible national struggle. Under such circumstances I was as it were forced to go to Cairo, and bore myself, under the circumstances, as much like Mark Tapley as my nature would permit. I was not jolly while I was there certainly, but I did not absolutely break down and perish in its mud.

Cairo is the southern terminus of the Illinois central railway. There is but one daily arrival there, namely, at half-past four in the morning, and but one despatch, which is at half-past three in the morning. Everything is thus done to assist that view of life which Mark Tapley took when he resolved to ascertain under what possible worst circumstances of existence he could still maintain his jovial character. Why anybody should ever arrive at Cairo at half-past four A.M., I cannot understand. The departure at any hour is easy of comprehension. The place is situated exactly at the point at which the Ohio and the Mississippi meet, and is, I should say, merely guessing on the matter, some ten or twelve feet lower than the winter level of the two rivers. This gives it naturally a depressed appearance, which must have much aided Mark Tapley in his endeavours. Who were the founders of Cairo I have never ascertained. They are probably buried fathoms deep in the mud, and their names will no doubt remain a mystery to the latest ages. They were brought thither, I presume, by the apparent water privileges of the place; but the water privileges have been too much for them, and by the excess of their powers have succeeded in drowning all the capital of the early Cairovians, and in throwing a wet blanket of thick, moist, glutinous dirt over all their energies.

The free State of Illinois runs down far south between the slave States of Kentucky to the east, and of Missouri to the west, and is the most southern point of the continuous free-soil territory of the Northern States. This point of it is a part of a district called Egypt, which is as fertile as the old country from whence it has borrowed a name; but it suffers under those afflictions which are common to all newly-settled lands which owe their fertility to the vicinity of great rivers. Fever and ague universally prevail. Men and women grow up with their lantern faces like spectres. The children are prematurely old; and the earth which is so fruitful is hideous in its fertility. Cairo and its immediate neighbourhood must, I suppose, have been subject to yearly inundation before it was "settled up." At present it is guarded on the shores of each river by high mud banks, built so as to protect the point of land. These are called the levees, and do perform their duty by keeping out the body of the waters. The shore between the banks is, I believe, never above breast deep with the inundation; and from the circumstances of the place, and the soft, half-liquid nature of the soil, this inundation generally takes the shape of mud instead of water.

Here, at the very point, has been built a town. Whether the town existed during Mr. Tapley's time I have not been able to learn. At the period of my visit, it was falling quickly into ruin; indeed I think I may pronounce it to have been on its last legs. At that moment a galvanic motion had been pumped into it by the war movements of General Halleck, but the true bearings of the town, as a town, were not less plainly to be read on that account. Every street was absolutely impassable from mud. I mean that in walking down the middle of any street in Cairo a moderately framed man would soon stick fast and not be able to move. The houses are generally built at considerable intervals and rarely face each other, and along one side of each street a plank boarding was laid, on which the mud had accumulated only up to one's ankles. I walked all over Cairo with big boots, and with my trousers tucked up to my knees; but at the crossings I found considerable danger, and occasionally had my doubts as to the possibility of progress. I was alone in my work, and saw no one else making any such attempt. A few only were moving about, and they moved in wretched carts, each drawn by two miserable, floundering horses. These carts were always empty, but were presumed to be engaged in some way on military service. No faces looked out at the windows of the houses, no forms stood in the doorways. A few shops were open, but only in the drinking shops did I see customers. In these silent, muddy men were sitting, —not with drink before them, as men sit with us, —but with the cud within their jaws, ruminating. Their drinking is always done on foot. They stand silent at a bar, with two small glasses before them. Out of one they swallow the whisky, and from the other they take a gulp of water, as though to rinse their mouths. After that, they again sit down and ruminate. It was thus that men enjoyed themselves at Cairo.

I cannot tell what was the existing population of Cairo. I asked one resident; but he only shook his head and said that the place was about "played out." And a miserable play it must have been. I tried to walk round the point on the levees, but I found that the mud was so deep and slippery on that which protected the town from the Mississippi, that I could not move on it. On the other, which forms the bank of the Ohio, the railway runs, and here was gathered all the life and movement of the place. But the life was galvanic in its nature, created by a war-galvanism of which the shocks were almost neutralized by mud.

As Cairo is of all towns in America the most desolate, so is its hotel the most forlorn and wretched. Not that it lacked custom. It was so full that no room was to be had on our first entry from the railway cars at five A.M., and we were reduced to the necessity of washing our hands and faces in the public wash-room. When I entered it the barber and his assistants were asleep there, and four or five citizens from the railway were busy at the basins. There is a fixed resolution in these places that you shall be drenched with dirt and drowned in abominations, which is overpowering to a mind less strong than Mark Tapley's. The filth is paraded and made to go as far as possible. The stranger is spared none of the elements of nastiness. I remember how an old woman once stood over me in my youth, forcing me to swallow the gritty dregs of her terrible medicine-cup. The treatment I received in the hotel at Cairo reminded me of that old woman. In that room I did not dare to brush my teeth lest I should give offence; and I saw at once that I was regarded with suspicion when I used my own comb instead of that provided for the public.

At length we got a room, one room for the two. I had become so depressed in spirits that I did not dare to object to this arrangement. My friend could not complain much, even to me, feeling that these miseries had been produced by his own obstinacy. "It is a new phase of life," he said. That, at any rate, was true. If nothing more be necessary for pleasurable excitement than a new phase of life, I would recommend all who require pleasurable excitement to go to Cairo. They will certainly find a new phase of life. But do not let them remain too long, or they may find something beyond a new phase of life. Within a week of that time my friend was taking quinine, looking hollow about the eyes, and whispering to me of fever and ague. To say that there was nothing eatable or drinkable in that hotel, would be to tell that which will be understood without telling. My friend, however, was a cautious man, carrying with him comfortable tin pots, hermetically sealed, from Fortnum & Mason's; and on the second day of our sojourn we were invited by two officers to join their dinner at a Cairo eating-house. We ploughed our way gallantly through the mud to a little shanty, at the door of which we were peremptorily demanded by the landlord to scrub ourselves before we entered with the stump of an old broom. This we did, producing on our nether persons the appearance of bread which has been carefully spread with treacle by an economic housekeeper. And the proprietor was right, for had we not done so, the treacle would have run off through the whole house. But after this we fared royally. Squirrel soup and prairie chickens regaled us. One of our new friends had laden his pockets with champagne and brandy; the other with glasses and a corkscrew; and as the bottle went round, I began to feel something of the spirit of Mark Tapley in my soul.

But our visit to Cairo had been made rather with reference to its present warlike character, than with any eye to the natural beauties of the place. A large force of men had been collected there, and also a fleet of gun-boats. We had come there fortified with letters to generals and commodores, and were prepared to go through a large amount of military inspection. But the bird had flown before our arrival; or rather the body and wings of the bird, leaving behind only a draggled tail and a few of its feathers. There were only a thousand soldiers at Cairo when we were there;—that is, a thousand stationed in the Cairo sheds. Two regiments passed through the place during the time, getting out of one steamer on to another, or passing from the railway into boats. One of these regiments passed before me down the slope of the river-bank, and the men as a body seemed to be healthy. Very many were drunk, and all were mud-clogged up to their shoulders and very caps. In other respects they appeared to be in good order. It must be understood that these soldiers, the volunteers, had never been made subject to any discipline as to cleanliness. They wore their hair long. Their hats or caps, though all made in some military form and with some military appendance, were various and ill-assorted. They all were covered with loose, thick, blue-gray great-coats, which no doubt were warm and wholesome, but which from their looseness and colour seemed to be peculiarly susceptible of receiving and showing a very large amount of mud. Their boots were always good; but each man was shod as he liked. Many wore heavy over-boots coming up the leg;—boots of excellent manufacture, and from their cost, if for no other reason, quite out of the reach of an English soldier; boots in which a man would be not at all unfortunate to find himself hunting; but from these, or from their high-lows, shoes, or whatever they might wear, the mud had never been even scraped. These men were all warmly clothed, but clothed apparently with an endeavour to contract as much mud as might be possible.

The generals and commodores were gone up the Ohio river and up the Tennessee in an expedition with gun-boats, which turned out to be successful, and of which we have all read in the daily history of this war. They had departed the day before our arrival, and though we still found at Cairo a squadron of gun-boats,—if gun-boats go in squadrons,—the bulk of the army had been moved. There was left there one regiment and one colonel, who kindly described to us the battles he had fought, and gave us permission to see everything that was to be seen. Four of these gun-boats were still lying in the Ohio, close under the terminus of the railway with their flat, ugly noses against the muddy bank, and we were shown over two of them. They certainly seemed to be formidable weapons for river warfare, and to have been "got up quite irrespective of expense." So much, indeed, may be said for the Americans throughout the war. They cannot be accused of parsimony. The largest of these vessels, called the "Benton," had cost £36,000. These boats are made with sides sloping inwards, at an angle of 45 degrees. The iron is two-and-a-half inches thick, and it has not, I believe, been calculated that this will resist cannon shot of great weight, should it be struck in a direct line. But the angle of the sides of the boat makes it improbable that any such shot should strike them; and the iron, bedded as it is upon oak, is supposed to be sufficient to turn a shot that does not hit it in a direct line. The boats are also roofed in with iron, and the pilots who steer the vessel stand encased, as it were, under an iron cupola. I imagine that these boats are well calculated for the river service, for which they have been built. Six or seven of them had gone up the Tennessee river the day before we reached Cairo, and while we were there they succeeded in knocking down Fort Henry, and in carrying off the soldiers stationed there and the officer in command. One of the boats, however, had been penetrated by a shot which made its way into the boiler, and the men on deck, six, I think, in number, were scalded to death by the escaping steam. The two pilots up in the cupola were destroyed in this terrible manner. As they were altogether closed in by the iron roof and sides, there was no escape for the steam. The boats, however, were well made and very powerfully armed, and will, probably, succeed in driving the secessionist armies away from the great river banks. By what machinery the secessionist armies are to be followed into the interior is altogether another question.

But there was also another fleet at Cairo, and we were informed that we were just in time to see the first essay made at testing the utility of this armada. It consisted of no less than thirty-eight mortar-boats, each of which had cost £1700. These mortar-boats were broad, flat-bottomed rafts, each constructed with a deck raised three feet above the bottom. They were protected by high iron sides, supposed to be proof against rifle balls, and when supplied had been furnished each with a little boat, a rope, and four rough sweeps or oars. They had no other furniture or belongings, and were to be moved either by steam tugs or by the use of the long oars which were sent with them. It was intended that one 13-inch mortar, of enormous weight, should be put upon each, that these mortars should be fired with twenty-three pounds of powder, and that the shell thrown should, at a distance of three miles, fall with absolute precision into any devoted town which the rebels might hold on the river banks. The grandeur of the idea is almost sublime. So large an amount of powder had, I imagine, never then been used for the single charge in any instrument of war; and when we were told that thirty-eight of them were to play at once on a city, and that they could be used with absolute precision, it seemed as though the fate of Sodom and Gomorrah could not be worse than the fate of that city. Could any city be safe when such implements of war were about upon the waters?

But when we came to inspect the mortar-boats, our misgivings as to any future destination for this fleet were relieved, and our admiration was given to the smartness of the contractor who had secured to himself the job of building them. In the first place they had all leaked till the spaces between the bottoms and the decks were filled with water. This space had been intended for ammunition, but now seemed hardly to be fitted for that purpose. The officer who was about to test them by putting a mortar into one and by firing it off with twenty-three pounds of powder, had the water pumped out of a selected raft, and we were towed by a steam-tug from their moorings a mile up the river, down to the spot where the mortar lay ready to be lifted in by a derrick. But as we turned on the river, the tug-boat which had brought us down, was unable to hold us up against the force of the stream. A second tug-boat was at hand, and with one on each side we were just able, in half-an-hour, to recover the 100 yards which we had lost down the river. The pressure against the stream was so great, owing partly to the weight of the raft, and partly to the fact that its flat head buried itself in the water, that it was almost immoveable against the stream, although the mortar was not yet on it.

It soon became manifest that no trial could be made on that day, and so we were obliged to leave Cairo without having witnessed the firing of the great gun. My belief is that very little evil to the enemy will result from those mortar-boats, and that they cannot be used with much effect. Since that time they have been used on the Mississippi, but as yet we do not know with what result. Island No. 10 has been taken, but I do not know that the mortar-boats contributed much to that success. The enormous cost of moving them against the stream of the river is in itself a barrier to their use. When we saw them—and then they were quite new—many of the rivets were already gone. The small boats had been stolen from some of them, and the ropes and oars from others. There they lay, thirty-eight in number, up against the mud-banks of the Ohio, under the boughs of the half-clad, melancholy forest trees, as sad a spectacle of reckless prodigality as the eye ever beheld. But the contractor who made them no doubt was a smart man.

This armada was moored on the Ohio against the low, reedy bank, a mile above the levee, where the old unchanged forest of nature came down to the very edge of the river, and mixed itself with the shallow overflowing waters. I am wrong in saying that it lay under the boughs of the trees, for such trees do not spread themselves out with broad branches. They stand thickly together, broken, stunted, spongy with rot, straight and ugly, with ragged tops and shattered arms, seemingly decayed, but still ever renewing themselves with the rapid moist life of luxuriant forest vegetation. Nothing to my eyes is sadder than the monotonous desolation of such scenery. We, in England, when we read and speak of the primeval forests of America, are apt to form pictures in our minds of woodland glades, with spreading oaks and green mossy turf beneath,—of scenes than which nothing that God has given us is more charming. But these forests are not after that fashion; they offer no allurement to the lover, no solace to the melancholy man of thought. The ground is deep with mud, or overflown with water. The soil and the river have no defined margins. Each tree, though full of the forms of life, has all the appearance of death. Even to the outward eye they seem to be laden with ague, fever, sudden chills, and pestilential malaria.

When we first visited the spot we were alone, and we walked across from the railway line to the place at which the boats were moored. They lay in treble rank along the shore, and immediately above them an old steam-boat was fastened against the bank. Her back was broken, and she was given up to ruin,—placed there that she might rot quietly into her watery grave. It was mid-winter, and every tree was covered with frozen sleet and small particles of snow which had drizzled through the air; for the snow had not fallen in hearty, honest flakes. The ground beneath our feet was crisp with frost, but traitorous in its crispness; not frozen manfully so as to bear a man's weight, but ready at every point to let him through into the fat, glutinous mud below. I never saw a sadder picture, or one which did more to awaken pity for those whose fate had fixed their abodes in such a locality. And yet there was a beauty about it too,—a melancholy, death-like beauty. The disordered ruin and confused decay of the forest was all gemmed with particles of ice. The eye reaching through the thin underwood could form for itself picturesque shapes and solitary bowers of broken wood, which were bright with the opaque brightness of the hoar-frost. The great river ran noiselessly along, rapid, but still with an apparent lethargy in its waters. The ground beneath our feet was fertile beyond compare, but as yet fertile to death rather than to life. Where we then trod man had not yet come with his axe and his plough; but the railroad was close to us, and within a mile of the spot thousands of dollars had been spent in raising a city which was to have been rich with the united wealth of the rivers and the land. Hitherto fever and ague, mud and malaria, had been too strong for man, and the dollars had been spent in vain. The day, however, will come when this promontory between the two great rivers will be a fit abode for industry. Men will settle there, wandering down from the North and East, and toil sadly, and leave their bones among the mud. Thin, pale-faced, joyless mothers will come there, and grow old before their time; and sickly children will be born, struggling up with wan faces to their sad life's labour. But the work will go on, for it is God's work; and the earth will be prepared for the people, and the fat rottenness of the still living forest will be made to give forth its riches.

We found that two days at Cairo were quite enough for us. We had seen the gun-boats and the mortar-boats, and gone through the sheds of the soldiers. The latter were bad, comfortless, damp, and cold; and certain quarters of the officers, into which we were hospitably taken, were wretched abodes enough; but the sheds of Cairo did not stink like those of Benton barracks at St. Louis, nor had illness been prevalent there to the same degree. I do not know why this should have been so, but such was the result of my observation. The locality of Benton barracks must, from its nature, have been the more healthy, but it had become by art the foulest place I ever visited. Throughout the army it seemed to be the fact, that the men under canvas were more comfortable, in better spirits, and also in better health than those who were lodged in sheds. We had inspected the Cairo army and the Cairo navy, and had also seen all that Cairo had to show us of its own. We were thoroughly disgusted with the hotel, and retired on the second night to bed, giving positive orders that we might be called at half-past two, with reference to that terrible start to be made at half-past three. As a matter of course we kept dozing and waking till past one, in our fear lest neglect on the part of the watcher should entail on us another day at this place; of course we went fast asleep about the time at which we should have roused ourselves; and of course we were called just fifteen minutes before the train started. Everybody knows how these things always go. And then the pair of us, jumping out of bed in that wretched chamber, went through the mockery of washing and packing which always takes place on such occasions;—a mockery indeed of washing, for there was but one basin between us! And a mockery also of packing, for I left my hair-brushes behind me! Cairo was avenged in that I had declined to avail myself of the privileges of free citizenship which had been offered to me in that barber's shop. And then, while we were in our agony, pulling at the straps of our portmanteaux and swearing at the faithlessness of the boots, up came the clerk of the hotel—the great man from behind the bar—and scolded us prodigiously for our delay. "Called! We had been called an hour ago!" Which statement, however, was decidedly untrue, as we remarked, not with extreme patience. "We should certainly be late," he said; "it would take us five minutes to reach the train, and the cars would be off in four." Nobody who has not experienced them can understand the agonies of such moments,—of such moments as regards travelling in general; but none who have not been at Cairo can understand the extreme agony produced by the threat of a prolonged sojourn in that city. At last we were out of the house, rushing through the mud, slush, and half-melted snow, along the wooden track to the railway, laden with bags and coats, and deafened by that melancholy, wailing sound, as though of a huge polar she-bear in the pangs of travail upon an iceberg, which proceeds from an American railway-engine before it commences its work. How we slipped and stumbled, and splashed and swore, rushing along in the dark night, with buttons loose, and our clothes half on! And how pitilessly we were treated! We gained our cars, and even succeeded in bringing with us our luggage; but we did not do so with the sympathy, but amidst the derision of the bystanders. And then the seats were all full, and we found that there was a lower depth even in the terrible deep of a railway train in a western State. There was a second-class carriage, prepared, I presume, for those who esteemed themselves too dirty for association with the aristocracy of Cairo; and into this we flung ourselves. Even this was a joy to us, for we were being carried away from Eden. We had acknowledged ourselves to be no fitting colleagues for Mark Tapley, and would have been glad to escape from Cairo even had we worked our way out of the place as assistant-stokers to the engine-driver. Poor Cairo! unfortunate Cairo! "It is about played out!" said its citizen to me. But in truth the play was commenced a little too soon.

Those players have played out; but another set will yet have their innings, and make a score that shall perhaps be talked of far and wide in the western world.

We were still bent upon army inspection, and with this purpose went back from Cairo to Louisville in Kentucky. I had passed through Louisville before, as told in my last chapter, but had not gone south from Louisville towards the Green River, and had seen nothing of General Buell's soldiers. I should have mentioned before that when we were at St. Louis, we asked General Halleck, the officer in command of the northern army of Missouri, whether he could allow us to pass through his lines to the South. This he assured us he was forbidden to do, at the same time offering us every facility in his power for such an expedition if we could obtain the consent of Mr. Seward, who at that time had apparently succeeded in engrossing into his own hands, for the moment, supreme authority in all matters of Government. Before leaving Washington we had determined not to ask Mr. Seward, having but little hope of obtaining his permission, and being unwilling to encounter his refusal. Before going to General Halleck we had considered the question of visiting the land of Dixie without permission from any of the men in authority. I ascertained that this might easily have been done from Kentucky to Tennessee, but that it could only be done on foot. There are very few available roads running North and South through these States. The railways came before roads; and even where the railways are far asunder, almost all the traffic of the country takes itself to them, preferring a long circuitous conveyance with steam, to short distances without. Consequently such roads as there are run laterally to the railways, meeting them at this point or that, and thus maintaining the communication of the country. Now the railways were of course in the hands of the armies. The few direct roads leading from North to South were in the same condition, and the bye-roads were impassable from mud. The frontier of the North therefore, though very extended, was not very easily to be passed, unless, as I have said before, by men on foot. For myself I confess that I was anxious to go South; but not to do so without my coats and trousers, or shirts and pocket-handkerchiefs. The readiest way of getting across the line,—and the way which was I believe the most frequently used,—was from below Baltimore in Maryland by boat across the Potomac. But in this there was a considerable danger of being taken, and I had no desire to become a state-prisoner in the hands of Mr. Seward under circumstances which would have justified our Minister in asking for my release only as a matter of favour. Therefore when at St. Louis, I gave up all hopes of seeing "Dixie" during my present stay in America. I presume it to be generally known that Dixie is the negro's heaven, and that the southern slave States, in which it is presumed that they have found a Paradise, have since the beginning of the war been so named.

We remained a few days at Louisville, and were greatly struck with the natural beauty of the country around it. Indeed, as far as I was enabled to see, Kentucky has superior attractions as a place of rural residence for an English gentleman, to any other State in the Union. There is nothing of landscape there equal to the banks of the upper Mississippi, or to some parts of the Hudson river. It has none of the wild grandeur of the White Mountains of New Hampshire, nor does it break itself into valleys equal to those of the Alleghanies in Pennsylvania. But all those are beauties for the tourist rather than for the resident. In Kentucky the land lies in knolls and soft sloping hills. The trees stand apart, forming forest openings. The herbage is rich, and the soil, though not fertile like the prairies of Illinois, or the river bottoms of the Mississippi and its tributaries, is good, steadfast, wholesome farming ground. It is a fine country for a resident gentleman farmer, and in its outward aspect reminds me more of England in its rural aspects, than any other State which I visited. Round Louisville there are beautiful sites for houses, of which advantage in some instances has been taken. But, nevertheless, Louisville though a well-built, handsome city, is not now a thriving city. I liked it because the hotel was above par, and because the country round it was good for walking; but it has not advanced as Cincinnati and St. Louis have advanced. And yet its position on the Ohio is favourable, and it is well circumstanced as regards the wants of its own State. But it is not a free-soil city. Nor indeed is St. Louis; but St. Louis is tending that way, and has but little to do with the "domestic institution." At the hotels in Cincinnati and St. Louis you are served by white men, and are very badly served. At Louisville the ministration is by black men, "bound to labour." The difference in the comfort is very great. The white servants are noisy, dirty, forgetful, indifferent, and sometimes impudent. The negroes are the very reverse of all this; you cannot hurry them; but in all other respects,— and perhaps even in that respect also,—they are good servants. This is the work for which they seem to have been intended. But nevertheless where they are, life and energy seem to languish, and prosperity cannot make any true advance. They are symbols of the luxury of the white men who employ them, and as such are signs of decay and emblems of decreasing power. They are good labourers themselves, but their very presence makes labour dishonourable. That Kentucky will speedily rid herself of the institution I believe firmly. When she has so done, the commercial city of that State may perhaps go a-head again like her sisters.

At this very time the Federal army was commencing that series of active movements in Kentucky and through Tennessee which led to such important results, and gave to the North the first solid victories which they had gained since the contest began. On the 19th of January one wing of General Buell's army, under General Thomas, had defeated the secessionists near Somerset, in the south-eastern district of Kentucky, under General Zollicoffer, who was there killed. But in that action the attack was made by Zollicoffer and the secessionists. When we were at Louisville we heard of the success of that gun-boat expedition up the Tennessee river by which Fort Henry was taken. Fort Henry had been built by the Confederates on the Tennessee,—exactly on the confines of the States of Tennessee and Kentucky. They had also another fort, Fort Donnelson, on the Cumberland river, which at that point runs parallel to the Tennessee, and is there distant from it but a very few miles. Both these rivers run into the Ohio. Nashville, which is the capital of Tennessee, is higher up on the Cumberland; and it was now intended to send the gun-boats down the Tennessee back into the Ohio, and thence up the Cumberland, there to attack Fort Donnelson, and afterwards to assist General Buell's army in making its way down to Nashville. The gun-boats were attached to General Halleck's army, and received their directions from St. Louis. General Buell's head-quarters were at Louisville, and his advanced position was on the Green River, on the line of the railway from Louisville to Nashville. The secessionists had destroyed the railway bridge over the Green River, and were now lying at Bowling Green, between the Green River and Nashville. This place it was understood that they had fortified.

Matters were in this position when we got a military pass to go down by the railway to the army on the Green River,—for the railway was open to no one without a military pass;—and we started, trusting that Providence would supply us with rations and quarters. An officer attached to General Buell's staff, with whom however our acquaintance was of the very slightest, had telegraphed down to say that we were coming. I cannot say that I expected much from the message, seeing that it simply amounted to a very thin introduction to a general officer to whom we were strangers even by name, from a gentleman to whom we had brought a note from another gentleman whose acquaintance we had chanced to pick up on the road. We manifestly had no right to expect much; but to us, expecting very little, very much was given. General Johnson was the officer to whose care we were confided, he being a brigadier under General M'Cook, who commanded the advance. We were met by an aide-de-camp and saddle-horses, and soon found ourselves in the General's tent, or rather in a shanty formed of solid upright wooden logs, driven into the ground with the bark still on, and having the interstices filled in with clay. This was roofed with canvas, and altogether made a very eligible military residence. The General slept in a big box about nine feet long and four broad which occupied one end of the shanty, and he seemed in all his fixings to be as comfortably put up as any gentleman might be when out on such a picnic as this. We arrived in time for dinner, which was brought in, table and all, by two negroes. The party was made up by a doctor, who carved, and two of the staff, and a very nice dinner we had. In half-an-hour we were intimate with the whole party, and as familiar with the things around us as though we had been living in tents all our lives. Indeed I had by this time been so often in the tents of the northern army, that I almost felt entitled to make myself at home. It has seemed to me that an Englishman has always been made welcome in these camps. There has been and is at this moment a terribly bitter feeling among Americans against England, and I have heard this expressed quite as loudly by men in the army as by civilians; but I think I may say that this has never been brought to bear upon individual intercourse. Certainly we have said some very sharp things of them, — words which, whether true or false, whether deserved or undeserved, must have been offensive to them. I have known this feeling of offence to amount almost to an agony of anger. But nevertheless I have never seen any falling off in the hospitality and courtesy generally shown by a civilized people to passing visitors. I have argued the matter of England's course throughout the war, till I have been hoarse with asseverating the rectitude of her conduct and her national unselfishness. I have met very strong opponents on the subject, and have been coerced into loud strains of voice; but I never yet met one American who was personally uncivil to me as an Englishman, or who seemed to be made personally angry by my remarks. I found no coldness in that hospitality to which as a stranger I was entitled, because of the national ill-feeling which circumstances have engendered. And while on this subject I will remark, that when travelling I have found it expedient to let those with whom I might chance to talk know at once that I was an Englishman. In fault of such knowledge things would be said which could not but be disagreeable to me; but not even from any rough western enthusiast in a railway carriage have I ever heard a word spoken insolently to England, after I had made my nationality known. I have learned that Wellington was beaten at Waterloo; that Lord Palmerston was so unpopular that he could not walk alone in the streets; that the House of Commons was an acknowledged failure; that starvation was the normal condition of the British people, and that the Queen was a bloodthirsty tyrant. But these assertions were not made with the intention that they should be heard by an Englishman. To us as a nation they are at the present moment unjust almost beyond belief; but I do not think that the feeling has ever taken the guise of personal discourtesy.

We spent two days in the camp close upon the Green River, and I do not know that I enjoyed any days of my trip more thoroughly than I did these. In truth for the last month, since I had left Washington, my life had not been one of enjoyment. I had been rolling in mud and had been damp with filth. Camp Wood, as they called this military settlement on the Green River, was also muddy; but we were excellently well-mounted; the weather was very cold, but peculiarly fine, and the soldiers around us, as far as we could judge, seemed to be better off in all respects than those we had visited at St. Louis, at Rolla, or at Cairo. They were all in tents, and seemed to be light-spirited and happy. Their rations were excellent,—but so much may, I think, be said of the whole northern army from Alexandria on the Potomac to Springfield in the west of Missouri. There was very little illness at that time in the camp in Kentucky, and the reports made to us led us to think that on the whole this had been the most healthy division of the army. The men, moreover, were less muddy than their brethren either east or west of them,—at any rate this may be said of them as regards the infantry.

But perhaps the greatest charm of the place to me was the beauty of the scenery. The Green River at this spot is as picturesque a stream as I ever remember to have seen in such a country. It lies low down between high banks, and curves hither and thither, never keeping a straight line. Its banks are wooded; but not, as is so common in America, by continuous, stunted, uninteresting forest, but by large single trees standing on small patches of meadow by the water-side, with the high banks rising over them, with glades through them open for the horseman. The rides here in summer must be very lovely. Even in winter they were so, and made me in love with the place in spite of that brown, dull, barren aspect which the presence of an army always creates. I have said that the railway bridge which crossed the Green River at this spot had been destroyed by the secessionists. This had been done effectually as regarded the passage of trains, but only in part as regarded the absolute fabric of the bridge. It had been, and still was when I saw it, a beautifully light construction, made of iron and supported over a valley, rather than over a river, on tall stone piers. One of these piers had been blown up; but when we were there, the bridge had been repaired with beams and wooden shafts. This had just been completed, and an engine had passed over it. I must confess that it looked to me most perilously insecure; but the eye uneducated in such mysteries is a bad judge of engineering work. I passed with a horse backwards and forwards on it, and it did not tumble down then; but I confess that on the first attempt I was glad enough to lead the horse by the bridle.

That bridge was certainly a beautiful fabric, and built in a most lovely spot. Immediately under it there was also a pontoon bridge. The tents of General M'Cook's division were immediately at the northern end of it, and the whole place was alive with soldiers, nailing down planks, pulling up temporary rails at each side, carrying over straw for the horses, and preparing for the general advance of the troops. It was a glorious day. There had been heavy frost at night; but the air was dry, and the sun though cold was bright. I do not know when I saw a prettier picture. It would perhaps have been nothing without the loveliness of the river scenery; but the winding of the stream at the spot, the sharp wooded hills on each side, the forest openings, and the busy, eager, strange life together filled the place with no common interest. The officers of the army at the spot spoke with bitterest condemnation of the vandalism of their enemy in destroying the bridge. The justice of the indignation, I ventured very strongly to question. "Surely you would have destroyed their bridge?" I said. "But they are rebels," was the answer. It has been so throughout the contest; and the same argument has been held by soldiers and by non-soldiers,—by women and by men. "Grant that they are rebels," I have answered. "But when rebels fight they cannot be expected to be more scrupulous in their mode of doing so than their enemies who are not rebels." The whole population of the North has from the beginning of this war considered themselves entitled to all the privileges of belligerents; but have called their enemies Goths and Vandals for even claiming those privileges for themselves. The same feeling was at the bottom of their animosity against England. Because the South was in rebellion, England should have consented to allow the North to assume all the rights of a belligerent, and should have denied all those rights to the South! Nobody has seemed to understand that any privilege which a belligerent can claim must depend on the very fact of his being in encounter with some other party having the same privilege. Our press has animadverted very strongly on the States government for the apparent untruthfulness of their arguments on this matter; but I profess that I believe that Mr. Seward and his colleagues,—and not they only but the whole nation,—have so thoroughly deceived themselves on this subject, have so talked and speechified themselves into a misunderstanding of the matter, that they have taught themselves to think that the men of the South could be entitled to no consideration from any quarter. To have rebelled against the stars and stripes seems to a northern man to be a crime putting the criminal altogether out of all courts,—a crime which should have armed the hands of all men against him, as the hands of all men are armed at a dog that is mad, or a tiger that has escaped from its keeper. It is singular that such a people, a people that has founded itself on rebellion, should have such a horror of rebellion; but, as far as my observation may have enabled me to read their feelings rightly, I do believe that it has been as sincere as it is irrational.

We were out riding early on the morning of the second day of our sojourn in the camp, and met the division of General Mitchell, a detachment of General Buell's army, which had been in camp between the Green River and Louisville, going forward to the bridge which was then being prepared for their passage. This division consisted of about 12,000 men, and the road was crowded throughout the whole day with them and their waggons. We first passed a regiment of cavalry, which appeared to be endless. Their cavalry regiments are, in general, more numerous than those of the infantry, and on this occasion we saw, I believe, about 1200 men pass by us. Their horses were strong and serviceable, and the men were stout and in good health; but the general appearance of everything about them was rough and dirty. The American cavalry have always looked to me like brigands. A party of them would, I think, make a better picture than an equal number of our dragoons; but if they are to be regarded in any other view than that of the picturesque, it does not seem to me that they have been got up successfully. On this occasion they were forming themselves into a picture for my behoof, and as the picture was, as a picture, very good, I at least have no reason to complain.

We were taken to see one German regiment, a regiment of which all the privates were German and all the officers save one,—I think the surgeon. We saw the men in their tents, and the food which they eat, and were disposed to think that hitherto things were going well with them. In the evening the colonel and lieutenant-colonel, both of whom had been in the Prussian service, if I remember rightly, came up to the general's quarters, and we spent the evening together in smoking cigars and discussing slavery round the stove. I shall never forget that night, or the vehement abolition enthusiasm of the two German colonels. Our host had told us that he was a slave-owner; and as our wants were supplied by two sable ministers, I concluded that he had brought with him a portion of his domestic institution. Under such circumstances I myself should have avoided such a subject, having been taught to believe that southern gentlemen did not generally take delight in open discussions on the subject. But had we been arguing the question of the population of the planet Jupiter, or the final possibility of the transmutation of metals, the matter could not have been handled with less personal feeling. The Germans, however, spoke the sentiments of all the Germans of the western States,—that is, of all the Protestant Germans, and to them is confined the political influence held by the German immigrants. They all regard slavery as an evil, holding on the matter opinions quite as strong as ours have ever been. And they argue that as slavery is an evil, it should therefore be abolished at once. Their opinions are as strong as ours have ever been, and they have not had our West Indian experience. Any one desiring to understand the present political position of the States should realize the fact of the present German influence on political questions. Many say that the present President was returned by German voters. In one sense this is true, for he certainly could not have been returned without them;

but for them, or for their assistance, Mr. Breckinridge would have been President, and this civil war would not have come to pass. As abolitionists they are much more powerful than the republicans of New England, and also more in earnest. In New England the matter is discussed politically; in the great western towns, where the Germans congregate by thousands, they profess to view it philosophically. A man, as a man, is entitled to freedom. That is their argument, and it is a very old one. When you ask them what they would propose to do with 4,000,000 of enfranchised slaves and with their ruined masters,—how they would manage the affairs of those 12,000,000 of people, all whose wealth and work and very life have hitherto been hinged and hung upon slavery, they again ask you whether slavery is not in itself bad, and whether anything acknowledged to be bad should be allowed to remain.

But the American Germans are in earnest, and I am strongly of opinion that they will so far have their way, that the country which for the future will be their country, will exist without the taint of slavery. In the northern nationality, which will reform itself after this war is over, there will, I think, be no slave State. That final battle of abolition will have to be fought among a people apart; and I must fear that while it lasts their national prosperity will not be great.

CHAPTER VII
THE ARMY OF THE NORTH

I trust that it may not be thought that in this chapter I am going to take upon myself the duties of a military critic. I am well aware that I have no capacity for such a task, and that my opinion on such matters would be worth nothing. But it is impossible to write of the American States as they were when I visited them, and to leave that subject of the American army untouched. It was all but impossible to remain for some months in the northern States without visiting the army. It was impossible to join in any conversation in the States without talking about the army. It was impossible to make inquiry as to the present and future condition of the people without basing such inquiries more or less upon the doings of the army. If a stranger visit Manchester with the object of seeing what sort of place Manchester is, he must visit the cotton mills and printing establishments, though he may have no taste for cotton and no knowledge on the subject of calicoes. Under pressure of this kind I have gone about from one army to another, looking at the drilling of regiments, of the manœuvres of cavalry, at the practice of artillery, and at the inner life of the camps. I do not feel that I am in any degree more fitted to take the command of a campaign than I was before I began, or even more fitted to say who can and who cannot do so. But I have obtained on my own mind's eye a tolerably clear impression of the outward appearance of the northern army; I have endeavoured to learn something of the manner in which it was brought together, and of its cost as it now stands; and I have learned—as any man in the States may learn, without much trouble or personal investigation—how terrible has been the peculation of the contractors and officers by whom that army has been supplied. Of these things, writing of the States at this moment, I must say something. In what I shall say as to that matter of peculation I trust that I may be believed to have spoken without personal ill-feeling or individual malice.

While I was travelling in the States of New England and in the North-west, I came across various camps at which young regiments were being drilled and new regiments were being formed. These lay in our way as we made our journeys, and therefore we visited them; but they were not objects of any very great interest. The men had not acquired even any pretence of soldierlike bearing. The officers for the most part had only just been selected, having hardly as yet left their civil occupations, and anything like criticism was disarmed by the very nature of the movement which had called the men together. I then thought, as I still think, that the men themselves were actuated by proper motives, and often by very high motives, in joining the regiments. No doubt they looked to the pay offered. It is not often that men are able to devote themselves to patriotism without any reference to their personal circumstances. A man has got before him the necessity of earning his bread, and very frequently the necessity of earning the bread of others besides himself. This comes before him not only as his first duty, but as the very law of his existence. His wages are his life, and when he proposes to himself to serve his country that subject of payment comes uppermost as it does when he proposes to serve any other master. But the wages given, though very high in comparison with those of any other army, have not been of a nature to draw together from their distant homes at so short a notice, so vast a cloud of men, had no other influence been at work. As far as I can learn, the average rate of wages in the country since the war began has been about 65 cents a day over and beyond the workmen's diet. I feel convinced that I am putting this somewhat too low, taking the average of all the markets from which the labour has been withdrawn. In large cities labour has been higher than this, and a considerable proportion of the army has been taken from large cities. But taking 65 cents a day as the average, labour has been worth about 17 dollars a month over and above the labourers' diet. In the army the soldier receives 13 dollars a month, and also receives his diet and clothes; in addition to this, in many States, 6 dollars a month have been paid by the State to the wives and families of those soldiers who have left wives and families in the States behind them. Thus for the married men the wages given by the army have been 2 dollars a month, or less than £5 a year, more than his earnings at home, and for the unmarried man they have been 4 dollars a month, or less than £10 a year below his earnings at home. But the army also gives clothing to the extent of 3 dollars a month. This would place the unmarried soldier, in a pecuniary point of view, worse off by one dollar a month, or £2 10s. a year, than he would have been at home; and would give the married man 5 dollars a month, or £12 a year more than his ordinary wages for absenting himself from his family. I cannot think therefore that the pecuniary attractions have been very great.

Our soldiers in England enlist at wages which are about one half that paid in the ordinary labour market to the class from whence they come. But labour in England is uncertain, whereas in the States it is certain. In England the soldier with his shilling gets better food than the labourer with his two shillings; and the Englishman has no objection to the rigidity of that discipline which is so distasteful to an American. Moreover, who in England ever dreamed of raising 600,000 new troops in six months, out of a population of thirty million? But this has been done in the northern States out of a population of eighteen million. If England were invaded, Englishmen would come forward in the same way, actuated, as I believe, by the same high motives. My object here is simply to show that the American soldiers have not been drawn together by the prospect of high wages, as has been often said since the war began.

They who inquire closely into the matter will find that hundreds and thousands have joined the army as privates, who in doing so have abandoned all their best worldly prospects, and have consented to begin the game of life again, believing that their duty to their country has now required their services. The fact has been that in the different States a spirit of rivalry has been excited. Indiana has endeavoured to show that she was as forward as Illinois; Pennsylvania has been unwilling to lag behind New York; Massachusetts, who has always struggled to be foremost in peace, has desired to boast that she was first in war also; the smaller States have resolved to make their names heard, and those which at first were backward in sending troops have been shamed into greater earnestness by the public voice. There has been a general feeling throughout the people that the thing should be done;—that the rebellion must be put down, and that it must be put down by arms. Young men have been ashamed to remain behind; and their elders, acting under that glow of patriotism which so often warms the hearts of free men, but which perhaps does not often remain there long in all its heat, have left their wives and have gone also. It may be true that the voice of the majority has been coercive on many;—that men have enlisted partly because the public voice required it of them, and not entirely through the promptings of individual spirit. Such public voice in America is very potent; but it is not, I think, true that the army has been gathered together by the hope of high wages.

Such was my opinion of the men when I saw them from State to State clustering into their new regiments. They did not look like soldiers; but I regarded them as men earnestly intent on a work which they believed to be right. Afterwards when I saw them in their camps, amidst all the pomps and circumstances of glorious war, positively converted into troops, armed with real rifles and doing actual military service, I believed the same of them,— but cannot say that I then liked them so well. Good motives had brought them there. They were the same men, or men of the same class that I had seen before. They were doing just that which I knew they would have to do. But still I found that the more I saw of them the more I lost of that respect for them which I had once felt. I think it was their dirt that chiefly operated upon me. Then, too, they had hitherto done nothing, and they seemed to be so terribly intent upon their rations! The great boast of this army was that they eat meat twice a day, and that their daily supply of bread was more than they could consume.

When I had been two or three weeks in Washington, I went over to the army of the Potomac and spent a few days with some of the officers. I had on previous occasions ridden about the camps, and had seen a review at which General Maclellan trotted up and down the lines with all his numerous staff at his heels. I have always believed reviews to be absurdly useless as regards the purpose for which they are avowedly got up,—that, namely, of military inspection. And I believed this especially of this review. I do not believe that any Commander-in-chief ever learns much as to the excellence or deficiencies of his troops by watching their manœuvres on a vast open space; but I felt sure that General Maclellan had learned nothing on this occasion. If before his review he did not know whether his men were good as soldiers, he did not possess any such knowledge after the review. If the matter may be regarded as a review of the general;—if the object was to show him off to the men, that they might know how well he rode, and how grand he looked with his staff of forty or fifty officers at his heels, then this review must be considered as satisfactory. General Maclellan does ride very well. So much I learned, and no more.

It was necessary to have a pass for crossing the Potomac either from one side or from the other, and such a pass I procured from a friend in the War-office, good for the whole period of my sojourn in Washington. The wording of the pass was more than ordinarily long, as it recommended me to the special courtesy of all whom I might encounter; but in this respect it was injurious to me rather than otherwise, as every picket by whom I was stopped found it necessary to read it to the end. The paper was almost invariably returned to me without a word; but the musket which was not unfrequently kept extended across my horse's nose by the reader's comrade would be withdrawn, and then I would ride on to the next barrier. It seemed to me that these passes were so numerous and were signed by so many officers, that there could have been no risk in forging them. The army of the Potomac into which they admitted the bearer lay in quarters which were extended over a length of twenty miles up and down on the Virginian side of the river, and the river could be traversed at five different places. Crowds of men and women were going over daily, and no doubt all the visitors who so went with innocent purposes were provided with proper passports; but any whose purposes were not innocent, and who were not so provided, could have passed the pickets with counterfeited orders. This, I have little doubt, was done daily. Washington was full of secessionists, and every movement of the Federal army was communicated to the Confederates at Richmond, at which city was now established the Congress and head-quarters of the Confederacy. But no such tidings of the Confederate army reached those in command at Washington. There were many circumstances in the contest which led to this result, and I do not think that General Maclellan had any power to prevent it. His system of passes certainly did not do so.

I never could learn from any one what was the true number of this army on the Potomac. I have been informed by those who professed to know that it contained over 200,000 men, and by others who also professed to know, that it did not contain 100,000. To me the soldiers seemed to be innumerable, hanging like locusts over the whole country, — a swarm desolating everything around them. Those pomps and circumstances are not glorious in my eyes. They affect me with a melancholy which I cannot avoid. Soldiers gathered together in a camp are uncouth and ugly when they are idle; and when they are at work their work is worse than idleness. When I have seen a thousand men together, moving their feet hither at one sound and thither at another, throwing their muskets about awkwardly, prodding at the air with their bayonets, trotting twenty paces here and backing ten paces there, wheeling round in uneven lines, and looking, as they did so, miserably conscious of the absurdity of their own performances, I have always been inclined to think how little the world can have advanced in civilization, while grown-up men are still forced to spend their days in such grotesque performances. Those to whom the "pomps and circumstances" are dear—nay, those by whom they are considered simply necessary—will be able to confute me by a thousand arguments. I readily own myself confuted. There must be soldiers, and soldiers must be taught. But not the less pitiful is it to see men of thirty undergoing the goose-step, and tortured by orders as to the proper mode of handling a long instrument which is half-gun and half-spear. In the days of Hector and Ajax, the thing was done in a more picturesque manner, and the songs of battle should, I think, be confined to those ages.

The ground occupied by the divisions on the further or south-western side of the Potomac was, as I have said, about twenty miles in length and perhaps seven in breadth. Through the whole of this district the soldiers were everywhere. The tents of the various brigades were clustered together in streets, the regiments being divided; and the divisions, combining the brigades, lay apart at some distance from each other. But everywhere, at all points, there were some signs of military life. The roads were continually thronged with waggons, and tracks were opened for horses wherever a shorter way might thus be made available. On every side the trees were falling, or had fallen. In some places whole woods had been felled with the express purpose of rendering the ground impracticable for troops, and firs and pines lay one over the other, still covered with their dark rough foliage, as though a mighty forest had grown there along the ground, without any power to raise itself towards the heavens. In other places the trees had been chopped off from their trunks about a yard from the ground, so that the soldier who cut it should have no trouble in stooping, and the tops had been dragged away for firewood, or for the erection of screens against the wind. Here and there in solitary places there were outlying tents, looking as though each belonged to some military recluse; and in the neighbourhood of every division was to be found a photographing-establishment upon wheels, in order that the men might send home to their sweethearts pictures of themselves in their martial costumes.

I wandered about through these camps both on foot and on horseback day after day, and every now and then I would come upon a farm-house that was still occupied by its old inhabitants. Many of such houses had been deserted, and were now held by the senior officers of the army; but some of the old families remained, living in the midst of this scene of war in a condition most forlorn. As for any tillage of their land, that under such circumstances might be pronounced as hopeless. Nor could there exist encouragement for farm-work of any kind. Fences had been taken down and burned; the ground had been overrun in every direction. The stock had of course disappeared; it had not been stolen, but had been sold in a hurry for what under such circumstances it might fetch. What farmer could work or have any hope for his land in the middle of such a crowd of soldiers? But yet there were the families. The women were in their houses, and the children playing at their doors, and the men, with whom I sometimes spoke, would stand around with their hands in their pockets. They knew that they were ruined; they expected no redress. In nine cases out of ten they were inimical in spirit to the soldiers around them. And yet it seemed that their equanimity was never disturbed. In a former chapter I have spoken of a certain general,—not a fighting general of the army, but a local farming general,—who spoke loudly and with many curses of the injury inflicted on him by the secessionists. With that exception, I heard no loud complaint of personal suffering. These Virginian farmers must have been deprived of everything,—of the very means of earning bread. They still hold by their houses, though they were in the very thick of the war, because there they had shelter for their families, and elsewhere they might seek it in vain. A man cannot move his wife and children if he have no place to which to move them, even though his house be in the midst of disease, of pestilence, or of battle. So it was with them then, but it seemed as though they were already used to it.

But there was a class of inhabitants in that same country to whom fate had been even more unkind than to those whom I saw. The lines of the northern army extended perhaps seven or eight miles from the Potomac, and the lines of the Confederate army were distant some four miles from those of their enemies. There was, therefore, an intervening space or strip of ground about four miles broad, which might be said to be no man's land. It was no man's land as to military possession, but it was still occupied by many of its old inhabitants. These people were not allowed to pass the lines either of one army or of the other; or if they did so pass they were not allowed to return to their homes. To these homes they were forced to cling, and there they remained. They had no market, no shops at which to make purchases even if they had money to buy; no customers with whom to deal even if they had produce to sell. They had their cows, if they could keep them from the Confederate soldiers, their pigs and their poultry; and on them they were living—a most forlorn life. Any advance made by either party must be over their homesteads. In the event of battle they would be in the midst of it; and in the meantime they could see no one, hear of nothing, go no whither beyond the limits of that miserable strip of ground!

The earth was hard with frost when I paid my visit to the camp, and the general appearance of things around my friend's quarters was on that account cheerful enough. It was the mud which made things sad and wretched. When the frost came it seemed as though the army had overcome one of its worst enemies. Unfortunately cold weather did not last long. I have been told in Washington that they rarely have had so open a season. Soon after my departure that terrible enemy, the mud, came back upon them, but during my stay the ground was hard and the weather very sharp. I slept in a tent, and managed to keep my body warm by an enormous overstructure of blankets and coats; but I could not keep my head warm. Throughout the night I had to go down, like a fish beneath the water, for protection, and come up for air at intervals, half-smothered. I had a stove in my tent, but the heat of that when lighted was more terrible than the severity of the frost.

The tents of the brigade with which I was staying had been pitched not without an eye to appearances. They were placed in streets as it were, each street having its name, and between them screens had been erected of fir-poles and fir-branches, so as to keep off the wind. The outside boundaries of the nearest regiment were ornamented with arches, crosses, and columns constructed in the same way; so that the quarters of the men were reached, as it were, through gateways. The whole thing was pretty enough, and while the ground was hard the camp was picturesque, and a visit to it was not unpleasant. But unfortunately the ground was in its nature soft and deep, composed of red clay, and as the frost went and the wet weather came, mud became omnipotent and destroyed all prettiness. And I found that the cold weather, let it be ever so cold, was not severe upon the men. It was wet which they feared and had cause to fear, both for themselves and for their horses. As to the horses, but few of them were protected by any shelter or covering whatsoever. Through both frost and wet they remained out, tied to the wheel of a waggon or to some temporary rack at which they were fed. In England we should imagine that any horse so treated must perish; but here the animals seemed to stand it. Many of them were miserable enough in appearance, but nevertheless they did the work required of them. I have observed that horses throughout the States are treated in a hardier manner than is usually the case with us.

At the period of which I am speaking, January, 1862, the health of the army of the Potomac was not as good as it had been, and was beginning to give way under the effects of the winter. Measles had become very prevalent, and also small-pox—though not of a virulent description; and men, in many instances, were sinking under fatigue. I was informed by various officers that the Irish regiments were on the whole the most satisfactory. Not that they made the best soldiers, for it was asserted that they were worse, as soldiers, than the Americans or Germans; not that they became more easily subject to rule, for it was asserted that they were unruly;—but because they were rarely ill. Diseases which seized the American troops on all sides seemed to spare them. The mortality was not excessive, but the men became sick and ailing, and fell under the doctor's hands.

Mr. Olmstead, whose name is well known in England as a writer on the southern States, was at this time secretary to a Sanitary Commission on the army, and published an abstract of the results of the inquiries made, on which I believe perfect reliance may be placed. This inquiry was extended to two hundred regiments, which were presumed to be included in the army of the Potomac; but these regiments were not all located on the Virginian side of the river, and must not therefore be taken as belonging exclusively to the divisions of which I have been speaking. Mr. Olmstead says, "The health of our armies is evidently not above the average of armies in the field. The mortality of the army of the Potomac during the summer months averaged 3½ per cent., and for the whole army it is stated at 5 per cent." "Of the camps inspected, 5 per cent.," he says, "were in admirable order; 44 per cent. fairly clean and well policed. The condition of 26 per cent. was negligent and slovenly, and of 24 per cent. decidedly bad, filthy, and dangerous." Thus 50 per cent. were either negligent and slovenly, or filthy and dangerous. I wonder what the report would have been had Camp Benton at St. Louis been surveyed! "In about 80 per cent. of the regiments the officers claimed to give systematic attention to the cleanliness of the men; but it is remarked that they rarely enforced the washing of the feet, and not always of the head and neck." I wish Mr. Olmstead had added that they never enforced the cutting of the hair. No single trait has been so decidedly disadvantageous to the appearance of the American army, as the long, uncombed, rough locks of hair which the men have appeared so loth to abandon. In reading the above one cannot but think of the condition of those other twenty regiments!

According to Mr. Olmstead two-thirds of the men were native-born, and one-third was composed of foreigners. These foreigners are either Irish or German. Had a similar report been made of the armies in the West, I think it would have been seen that the proportion of foreigners was still greater. The average age of the privates was something under twenty-five, and that of the officers thirty-four. I may here add, from my own observation, that an officer's rank could in no degree be predicated from his age. Generals, colonels, majors, captains, and lieutenants, had been all appointed at the same time and without reference to age or qualification. Political influence or the power of raising recruits had been the standard by which military rank was distributed. The old West Point officers had generally been chosen for high commands, but beyond this everything was necessarily new. Young colonels and ancient captains abounded without any harsh feeling as to the matter on either side. Indeed in this respect the practice of the country generally was simply carried out. Fathers and mothers in America seem to obey their sons and daughters naturally, and as they grow old become the slaves of their grandchildren.

Mr. Olmstead says that food was found to be universally good and abundant. On this matter Mr. Olmstead might have spoken in stronger language without exaggeration. The food supplied to the American armies has been extravagantly good, and certainly has been wastefully abundant. Very much has been said of the cost of the American army, and it has been made a matter of boasting that no army so costly has ever been put into the field by any other nation. The assertion is, I believe, at any rate true. I have found it impossible to ascertain what has hitherto been expended on the army. I much doubt whether even Mr. Chase, the Secretary of the Treasury, or Mr. Stanton, the Secretary-at-War, know themselves, and I do not suppose that Mr. Stanton's predecessor much cared. Some approach, however, may be reached to the amount actually paid in wages and for clothes and diet, and I give below a statement which I have seen of the actual annual sum proposed to be expended on these heads, presuming the army to consist of 500,000 men. The army is stated to contain 660,000 men, but the former numbers given would probably be found to be nearer the mark.

	Dollars
Wages of privates, including sergeants and corporals	86,640,000
Salaries of regimental officers	23,784,000
Extra wages of privates; extra pay to mounted officers, and salary of officers above the rank of colonel	17,000,000
	127,424,000
	or
	£25,484,000
	sterling.

To this must be added the cost of diet and clothing. The food of the men, I was informed, was supplied at an average cost of 17 cents a day, which, for an army of 500,000 men, would amount to £6,200,000 per annum. The clothing of the men is shown by the printed statement of their war department to amount to 3 dollars a month for a period of five years. That, at least, is the amount allowed to a private of infantry or artillery. The cost of the cavalry uniforms and of the dress of the non-commissioned officers is something higher, but not sufficiently so to make it necessary to make special provision for the difference in a statement so rough as this. At 3 dollars a month the clothing of the army would amount to £3,600,000. The actual annual cost would therefore be as follows:—

Salaries and wages	£25,484,400
Diet of the soldiers	6,200,000
Clothing for the soldiers	3,600,000
	£35,284,400

I believe that these figures may be trusted, unless it be with reference to that sum of $17,000,000 or £3,400,000, which is presumed to include the salaries of all general-officers with their staffs, and also the extra wages paid to soldiers in certain cases. This is given as an estimate, and may be over or under the mark. The sum named as the cost of clothing would be correct, or nearly so, if the army remained in its present force for five years. If it so remained for only one year the cost would be one-fifth higher. It must of course be remembered that the sum above named includes simply the wages, clothes, and food of the men. It does not comprise the purchase of arms, horses, ammunition, or waggons; the forage of horses; the transport of troops, or any of those incidental expenses of warfare which are always, I presume, heavier than the absolute cost of the men, and which in this war have been probably heavier than in any war ever waged on the face of God's earth. Nor does it include that terrible item of peculation as to which I will say a word or two before I finish this chapter.

The yearly total payment of the officers and soldiers of the armies is as follows. As regards the officers it must be understood that this includes all the allowances made to them, except as regards those on the staff. The sums named apply only to the infantry and artillery. The pay of the cavalry is about ten per cent. higher.

Lieutenant-General.	£1,850
General Scott alone holds that rank in the States' army	
Major-General	1,150
Brigadier-General	800
*Colonel	530
*Lieutenant-Colonel	475
Major	430
Captain	300
First Lieutenant	265
Second Lieutenant	245
First Sergeant	48
Sergeant	40
Corporal	34
Private	31

*A Colonel and Lieutenant-Colonel are attached to each regiment.

In every grade named the pay is, I believe, higher than that given by us, or, as I imagine, by any other nation. It is, however, probable that the extra allowances paid to some of our higher officers when on duty may give to their positions for a time a higher pecuniary remuneration. It will of course be understood that there is nothing in the American army answering to our colonel of a regiment. With us the officer so designated holds a nominal command of high dignity and emolument as a reward for past services.

I have already spoken of my visits to the camps of the other armies in the field, that of General Halleck, who held his head-quarters at St. Louis, in Missouri, and that of General Buell, who was at Louisville, in Kentucky. There was also a fourth army under General Hunter, in Kansas, but I did not make my way as far west as that. I do not pretend to any military knowledge, and should be foolish to attempt military criticism; but as far as I could judge by appearance, I should say that the men in Buell's army were, of the three, in the best order. They seemed to me to be cleaner than the others, and, as far as I could learn, were in better health. Want of discipline and dirt have, no doubt, been the great faults of the regiments generally, and the latter drawback may probably be included in the former. These men have not been accustomed to act under the orders of superiors, and when they entered on the service hardly recognized the fact that they would have to do so in ought else than in their actual drill and fighting. It is impossible to conceive any class of men to whom the necessary discipline of a soldier would come with more difficulty than to an American citizen. The whole training of his life has been against it. He has never known respect for a master, or reverence for men of a higher rank than himself. He has probably been made to work hard for his wages,—harder than an Englishman works,—but he has been his employer's equal. The language between them has been the language of equals, and their arrangement as to labour and wages has been a contract between equals. If he did not work he would not get his money,—and perhaps not if he did. Under these circumstances he has made his fight with the world; but those circumstances have never taught him that special deference to a superior, which is the first essential of a soldier's duty. But probably in no respect would that difficulty be so severely felt as in all matters appertaining to personal habits. Here at any rate the man would expect to be still his own master, acting for himself and independent of all outer control. Our English Hodge, when taken from the plough to the camp, would, probably, submit without a murmur to soap and water and a barber's shears; he would have received none of that education which would prompt him to rebel against such ordinances; but the American citizen, who for a while expects to shake hands with his captain whenever he sees him, and is astonished when he learns that he must not offer him drinks, cannot at once be brought to understand that he is to be treated like a child in the nursery;—that he must change his shirt so often, wash himself at such and such intervals, and go through a certain process of cleansing his outward garments daily. I met while travelling a sergeant of an old regular American regiment, and he spoke of the want of discipline among the volunteers as hopeless. But even he instanced it chiefly by their want of cleanliness. "They wear their shirts till they drop off their backs," said he; "and what can you expect from such men as that?" I liked that sergeant for his zeal and intelligence, and also for his courtesy when he found that I was an Englishman; for previous to his so finding he had begun to abuse the English roundly,—but I did not quite agree with him about the volunteers. It is very bad that soldiers should be dirty, bad also that they should treat their captains with familiarity and desire to exchange drinks with the majors. But even discipline is not everything; and discipline will come at last even to the American soldiers, distasteful as it may be, when the necessity for it is made apparent. But these volunteers have great military virtues. They are intelligent, zealous in their cause, handy with arms, willing enough to work at all military duties, and personally brave. On the other hand they are sickly, and there has been a considerable amount of drunkenness among them. No man who has looked to the subject can, I think, doubt that a native American has a lower physical development than an Irishman, a German, or an Englishman. They become old sooner, and die at an earlier age. As to that matter of drink, I do not think that much need be said against them. English soldiers get drunk when they have the means of doing so, and American soldiers would not get drunk if the means were taken away from them. A little drunkenness goes a long way in a camp, and ten drunkards will give a bad name to a company of a hundred. Let any man travel with twenty men of whom four are tipsy, and on leaving them he will tell you that every man of them was a drunkard.

I have said that these men are brave, and I have no doubt that they are so. How should it be otherwise with men of such a race? But it must be remembered that there are two kinds of courage, one of which is very common and the other very uncommon. Of the latter description of courage it cannot be expected that much should be found among the privates of any army, and perhaps not very many examples among the officers. It is a courage self-sustained, based on a knowledge of the right and on a life-long calculation that any results coming from adherence to the right will be preferable to any that can be produced by a departure from it. This is the courage which will enable a man to stand his ground in battle or elsewhere, though broken worlds should fall around him. The other courage, which is mainly an affair of the heart or blood and not of the brain, always requires some outward support. The man who finds himself prominent in danger bears himself gallantly, because the eyes of many will see him; whether as an old man he leads an army, or as a young man goes on a forlorn hope, or as a private carries his officer on his back out of the fire, he is sustained by the love of praise. And the men who are not individually prominent in danger, who stand their ground shoulder to shoulder, bear themselves gallantly also, each trusting in the combined strength of his comrades. When such combined strength has been acquired, that useful courage is engendered which we may rather call confidence, and which of all courage is the most serviceable in the army. At the battle of Bull's Run the army of the North became panic-stricken and fled. From this fact many have been led to believe that the American soldiers would not fight well, and that they could not be brought to stand their ground under fire. This I think has been an unfair conclusion. In the first place the history of the battle of Bull's Run has yet to be written; as yet the history of the flight only has been given to us. As far as I can learn, the northern soldiers did at first fight well;—so well, that the army of the South believed itself to be beaten. But a panic was created—at first, as it seems, among the teamsters and waggons. A cry was raised, and a rush was made by hundreds of drivers with their carts and horses; and then men who had never seen war before, who had not yet had three months' drilling as soldiers, to whom the turmoil of that day must have seemed as though hell were opening upon them, joined themselves to the general clamour, and fled to Washington, believing that all was lost. But at the same time the regiments of the enemy were going through the same farce in the other direction! It was a battle between troops who knew nothing of battles; of soldiers who were not yet soldiers. That individual high-minded courage, which would have given to each individual recruit the self-sustained power against a panic, which is to be looked for in a general, was not to be looked for in them. Of the other courage of which I have spoken, there was as much as the circumstances of the battle would allow.

On subsequent occasions the men have fought well. We should, I think, admit that they have fought very well when we consider how short has been their practice at such work. At Somerset, at Fort Henry, at Fort Donnelson, at Corinth, the men behaved with courage, standing well to their arms, though at each place the slaughter among them was great. They have always gone well into fire, and have generally borne themselves well under fire. I am convinced that we in England can make no greater mistake than to suppose that the Americans as soldiers are deficient in courage.

But now I must come to a matter in which a terrible deficiency has been shown, not by the soldiers, but by those whose duty it has been to provide for the soldiers. It is impossible to speak of the army of the North and to leave untouched that hideous subject of army contracts. And I think myself the more specially bound to allude to it because I feel that the iniquities which have prevailed, prove with terrible earnestness the demoralizing power of that dishonesty among men in high places, which is the one great evil of the American States. It is there that the deficiency exists, which must be supplied before the public men of the nation can take a high rank among other public men. There is the gangrene, which must be cut out before the government, as a government, can be great. To make money is the one thing needful, and men have been anxious to meddle with the affairs of government, because there might money be made with the greatest ease.

"Make money," the Roman satirist said; "make it honestly if you can, but at any rate make money." That first counsel would be considered futile and altogether vain by those who have lately dealt with the public wants of the American States.

This is bad in a most fatal degree, not mainly because men in high places have been dishonest, or because the government has been badly served by its own paid officers. That men in high places should be dishonest, and that the people should be cheated by their rulers is very bad. But there is worse than this. The thing becomes so common, and so notorious, that the American world at large is taught to believe that dishonesty is in itself good. "It behoves a man to be smart, sir!" Till the opposite doctrine to that be learned; till men in America,—ay, and in Europe, Asia, and Africa,—can learn that it specially behoves a man not to be smart, they will have learned little of their duty towards God, and nothing of their duty towards their neighbour.

In the instances of fraud against the States' government to which I am about to allude, I shall take all my facts from the report made to the House of Representatives at Washington by a Committee of that House in December, 1861. "Mr. Washbourne, from the Select Committee to inquire into the Contracts of the Government, made the following Report." That is the heading of the pamphlet. The Committee was known as the Van Wyck Committee, a gentleman of that name having acted as chairman.

The Committee first went to New York, and began their inquiries with reference to the purchase of a steam-boat called the "Catiline." In this case a certain Captain Comstock had been designated from Washington as the agent to be trusted in the charter or purchase of the vessel. He agreed on behalf of the Government to hire that special boat for £2000 a month for three months, having given information to friends of his on the matter, which enabled them to purchase it out-and-out for less than £4000. These friends were not connected with shipping matters, but were lawyers and hotel proprietors. The Committee conclude "that the vessel was chartered to the Government at an unconscionable price; and that Captain Comstock, by whom this was effected, while enjoying *the peculiar confidence of the Government*, was acting for and in concert with the parties who chartered the vessel, and was in fact their agent." But the report does not explain why Captain Comstock was selected for this work by authority from Washington, nor does it recommend that he be punished. It does not appear that Captain Comstock had ever been in the regular service of the Government, but that he had been master of a steamer.

In the next place one Starbuck is employed to buy ships. As a government agent he buys two for £1300, and sells them to the government for £2900. The vessels themselves, when delivered at the Navy Yard, were found to be totally unfit for the service for which they had been purchased. But why was Starbuck employed, when, as appears over and over again in the report, New York was full of paid government servants ready and fit to do the work? Starbuck was merely an agent, and who will believe that he was allowed to pocket the whole difference of £1600? The greater part of the plunder was, however, in this case refunded.

Then we come to the case of Mr. George D. Morgan, brother-in-law of Mr. Welles, the Secretary of the Navy. I have spoken of this gentleman before, and of his singular prosperity. He amassed a large fortune in five months, as a government agent for the purchase of vessels, he having been a wholesale grocer by trade. This gentleman had had no experience whatsoever with reference to ships. It is shown by the evidence that he had none of the requisite knowledge, and that there were special servants of the government in New York at that time, sent there specially for such services as these, who were in every way trustworthy, and who had the requisite knowledge. Yet Mr. Morgan was placed in this position by his brother-in-law the Secretary of the Navy, and in that capacity made about £20,000 in five months, all of which was paid by the government, as is well shown to have been the fact in the report before me. One result of such a mode of agency is given;—one other result, I mean, besides the £20,000 put into the pocket of the brother of the Secretary of the Navy. A ship called the "Stars and Stripes" was bought by Mr. Morgan for £11,000, which had been built some months before for £7000. This vessel was bought from a company which was blessed with a President. The President made the bargain with the government agent, but insisted on keeping back from his own company £2000 out of the £11,000 for expenses incident to the purchase. The company did not like being mulcted of its prey, and growled heavily; but their President declared that such bargains were not got at Washington for nothing. Members of Congress had to be paid to assist in such things. At least he could not reduce his little private bill for such assistance below £1600. He had, he said, positively paid out so much to those venal Members of Congress, and had made nothing for himself to compensate him for his own exertions. When this President came to be examined, he admitted that he had really made no payments to Members of Congress. His own capacity had been so great that no such assistance had been found necessary. But he justified his charge on the ground that the sum taken by him was no more than the company might have expected him to lay out on Members of Congress, or on ex-Members who are specially mentioned, had he not himself carried on the business with such consummate discretion! It seems to me that the Members or ex-Members of Congress were shamefully robbed in this matter.

The report deals manfully with Mr. Morgan, showing that for five months' work,—which work he did not do and did not know how to do,—he received as large a sum as the President's salary for the whole Presidential term of four years. So much better is it to be an agent of government than simply an officer! And the Committee adds, that they "do not find in this transaction the less to censure in the fact that this arrangement between the Secretary of the Navy and Mr. Morgan was one between brothers-in-law." After that who will believe that Mr. Morgan had the whole of that £20,000 for himself? And yet Mr. Welles still remains Secretary of the Navy, and has justified the whole transaction in an explanation admitting everything, and which is considered by his friends to be an able State paper. "It behoves a man to be smart, sir." Mr. Morgan and Secretary Welles will no doubt be considered by their own party to have done their duty well as high trading public functionaries. The faults of Mr. Morgan and of Secretary Welles are nothing to us in England; but the light in which such faults may be regarded by the American people is much to us.

I will now go on to the case of a Mr. Cummings. Mr. Cummings, it appears, had been for many years the editor of a newspaper in Philadelphia, and had been an intimate political friend and ally of Mr. Cameron. Now at the time of which I am writing, April, 1861, Mr. Cameron was Secretary-at-War, and could be very useful to an old political ally living in his own State. The upshot of the present case will teach us to think well of Mr. Cameron's gratitude.

In April, 1861, stores were wanted for the army at Washington, and Mr. Cameron gave an order to his old friend Cummings to expend 2,000,000 dollars, pretty much according to his fancy, in buying stores. Governor Morgan, the Governor of New York State and a relative of our other friend Morgan, was joined with Mr. Cummings in this commission, Mr. Cameron no doubt having felt himself bound to give the friends of his colleague at the Navy a chance. Governor Morgan at once made over his right to his relative; but better things soon came in Mr. Morgan's way, and he relinquished his share in this partnership at an early date. In this transaction he did not himself handle above 25,000 dollars. Then the whole job fell into the hands of Mr. Cameron's old political friend.

The 2,000,000 of dollars, or £400,000, were paid into the hands of certain government treasurers at New York, but they had orders to honour the draft of the political friend of the Secretary-at-War, and consequently £50,000 was immediately withdrawn by Mr. Cummings, and with this he went to work. It is shown that he knew nothing of the business; that he employed a clerk from Albany whom he did not know, and confided to this clerk the duty of buying such stores as were bought; that this clerk was recommended to him by Mr. Weed, the editor of a newspaper at Albany, who is known in the States as the special political friend of Mr. Seward, the Secretary of State; and that in this way he spent £32,000. He bought linen pantaloons and straw hats to the amount of £4200, because he thought the soldiers looked hot in the warm weather; but he afterwards learned that they were of no use. He bought groceries of a hardware dealer named Davidson, at Albany, that town whence came Mr. Weed's clerk. He did not know what was Davidson's trade, nor did he know exactly what he was going to buy; but Davidson proposed to sell him something which Mr. Cummings believed to be some kind of provisions, and he bought it. He did not know for how much, —whether over £2000 or not. He never saw the articles and had no knowledge of their quality. It was out of the question that he should have such knowledge, as he naïvely remarks. His clerk Humphreys saw the articles. He presumed they were brought from Albany, but did not know. He afterwards bought a ship, —or two or three ships. He inspected one ship "by a mere casual visit:" that is to say, he did not examine her boilers; he did not know her tonnage, but he took the word of the seller for everything. He could not state the terms of the charter, or give the substance of it. He had had no former experience in buying or chartering ships. He also bought 75,000 pair of shoes at only 25 cents, or one shilling a pair, more than their proper price. He bought them of a Mr. Hall, who declares that he paid Mr. Cummings nothing for the job, but regarded it as a return for certain previous favours conferred by him on Mr. Cummings in the occasional loans of £100 or £200.

At the end of the examination it appears that Mr. Cummings still held in his hand a slight balance of £28,000, of which he had forgotten to make mention in the body of his own evidence. "This item seems to have been overlooked by him in his testimony," says the report. And when the report was made nothing had yet been learned of the destiny of this small balance.

Then the report gives a list of the army supplies miscellaneously purchased by Mr. Cummings:—280 dozen pints of ale at 9s. 6d. a dozen; a lot of codfish and herrings; 200 boxes of cheeses and a large assortment of butter; some tongues; straw hats and linen "pants;" 23 barrels of pickles; 25 casks of Scotch ale, price not stated; a lot of London porter, price not stated; and some Hall carbines of which I must say a word more further on. It should be remembered that no requisition had come from the army for any of the articles named; that the purchase of herrings and straw hats was dictated solely by the discretion of Cummings and his man Humphreys, — or, as is more probable, by the fact that some other person had such articles by him for sale; and that the government had its own established officers for the supply of things properly ordered by military requisition. These very same articles also were apparently procured, in the first place, as a private speculation, and were made over to the government on the failure of that speculation. "Some of the above articles," says the report, "were shipped by the 'Catiline,' which were probably loaded on private account, and not being able to obtain a clearance was in some way, through Mr. Cummings, transferred over to the government, — *Scotch ale, London porter, selected herrings*, and all." The italics as well as the words are taken from the report.

This was the confidential political friend of the Secretary-at-War, by whom he was intrusted with £400,000 of public money! £28,000 had not been accounted for when the report was made, and the army supplies were bought after the fashion above named. That Secretary-at-War, Mr. Cameron, has since left the Cabinet; but he has not been turned out in disgrace; he has been nominated as minister to Russia, and the world has been told that there was some difference of opinion between him and his colleagues respecting slavery! Mr. Cameron in some speech or paper declared on his leaving the Cabinet that he had not intended to remain long as Secretary-at-War. This assertion, I should think, must have been true.

And now about the Hall carbines, as to which the gentlemen on this Committee tell their tale with an evident delight in the richness of its incidents which at once puts all their readers in accord with them. There were altogether some five thousand of these, all of which the government sold to a Mr. Eastman in June, 1861, for 14s. each, as perfectly useless, and afterwards bought in August for £4 8s. each, about 4s. a carbine having been expended in their repair in the mean time. But as regards 790 of these now famous weapons, it must be explained they had been sold by the government as perfectly useless, and at a nominal price, previously to this second sale made by the government to Mr. Eastman. They had been so sold, and then, in April, 1861, they had been bought again for the government by the indefatigable Cummings for £3 each. Then they were again sold as useless for 14s. each to Eastman, and instantly rebought on behalf of the government for £4 8s. each! Useless for war purposes they may have been, but as articles of commerce it must be confessed that they were very serviceable.

This last purchase was made by a man named Stevens on behalf of General Fremont, who at that time commanded the army of the United States in Missouri. Stevens had been employed by General Fremont as an agent on the behalf of government, as is shown with clearness in the report, and on hearing of these muskets telegraphed to the General at once. "I have 5000 Hall's rifled cast-steel muskets, breech-loading, new, at 22 dollars." General Fremont telegraphed back instantly, "I will take the whole 5000 carbines ... I will pay all extra charges ..." And so the purchase was made. The muskets, it seems, were not absolutely useless even as weapons of war. "Considering the emergency of the times," a competent witness considered them to be worth "10 or 12 dollars." The government had been as much cheated in selling them as it had in buying them. But the nature of the latter transaction is shown by the facts that Stevens was employed, though irresponsibly employed, as a government agent by General Fremont; that he bought the muskets in that character himself, making on the transaction £1 18s. on each musket; and that the same man afterwards appeared as an aide-de-camp on General Fremont's staff. General Fremont had no authority himself to make such a purchase, and when the money was paid for the first instalment of the arms, it was so paid by the special order of General Fremont himself out of moneys intended to be applied to other purposes. The money was actually paid to a gentleman known at Fremont's head-quarters as his special friend, and was then paid in that irregular way because this friend desired that that special bill should receive immediate payment. After that who can believe that Stevens was himself allowed to pocket the whole amount of the plunder?

There is a nice little story of a clergyman in New York who sold for £40 and certain further contingencies, the right to furnish 200 cavalry horses; but I should make this too long if I told all the nice little stories. As the frauds at St. Louis were, if not in fact the most monstrous, at any rate the most monstrous which have as yet been brought to the light, I cannot finish this account without explaining something of what was going on at that western Paradise in those halcyon days of General Fremont.

General Fremont, soon after reaching St. Louis, undertook to build ten forts for the protection of that city. These forts have since been pronounced as useless, and the whole measure has been treated with derision by officers of his own army. But the judgment displayed in the matter is a military question with which I do not presume to meddle. Even if a general be wrong in such a matter, his character as a man is not disgraced by such error. But the manner of building them was the affair with which Mr. Van Wyck's committee had to deal. It seems that five of the forts, the five largest, were made under the orders of a certain Major Kappner at a cost of £12,000, and that the other five could have been built at least for the same sum. Major Kappner seems to have been a good and honest public servant, and therefore quite unfit for the superintendence of such work at St. Louis. The other five smaller forts were also in progress, the works on them having been continued from 1st September to 25th September, 1861; but on the 25th September General Fremont himself gave special orders that a contract should be made with a man named Beard, a Californian, who had followed him from California to St. Louis. This contract is dated the 25th of September. But nevertheless the work specified in that contract was done previous to that date, and most of the money paid was paid previous to that date. The contract did not specify any lump sum, but agreed that the work should be paid for by the yard and by the square foot. No less a sum was paid to Beard for this work—the cormorant Beard, as the report calls him— than £24,200, the last payment only, amounting to £4000, having been made subsequent to the date of the contract. £20,200 was paid to Beard before the date of the contract! The amounts were paid at five times, and the last four payments were made on the personal order of General Fremont. This Beard was under no bond, and none of the officers of the government knew anything of the terms under which he was working. On the 14th of October General Fremont was ordered to discontinue these works, and to abstain from making any further payments on their account. But, disobeying this order, he directed his Quartermaster to pay a further sum of £4000 to Beard out of the first sums he should receive from Washington, he then being out of money. This however was not paid. "It must be understood," says the report, "that every dollar ordered to be paid by General Fremont on account of these works was diverted from a fund specially appropriated for another purpose." And then again, "The money appropriated by Congress to subsist and clothe and transport our armies was then, in utter contempt of all law and of the army regulations, as well as in defiance of superior authority, ordered to be diverted from its lawful purpose and turned over to the cormorant Beard. While he had received 170,000 dollars (£24,200) from the Government, it will be seen from the testimony of Major Kappner that there had only been paid to the honest German labourers, who did the work on the first five forts built under his directions, the sum of 15,500 dollars (£3100), leaving from 40,000 to 50,000 dollars (£8000 to £10,000) still due; and while these labourers, whose families were clamouring for bread, were besieging the Quartermaster's department for their pay, this infamous contractor Beard is found following up the army and in the confidence of the Major-General, who gives him orders for large purchases, which could only have been legally made through the Quartermaster's department." After that who will believe that all the money went into Beard's pocket? Why should General Fremont have committed every conceivable breach of order against his government, merely with the view of favouring such a man as Beard?

The collusion of the Quartermaster M'Instry with fraudulent knaves in the purchase of horses is then proved. M'Instry was at this time Fremont's Quartermaster at St. Louis. I cannot go through all these. A man of the name of Jim Neil comes out in beautiful pre-eminence. No dealer in horses could get to the Quartermaster except through Jim Neil, or some such go-between. The Quartermaster contracted with Neil and Neil with the owners of horses; Neil at the time being also military inspector of horses for the Quartermaster. He bought horses as cavalry horses for £24 or less, and passed them himself as artillery horses for £30. In other cases the military inspectors were paid by the sellers to pass horses. All this was done under Quartermaster M'Instry, who would himself deal with none but such as Neil. In one instance, one Elleard got a contract from M'Instry, the profit of which was £8000. But there was a man named Brady. Now Brady was a friend of M'Instry's, who, scenting the carrion afar off, had come from Detroit, in Michigan, to St. Louis. M'Instry himself had also come from Detroit. In this case Elleard was simply directed by M'Instry to share his profits with Brady, and consequently paid to Brady £4000, although Brady gave to the business neither capital nor labour. He simply took the £4000 as the Quartermaster's friend. This Elleard, it seems, also gave a carriage and horses to Mrs. Fremont. Indeed Elleard seems to have been a civil and generous fellow. Then there is a man named Thompson, whose case is very amusing. Of him the Committee thus speaks:—"It must be said that Thompson was not forgetful of the obligations of gratitude, for, after he got through with the contract, he presented the son of Major M'Instry with a riding pony. That was the only mark of respect," to use his own words, "that he showed to the family of Major M'Instry."

General Fremont himself desired that a contract should be made with one Augustus Sacchi for a thousand Canadian horses. It turned out that Sacchi was "nobody: a man of straw living in a garret in New York whom nobody knew, a man who was brought out there"—to St. Louis—"as a good person through whom to work." "It will hardly be believed," says the report, "that the name of this same man Sacchi appears in the newspapers as being on the staff of General Fremont, at Springfield, with the rank of captain."

I do not know that any good would result from my pursuing further the details of this wonderful report. The remaining portion of it refers solely to the command held by General Fremont in Missouri, and adds proof upon proof of the gross robberies inflicted upon the government of the States by the very persons set in high authority to protect the government. We learn how all utensils for the camp, kettles, blankets, shoes, mess-pans, &c., were supplied by one firm, without a contract, at an enormous price, and of a quality so bad as to be almost useless, because the Quartermaster was under obligations to the partners. We learn that one partner in that firm gave £40 towards a service of plate for the Quartermaster, and £60 towards a carriage for Mrs. Fremont. We learn how futile were the efforts of any honest tradesman to supply good shoes to soldiers who were shoeless, and the history of one special pair of shoes which was thrust under the nose of the Quartermaster is very amusing. We learn that a certain paymaster properly refused to settle an account for matters with which he had no concern, and that General Fremont at once sent down soldiers to arrest him unless he made the illegal payment. In October £1000 was expended in ice, all which ice was wasted. Regiments were sent hither and thither with no military purpose, merely because certain officers, calling themselves generals, desired to make up brigades for themselves. Indeed every description of fraud was perpetrated, and this was done not through the negligence of those in high command, but by their connivance and often with their express authority.

It will be said that the conduct of General Fremont during the days of his command in Missouri is not a matter of much moment to us in England; that it has been properly handled by the Committee of Representatives appointed by the American Congress to inquire into the matter; and that after the publication of such a report by them, it is ungenerous in a writer from another nation to speak upon the subject. This would be so if the inquiries made by that Committee and their report had resulted in any general condemnation of the men whose misdeeds and peculations have been exposed. This, however, is by no means the case. Those who were heretofore opposed to General Fremont on political principles are opposed to him still; but those who heretofore supported him are ready to support him again. * He has not been placed beyond the pale of public favour by the record which has been made of his public misdeeds. He is decried by the democrats because he is a republican, and by the anti-abolitionists because he is an abolitionist; but he is not decried because he has shown himself to be dishonest in the service of his government. He was dismissed from his command in the West, but men on his side of the question declare that he was so dismissed because his political opponents had prevailed. Now, at the moment that I am writing this, men are saying that the President must give him another command. He is still a major-general in the army of the States, and is as probable a candidate as any other that I could name for the next Presidency.

> *Since this was written General Fremont has been restored
> to high military command, and now holds equal rank and
> equal authority with Maclellan and Halleck. In fact, the
> charges made against him by the Committee of the House of

Representatives have not been allowed to stand in his way. He is politically popular with a large section of the nation, and therefore it has been thought well to promote him to high place. Whether he be fit for such place, either as regards capability or integrity, seems to be considered of no moment.

The same argument must be used with reference to the other gentlemen named. Mr. Welles is still a Cabinet Minister and Secretary for the Navy. It has been found impossible to keep Mr. Cameron in the Cabinet, but he was named as the Minister of the States government to Russia after the publication of the Van Wyck report, when the result of his old political friendship with Mr. Alexander Cummings was well known to the President who appointed him and to the Senate who sanctioned his appointment. The individual corruption of any one man—of any ten men—is not much. It should not be insisted on loudly by any foreigner in making up a balance-sheet of the virtues and vices of the good and bad qualities of any nation. But the light in which such corruption is viewed by the people whom it most nearly concerns is very much. I am far from saying that democracy has failed in America. Democracy there has done great things for a numerous people, and will yet, as I think, be successful. But that doctrine as to the necessity of smartness must be eschewed before a verdict in favour of American democracy can be pronounced. "It behoves a man to be smart, sir." In those words are contained the curse under which the States' government has been suffering for the last thirty years. Let us hope that the people will find a mode of ridding themselves of that curse. I, for one, believe that they will do so.

CHAPTER VIII
BACK TO BOSTON

From Louisville we returned to Cincinnati, in making which journey we were taken to a place called Seymour in Indiana, at which spot we were to "make connection" with the train running on the Mississippi and Ohio line from St. Louis to Cincinnati. We did make the connection, but were called upon to remain four hours at Seymour in consequence of some accident on the line. In the same way, when going eastwards from Cincinnati to Baltimore a few days later, I was detained another four hours at a place called Crossline, in Ohio. On both occasions I spent my time in realizing, as far as that might be possible, the sort of life which men lead who settle themselves at such localities. Both these towns,—for they call themselves towns,—had been created by the railways. Indeed this has been the case with almost every place at which a few hundred inhabitants have been drawn together in the western States. With the exception of such cities as Chicago, St. Louis, and Cincinnati, settlers can hardly be said to have chosen their own localities. These have been chosen for them by the originators of the different lines of railway. And there is nothing in Europe in any way like to these western railway settlements. In the first place the line of the rails runs through the main street of the town, and forms not unfrequently the only road. At Seymour I could find no way of getting away from the rails unless I went into the fields. At Crossline, which is a larger place, I did find a street in which there was no railroad, but it was deserted, and manifestly out of favour with the inhabitants. As there were railway junctions at both these posts, there were of course cross-streets, and the houses extended themselves from the centre thus made along the lines, houses being added to houses at short intervals as new comers settled themselves down. The panting and groaning, and whistling of engines is continual; for at such places freight trains are always kept waiting for passenger trains, and the slower freight trains for those which are called fast. This is the life of the town; and indeed as the whole place is dependent on the railway, so is the railway held in favour and beloved. The noise of the engines is not disliked, nor are its puffings and groanings held to be unmusical. With us a locomotive steam-engine is still, as it were, a beast of prey, against which one has to be on one's guard,—in respect to which one specially warns the children. But there, in the western States, it has been taken to the bosoms of them all as a domestic animal; no one fears it, and the little children run about almost among its wheels. It is petted and made much of on all sides,— and, as far as I know, it seldom bites or tears. I have not heard of children being destroyed wholesale in the streets, or of drunken men becoming frequent sacrifices. But had I been consulted beforehand as to the natural effects of such an arrangement, I should have said that no child could have been reared in such a town, and that any continuance of population under such circumstances must have been impracticable.

Such places, however, do thrive and prosper with a prosperity especially their own, and the boys and girls increase and multiply in spite of all dangers. With us in England, it is difficult to realize the importance which is attached to a railway in the States, and the results which a railway creates. We have roads everywhere, and our country had been cultivated throughout, with more or less care, before our system of railways had been commenced; but in America, especially in the North, the railways have been the precursors of cultivation. They have been carried hither and thither, through primeval forests and over prairies, with small hope of other traffic than that which they themselves would make by their own influences. The people settling on their edges have had the very best of all roads at their service; but they have had no other roads. The face of the country between one settlement and another is still in many cases utterly unknown; but there is the connecting road by which produce is carried away, and new comers are brought in. The town that is distant a hundred miles by the rail is so near that its inhabitants are neighbours; but a settlement twenty miles distant across the uncleared country is unknown, unvisited, and probably unheard of by the women and children. Under such circumstances the railway is everything. It is the first necessity of life, and gives the only hope of wealth. It is the backbone of existence from whence spring, and by which are protected, all the vital organs and functions of the community. It is the right arm of civilization for the people, and the discoverer of the fertility of the land. It is all in all to those people, and to those regions. It has supplied the wants of frontier life with all the substantial comfort of the cities, and carried education, progress, and social habits into the wilderness. To the eye of the stranger such places as Seymour and Crossline are desolate and dreary. There is nothing of beauty in them, given either by nature or by art. The railway itself is ugly, and its numerous sidings and branches form a mass of iron road which is bewildering and, according to my ideas, in itself disagreeable. The wooden houses open down upon the line, and have no gardens to relieve them. A foreigner, when first surveying such a spot, will certainly record within himself a verdict against it; but in doing so he probably commits the error of judging it by a wrong standard. He should compare it with the new settlements which men have opened up in spots where no railway has assisted them, and not with old towns in which wealth has long been congregated. The traveller may see what is the place with the railway; then let him consider how it might have thriven without the railway.

I confess that I became tired of my sojourn at both the places I have named. At each I think that I saw every house in the place, although my visit to Seymour was made in the night; and at both I was lamentably at a loss for something to do. At Crossline I was all alone, and began to feel that the hours which I knew must pass before the missing train could come, would never make away with themselves. There were many others stationed there as I was, but to them had been given a capability for loafing which niggardly Nature has denied to me. An American has the power of seating himself in the close vicinity of a hot stove and feeding in silence on his own thoughts by the hour together. It may be that he will smoke; but after a while his cigar will come to an end. He sits on, however, certainly patient, and apparently contented. It may be that he chews, but if so, he does it with motionless jaws, and so slow a mastication of the pabulum on which he feeds, that his employment in this respect only disturbs the absolute quiet of the circle when, at certain long, distant intervals, he deposits the secretion of his tobacco in an ornamental utensil which may probably be placed in the furthest corner of the hall. But during all this time he is happy. It does not fret him to sit there and think and do nothing. He is by no means an idle man,—probably one much given to commercial enterprise. Idle men out there in the West we may say there are none. How should any idle man live in such a country? All who were sitting hour after hour in that circle round the stove of the Crossline Hotel hall,—sitting there hour after hour in silence, as I could not sit,—were men who earned their bread by labour. They were farmers, mechanics, storekeepers; there was a lawyer or two, and one clergyman. Sufficient conversation took place at first to indicate the professions of many of them. One may conclude that there could not be place there for an idle man. But they all of them had a capacity for a prolonged state of doing nothing, which is to me unintelligible, and which is very much to be envied. They are patient as cows, which from hour to hour lie on the grass chewing their cud. An Englishman, if he be kept waiting by a train in some forlorn station in which he can find no employment, curses his fate and all that has led to his present misfortune with an energy which tells the story of his deep and thorough misery. Such, I confess, is my state of existence under such circumstances. But a western American gives himself up to "loafing," and is quite happy. He balances himself on the back legs of an arm-chair, and remains so, without speaking, drinking, or smoking for an hour at a stretch; and while he is doing so he looks as though he had all that he desired. I believe that he is happy, and that he has all that he wants for such an occasion;—an arm-chair in which to sit, and a stove on which he can put his feet, and by which he can make himself warm.

Such was not the phase of character which I had expected to find among the people of the West. Of all virtues, patience would have been the last which I should have thought of attributing to them. I should have expected to see them angry when robbed of their time, and irritable under the stress of such grievances as railway delays; but they are never irritable under such circumstances as I have attempted to describe, nor, indeed, are they a people prone to irritation under any grievances. Even in political matters they are long-enduring, and do not form themselves into mobs for the expression of hot opinion. We in England thought that masses of the people would rise in anger if Mr. Lincoln's government should consent to give up Slidell and Mason; but the people bore it without any rising. The habeas corpus has been suspended, the liberty of the press has been destroyed for a time, the telegraph wires have been taken up by the government into their own hands; but nevertheless the people have said nothing. There has been no rising of a mob, and not even an expression of an adverse opinion. The people require to be allowed to vote periodically, and having acquired that privilege permit other matters to go by the board. In this respect we have, I think, in some degree misunderstood their character. They have all been taught to reverence the nature of that form of government under which they live, but they are not specially addicted to hot political fermentation. They have learned to understand that democratic institutions have given them liberty, and on that subject they entertain a strong conviction which is universal. But they have not habitually interested themselves deeply in the doings of their legislators or of their government. On the subject of slavery there have been and are different opinions, held with great tenacity and maintained occasionally with violence; but on other subjects of daily policy the American people have not, I think, been eager politicians. Leading men in public life have been much less trammelled by popular will than among us. Indeed with us the most conspicuous of our statesmen and legislators do not lead, but are led. In the States the noted politicians of the day have been the leaders, and not unfrequently the coercers of opinion. Seeing this, I claim for England a broader freedom in political matters than the States have as yet achieved. In speaking of the American form of government, I will endeavour to explain more clearly the ideas which I have come to hold on this matter.

I survived my delay at Seymour, after which I passed again through Cincinnati, and then survived my subsequent delay at Crossline. As to Cincinnati, I must put on record the result of a country walk which I took there,—or rather on which I was taken by my friend. He professed to know the beauties of the neighbourhood, and to be well acquainted with all that was attractive in its vicinity. Cincinnati is built on the Ohio, and is closely surrounded by picturesque hills which overhang the suburbs of the city. Over these I was taken, ploughing my way through a depth of mud which cannot be understood by any ordinary Englishman. But the depth of mud was not the only impediment, nor the worst which we encountered. As we began to ascend from the level of the outskirts of the town we were greeted by a rising flavour in the air, which soon grew into a strong odour, and at last developed itself into a stench that surpassed in offensiveness anything that my nose had ever hitherto suffered. When we were at the worst we hardly knew whether to descend or to proceed. It had so increased in virulence, that at one time I felt sure that it arose from some matter buried in the ground beneath my feet. But my friend, who declared himself to be quite at home in Cincinnati matters, and to understand the details of the great Cincinnati trade, declared against this opinion of mine. Hogs, he said, were at the bottom of it. It was the odour of hogs going up to the Ohio heavens;—of hogs in a state of transit from hoggish nature to clothes-brushes, saddles, sausages, and lard. He spoke with an authority that constrained belief; but I can never forgive him in that he took me over those hills, knowing all that he professed to know. Let the visitors to Cincinnati keep themselves within the city, and not wander forth among the mountains. It is well that the odour of hogs should ascend to heaven and not hang heavy over the streets; but it is not well to intercept that odour in its ascent. My friend became ill with fever, and had to betake himself to the care of nursing friends; so that I parted company with him at Cincinnati. I did not tell him that his illness was deserved as well as natural, but such was my feeling on the matter. I myself happily escaped the evil consequences which his imprudence might have entailed on me.

I passed again through Pittsburg, and over the Alleghany mountains by Altoona, and down to Baltimore,—back into civilization, secession, conversation, and gastronomy. I never had secessionist sympathies and never expressed them. I always believed in the North as a people,—discrediting, however, to the utmost the existing northern Government, or, as I should more properly say, the existing northern Cabinet; but nevertheless, with such feelings and such belief, I found myself very happy at Baltimore. Putting aside Boston, which must, I think, be generally preferred by Englishmen to any other city in the States, I should choose Baltimore as my residence if I were called upon to live in America. I am not led to this opinion, if I know myself, solely by the canvas-back ducks; and as to the terrapins, I throw them to the winds. The madeira, which is still kept there with a reverence which I should call superstitious were it not that its free circulation among outside worshippers prohibits the just use of such a word, may have something to do with it; as may also the beauty of the women, — to some small extent. Trifles do bear upon our happiness in a manner that we do not ourselves understand, and of which we are unconscious. But there was an English look about the streets and houses which I think had as much to do with it as either the wine, the women, or the ducks; and it seemed to me as though the manners of the people of Maryland were more English than those of other Americans. I do not say that they were on this account better. My English hat is, I am well aware, less graceful, and I believe less comfortable, than a Turkish fez and turban; nevertheless I prefer my English hat. New York I regard as the most thoroughly American of all American cities. It is by no means the one in which I should find myself the happiest, but I do not on that account condemn it.

I have said that in returning to Baltimore I found myself among secessionists. In so saying, I intend to speak of a certain set whose influence depends perhaps more on their wealth, position, and education than on their numbers. I do not think that the population of the city was then in favour of secession, even if it had ever been so. I believe that the mob of Baltimore is probably the roughest mob in the States, — is more akin to a Paris mob, and I may, perhaps, also say to a Manchester mob, than that of any other American city. There are more roughs in Baltimore than elsewhere, and the roughs there are rougher. In those early days of secession, when the troops were being first hurried down from New England for the protection of Washington, this mob was vehemently opposed to its progress. Men had been taught to think that the rights of the State of Maryland were being invaded by the passage of the soldiers; and they also were undoubtedly imbued with a strong prepossession for the southern cause. The two ideas had then gone together. But the mob of Baltimore had ceased to be secessionists within twelve months of their first exploit. In April, 1861, they had refused to allow Massachusetts soldiers to pass through the town on their way to Washington; and in February, 1862, they were nailing Union flags on the door-posts of those who refused to display such banners as signs of triumph at the northern victories!

That Maryland can ever go with the South, even in the event of the South succeeding in secession, no Marylander can believe. It is not pretended that there is any struggle now going on with such an object. No such result has been expected, certainly since the possession of Washington was secured to the North by the army of the Potomac. By few, I believe, was such a result expected even when Washington was insecure. And yet the feeling for secession among a certain class in Baltimore is as strong now as ever it was. And it is equally strong in certain districts of the State, — in those districts which are most akin to Virginia in their habits, modes of thought, and ties of friendship. These men, and these women also, pray for the South if they be pious, give their money to the South if they be generous, work for the South if they be industrious, fight for the South if they be young, and talk for the South morning, noon, and night in spite of General Dix and his columbiads on Federal Hill. It is in vain to say that such men and women have no strong feeling on the matter, and that they are praying, working, fighting, and talking under dictation. Their hearts are in it. And judging from them, even though there were no other evidence from which to judge, I have no doubt that a similar feeling is strong through all the seceding States. On this subject the North, I think, deceives itself in supposing that the southern rebellion has been carried on without any strong feeling on the part of the southern people. Whether the mob of Charleston be like the mob of Baltimore I cannot tell; but I have no doubt as to the gentry of Charleston and the gentry of Baltimore being in accord on the subject.

In what way, then, when the question has been settled by the force of arms, will these classes find themselves obliged to act? In Virginia and Maryland they comprise, as a rule, the highest and best educated of the people. As to parts of Kentucky the same thing may be said, and probably as to the whole of Tennessee. It must be remembered that this is not as though certain aristocratic families in a few English counties should find themselves divided off from the politics and national aspirations of their countrymen, — as was the case long since with reference to the Roman Catholic adherents of the Stuarts, and as has been the case since then in a lesser degree with the firmest of the old Tories who had allowed themselves to be deceived by Sir Robert Peel. In each of these cases the minority of dissentients was so small that the nation suffered nothing, though individuals were all but robbed of their nationality. But as regards America it must be remembered that each State has in itself a governing power, and is in fact a separate people. Each has its own legislature, and must have its own line of politics.

The secessionists of Maryland and of Virginia may consent to live in obscurity; but if this be so, who is to rule in those States? From whence are to come the senators and the members of Congress; the governors and attorney-generals? From whence is to come the national spirit of the two States, and the salt that shall preserve their political life? I have never believed that these States would succeed in secession. I have always felt that they would be held within the Union, whatever might be their own wishes. But I think that they will be so held in a manner and after a fashion that will render any political vitality almost impossible till a new generation shall have sprung up. In the meantime life goes on pleasantly enough in Baltimore, and ladies meet together, knitting stockings and sewing shirts for the southern soldiers, while the gentlemen talk southern politics and drink the health of the (southern) President in ambiguous terms, as our Cavaliers used to drink the health of the king.

During my second visit to Baltimore I went over to Washington for a day or two, and found the capital still under the empire of King Mud. How the elite of a nation—for the inhabitants of Washington consider themselves to be the elite—can consent to live in such a state of thraldom, a foreigner cannot understand. Were I to say that it was intended to be typical of the condition of the government, I might be considered cynical; but undoubtedly the sloughs of despond which were deepest in their despondency were to be found in localities which gave an appearance of truth to such a surmise. The Secretary of State's office in which Mr. Seward was still reigning, though with diminished glory, was divided from the Head-Quarters of the Commander-in-Chief, which are immediately opposite to it, by an opaque river which admitted of no transit. These buildings stand at the corner of President Square, and it had been long understood that any close intercourse between them had not been considered desirable by the occupants of the military side of the causeway. But the Secretary of State's office was altogether unapproachable without a long circuit and begrimed legs. The Secretary-at-War's department was, if possible, in a worse condition. This is situated on the other side of the President's house, and the mud lay, if possible, thicker in this quarter than it did round Mr. Seward's chambers. The passage over Pennsylvania Avenue, immediately in front of the War Office, was a thing not to be attempted in those days. Mr. Cameron, it is true, had gone, and Mr. Stanton was installed; but the labour of cleansing the interior of that establishment had hitherto allowed no time for a glance at the exterior dirt, and Mr. Stanton should, perhaps, be held as excused. That the Navy Office should be buried in mud, and quite debarred from approach, was to be expected. The space immediately in front of Mr. Lincoln's own residence was still kept fairly clean, and I am happy to be able to give testimony to this effect. Long may it remain so. I could not, however, but think that an energetic and careful President would have seen to the removal of the dirt from his own immediate neighbourhood. It was something that his own shoes should remain unpolluted; but the foul mud always clinging to the boots and leggings of those by whom he was daily surrounded must, I should think, have been offensive to him. The entrance to the Treasury was difficult to achieve by those who had not learned by practice the ways of the place; but I must confess that a tolerably clear passage was maintained on that side which led immediately down to the halls of Congress. Up at the Capitol the mud was again triumphant in the front of the building; this however was not of great importance, as the legislative chambers of the States are always reached by the back-door. I, on this occasion, attempted to leave the building by the grand entrance, but I soon became entangled among rivers of mud and mazes of shifting sand. With difficulty I recovered my steps, and finding my way back to the building was forced to content myself by an exit among the crowd of senators and representatives who were thronging down the back-stairs.

Of dirt of all kinds it behoves Washington and those concerned in Washington to make themselves free. It is the Augean stables through which some American Hercules must turn a purifying river before the American people can justly boast either of their capital or of their government. As to the material mud, enough has been said. The presence of the army perhaps caused it, and the excessive quantity of rain which had fallen may also be taken as a fair plea. But what excuse shall we find for that other dirt? It also had been caused by the presence of the army, and by that long-continued down-pouring of contracts which had fallen like Danaë's golden shower into the laps of those who understood how to avail themselves of such heavenly waters. The leaders of the rebellion are hated in the North. The names of Jefferson Davis, of Cobb, Tombes, and Floyd are mentioned with execration by the very children. This has sprung from a true and noble feeling; from a patriotic love of national greatness and a hatred of those who, for small party purposes, have been willing to lessen the name of the United States. I have reverenced the feeling even when I have not shared it. But, in addition to this, the names of those also should be execrated who have robbed their country when pretending to serve it; who have taken its wages in the days of its great struggle, and at the same time have filched from its coffers; who have undertaken the task of steering the ship through the storm in order that their hands might be deep in the meal-tub and the bread-basket, and that they might stuff their own sacks with the ship's provisions. These are the men who must be loathed by the nation,—whose fate must be held up as a warning to others before good can come! Northern men and women talk of hanging Davis and his accomplices. I myself trust that there will be no hanging when the war is over. I believe there will be none, for the Americans are not a blood-thirsty people. But if punishment of any kind be meted out, the men of the North should understand that they have worse offenders among them than Davis and Floyd.

At the period of which I am now speaking, there had come a change over the spirit of Mr. Lincoln's cabinet. Mr. Seward was still his Secretary of State, but he was, as far as outside observers could judge, no longer his Prime Minister. In the early days of the war, and up to the departure of Mr. Cameron from out of the cabinet, Mr. Seward had been the Minister of the nation. In his despatches he talks ever of We or of I. In every word of his official writings, of which a large volume has been published, he shows plainly that he intends to be considered as the man of the day,—as the hero who is to bring the States through their difficulties. Mr. Lincoln may be King, but Mr. Seward is Mayor of the Palace and carries the King in his pocket. From the depth of his own wisdom he undertakes to teach his ministers in all parts of the world, not only their duties, but their proper aspiration. He is equally kind to foreign statesmen, and sends to them messages as though from an altitude which no European politician had ever reached. At home he has affected the Prime Minister in everything, dropping the We and using the I in a manner that has hardly made up by its audacity for its deficiency in discretion. It is of course known everywhere that he had run Mr. Lincoln very hard for the position of republican candidate for the Presidency. Mr. Lincoln beat him, and Mr. Seward is well aware that in the States a man has never a second chance for the Presidential chair. Hence has arisen his ambition to make for himself a new place in the annals of American politics. Hitherto there has been no Prime Minister known in the Government of the United States. Mr. Seward has attempted a revolution in that matter, and has essayed to fill the situation. For awhile it almost seemed that he was successful. He interfered with the army, and his interferences were endured. He took upon himself the business of the police, and arrested men at his own will and pleasure. The habeas corpus was in his hand, and his name was current through the States as a covering authority for every outrage on the old laws. Sufficient craft, or perhaps cleverness, he possessed to organize a position which should give him a power greater than the power of the President; but he had not the genius which would enable him to hold it. He made foolish prophecies about the war, and talked of the triumphs which he would win. He wrote state papers on matters which he did not understand, and gave himself the airs of diplomatic learning while he showed himself to be sadly ignorant of the very rudiments of diplomacy. He tried to joke as Lord Palmerston jokes, and nobody liked his joking. He was greedy after the little appanages of power, taking from others who loved them as well as he did, privileges with which he might have dispensed. And then, lastly, he was successful in nothing. He had given himself out as the commander of the Commander-in-Chief; but then under his command nothing got itself done. For a month or two some men had really believed in Mr. Seward. The policemen of the country had come to have an absolute trust in him, and the underlings of the public offices were beginning to think that he might be a great man. But then, as is ever the case with such men, there came suddenly a downfall. Mr. Cameron went from the cabinet, and everybody knew that Mr. Seward would be no longer commander of the Commander-in-Chief. His prime ministership was gone from him, and he sank down into the comparatively humble position of Minister for Foreign Affairs. His lettres de cachet no longer ran. His passport system was repealed. His prisoners were released. And though it is too much to say that writs of habeas corpus were no longer suspended, the effect and very meaning of the suspension were at once altered. When I first left Washington Mr. Seward was the only minister of the cabinet whose name was ever mentioned with reference to any great political measure. When I returned to Washington Mr. Stanton was Mr. Lincoln's leading minister, and, as Secretary-at-War, had practically the management of the army and of the internal police.

I have spoken here of Mr. Seward by name, and in my preceding paragraphs I have alluded with some asperity to the dishonesty of certain men who had obtained political power under Mr. Lincoln and used it for their own dishonest purposes. I trust that I may not be understood as bringing any such charges against Mr. Seward. That such dishonesty has been frightfully prevalent all men know who knew anything of Washington during the year 1861. In a former chapter I have alluded to this more at length, stating circumstances and in some cases giving the names of the persons charged with offences. Whenever I have done so, I have based my statements on the Van Wyck Report, and the evidence therein given. This is the published report of a Committee appointed by the House of Representatives; and as it has been before the world for some months without refutation, I think that I have a right to presume it to be true. * On no less authority than this would I consider myself justified in bringing any such charge. Of Mr. Seward's incompetency I have heard very much among American politicians; much also of his ambition. With worse offences than these I have not heard him charged.

> *I ought perhaps to state that General Fremont has published
> an answer to the charges preferred against him. That answer
> refers chiefly to matters of military capacity or incapacity, as
> to which I have expressed no opinion. General Fremont does
> allude to the accusations made against him regarding the
> building of the forts;—but in doing so he seems to me rather
> to admit than to deny the facts as stated by the Committee.

At the period of which I am writing, February, 1862, the long list of military successes which attended the northern army through the late winter and early spring had commenced. Fort Henry, on the Tennessee river, had first been taken, and after that, Fort Donnelson on the Cumberland river, also in the State of Tennessee. Price had been driven out of Missouri into

Arkansas by General Curtis, acting under General Halleck's orders. The chief body of the Confederate army in the West had abandoned the fortified position which they had long held at Bowling Green, in the south-western district of Kentucky. Roanoke Island, on the coast of North Carolina, had been taken by General Burnside's expedition, and a belief had begun to manifest itself in Washington that the army of the Potomac was really about to advance. It is impossible to explain in what way the renewed confidence of the northern party showed itself, or how one learned that the hopes of the secessionists were waxing dim; but it was so; and even a stranger became aware of the general feeling as clearly as though it were a defined and established fact. In the early part of the winter, when I reached Washington, the feeling ran all the other way. Northern men did not say that they were despondent; they did not with spoken words express diffidence as to their success; but their looks betrayed diffidence, and the moderation of their self-assurance almost amounted to despondency. In the capital the parties were very much divided. The old inhabitants were either secessionists or influenced by "secession proclivities," as the word went; but the men of the government and of the two houses of Congress were, with a few exceptions, of course northern. It should be understood that these parties were at variance with each other on almost every point as to which men can disagree. In our civil war it may be presumed that all Englishmen were at any rate anxious for England. They desired and fought for different modes of government; but each party was equally English in its ambition. In the States there is the hatred of a different nationality added to the rancour of different politics. The Southerners desire to be a people of themselves,—to divide themselves by every possible mark of division from New England; to be as little akin to New York as they are to London,—or if possible less so. Their habits, they say, are different; their education, their beliefs, their propensities, their very virtues and vices are not the education, or the beliefs, or the propensities, or the virtues and vices of the North. The bond that ties them to the North is to them a Mezentian marriage, and they hate their northern spouses with a Mezentian hatred. They would be anything sooner than citizens of the United States. They see to what Mexico has come, and the republics of Central America; but the prospect of even that degradation is less bitter to them than a share in the glory of the stars and stripes. Better, with them, to reign in hell than serve in heaven! It is not only in politics that they will be beaten, if they be beaten,—as one party with us may be beaten by another; but they will be beaten as we should be beaten if France annexed us, and directed that we should live under French rule. Let an Englishman digest and realize that idea, and he will comprehend the feelings of a southern gentleman as he contemplates the probability that his State will be brought back into the Union. And the northern feeling is as strong. The northern man has founded his national ambition on the territorial greatness of his nation. He has panted for new lands, and for still extended boundaries. The western world has opened her arms to him, and has seemed to welcome him as her only lord. British America has tempted him towards the north, and Mexico has been as a prey to him on the south. He has made maps of his empire, including all the continent, and has preached the Monroe doctrine as though it had been decreed by the gods. He has told the world of his increasing millions, and has never yet known his store to diminish. He has pawed in the valley, and rejoiced in his strength. He has said among the trumpets, Ha, ha! He has boasted aloud in his pride, and called on all men to look at his glory. And now shall he be divided and shorn? Shall he be hemmed in from his ocean and shut off from his rivers? Shall he have a hook run into his nostrils, and a thorn driven into his jaw? Shall men say that his day is over, when he has hardly yet tasted the full cup of his success? Has his young life been a dream, and not a truth? Shall he never reach that giant manhood which the growth of his boyish years has promised him? If the South goes from him, he will be divided, shorn, and hemmed in. The hook will have pierced his nose, and the thorn will fester in his jaw. Men will taunt him with his former boastings, and he will awake to find himself but a mortal among mortals.

Such is the light in which the struggle is regarded by the two parties, and such the hopes and feelings which have been engendered. It may therefore be surmised with what amount of neighbourly love secessionist and northern neighbours regarded each other in such towns as Baltimore and Washington. Of course there was hatred of the deepest dye; of course there were muttered curses, or curses which sometimes were not simply muttered. Of course there were wretchedness, heart-burnings, and fearful divisions in families. That, perhaps, was the worst of all. The daughter's husband would be in the northern ranks, while the son was fighting in the South; or two sons would hold equal rank in the two armies, sometimes sending to each other frightful threats of personal vengeance. Old friends would meet each other in the street, passing without speaking; or, worse still, would utter words of insult for which payment is to be demanded when a southern gentleman may again be allowed to quarrel in his own defence.

And yet society went on. Women still smiled, and men were happy to whom such smiles were given. Cakes and ale were going and ginger was still hot in the mouth. When many were together no words of unhappiness were heard. It was at those small meetings of two or three that women would weep instead of smiling, and that men would run their hands through their hair and sit in silence, thinking of their ruined hopes and divided children.

I have spoken of southern hopes and northern fears, and have endeavoured to explain the feelings of each party. For myself I think that the Southerners have been wrong in their hopes, and that those of the North have been wrong in their fears. It is not better to rule in hell than serve in heaven. Of course a southern gentleman will not admit the premises which are here by me taken for granted. The hell to which I allude is, the sad position of a low and debased nation. Such, I think, will be the fate of the Gulf States, if they succeed in obtaining secession,—of a low and debased nation, or, worse still, of many low and debased nations. They will have lost their cotton monopoly by the competition created during the period of the war, and will have no material of greatness on which either to found themselves or to flourish. That they had much to bear when linked with the North, much to endure on account of that slavery from which it was all but impossible that they should disentangle themselves, may probably be true. But so have all political parties among all free nations much to bear from political opponents, and yet other free nations do not go to pieces. Had it been possible that the slave-owners and slave properties should have been scattered in parts through all the States and not congregated in the South, the slave party would have maintained itself as other parties do; but in such case, as a matter of course, it would not have thought of secession. It has been the close vicinity of slave-owners to each other, the fact that their lands have been coterminous, that theirs was especially a cotton district, which has tempted them to secession. They have been tempted to secession, and will, as I think, still achieve it in those Gulf States,—much to their misfortune.

And the fears of the North are, I think, equally wrong. That they will be deceived as to that Monroe doctrine is no doubt more than probable. That ambition for an entire continent under one rule will not, I should say, be gratified. But not on that account need the nation be less great, or its civilization less extensive. That hook in its nose and that thorn in its jaw will, after all, be but a hook of the imagination and an ideal thorn. Do not all great men suffer such ere their greatness be established and acknowledged? There is scope enough for all that manhood can do between the Atlantic and the Pacific, even though those hot, swampy cotton-fields be taken away; even though the snows of the British provinces be denied to them. And as for those rivers and that sea-board, the Americans of the North will have lost much of their old energy and usual force of will, if any southern Confederacy be allowed to deny their right of way or to stop their commercial enterprises. I believe that the South will be badly off without the North; but I feel certain that the North will never miss the South when once the wounds to her pride have been closed.

From Washington I journeyed back to Boston through the cities which I had visited in coming thither, and stayed again on my route for a few days at Baltimore, at Philadelphia, and at New York. At each town there were those whom I now regarded almost as old friends, and as the time of my departure drew near I felt a sorrow that I was not to be allowed to stay longer. As the general result of my sojourn in the country, I must declare that I was always happy and comfortable in the eastern cities, and generally unhappy and uncomfortable in the West. I had previously been inclined to think that I should like the roughness of the West, and that in the East I should encounter an arrogance which would have kept me always on the verge of hot water; but in both these surmises I found myself to have been wrong. And I think that most English travellers would come to the same conclusion. The western people do not mean to be harsh or uncivil, but they do not make themselves pleasant. In all the eastern cities,—I speak of the eastern cities north of Washington,—a society may be found which must be esteemed as agreeable by Englishmen who like clever genial men, and who love clever pretty women.

I was forced to pass twice again over the road between New York and Boston, as the packet by which I intended to leave America was fixed to sail from the former port. I had promised myself, and had promised others, that I would spend in Boston the last week of my sojourn in the States, and this was a promise which I was by no means inclined to break. If there be a gratification in this world which has no alloy, it is that of going to an assured welcome. The belief that men's arms and hearts are open to receive one,— and the arms and hearts of women, too, as far as they allow themselves to open them,—is the salt of the earth, the sole remedy against sea-sickness, the only cure for the tedium of railways, the one preservative amidst all the miseries and fatigue of travel. These matters are private, and should hardly be told of in a book; but in writing of the States, I should not do justice to my own convictions of the country if I did not say how pleasantly social intercourse there will ripen into friendship, and how full of love that friendship may become. I became enamoured of Boston at last. Beacon Street was very pleasant to me, and the view over Boston Common was dear to my eyes. Even the State House, with its great yellow-painted dome, became sightly; and the sunset over the western waters that encompass the city beats all other sunsets that I have seen.

During my last week there the world of Boston was moving itself on sleighs. There was not a wheel to be seen in the town. The omnibuses and public carriages had been dismounted from their axles and put themselves upon snow runners, and the private world had taken out its winter carriages, and wrapped itself up in buffalo robes. Men now spoke of the coming thaw as of a misfortune which must come, but which a kind Providence might perhaps postpone,—as we all, in short, speak of death. In the morning the snow would have been hardened by the night's frost, and men would look happy and contented. By an hour after noon the streets would be all wet, and the ground would be slushy and men would look gloomy and speak of speedy dissolution. There were those who would always prophesy that the next day would see the snow converted into one dull, dingy river. Such I regarded as seers of tribulation, and endeavoured with all my mind to disbelieve their interpretations of the signs. That sleighing was excellent fun. For myself I must own that I hardly saw the best of it at Boston, for the coming of the end was already at hand when I arrived there, and the fresh beauty of the hard snow was gone. Moreover when I essayed to show my prowess with a pair of horses on the established course for such equipages, the beasts ran away, knowing that I was not practised in the use of snow chariots, and brought me to grief and shame. There was a lady with me on the sleigh whom, for a while, I felt that I was doomed to consign to a snowy grave,—whom I would willingly have overturned into a drift of snow, so as to avoid worse consequences, had I only known how to do so. But Providence, even though without curbs and assisted only by simple snaffles, did at last prevail; and I brought the sleigh, horses, and lady alive back to Boston, whether with or without permanent injury I have never yet ascertained.

At last the day of tribulation came, and the snow was picked up and carted out of Boston. Gangs of men, standing shoulder to shoulder, were at work along the chief streets, picking, shovelling, and disposing of the dirty blocks. Even then the snow seemed to be nearly a foot thick; but it was dirty, rough, half-melted in some places, though hard as stone in others. The labour and cost of cleansing the city in this way must be very great. The people were at it as I left, and I felt that the day of tribulation had in truth come.

Farewell to thee, thou western Athens! When I have forgotten thee my right hand shall have forgotten its cunning, and my heart forgotten its pulses. Let us look at the list of names with which Boston has honoured itself in our days, and then ask what other town of the same size has done more. Prescott, Bancroft, Motley, Longfellow, Lowell, Emerson, Dana, Agassiz, Holmes, Hawthorne! Who is there among us in England who has not been the better for these men? Who does not owe to some of them a debt of gratitude? In whose ears is not their names familiar? It is a bright galaxy and far extended, for so small a city. What city has done better than this? All these men, save one, are now alive and in the full possession of their powers. What other town of the same size has done as well in the same short space of time? It may be that this is the Augustan æra of Boston,—its Elizabethan time. If so, I am thankful that my steps have wandered thither at such a period.

While I was at Boston I had the sad privilege of attending the funeral of President Felton, the head of Harvard College. A few months before I had seen him a strong man, apparently in perfect health and in the pride of life. When I reached Boston, I heard of his death. He also was an accomplished scholar, and as a Grecian has left few behind him who were his equals. At his installation as President, four ex-Presidents of Harvard College assisted. Whether they were all present at his funeral I do not know, but I do know that they were all still living. These are Mr. Quincy, who is now over ninety; Mr. Sparks; Mr. Everett, the well-known orator; and Mr. Walker. They all reside in Boston or its neighbourhood, and will probably all assist at the installation of another President.

CHAPTER IX
THE CONSTITUTION OF THE UNITED STATES

It is, I presume, universally known that the citizens of the Western American colonies of Great Britain which revolted, declared themselves to be free from British dominion by an Act which they called the Declaration of Independence. This was done on the 4th of July, 1776, and was signed by delegates from the thirteen colonies, or States as they then called themselves. These delegates in this document declare themselves to be the representatives of the United States of America in general Congress assembled. The opening and close of this declaration have in them much that is grand and striking; the greater part of it, however, is given up to enumerating, in paragraph after paragraph, the sins committed by George III. against the colonies. Poor George III.! There is no one now to say a good word for him; but of all those who have spoken ill of him, this declaration is the loudest in its censure.

In the following year, on the 15th November, 1777, were drawn up the Articles of Confederation between the States, by which it was then intended that a sufficient bond and compact should be made for their future joint existence and preservation. A reference to this document, which, together with the Declaration of Independence and the subsequently framed Constitution of the United States, is given in the Appendix, will show how slight was the then intended bond of union between the States. The second article declares that each State retains its sovereignty, freedom, and independence. The third article avows that "the said States hereby severally enter into a firm league of friendship with each other for their common defence, the security of their liberties, and their mutual and general welfare, binding themselves to assist each other against all force offered to, or attacks made upon, them, or any of them, on account of religion, sovereignty, trade, or any other pretext whatever." And the third article, "the better to secure and perpetuate mutual friendship," declares that the free citizens of one State shall be free citizens of another. From this it is, I think, manifest that no idea of one united nation had at that time been received and adopted by the citizens of the States. The articles then go on to define the way in which Congress shall assemble and what shall be its powers. This Congress was to exercise the authority of a national Government rather than perform the work of a national Parliament. It was intended to be executive rather than legislative. It was to consist of delegates, the very number of which within certain limits was to be left to the option of the individual States, and to this Congress was to be confided certain duties and privileges, which could not be performed or exercised separately by the Governments of the individual States. One special article, the eleventh, enjoins that "Canada, acceding to the Confederation, and joining in the measures of the United States, shall be admitted into and entitled to all the advantages of this Union; but no other colony shall be admitted into the same unless such admission be agreed to by nine States." I mention this to show how strong was the expectation at that time that Canada also would revolt from England. Up to this day few Americans can understand why Canada has declined to join her lot to them.

But the compact between the different States made by the Articles of Confederation, and the mode of national procedure therein enjoined, were found to be inefficient for the wants of a people who to be great must be united in fact as well as in name. The theory of the most democratic among the Americans of that day was in favour of self-government carried to an extreme. Self-government was the Utopia which they had determined to realize, and they were unwilling to diminish the reality of the self-government of the individual States by any centralization of power in one head, or in one Parliament, or in one set of ministers for the nation. For ten years, from 1777 to 1787, the attempt was made; but then it was found that a stronger bond of nationality was indispensable, if any national greatness was to be regarded as desirable. Indeed, all manner of failure had attended the mode of national action ordained by the Articles of Confederation. I am not attempting to write a history of the United States, and will not therefore trouble my readers with historic details, which are not of value unless put forward with historic weight. The fact of the failure is however admitted, and the present written constitution of the United States, which is the splendid result of that failure, was "Done in Convention by the unanimous consent of the States present." * Twelve States were present,—Rhode Island apparently having had no representative on the occasion,—on the 17th September, 1787, and in the twelfth year of the Independence of the United States.

> *It must not, however, be supposed that by this "doing in convention," the constitution became an accepted fact. It simply amounted to the adoption of a proposal of the constitution. The constitution itself was formally adopted by the people in conventions held in their separate State capitals. It was agreed to by the people in 1788, and came into operation in 1789.

I call the result splendid, seeing that under this constitution so written a nation has existed for three quarters of a century and has grown in numbers, power, and wealth till it has made itself the political equal of the other greatest nations of the earth. And it cannot be said that it has so grown in spite of the constitution, or by ignoring the constitution. Hitherto the laws there laid down for the national guidance have been found adequate for the great purpose assigned to them, and have done all that which the framers of them hoped that they might effect. We all know what has been the fate of the constitutions which were written throughout the French revolution for the use of France. We all, here in England, have the same ludicrous conception of Utopian theories of government framed by philosophical individuals who imagine that they have learned from books a perfect system of managing nations. To produce such theories is especially the part of a Frenchman; to disbelieve in them is especially the part of an Englishman. But in the States a system of government has been produced, under a written constitution, in which no Englishman can disbelieve, and which every Frenchman must envy. It has done its work. The people have been free, well-educated, and politically great. Those among us who are most inclined at the present moment to declare that the institutions of the United States have failed, can at any rate only declare that they have failed in their finality; that they have shown themselves to be insufficient to carry on the nation in its advancing strides through all times. They cannot deny that an amount of success and prosperity, much greater than the nation even expected for itself, has been achieved under this constitution and in connection with it. If it be so they cannot disbelieve in it. Let those who now say that it is insufficient, consider what their prophecies regarding it would have been had they been called on to express their opinions concerning it when it was proposed in 1787. If the future as it has since come forth had then been foretold for it, would not such a prophecy have been a prophecy of success? That constitution is now at the period of its hardest trial, and at this moment one may hardly dare to speak of it with triumph; but looking at the nation even in its present position, I think I am justified in saying that its constitution is one in which no Englishman can disbelieve. When I also say that it is one which every Frenchman must envy, perhaps I am improperly presuming that Frenchmen could not look at it with Englishmen's eyes.

When the constitution came to be written, a man had arisen in the States who was peculiarly suited for the work in hand; he was one of those men to whom the world owes much, and of whom the world in general knows but little. This was Alexander Hamilton, who alone on the part of the great State of New York signed the constitution of the United States. The other States sent two, three, four, or more delegates; New York sent Hamilton alone; but in sending him New York sent more to the constitution than all the other States together. I should be hardly saying too much for Hamilton if I were to declare that all those parts of the constitution emanated from him in which permanent political strength has abided. And yet his name has not been spread abroad widely in men's mouths. Of Jefferson, Franklin, and Madison, we have all heard; our children speak of them and they are household words in the nursery of history. Of Hamilton however it may, I believe, be said that he was greater than any of those.

Without going with minuteness into the early contests of democracy in the United States, I think I may say that there soon arose two parties, each probably equally anxious in the cause of freedom, one of which was conspicuous for its French predilections, and the other for its English aptitudes. It was the period of the French revolution,—the time when the French revolution had in it as yet something of promise, and had not utterly disgraced itself. To many in America the French theory of democracy not unnaturally endeared itself, and foremost among these was Thomas Jefferson. He was the father of those politicians in the States who have since taken the name of democrats, and in accordance with whose theory it has come to pass that everything has been referred to the universal suffrage of the people. James Madison, who succeeded Jefferson as President, was a pupil in this school, as indeed have been most of the Presidents of the United States. At the head of the other party, from which through various denominations have sprung those who now call themselves republicans, was Alexander Hamilton. I believe I may say that all the political sympathies of George Washington were with the same school. Washington, however, was rather a man of feeling and of action, than of theoretical policy or speculative opinion. When the constitution was written, Jefferson was in France, having been sent thither as minister from the United States, and he therefore was debarred from concerning himself personally in the matter. His views, however, were represented by Madison, and it is now generally understood that the Constitution, as it stands, is the joint work of Madison and Hamilton. * The democratic bias, of which it necessarily contains much, and without which it could not have obtained the consent of the people, was furnished by Madison; but the conservative elements, of which it possesses much more than superficial observers of the American form of government are wont to believe, came from Hamilton.

> *It should, perhaps, be explained that the views of Madison were originally not opposed to those of Hamilton. Madison, however, gradually adopted the policy of Jefferson,—his policy rather than his philosophy.

The very preamble of the constitution at once declares that the people of the different States do hereby join themselves together with the view of forming themselves into one nation. "We, the people of the United States, in order to form a more perfect Union, establish justice, ensure domestic tranquillity, provide for the common defence, promote the general welfare, and secure the blessings of liberty to ourselves and our posterity, do ordain and establish this constitution for the United States of America." Here a great step was made towards centralization,—towards one national government and the binding together of the States into one nation. But from that time down to the present, the contest has been going on, sometimes openly and sometimes only within the minds of men, between the still alleged sovereignty of the individual States and the acknowledged sovereignty of the central Congress and central Government. The disciples of Jefferson,— even though they have not known themselves to be his disciples,—have been carrying on that fight for State rights which has ended in secession; and the disciples of Hamilton,—certainly not knowing themselves to be his disciples,—have been making that stand for central government, and for the one acknowledged republic, which is now at work in opposing secession, and which, even though secession should to some extent be accomplished, will, we may hope, nevertheless, and not the less on account of such secession, conquer and put down the spirit of democracy.

The political contest of parties which is being waged now, and which has been waged throughout the history of the United States, has been pursued on one side in support of that idea of an undivided nationality of which I have spoken,—of a nationality in which the interests of a part should be esteemed as the interests of the whole; and on the other side it has been pursued in opposition to that idea. I will not here go into the interminable question of slavery,—though it is on that question that the southern or democratic States have most loudly declared their own sovereign rights and their aversion to national interference. Were I to do so I should fail in my present object of explaining the nature of the constitution of the United States. But I protest against any argument which shall be used to show that the constitution has failed because it has allowed slavery to produce the present division among the States. I myself think that the Southern or Gulf States will go. I will not pretend to draw the exact line, or to say how many of them are doomed; but I believe that South Carolina with Georgia, and perhaps five or six others, will be extruded from the Union. But their very extrusion will be a political success, and will, in fact, amount to a virtual acknowledgment in the body of the Union of the truth of that system for which the conservative republican party has contended. If the North obtain the power of settling that question of boundary, the abandonment of those southern States will be a success, even though the privilege of retaining them be the very point for which the North is now in arms.

The first clause of the constitution declares that all the legislative powers granted by the constitution shall be vested in a Congress, which shall consist of a Senate and of a House of Representatives. The House of Representatives is to be rechosen every two years, and shall be elected by the people, such persons in each State having votes for the national Congress as have votes for the legislature of their own States. If therefore South Carolina should choose—as she has chosen—to declare that the electors of her own legislature shall possess a property qualification, the electors of members of Congress from South Carolina must also have that qualification. In Massachusetts universal suffrage now prevails, although it is not long since a low property qualification prevailed even in Massachusetts. It therefore follows that members of the House of Representatives in Congress need by no means be all chosen on the same principle. As a fact, universal suffrage * and vote by ballot, that is by open voting papers, prevail in the States, but they do not so prevail by virtue of any enactment of the constitution. The laws of the States, however, require that the voter shall have been a resident in the State for some period, and generally either deny the right of voting to negroes, or so hamper that privilege that practically it amounts to the same thing.

> *Perhaps the better word would have been manhood suffrage; and even that word should be taken with certain restrictions. Aliens, minors, convicts, and men who pay no taxes cannot vote. In some States none can vote unless they can read and write. In some there is a property qualification. In all there are special restrictions against negroes. There is in none an absolutely universal suffrage. But I keep the name as it best expresses to us in England the system of franchise which has practically come to prevail in the United States.

The Senate of the United States is composed of two senators from each State. These senators are chosen for six years, and are elected in a manner which shows the conservative tendency of the constitution with more signification than perhaps any other rule which it contains. This branch of Congress, which, as I shall presently endeavour to show, is by far the more influential of the two, is not in any way elected by the people. "The Senate of the United States shall be composed of two senators from each State, *chosen by the legislature thereof,* for six years, and each senator shall have one voice." The Senate sent to Congress is therefore elected by the State legislatures. Each State legislature has two Houses; and the senators sent from that State to Congress are either chosen by vote of the two Houses voting together—which is, I believe, the mode adopted in most States, or are voted for in the two Houses separately—in which cases, when different candidates have been nominated, the two Houses confer by committees and settle the matter between them. The conservative purpose of the constitution is here sufficiently evident. The intention has been to take the election of the senators away from the people, and to confide it to that body in each State which may be regarded as containing its best trusted citizens. It removes the senators far away from the democratic element, and renders them liable to the necessity of no popular canvas. Nor am I aware that the constitution has failed in keeping the ground which it intended to hold in this matter. On some points its selected rocks and chosen standing ground have slipped from beneath its feet, owing to the weakness of words in defining and making solid the intended prohibitions against democracy. The wording of the constitution has been regarded by the people as sacred; but the people has considered itself justified in opposing the spirit as long as it revered the letter of the constitution. And this was natural. For the letter of the constitution can be read by all men; but its spirit can be understood comparatively but by few. As regards the election of the senators, I believe that it has been fairly made by the legislatures of the different States. I have not heard it alleged that members of the State legislatures have been frequently constrained by the outside popular voice to send this or that man as senator to Washington. It was clearly not the intention of those who wrote the constitution that they should be so constrained. But the Senators themselves in Washington have submitted to restraint. On subjects in which the people are directly interested they submit to instructions from the legislatures which have sent them as to the side on which they shall vote, and justify themselves in voting against their convictions by the fact that they have received such instructions. Such a practice, even with the members of a House which has been directly returned by popular election, is, I think, false to the intention of the system. It has clearly been intended that confidence should be put in the chosen candidate for the term of his duty, and that the electors are to be bound in the expression of their opinion by his sagacity and patriotism for that term. A member of a representative House so chosen, who votes at the bidding of his constituency in opposition to his convictions, is manifestly false to his charge, and may be presumed to be thus false in deference to his own personal interests, and with a view to his own future standing with his constituents. Pledges before election may be fair, because a pledge given is after all but the answer to a question asked. A voter may reasonably desire to know a candidate's opinion on any matter of political interest before he votes for or against him. The representative when returned should be free from the necessity of further pledges. But if this be true with a House elected by popular suffrage, how much more than true must it be with a chamber collected together as the Senate of the United States is collected! Nevertheless it is the fact that many senators, especially those who have been sent to the House as democrats, do allow the State legislatures to dictate to them their votes, and that they do hold themselves absolved from the personal responsibility of their votes by such dictation. This is one place in which the rock which was thought to have been firm has slipped away, and the sands of democracy have made their way through. But with reference to this it is always in the power of the Senate to recover its own ground, and re-establish its own dignity; to the people in this matter the words of the constitution give no authority, and all that is necessary for the recovery of the old practice is a more conservative tendency throughout the country generally. That there is such a conservative tendency no one can doubt; the fear is whether it may not work too quickly and go too far.

In speaking of these instructions given to senators at Washington, I should explain that such instructions are not given by all States, nor are they obeyed by all senators. Occasionally they are made in the form of requests, the word "instruct" being purposely laid aside. Requests of the same kind are also made to representatives, who, as they are not returned by the State legislatures, are not considered to be subject to such instructions. The form used is as follows: "We instruct our senators and request our representatives," &c. &c.

The senators are elected for six years, but the same Senate does not sit entire throughout that term. The whole chamber is divided into three equal portions or classes, and a portion goes out at the end of every second year; so that a third of the Senate comes in afresh with every new House of Representatives. The Vice-President of the United States, who is elected with the President, and who is not a senator by election from any State, is the ex-officio President of the Senate. Should the President of the United States vacate his seat by death or otherwise, the Vice-President becomes President of the United States; and in such case the Senate elects its own President pro tempore.

In speaking of the Senate, I must point out a matter to which the constitution does not allude, but which is of the gravest moment in the political fabric of the nation. Each State sends two senators to Congress. These two are sent altogether independently of the population which they represent, or of the number of members which the same State supplies to the Lower House. When the constitution was framed, Delaware was to send one member to the House of Representatives, and Pennsylvania eight; nevertheless, each of these States sent two senators. It would seem strange that a young people, commencing business as a nation on a basis intended to be democratic, should consent to a system so directly at variance with the theory of popular representation. It reminds one of the old days when Yorkshire returned two members, and Rutlandshire two also. And the discrepancy has greatly increased as young States have been added to the Union, while the old States have increased in population. New York, with a population of about 4,000,000, and with thirty-three members in the House of Representatives, sends two senators to Congress. The new State of Oregon, with a population of 50,000 or 60,000, and with one member in the House of Representatives, sends also two senators to Congress. But though it would seem that in such a distribution of legislative power, the young nation was determined to preserve some of the old fantastic traditions of the mother-country which it had just repudiated; the fact, I believe, is that this system, apparently so opposed to all democratic tendencies, was produced and specially insisted upon by democracy itself. Where would be the State sovereignty and individual existence of Rhode Island and Delaware, unless they could maintain, in at least one House of Congress, their State equality with that of all other States in the Union? In those early days, when the constitution was being framed, there was nothing to force the small States into a Union with those whose populations preponderated. Each State was sovereign in its municipal system, having preserved the boundaries of the old colony, together with the liberties and laws given to it under its old colonial charter. A union might be, and no doubt was, desirable; but it was to be a union of sovereign States, each retaining equal privileges in that union, and not a fusion of the different populations into one homogeneous whole. No State was willing to abandon its own individuality, and least of all were the small States willing to do so. It was therefore ordained that the House of Representatives should represent the people, and that the Senate should represent the States.

From that day to the present time the arrangement of which I am speaking has enabled the democratic or southern party to contend at a great advantage with the republicans of the North. When the constitution was founded, the seven northern States—I call those northern which are now free-soil States, and those southern in which the institution of slavery now prevails—the seven northern States were held to be entitled by their population to send thirty-five members to the House of Representatives, and they sent fourteen members to the Senate. The six southern States were entitled to thirty members in the Lower House, and to twelve senators. Thus the proportion was about equal for the North and South. But now,—or rather in 1860, when secession commenced,—the northern States, owing to the increase of population in the North, sent one hundred and fifty representatives to Congress, having nineteen States and thirty-eight senators; whereas the South, with fifteen States and thirty senators, was entitled by its population to only ninety representatives, although by a special rule in its favour, which I will presently explain, it was in fact allowed a greater number of representatives in proportion to its population than the North. Had an equal balance been preserved, the South, with its ninety representatives in the Lower House, would have but twenty-three senators, instead of thirty, in the Upper. * But these numbers indicate to us the recovery of political influence in the North, rather than the pride of the power of the South; for the South, in its palmy days, had much more in its favour than I have above described as its position in 1860. Kansas had then just become a free-soil State, after a terrible struggle, and shortly previous to that Oregon and Minnesota, also free States, had been added to the Union. Up to that date the slave States sent thirty senators to Congress, and the free States only thirty-two. In addition to this when Texas was annexed and converted into a State, a clause was inserted into the Act giving authority for the future subdivision of that State into four different States as its population should increase, thereby enabling the South to add senators to its own party from time to time, as the northern States might increase in number.

> *It is worthy of note that the new northern and western States have been brought into the Union by natural increase and the spread of population. But this has not been so with the new southern States. Louisiana and Florida were purchased, and Texas was—annexed.

And here I must explain, in order that the nature of the contest may be understood, that the senators from the South maintained themselves ever in a compact body, voting together, true to each other, disciplined as a party, understanding the necessity of yielding in small things in order that their general line of policy might be maintained. But there was no such system, no such observance of political tactics among the senators of the North. Indeed, they appear to have had no general line of politics, having been divided among themselves on various matters. Many had strong southern tendencies, and many more were willing to obtain official power by the help of southern votes. There was no great bond of union among them, as slavery was among the senators from the South. And thus, from these causes, the power of the Senate and the power of the Government fell into the hands of the southern party.

I am aware that in going into these matters here I am departing somewhat from the subject of which this chapter is intended to treat; but I do not know that I could explain in any shorter way the manner in which those rules of the constitution have worked by which the composition of the Senate is fixed. That State basis, as opposed to a basis of population in the

Upper House of Congress, has been the one great political weapon, both of offence and defence, in the hands of the democratic party. And yet I am not prepared to deny that great wisdom was shown in the framing of the constitution of the Senate. It was the object of none of the politicians then at work to create a code of rules for the entire governance of a single nation such as is England or France. Nor, had any American politician of the time so desired, would he have had reasonable hope of success. A federal union of separate sovereign States was the necessity, as it was also the desire, of all those who were concerned in the American policy of the day; and I think it may be understood and maintained that no such federal union would have been just, or could have been accepted by the smaller States, which did not in some direct way recognize their equality with the larger States. It is moreover to be observed, that in this, as in all matters, the claims of the minority were treated with indulgence. No ordinance of the constitution is made in a niggardly spirit. It would seem as though they who met together to do the work had been actuated by no desire for selfish preponderance or individual influence. No ambition to bind close by words which shall be exacting as well as exact is apparent. A very broad power of interpretation is left to those who were to be the future interpreters of the written document.

It is declared that "Representation and direct taxes shall be apportioned among the several States which may be included within this Union according to their respective numbers," thereby meaning that representation and taxation in the several States shall be adjusted according to the population. This clause ordains that throughout all the States a certain amount of population shall return a member to the Lower House of Congress,—say one member to 100,000 persons, as is I believe about the present proportion,—and that direct taxation shall be levied according to the number of representatives. If New York return thirty-three members and Kansas one, on New York shall be levied, for the purposes of the United States' revenue, thirty-three times as much direct taxation as on Kansas. This matter of direct taxation was not then, nor has it been since, matter of much moment. No direct taxation has hitherto been levied in the United States for national purposes. But the time has now come when this proviso will be a terrible stumbling-block in the way.

But before we go into that matter of taxation, I must explain how the South was again favoured with reference to its representation. As a matter of course no slaves, or even negroes—no men of colour—were to vote in the southern States. Therefore, one would say, that in counting up the people with reference to the number of the representatives, the coloured population should be ignored altogether. But it was claimed on behalf of the South that their property in slaves should be represented, and in compliance with this claim, although no slave can vote or in any way demand the services of a representative, the coloured people are reckoned among the population. When the numbers of the free persons are counted, to this number is added "three-fifths of all other persons." Five slaves are thus supposed to represent three white persons. From the wording, one would be led to suppose that there was some other category into which a man might be put besides that of free or slave! But it may be observed, that on this subject of slavery the framers of the constitution were tender-mouthed. They never speak of slavery or of a slave. It is necessary that the subject should be mentioned, and therefore we hear first of persons other than free, and then of persons bound to labour!

Such were the rules laid down for the formation of Congress, and the letter of those rules has, I think, been strictly observed. I have not thought it necessary to give all the clauses, but I believe I have stated those which are essential to a general understanding of the basis upon which Congress is founded. A reference to the Appendix will show all those which I have omitted.

The constitution ordains that members of both the Houses shall be paid for their time, but it does not decree the amount. "The senators and representatives shall receive a compensation for their services, to be ascertained by law, and paid out of the Treasury of the United States." In the remarks which I have made as to the present Congress I have spoken of the amount now allowed. The understanding, I believe, is that the pay shall be enough for the modest support of a man who is supposed to have raised himself above the heads of the crowd. Much may be said in favour of this payment of legislators, but very much may also be said against it. There was a time when our members of the House of Commons were entitled to payment for their services, and when, at any rate, some of them took the money. It may be that with a new nation such an arrangement was absolutely necessary. Men whom the people could trust, and who would have been able to give up their time without payment, would not have probably been found in a new community. The choice of senators and of representatives would have been so limited that the legislative power would have fallen into the hands of a few rich men. Indeed it may be said that such payment was absolutely necessary in the early days of the life of the Union. But no one, I think, will deny that the tone of both Houses would be raised by the gratuitous service of the legislators. It is well known that politicians find their way into the Senate and into the Chamber of Representatives solely with a view to the loaves and fishes. The very word "politician" is foul and unsavoury throughout the States, and means rather a political blackleg than a political patriot. It is useless to blink this matter in speaking of the politics and policy of the United States. The corruption of the venial politicians of the nation stinks aloud in the nostrils of all men. It behoves the country to look to this. It is time now that she should do so. The people of the nation are educated and clever. The women are bright and beautiful. Her charity is profuse; her philanthropy is eager and true; her national ambition is noble and honest,—honest in the cause of civilization. But she has soiled herself with political corruption, and has disgraced the cause of republican government by the dirt of those whom she has placed in her high places. Let her look to it now. She is nobly ambitious of reputation throughout the earth; she desires to be called good as well as great; to be regarded not only as powerful, but also as beneficent. She is creating an army; she is forging cannon and preparing to build impregnable ships of war. But all these will fail to satisfy her pride, unless she can cleanse herself from that corruption by which her political democracy has debased itself. A politician should be a man worthy of all honour, in that he loves his country; and not one worthy of all contempt, in that he robs his country.

I must not be understood as saying that every senator and representative who takes his pay is wrong in taking it. Indeed, I have already expressed an opinion that such payments were at first necessary, and I by no means now say that the necessity has as yet disappeared. In the minds of thorough democrats it will be considered much that the poorest man of the people should be enabled to go into the legislature, if such poorest man be worthy of that honour. I am not a thorough democrat, and consider that more would be gained by obtaining in the legislature that education, demeanour, and freedom from political temptation which easy circumstances produce. I am not, however, on this account inclined to quarrel with the democrats,—not on that account if they can so manage their affairs that their poor and popular politicians shall be fairly honest men. But I am a thorough republican, regarding our own English form of government as the most purely republican that I know, and as such I have a close and warm sympathy with those trans-Atlantic anti-monarchical republicans who are endeavouring to prove to the world that they have at length founded a political Utopia. I for one do not grudge them all the good they can do, all the honour they can win. But I grieve over the evil name which now taints them, and which has accompanied that wider spread of democracy which the last twenty years has produced. This longing for universal suffrage in all things—in voting for the President, in voting for judges, in voting for the representatives, in dictating to senators, has come up since the days of President Jackson, and with it has come corruption and unclean hands. Democracy must look to it, or the world at large will declare her to have failed.

One would say that at any rate the Senate might be filled with unpaid servants of the public. Each State might surely find two men who could afford to attend to the public weal of their country without claiming a compensation for their time. In England we find no difficulty in being so served. Those cities among us in which the democratic element most strongly abounds, can procure representatives to their mind—even though the honour of filling the position is not only not remunerative, but is very costly. I cannot but think that the Senate of the United States would stand higher in the public estimation of its own country if it were an unpaid body of men.

It is enjoined that no person holding any office under the United States shall be a member of either House during his continuance in office. At first sight such a rule as this appears to be good in its nature; but a comparison of the practice of the United States' Government with that of our own makes me think that this embargo on members of the legislative bodies is a mistake. It prohibits the President's ministers from a seat in either House, and thereby relieves them from the weight of that responsibility to which our ministers are subjected. It is quite true that the United States' ministers cannot be responsible as are our ministers, seeing that the President himself is responsible and that the Queen is not so. Indeed, according to the theory of the American constitution, the President has no ministers. The constitution speaks only of the principal officers of the executive departments. "He," the President, "may require the opinion in writing of the principal officer in each of the executive departments." But in practice he has his cabinet, and the irresponsibility of that cabinet would practically cease if the members of it were subjected to the questionings of the two Houses. With us the rule which prohibits servants of the State from going into Parliament is, like many of our constitutional rules, hard to be defined, and yet perfectly understood. It may perhaps be said, with the nearest approach to a correct definition, that permanent servants of the State may not go into Parliament, and that those may do so whose services are political, depending for the duration of their term on the duration of the existing ministry. But even this would not be exact, seeing that the Master of the Rolls and the officers of the army and navy can sit in Parliament. The absence of the President's ministers from Congress certainly occasions much confusion, or rather prohibits a more thorough political understanding between the executive and the legislative than now exists. In speaking of the Government of the United States in the next chapter, I shall be constrained to allude again to this subject. *

*It will be alleged by Americans that the introduction
into Congress of the President's ministers would alter all
the existing relations of the President and of Congress,

and would at once produce that Parliamentary form of Government which England possesses, and which the States have chosen to avoid. Such a change would elevate Congress, and depress the President. No doubt this is true. Such elevation, however, and such depression seem to me to be the two things needed.

The duties of the House of Representatives are solely legislative. Those of the Senate are legislative and executive—as with us those of the Upper House are legislative and judicial. The House of Representatives is always open to the public. The Senate is so open when it is engaged on legislative work; but it is closed to the public when engaged in executive session. No treaties can be made by the President, and no appointments to high offices confirmed without the consent of the Senate; and this consent must be given—as regards the confirmation of treaties—by two-thirds of the members present. This law gives to the Senate the power of debating with closed doors upon the nature of all treaties, and upon the conduct of the Government as evinced in the nomination of the officers of State. It also gives to the Senate a considerable control over the foreign relations of the Government. I believe that this power is often used, and that by it the influence of the Senate is raised much above that of the Lower House. This influence is increased again by the advantage of that superior statecraft and political knowledge which the six years of the senator gives him over the two years of the representative. The tried representative, moreover, very frequently blossoms into a senator; but a senator does not frequently fade into a representative. Such occasionally is the case, and it is not even unconstitutional for an ex-President to re-appear in either House. Mr. Benton, after thirty years' service in the Senate, sat in the House of Representatives. Mr. Crittenden, who was returned as senator by Kentucky, I think seven times, now sits in the Lower House; and John Quincy Adams appeared as a representative from Massachusetts after he had filled the Presidential chair.

And, moreover, the Senate of the United States is not debarred from an interference with money bills, as the House of Lords is debarred with us. "All bills for raising revenue," says the seventh section of the first article of the constitution, "shall originate with the House of Representatives, but the Senate may propose or concur with amendments as on other bills." By this the Senate is enabled to have an authority in the money matters of the nation almost equal to that held by the Lower House,—an authority quite sufficient to preserve to it the full influence of its other powers. With us the House of Commons is altogether in the ascendant, because it holds and jealously keeps to itself the exclusive command of the public purse.

Congress can levy custom duties in the United States, and always has done so; hitherto the national revenue has been exclusively raised from custom duties. It cannot levy duties on imports. It can levy excise duties, and is now doing so; hitherto it has not done so. It can levy direct taxes, such as an income-tax and a property-tax; it hitherto has not done so, but now must do so. It must do so, I think I am justified in saying; but its power of doing this is so hampered by constitutional enactment, that it would seem that the constitution as regards this heading must be altered before any scheme can be arranged by which a moderately just income-tax can be levied and collected. This difficulty I have already mentioned, but perhaps it will be well that I should endeavour to make the subject more plain. It is specially declared, "That all duties, imposts, and excises shall be uniform throughout the United States." And again, "That no capitation or other direct tax shall be laid, unless in proportion to the census or enumeration hereinbefore directed to be taken." And again, in the words before quoted, "Representatives and direct taxes shall be apportioned among the several States which shall be included in this Union, according to their respective numbers." By these repeated rules it has been intended to decree that the separate States shall bear direct taxation according to their population and the consequent number of their representatives; and this intention has been made so clear, that no direct taxation can be levied in opposition to it without an evident breach of the constitution. To explain the way in which this will work, I will name the two States of Rhode Island and Iowa as opposed to each other, and the two States of Massachusetts and Indiana as opposed to each other. Rhode Island and Massachusetts are wealthy Atlantic States, containing, as regards enterprise and commercial success, the cream of the population of the United States. Comparing them in the ratio of population, I believe that they are richer than any other States. They return between them thirteen representatives, Rhode Island sending two and Massachusetts eleven. Iowa and Indiana also send thirteen representatives, Iowa sending two, and being thus equal to Rhode Island; Indiana sending eleven and being thus equal to Massachusetts. Iowa and Indiana are western States; and though I am not prepared to say that they are the poorest States of the Union, I can assert that they are exactly opposite in their circumstances to Rhode Island and Massachusetts. The two Atlantic States of New England are old established, rich, and commercial. The two western States I have named are full of new immigrants, are comparatively poor, and are agricultural. Nevertheless any direct taxation levied on those in the East and on those in the West must be equal in its weight. Iowa must pay as much as Rhode Island; Indiana must pay as much as Massachusetts. But Rhode Island and Massachusetts could pay without the sacrifice of any comfort to its people, without any sensible suffering, an amount of direct taxation which would crush the States of Iowa and Indiana, — which indeed no tax-gatherer could collect out of those States. Rhode Island and Massachusetts could with their ready money buy Iowa and Indiana; and yet the income-tax to be collected from the poor States is to be the same in amount as that collected from the rich States. Within each individual State the total amount of income-tax or of other direct taxation to be levied from that State may be apportioned as the State may think fit; but an income-tax of two per cent. on Rhode Island would probably produce more than an income-tax of ten per cent. in Iowa; whereas Rhode Island could pay an income-tax of ten per cent. easier than could Iowa one of two per cent.

It would in fact appear that the constitution as at present framed is fatal to all direct taxation. Any law for the collection of direct taxation levied under the constitution would produce internecine quarrel between the western States and those which border on the Atlantic. The western States would not submit to the taxation. The difficulty which one here feels is that which always attends an attempt at finality in political arrangements. One would be inclined to say at once that the law should be altered, and that as the money required is for the purposes of the Union and for State purposes, such a change should be made as would enable Congress to levy an income-tax on the general income of the nation. But Congress cannot go beyond the constitution.

It is true that the constitution is not final, and that it contains an express article ordaining the manner in which it may be amended. And perhaps I may as well explain here the manner in which this can be done, although by doing so, I am departing from the order in which the constitution is written. It is not final, and amendments have been made to it. But the making of such amendments is an operation so ponderous and troublesome, that the difficulty attached to any such change envelops the constitution with many of the troubles of finality. With us there is nothing beyond an act of parliament. An act of parliament with us cannot be unconstitutional. But no such power has been confided to Congress, or to Congress and the President together. No amendment of the constitution can be made without the sanction of the State legislatures. Congress may propose any amendments, as to the expediency of which two-thirds of both Houses shall be agreed; but before such amendments can be accepted they must be ratified by the legislatures of three-fourths of the States, or by conventions in three-fourths of the States, "as the one or the other mode of ratification may be proposed by Congress." Or Congress, instead of proposing the amendments, may, on an application from the legislatures of two-thirds of the different States, call a convention for the proposing of them. In which latter case the ratification by the different States must be made after the same fashion as that required in the former case. I do not know that I have succeeded in making clearly intelligible the circumstances under which the constitution can be amended; but I think I may have succeeded in explaining that those circumstances are difficult and tedious. In a matter of taxation why should States agree to an alteration proposed with the very object of increasing their proportion of the national burden? But unless such States will agree,—unless Rhode Island, Massachusetts, and New York will consent to put their own necks into the yoke,—direct taxation cannot be levied on them in a manner available for national purposes. I do believe that Rhode Island and Massachusetts at present possess a patriotism sufficient for such an act. But the mode of doing the work will create disagreement, or at any rate, tedious delay and difficulty. How shall the constitution be constitutionally amended while one-third of the States are in revolt?

In the eighth section of its first article the Constitution gives a list of the duties which Congress shall perform,—of things, in short, which it shall do, or shall have power to do:—To raise taxes; to regulate commerce and the naturalization of citizens; to coin money and protect it when coined; to establish postal communication; to make laws for defence of patents and copyrights; to constitute national courts of law inferior to the Supreme Court; to punish piracies; to declare war; to raise, pay for, and govern armies, navies, and militia; and to exercise exclusive legislation in a certain district which shall contain the seat of Government of the United States, and which is therefore to be regarded as belonging to the nation at large, and not to any particular State. This district is now called the district of Columbia. It is situated on the Potomac and contains the city of Washington.

Then the ninth section of the same article declares what Congress shall not do. Certain immigration shall not be prohibited; *the privilege of the writ of habeas corpus shall not be suspended*, except under certain circumstances; no ex post facto law shall be passed; no direct tax shall be laid unless in proportion to the census; no tax shall be laid on exports; no money shall be drawn from the treasury but by legal appropriation; no title of nobility shall be granted.

The above are lists or catalogues of the powers which Congress has, and of the powers which Congress has not; of what Congress may do, and of what Congress may not do; and having given them thus seriatim, I may here perhaps be best enabled to say a few words as to the suspension of the privilege of the writ of habeas corpus in the United States. It is generally known that this privilege has been suspended during the existence of the present rebellion very many times; that this has been done by the executive, and not by Congress; and that it is maintained by the executive, and by those who defend the conduct of the now acting executive of the United States, that the power of suspending the writ has been given by the constitution to the President, and not to Congress. I confess that I cannot understand how any man, familiar either with the wording or with the spirit of the constitution should hold such an argument. To me it appears manifest that the executive, in suspending the privilege of the writ without the authority of Congress, has committed a breach of the constitution. Were the case one referring to our British constitution, a plain man, knowing little of Parliamentary usage, and nothing of law lore, would probably feel some hesitation in expressing any decided opinion on such a subject, seeing that our constitution is unwritten. But the intention has been that every citizen of the United States should know and understand the rules under which he is to live,—and he that runs may read.

As this matter has been argued by Mr. Horace Binney, a lawyer of Philadelphia, much trusted, of very great and of deserved eminence throughout the States, in a pamphlet in which he defends the suspension of the privilege of the writ by the President, I will take the position of the question as summed up by him in his last page, and compare it with that clause in the constitution by which the suspension of the privilege under certain circumstances is decreed; and to enable me to do this I will, in the first place, quote the words of the clause in question:—

"The privilege of the writ of habeas corpus shall not be suspended unless when, in case of rebellion or invasion, the public safety may require it." It is the second clause of that section which states what Congress shall not do.

Mr. Binney argues as follows:—"The conclusion of the whole matter is this: that the constitution itself is the law of the privilege, and of the exception to it; that the exception is expressed in the constitution, and that the constitution gives effect to the act of suspension when the conditions occur; that the conditions consist of two matters of fact,—one a naked matter of fact, and the other a matter-of-fact conclusion from facts, that is to say, rebellion and the public danger, or the requirement of public safety." By these words Mr. Binney intends to imply that the constitution itself gave the privilege of the writ of habeas corpus, and itself prescribes the taking away of that privilege under certain circumstances. But this is not so. The constitution does not prescribe the suspension of the privilege of the writ under any circumstances. It says that it shall not be suspended except under certain circumstances. Mr. Binney's argument, if I understand it, then goes on as follows. As the constitution prescribes the circumstances under which the privilege of the writ shall be suspended, the one circumstance being the naked matter-of-fact rebellion, and the other circumstance the public safety supposed to have been endangered by such rebellion,—which Mr.

Binney calls a matter-of-fact conclusion from facts, the constitution must be presumed itself to suspend the privilege of the writ. Whether the President or Congress be the agent of the constitution in this suspension is not matter of moment. Either can only be an agent, and as Congress cannot act executively, whereas the President must ultimately be charged with the executive administration of the order for that suspension, which has in fact been issued by the constitution itself, therefore the power of exercising the suspension of the writ may properly be presumed to be in the hands of the President, and not to be in the hands of Congress.

If I follow Mr. Binney's argument, it amounts to so much. But it seems to me that Mr. Binney is wrong in his premises, and wrong in his conclusion. The article of the constitution in question does not define the conditions under which the privilege of the writ shall be suspended. It simply states that this privilege shall never be suspended, except under certain conditions. It shall not be suspended unless when the public safety may require such suspension on account of rebellion or invasion. Rebellion or invasion is not necessarily to produce such suspension. There is indeed no naked matter of fact to guide either President or Congress in the matter, and therefore I say that Mr. Binney is wrong in his premises. Rebellion or invasion might occur twenty times over, and might even endanger the public safety, without justifying the suspension of the privilege of the writ under the constitution. I say also that Mr. Binney is wrong in his conclusion. The public safety must require the suspension before the suspension can be justified, and such requirement must be a matter for judgment, and for the exercise of discretion. Whether or no there shall be any suspension is a matter for deliberation,—not one simply for executive action, as though it were already ordered. There is no matter-of-fact conclusion from facts. Should invasion or rebellion occur, and should the public safety, in consequence of such rebellion or invasion, require the suspension of the privilege of the writ, then, and only then, may the privilege be suspended. But to whom is the power, or rather the duty, of exercising this discretion delegated? Mr. Binney says that "there is no express delegation of the power in the constitution." I maintain that Mr. Binney is again wrong, and that the constitution does expressly delegate the power, not to the President, but to Congress. This is done so clearly, to my mind, that I cannot understand the misunderstanding which has existed in the States upon the subject. The first article of the constitution treats "of the legislature." The second article treats "of the executive." The third treats "of the judiciary." After that there are certain "miscellaneous articles," so called. The eighth section of the first article gives, as I have said before, a list of things which the legislature or Congress shall do. The ninth section gives a list of things which the legislature or Congress shall not do. The second item in this list is the prohibition of any suspension of the privilege of the writ of habeas corpus, except under certain circumstances. This prohibition is therefore expressly placed upon Congress, and this prohibition contains the only authority under which the privilege can be constitutionally suspended. Then comes the article on the executive, which defines the powers that the President shall exercise. In that article there is no word referring to the suspension of the privilege of the writ. He that runs may read.

I say, therefore, that Mr. Lincoln's Government has committed a breach of the constitution in taking upon itself to suspend the privilege;—a breach against the letter of the constitution. It has assumed a power which the constitution has not given it,—which, indeed, the constitution, by placing it in the hands of another body, has manifestly declined to put into the hands of the executive; and it has also committed a breach against the spirit of the constitution. The chief purport of the constitution is to guard the liberties of the people, and to confide to a deliberative body the consideration of all circumstances by which those liberties may be affected. The President shall command the army; but Congress shall raise and support the army. Congress shall declare war. Congress shall coin money. Congress, by one of its bodies, shall sanction treaties. Congress shall establish such law courts as are not established by the constitution. Under no circumstances is the President to decree what shall be done. But he is to do those things which the constitution has decreed or which Congress shall decree. It is monstrous to suppose that power over the privilege of the writ of habeas corpus would, among such a people, and under such a constitution, be given without limit to the chief officer, the only condition being that there should be some rebellion. Such rebellion might be in Utah territory; or some trouble in the uttermost bounds of Texas would suffice. Any invasion, such as an inroad by the savages of Old Mexico upon New Mexico, would justify an arbitrary President in robbing all the people of all the States of their liberties! A squabble on the borders of Canada would put such a power into the hands of the President for four years; or the presence of an English frigate in the St. Juan channel might be held to do so. I say that such a theory is monstrous.

And the effect of this breach of the constitution at the present day has been very disastrous. It has taught those who have not been close observers of the American struggle to believe that, after all, the Americans are indifferent as to their liberties. Such pranks have been played before high heaven by men utterly unfitted for the use of great power, as have scared all the nations. Mr. Lincoln, the President by whom this unconstitutional act has been done, apparently delegated his assumed authority to his minister, Mr. Seward. Mr. Seward has revelled in the privilege of unrestrained arrests, and has locked men up with reason and without. He has instituted passports and surveillance; and placed himself at the head of an omnipresent police system with all the gusto of a Fouché, though luckily without a Fouché's craft or cunning. The time will probably come when Mr. Seward must pay for this,—not with his life or liberty, but with his reputation and political name. But in the mean time his lettres de cachet have run everywhere through the States. The pranks which he played were absurd, and the arrests which he made were grievous. After a while, when it became manifest that Mr. Seward had not found a way to success, when it was seen that he had inaugurated no great mode of putting down rebellion, he apparently lost his power in the cabinet. The arrests ceased, the passports were discontinued, and the prison-doors were gradually opened. Mr. Seward was deposed, not from the cabinet, but from the premiership of the cabinet. The suspension of the privilege of the writ of habeas corpus was not countermanded, but the operation of the suspension was allowed to become less and less onerous; and now, in April, 1862, within a year of the commencement of the suspension, it has, I think, nearly died out. The object in hand now is rather that of getting rid of political prisoners, than of taking others.

This assumption by the government of an unconstitutional power has, as I have said, taught many lookers-on to think that the Americans are indifferent to their liberties. I myself do not believe that such a conclusion would be just. During the present crisis the strong feeling of the people— that feeling which for the moment has been dominant—has been one in favour of the government as against rebellion. There has been a passionate resolution to support the nationality of the nation. Men have felt that they must make individual sacrifices, and that such sacrifices must include a temporary suspension of some of their constitutional rights. But I think that this temporary suspension is already regarded with jealous eyes;— with an increasing jealousy which will have created a reaction against such policy as that which Mr. Seward has attempted, long before the close of Mr. Lincoln's Presidency. I know that it is wrong in a writer to commit himself to prophecies, but I find it impossible to write upon this subject without doing so. As I must express a surmise on this subject, I venture to prophesy that the Americans of the States will soon show that they are not indifferent to the suspension of the privilege of the writ of habeas corpus. On that matter of the illegality of the suspension by the President I feel in my own mind that there is no doubt.

The second article of the constitution treats of the executive, and is very short. It places the whole executive power in the hands of the President, and explains with more detail the mode in which the President shall be chosen, than the manner after which the duties shall be performed. The first section states that the executive shall be vested in a President, who shall hold his office for four years. With him shall be chosen a Vice-President. I may here explain that the Vice-President, as such, has no power either political or administrative. He is, ex officio, the speaker of the Senate; and should the President die, or be by other cause rendered unable to act as President, the Vice-President becomes President either for the remainder of the Presidential term or for the period of the President's temporary absence. Twice since the constitution was written, the President has died and the Vice-President has taken his place. No President has vacated his position, even for a period, through any cause other than death.

Then come the rules under which the President and Vice-President shall be elected,—with reference to which there has been an amendment of the constitution subsequent to the fourth presidential election. This was found to be necessary by the circumstances of the contest between John Adams, Thomas Jefferson, and Aaron Burr. It was then found that the complications in the method of election created by the original clause were all but unendurable, and the constitution was amended.

I will not describe in detail the present mode of election, as the doing so would be tedious and unnecessary. Two facts I wish, however, to make specially noticeable and clear. The first is, that the President of the United States is now chosen by universal suffrage; and the second is, that the constitution expressly intended that the President should not be chosen by universal suffrage, but by a body of men who should enjoy the confidence and fairly represent the will of the people. The framers of the constitution intended so to write the words, that the people themselves should have no more immediate concern in the nomination of the President than in that of the Senate. They intended to provide that the election should be made in a manner which may be described as thoroughly conservative. Those words, however, have been inefficient for their purpose. They have not been violated. But the spirit has been violated, while the words have been held sacred,—and the Presidential elections are now conducted on the widest principles of universal suffrage. They are essentially democratic.

The arrangement, as written in the constitution, is that each State shall appoint a body of electors equal in number to the senators and representatives sent by that State to Congress, and that thus a body or college of electors shall be formed equal in number to the two joint Houses of Congress, by which the President shall be elected. No member of Congress, however, can be appointed an elector. Thus New York, with thirty-three representatives in the Lower House, would name thirty-five electors; and Rhode Island, with two members in the Lower House, would name four electors;—in each case two being added for the two senators.

It may perhaps be doubted whether this theory of an election by electors has ever been truly carried out. It was probably the case even at the election of the first Presidents after Washington, that the electors were pledged in some informal way as to the candidate for whom they should vote; but the very idea of an election by electors has been abandoned since the Presidency of General Jackson. According to the theory of the constitution the privilege and the duty of selecting a best man as President was to be delegated to certain best men chosen for that purpose. This was the intention of those who framed the constitution. It may, as I have said, be doubted whether this theory has ever availed for action; but since the days of Jackson it has been absolutely abandoned. The intention was sufficiently conservative. The electors to whom was to be confided this great trust, were to be chosen in their own States as each State might think fit. The use of universal suffrage for this purpose was neither enjoined nor forbidden in the separate States,— was neither treated as desirable or undesirable by the constitution. Each State was left to judge how it would elect its own electors. But the President himself was to be chosen by those electors and not by the people at large. The intention is sufficiently conservative, but the intention is not carried out.

The electors are still chosen by the different States in conformity with the bidding of the constitution. The constitution is exactly followed in all its biddings, as far as the wording of it is concerned; but the whole spirit of the document has been evaded in the favour of democracy, and universal suffrage in the Presidential elections has been adopted. The electors are still chosen, it is true; but they are only chosen as the mouthpiece of the people's choice, and not as the mind by which that choice shall be made. We have all heard of Americans voting for a ticket,—for the democratic ticket, or the republican ticket. All political voting in the States is now managed by tickets. As regards these Presidential elections, each party decides on a candidate. Even this primary decision is a matter of voting among the party itself. When Mr. Lincoln was nominated as its candidate by the republican party, the names of no less than thirteen candidates were submitted to the delegates who were sent to a convention at Chicago, assembled for the purpose of fixing upon a candidate. At that convention, Mr. Lincoln was chosen as the republican candidate; and in that convention was in fact fought the battle which was won in Mr. Lincoln's favour, although that convention was what we may call a private arrangement, wholly irrespective of any constitutional enactment. Mr. Lincoln was then proclaimed as the republican candidate, and all republicans were held as bound to support him. When the time came for the constitutional election of the electors, certain names were got together in each State as representing the republican interest. These names formed the republican ticket, and any man voting for them voted in fact for Lincoln. There were three other parties, each represented by a candidate, and each had its own ticket in the different States. It is not to be supposed that the supporters of Mr. Lincoln were very anxious about their ticket in Alabama, or those of Mr. Breckinridge as to theirs in Massachusetts. In Alabama, a democratic slave-ticket would of course prevail. In Massachusetts, a republican free-soil ticket would do so. But it may, I think, be seen that in this way the electors have in reality ceased to have any weight in the elections, — have in very truth ceased to have the exercise of any will whatever. They are mere names, and no more. Stat nominis umbra. The election of the President is made by universal suffrage, and not by a college of electors. The words as they are written are still obeyed; but the constitution in fact has been violated, for the spirit of it has been changed in its very essence.

The President must have been born a citizen of the United States. This is not necessary for the holder of any other office or for a senator or representative; he must be thirty-four years old at the time of his election.

His executive power is almost unbounded. He is much more powerful than any minister can be with us, and is subject to a much lighter responsibility. He may be impeached by the House of Representatives before the Senate, but that impeachment only goes to the removal from office and permanent disqualification for office. But in these days, as we all practically understand, responsibility does not mean the fear of any great punishment, but the necessity of accounting from day to day for public actions. A leading statesman has but slight dread of the axe, but is in hourly fear of his opponent's questions. The President of the United States is subject to no such questionings; and as he does not even require a majority in either House for the maintenance of his authority, his responsibility sits upon him very slightly. Seeing that Mr. Buchanan has escaped any punishment for maladministration, no President need fear the anger of the people.

The President is Commander-in-chief of the army and of the navy. He can grant pardons, — as regards all offences committed against the United States. He has no power to pardon an offence committed against the laws of any State, and as to which the culprit has been tried before the tribunals of that State. He can make treaties; but such treaties are not valid till they have been confirmed by two-thirds of the senators present in executive session. He appoints all ambassadors and other public officers, — but subject to the confirmation of the Senate. He can convene either or both Houses of Congress at irregular times, and under certain circumstances can adjourn them. His executive power is in fact almost unlimited; and this power is solely in his own hands, as the constitution knows nothing of the President's ministers. According to the constitution these officers are merely the heads of his bureaux. An Englishman, however, in considering the executive power of the President, and in making any comparison between that and the executive power of any officer or officers attached to the Crown in England, should always bear in mind that the President's power, and even authority, is confined to the Federal Government, and that he has none with reference to the individual States. Religion, education, the administration of the general laws which concern every man and woman, and the real de facto Government which comes home to every house; — these things are not in any way subject to the President of the United States.

His legislative power is also great. He has a veto upon all acts of Congress. This veto is by no means a dead letter, as is the veto of the Crown with us; but it is not absolute. The President, if he refuses his sanction to a bill sent up to him from Congress, returns it to that House in which it originated, with his objections in writing. If, after that, such bill shall again pass through both the Senate and the House of Representatives, receiving in each House the approvals of two-thirds of those present, then such bill becomes law without the President's sanction. Unless this be done the President's veto stops the bill. This veto has been frequently used, but no bill has yet been passed in opposition to it.

The third article of the constitution treats of the judiciary of the United States, but as I purpose to write a chapter devoted to the law courts and lawyers of the States, I need not here describe at length the enactments of the constitution on this head. It is ordained that all criminal trials, except in cases of impeachment, shall be by jury.

There are after this certain miscellaneous articles, some of which belong to the constitution as it stood at first, and others of which have been since added as amendments. A citizen of one State is to be a citizen of every State. Criminals from one State shall not be free from pursuit in other States. Then comes a very material enactment:—"No person held to service or labour in one State, under the laws thereof, escaping into another, shall, in consequence of any law or regulation therein, be discharged from such service or labour; but shall be delivered up on claim of the party to whom such service or labour may be due." In speaking of a person held to labour the constitution intends to speak of a slave, and the article amounts to a fugitive slave law. If a slave run away out of South Carolina and find his way into Massachusetts, Massachusetts shall deliver him up when called upon to do so by South Carolina. The words certainly are clear enough. But Massachusetts strongly objects to the delivery of such men when so desired. Such men she has delivered up, with many groanings and much inward perturbation of spirit. But it is understood, not in Massachusetts only, but in the free-soil States generally, that fugitive slaves shall not be delivered up by the ordinary action of the laws. There is a feeling strong as that which we entertain with reference to the rendition of slaves from Canada. With such a clause in the constitution as that, it is hardly too much to say that no free-soil State will consent to constitutional action. Were it expunged from the constitution, no slave State would consent to live under it. It is a point as to which the advocates of slavery and the enemies of slavery cannot be brought to act in union. But on this head I have already said what little I have to say.

New States may be admitted by Congress, but the bounds of no old State shall be altered without the consent of such State. Congress shall have power to rule and dispose of the territories and property of the United States. The United States guarantee every State a republican form of Government; but the constitution does not define that form of Government. An ordinary citizen of the United States, if asked, would probably say that it included that description of franchise which I have called universal suffrage. Such, however, was not the meaning of those who framed the constitution. The ordinary citizen would probably also say that it excluded the use of a king, though he would, I imagine, be able to give no good reason for saying so. I take a republican government to be that in which the care of the people is in the hands of the people. They may use an elected President, an hereditary king, or a chief magistrate called by any other name. But the magistrate, whatever be his name, must be the servant of the people and not their lord. He must act for them and at their bidding,—not they at his. If he do so, he is the chief officer of a republic;—as is our Queen with us.

The United States' constitution also guarantees to each State protection against invasion, and, if necessary, against domestic violence,—meaning, I presume, internal violence. The words domestic violence might seem to refer solely to slave insurrections; but such is not the meaning of the words. The free State of New York would be entitled to the assistance of the Federal Government in putting down internal violence, if unable to quell such violence by her own power.

This constitution, and the laws of the United States made in pursuance of it, are to be held as the supreme law of the land. The judges of every State are to be bound thereby, let the laws or separate constitution of such State say what they will to the contrary. Senators and others are to be bound by oath to support the constitution; but no religious test shall be required as a qualification to any office.

In the amendments to the constitution, it is enacted that Congress shall make no law as to the establishment of any religion, or prohibiting the free exercise thereof; and also that it shall not abridge the freedom of speech, or of the press, or of petition.—The Government, however, as is well known, has taken upon itself to abridge the freedom of the press.—The right of the people to bear arms shall not be infringed. Then follow various clauses intended for the security of the people in reference to the administration of the laws. They shall not be troubled by unreasonable searches. They shall not be made to answer for great offences except by indictment of a grand jury. They shall not be put twice in jeopardy for the same offence. They shall not be compelled to give evidence against themselves. Private property shall not be taken for public use without compensation. Accused persons in criminal proceedings shall be entitled to speedy and public trial. They shall be confronted with the witnesses against them, and shall have assistance of counsel. Suits in which the value controverted is above 20 dollars (£4) shall be tried before juries. Excessive bail shall not be required, nor cruel and unusual punishments inflicted. In all which enactments we see, I think, a close resemblance to those which have been time-honoured among ourselves.

The remaining amendments apply to the mode in which the President and Vice-President shall be elected, and of them I have already spoken.

The constitution is signed by Washington as President,—as President and Deputy from Virginia. It is signed by deputies from all the other States, except Rhode Island. Among the signatures is that of Alexander Hamilton, from New York; of Franklin, heading a crowd in Pennsylvania, in the capital of which State the convention was held; and that of James Madison, the future President, from Virginia.

In the beginning of this chapter I have spoken of the splendid results attained by those who drew up the constitution; and then, as though in opposition to the praise thus given to their work, I have insisted throughout the chapter both on the insufficiency of the constitution and on the breaches to which it has been subjected. I have declared my opinion that it is inefficient for some of its required purposes, and have said that, whether inefficient or efficient, it has been broken and in some degree abandoned. I maintain, however, that in this I have not contradicted myself. A boy, who declares his purpose of learning the Æneid by heart, will be held as being successful if at the end of the given period he can repeat eleven books out of the twelve. Nevertheless the reporter, in summing up the achievement, is bound to declare that that other book has not been learned. Under this constitution of which I have been speaking, the American people have achieved much material success and great political power. As a people they have been happy and prosperous. Their freedom has been secured to them, and for a period of seventy-five years they have lived and prospered without subjection to any form of tyranny. This in itself is much, and should, I think, be held as a preparation for greater things to follow. Such, I think, should be our opinion, although the nation is at the present burdened by so heavy a load of troubles. That any written constitution should serve its purposes and maintain its authority in a nation for a dozen years is in itself much for its framers. Where are now the constitutions which were written for France? But this constitution has so wound itself into the affections of the people, has become a mark for such reverence and love, has, after a trial of three quarters of a century, so recommended itself to the judgment of men, that the difficulty consists in touching it, not in keeping it. Eighteen or twenty millions of people who have lived under it,—in what way do they regard it? Is not that the best evidence that can be had respecting it? Is it to them an old woman's story, a useless parchment, a thing of old words at which all must now smile? Heaven mend them, if they reverence it more, as I fear they do, than they reverence their Bible. For them, after seventy-five years of trial, it has almost the weight of inspiration. In this respect,—with reference to this worship of the work of their forefathers, they may be in error. But that very error goes far to prove the excellence of the code. When a man has walked for six months over stony ways in the same boots, he will be believed when he says that his boots are good boots. No assertion to the contrary from any bystander will receive credence, even though it be shown that a stitch or two has come undone, and that some required purpose has not effectually been carried out. The boots have carried the man over his stony roads for six months, and they must be good boots. And so I say that the constitution must be a good constitution.

As to that positive breach of the constitution which has, as I maintain, been committed by the present Government, although I have been at some trouble to prove it, I must own that I do not think very much of it. It is to be lamented, but the evil admits, I think, of easy repair. It has happened at a period of unwonted difficulty, when the minds of men were intent rather on the support of that nationality which guarantees their liberties, than on the enjoyment of those liberties themselves, and the fault may be pardoned if it be acknowledged. But it is essential that it should be acknowledged. In such a matter as that there should at any rate be no doubt. Now, in this very year of the rebellion, it may be well that no clamour against Government should arise from the people, and thus add to the difficulties of the nation. But it will be bad, indeed, for the nation if such a fault shall have been committed by this Government and shall be allowed to pass unacknowledged, unrebuked,—as though it were a virtue and no fault. I cannot but think that the time will soon come in which Mr. Seward's reading of the constitution and Mr. Lincoln's assumption of illegal power under that reading will receive a different construction in the States than that put upon it by Mr. Binney.

But I have admitted that the constitution itself is not perfect. It seems to me that it requires to be amended on two separate points;—especially on two; and I cannot but acknowledge that there would be great difficulty in making such amendments. That matter of direct taxation is the first. As to that I shall speak again in referring to the financial position of the country. I think, however, that it must be admitted, in any discussion held on the constitution of the United States, that the theory of taxation as there laid down will not suffice for the wants of a great nation. If the States are to maintain their ground as a great national power, they must agree among themselves to bear the cost of such greatness. While a custom duty was sufficient for the public wants of the United States, this fault in the constitution was not felt. But now that standing armies have been inaugurated, that iron-clad ships are held as desirable, that a great national debt has been founded, custom duties will suffice no longer, nor will excise duties suffice. Direct taxation must be levied, and such taxation cannot be fairly levied without a change in the constitution. But such a change may be made in direct accordance with the spirit of the constitution, and the necessity for such an alteration cannot be held as proving any inefficiency in the original document for the purposes originally required.

As regards the other point which seems to me to require amendment, I must acknowledge that I am about to express simply my own opinion. Should Americans read what I write, they may probably say that I am recommending them to adopt the blunders made by the English in their practice of government. Englishmen, on the other hand, may not improbably conceive that a system which works well here under a monarchy, would absolutely fail under a presidency of four years' duration. Nevertheless I will venture to suggest that the government of the United States would be improved in all respects, if the gentlemen forming the President's cabinet were admitted to seats in Congress. At present they are virtually irresponsible. They are constitutionally little more than head clerks. This was all very well while the Government of the United States was as yet a small thing; but now it is no longer a small thing. The President himself cannot do all, nor can he be, in truth, responsible for all. A cabinet, such as is our cabinet, is necessary to him. Such a cabinet does exist, and the members of it take upon themselves the honours which are given to our cabinet ministers. But they are exempted from all that parliamentary contact which, in fact, gives to our cabinet ministers their adroitness, their responsibility, and their position in the country. On this subject also I must say another word or two further on.

But how am I to excuse the constitution on those points as to which it has, as I have said, fallen through,—in respect to which it has shown itself to be inefficient by the weakness of its own words? Seeing that all the executive power is intrusted to the President, it is especially necessary that the choice of the President should be guarded by constitutional enactments;—that the President should be chosen in such a manner as may seem best to the concentrated wisdom of the country. The President is placed in his seat for four years. For that term he is irremovable. He acts without any majority in either of the legislative Houses. He must state reasons for his conduct, but he is not responsible for those reasons. His own judgment is his sole guide. No desire of the people can turn him out; nor need he fear any clamour from the press. If an officer so high in power be needed, at any rate the choice of such an officer should be made with the greatest care. The constitution has decreed how such care should be exercised, but the constitution has not been able to maintain its own decree. The constituted electors of the President have become a mere name; and that officer is chosen by popular election, in opposition to the intention of those who framed the constitution. The effect of this may be seen in the characters of the men so chosen. Washington, Jefferson, Madison, the two Adamses, and Jackson were the owners of names that have become known in history. They were men who have left their marks behind them. Those in Europe who have read of anything, have read of them. Americans, whether as republicans they admire Washington and the Adamses, or as democrats hold by Jefferson, Madison, and Jackson, do not at any rate blush for their old Presidents. But who has heard of Polk, of Pierce, and of Buchanan? What American is proud of them? In the old days the name of a future President might be surmised. He would probably be a man honoured in the nation; but who now can make a guess as to the next President? In one respect a guess may be made with some safety. The next President will be a man whose name has as yet offended no one by its prominence. But one requisite is essential for a President; he must be a man whom none as yet have delighted to honour.

This has come of universal suffrage; and seeing that it has come in spite of the constitution, and not by the constitution, it is very bad. Nor in saying this am I speaking my own conviction so much as that of all educated Americans with whom I have discussed the subject. At the present moment universal suffrage is not popular. Those who are the highest among the people certainly do not love it. I doubt whether the masses of the people have ever craved it. It has been introduced into the Presidential elections by men called politicians—by men who have made it a matter of trade to dabble in state affairs, and who have gradually learned to see how the constitutional law, with reference to the Presidential electors, could be set aside without any positive breach of the constitution. *

*On this matter one of the best, and best informed Americans that I have known told me that he differed from me. "It introduced itself," said he. "It was the result of social and political forces. Election of the President by popular choice became a necessity." The meaning of this is, that in regard to their Presidential elections the United States drifted into universal suffrage. I do not know that his theory is one more comfortable for his country than my own.

Whether or no any backward step can now be taken,—whether these elections can again be put into the hands of men fit to exercise a choice in such a matter,—may well be doubted. Facilis descensus Averni. But the recovery of the downward steps is very difficult. On that subject, however, I hardly venture here to give an opinion. I only declare what has been done, and express my belief that it has not been done in conformity with the wishes of the people,—as it certainly has not been done in conformity with the intention of the constitution.

In another matter a departure has been made from the conservative spirit of the constitution. This departure is equally grave with the other, but it is one which certainly does admit of correction. I allude to the present position assumed by many of the senators, and to the instructions given to them by the State legislatures, as to the votes which they shall give in the Senate. An obedience on their part to such instructions is equal in its effects to the introduction of universal suffrage into the elections. It makes them hang upon the people, divests them of their personal responsibility, takes away all those advantages given to them by a six years' certain tenure of office, and annuls the safety secured by a conservative method of election. Here again I must declare my opinion that this democratic practice has crept into the Senate without any expressed wish of the people. In all such matters the people of the nation has been strangely undemonstrative. It has been done as part of a system which has been used for transferring the political power of the nation to a body of trading politicians who have become known and felt as a mass, and not known and felt as individuals. I find it difficult to describe the present political position of the States in this respect. The millions of the people are eager for the constitution, are proud of their power as a nation, and are ambitious of national greatness. But they are not, as I think, especially desirous of retaining political influences in their own hands. At many of the elections it is difficult to induce them to vote. They have among them a half-knowledge that politics is a trade in the hands of the lawyers, and that they are the capital by which those political tradesmen carry on their business. These politicians are all lawyers. Politics and law go together as naturally as the possession of land and the exercise of magisterial powers do with us. It may be well that it should be so, as the lawyers are the best educated men of the country, and need not necessarily be the most dishonest. Political power has come into their hands, and it is for their purposes and by their influences that the spread of democracy has been encouraged.

As regards the Senate, the recovery of their old dignity and former position is within their own power. No amendment of the constitution is needed here, nor has the weakness come from any insufficiency of the constitution. The Senate can assume to itself to-morrow its own glories, and can, by doing so, become the saviours of the honour and glory of the nation. It is to the Senate that we must look for that conservative element which may protect the United States from the violence of demagogues on one side and from the despotism of military power on the other. The Senate, and the Senate only, can keep the President in check. The Senate also has a power over the Lower House with reference to the disposal of money, which deprives the House of Representatives of that exclusive authority which belongs to our House of Commons. It is not simply that the House of Representatives cannot do what is done by the House of Commons. There is more than this. To the Senate, in the minds of all Americans, belongs that superior prestige, that acknowledged possession of the greater power and fuller scope for action, which is with us as clearly the possession of the House of Commons. The United States' Senate can be conservative, and can be so by virtue of the constitution. The love of the constitution in the hearts of all Americans is so strong that the exercise of such power by the Senate would strengthen rather than endanger its position. I could wish that the senators would abandon their money payments, but I do not imagine that that will be done exactly in these days.

I have now endeavoured to describe the strength of the constitution of the United States, and to explain its weakness. The great question is at this moment being solved, whether or no that constitution will still be found equal to its requirements. It has hitherto been the mainspring in the government of the people. They have trusted with almost childlike confidence to the wisdom of their founders, and have said to their rulers,—"There; in those words, you must find the extent and the limit of your powers. It is written down for you, so that he who runs may read." That writing down, as it were, at a single sitting, of a sufficient code of instructions for the governors of a great nation, had not hitherto in the world's history been found to answer. In this instance it has, at any rate, answered better than in any other, probably because the words so written contained in them less pretence of finality in political wisdom than other written constitutions have assumed. A young tree must bend, or the winds will certainly break it. For myself I can honestly express my hope that no storm may destroy this tree.

CHAPTER X
THE GOVERNMENT

In speaking of the American constitution I have said so much of the American form of government that but little more is left to me to say under that heading. Nevertheless, I should hardly go through the work which I have laid out for myself if I did not endeavour to explain more continuously, and perhaps more graphically, than I found myself able to do in the last chapter, the system on which public affairs are managed in the United States.

And here I must beg my readers again to bear in mind how moderate is the amount of governing which has fallen to the lot of the government of the United States; how moderate, as compared with the amount which has to be done by the Queen's officers of state for Great Britain, or by the Emperor, with such assistance as he may please to accept from his officers of state, for France. That this is so must be attributed to more than one cause; but the chief cause is undoubtedly to be found in the very nature of a federal government. The States are individually sovereign, and govern themselves as to all internal matters. All the judges in England are appointed by the Crown; but in the United States only a small proportion of the judges are nominated by the President. The greater number are servants of the different States. The execution of the ordinary laws for the protection of men and property does not fall on the government of the United States, but on the executives of the individual States,—unless in some special matters, which will be defined in the next chapter. Trade, education, roads, religion, the passing of new measures for the internal or domestic comfort of the people,—all these things are more or less matters of care to our government. In the States they are matters of care to the governments of each individual State, but are not so to the central government at Washington.

But there are other causes which operate in the same direction, and which have hitherto enabled the Presidents of the United States, with their ministers, to maintain their positions without much knowledge of statecraft, or the necessity for that education in state matters which is so essential to our public men. In the first place, the United States have hitherto kept their hands out of foreign politics. If they have not done so altogether, they have so greatly abstained from meddling in them that none of that thorough knowledge of the affairs of other nations has been necessary to them which is so essential with us, and which seems to be regarded as the one thing needed in the cabinets of other European nations. This has been a great blessing to the United States, but it has not been an unmixed blessing. It has been a blessing because the absence of such care has saved the country from trouble and from expense. But such a state of things was too good to last; and the blessing has not been unmixed, seeing that now, when that absence of concern in foreign matters has been no longer possible, the knowledge necessary for taking a dignified part in foreign discussions has been found wanting. Mr. Seward is now the Minister for Foreign Affairs in the States, and it is hardly too much to say that he has made himself a laughing-stock among the diplomatists of Europe, by the mixture of his ignorance and his arrogance. His reports to his own ministers during the single year of his office, as published by himself apparently with great satisfaction, are a monument not so much of his incapacity as of his want of training for such work. We all know his long state papers on the "Trent" affair. What are we to think of a statesman who acknowledges the action of his country's servant to have been wrong, and in the same breath declares that he would have held by that wrong, had the material welfare of his country been thereby improved? The United States have now created a great army and a great debt. They will soon also have created a great navy. Affairs of other nations will press upon them, and they will press against the affairs of other nations. In this way statecraft will become necessary to them; and by degrees their ministers will become habile, graceful, adroit;—and perhaps crafty, as are the ministers of other nations.

And, moreover, the United States have had no outlying colonies or dependencies, such as an India and Canada are to us, as Cuba is and Mexico was to Spain, and as were the provinces of the Roman empire. Territories she has had, but by the peculiar beneficence of her political arrangements, these territories have assumed the guise of sovereign States, and been admitted into federal partnership on equal terms, with a rapidity which has hardly left to the central Government the reality of any dominion of its own. We are inclined to suppose that these new States have been allowed to assume their equal privileges and State rights because they have been contiguous to the old States—as though it were merely an extension of frontier. But this has not been so. California and Oregon have been very much further from Washington than the Canadas are from London. Indeed they are still further, and I hardly know whether they can be brought much nearer than Canada is to us, even with the assistance of railways. But nevertheless California and Oregon were admitted as States, the former as quickly and the latter much more quickly than its population would seem to justify Congress in doing, according to the received ratio of population. A preference in this way has been always given by the United States to a young population over one that was older. Oregon with its 60,000 inhabitants has one representative. New York with 4,000,000 inhabitants has thirty-three. But in order to be equal with Oregon, New York should have sixty-six. In this way the outlying populations have been encouraged to take upon themselves their own governance, and the governing power of the President and his cabinet has been kept within moderate limits.

But not the less is the position of the President very dominant in the eyes of us Englishmen by reason of the authority with which he is endowed. It is not that the scope of his power is great, but that he is so nearly irresponsible in the exercise of that power. We know that he can be impeached by the representatives and expelled from his office by the verdict of the Senate; but this, in fact, does not amount to much. Responsibility of this nature is doubtless very necessary, and prevents ebullitions of tyranny such as those in which a Sultan or an Emperor may indulge; but it is not that responsibility which especially recommends itself to the minds of free men. So much of responsibility they take as a matter of course, as they do the air which they breathe. It would be nothing to us to know that Lord Palmerston could be impeached for robbing the Treasury, or Lord Russell punished for selling us to Austria. It is well that such laws should exist, but we do not in the least suspect those noble lords of such treachery. We are anxious to know, not in what way they may be impeached and beheaded for great crimes, but by what method they may be kept constantly straight in small matters. That they are true and honest is a matter of course. But they must be obedient also, discreet, capable, and above all things of one mind with the public. Let them be that; or if not they, then with as little delay as may be, some others in their place. That with us is the meaning of ministerial responsibility. To that responsibility all the cabinet is subject. But in the Government of the United States there is no such responsibility. The President is placed at the head of the executive for four years, and while he there remains no man can question him. It is not that the scope of his power is great. Our own Prime Minister is doubtless more powerful,—has a wider authority. But it is that within the scope of his power the President is free from all check. There are no reins, constitutional or unconstitutional, by which he can be restrained. He can absolutely repudiate a majority of both Houses, and refuse the passage of any act of Congress even though supported by those majorities. He can retain the services of ministers distasteful to the whole country. He can place his own myrmidons at the head of the army and navy,—or can himself take the command immediately on his own shoulders. All this he can do, and there is no one that can question him.

It is hardly necessary that I should point out the fundamental difference between our King or Queen, and the President of the United States. Our Sovereign, we all know, is not responsible. Such is the nature of our constitution. But there is not on that account any analogy between the irresponsibility of the Queen and that of the President. The Queen can do no wrong; but therefore, in all matters of policy and governance, she must be ruled by advice. For that advice her ministers are responsible; and no act of policy or governance can be done in England as to which responsibility does not immediately settle on the shoulders appointed to bear it. But this is not so in the States. The President is nominally responsible. But from that every-day working responsibility, which is to us so invaluable, the President is in fact free.

I will give an instance of this. Now, at this very moment of my writing, news has reached us that President Lincoln has relieved General Maclellan from the command of the whole army, that he has given separate commands to two other generals,—to General Halleck, namely, and alas! to General Fremont, and that he has altogether altered the whole organization of the military command as it previously existed. This he did not only during war, but with reference to a special battle, for the special fighting of which he, as ex-officio Commander-in-Chief of the forces, had given orders. I do not hereby intend to criticise this act of the President's, or to point out that that has been done which had better have been left undone. The President, in a strategetical point of view, may have been,—very probably has been, quite right. I, at any rate, cannot say that he has been wrong. But then neither can anybody else say so with any power of making himself heard. Of this action of the President's, so terribly great in its importance to the nation, no one has the power of expressing any opinion to which the President is bound to listen. For four years he has this sway, and at the end of four years he becomes so powerless that it is not then worth the while of any demagogue in a fourth-rate town to occupy his voice with that President's name. The anger of the country as to the things done both by Pierce and Buchanan is very bitter. But who wastes a thought upon either of these men? A past President in the United States is of less consideration than a past Mayor in an English borough. Whatever evil he may have done during his office, when out of office he is not worth the powder which would be expended in an attack.

But the President has his ministers as our Queen has hers. In one sense he has such ministers. He has high state servants who under him take the control of the various departments, and exercise among them a certain degree of patronage and executive power. But they are the President's ministers, and not the ministers of the people. Till lately there has been no chief minister among them, nor am I prepared to say that there is any such chief at present. According to the existing theory of the government these gentlemen have simply been the confidential servants of the commonwealth under the President, and have been attached each to his own department without concerted political alliance among themselves, without any acknowledged chief below the President, and without any combined responsibility even to the President. If one minister was in fault—let us say the Postmaster-General,—he alone was in fault, and it did not fall to the lot of any other minister either to defend him, or to declare that his conduct was indefensible. Each owed his duty and his defence to the President alone; and each might be removed alone, without explanation given by the President to the others. I imagine that the late practice of the President's cabinet has in some degree departed from this theory; but if so, the departure has sprung from individual ambition rather than from any preconcerted plan. Some one place in the cabinet has seemed to give to some one man an opportunity of making himself pre-eminent, and of this opportunity advantage has been taken. I am not now intending to allude to any individual, but am endeavouring to indicate the way in which a ministerial cabinet, after the fashion of our British cabinet, is struggling to get itself created. No doubt the position of Foreign Secretary has for some time past been considered as the most influential under the President. This has been so much the case that many have not hesitated to call the Secretary of State the chief minister. At the present moment, May, 1862, the gentleman who is at the head of the war department has, I think, in his own hands greater power than any of his colleagues.

It will probably come to pass before long that one special minister will be the avowed leader of the cabinet, and that he will be recognized as the chief servant of the State under the President. Our own cabinet, which now-a-days seems with us to be an institution as fixed as Parliament and as necessary as the throne, has grown by degrees into its present shape, and is not, in truth, nearly so old as many of us suppose it to be. It shaped itself, I imagine, into its present form, and even into its present joint responsibility, during the reign of George III. It must be remembered that even with us there is no such thing as a constitutional Prime Minister, and that our Prime Minister is not placed above the other ministers in any manner that is palpable to the senses. He is paid no more than the others; he has no superior title; he does not take the highest rank among them; he never talks of his subordinates, but always of his colleagues; he has a title of his own, that of First Lord of the Treasury, but it implies no headship in the cabinet. That he is the head of all political power in the nation, the Atlas who has to bear the globe, the god in whose hands rest the thunderbolts and the showers, all men do know. No man's position is more assured to him. But the bounds of that position are written in no book, are defined by no law, have settled themselves not in accordance with the recorded wisdom of any great men, but as expediency and the fitness of political things in Great Britain have seemed from time to time to require. This drifting of great matters into their proper places is not as closely in accordance with the idiosyncrasies of the American people as it is with our own. They would prefer to define by words, as the French do, what shall be the exact position of every public servant connected with their Government; or rather of every public servant with whom the people shall be held as having any concern. But nevertheless, I think it will come to pass that a cabinet will gradually form itself at Washington as it has done at London, and that of that cabinet there will be some recognized and ostensible chief.

But a Prime Minister in the United States can never take the place there which is taken here by our Premier. Over our Premier there is no one politically superior. The highest political responsibility of the nation rests on him. In the States this must always rest on the President, and any minister, whatever may be his name or assumed position, can only be responsible through the President. And it is here especially that the working of the United States system of Government seems to me deficient, —appears as though it wanted something to make it perfect and round at all points. Our ministers retire from their offices, as do the Presidents; and indeed the ministerial term of office with us, though of course not fixed, is in truth much shorter than the Presidential term of four years. But our ministers do not, in fact, ever go out. At one time they take one position, with pay, patronage, and power; and at another time another position, without these good things; but in either position they are acting as public men, and are, in truth, responsible for what they say and do. But the President, on whom it is presumed that the whole of the responsibility of the United States Government rests, goes out at a certain day, and of him no more is heard. There is no future before him to urge him on to constancy; no hope of other things beyond, of greater honours and a wider fame, to keep him wakeful in his country's cause. He has already enrolled his name on the list of his country's rulers, and received what reward his country can give him. Conscience, duty, patriotism may make him true to his place. True to his place, in a certain degree, they will make him. But ambition and hope of things still to come are the moving motives in the minds of most men. Few men can allow their energies to expand to their fullest extent in the cold atmosphere of duty alone. The President of the States must feel that he has reached the top of the ladder, and that he soon will have done with life. As he goes out he is a dead man. And what can be expected from one who is counting the last lingering hours of his existence? "It will not be in my time," Mr. Buchanan is reported to have said, when a friend spoke to him with warning voice of the coming rebellion. "It will not be in my time." In the old days, before democracy had prevailed in upsetting that system of Presidential election which the constitution had intended to fix as permanent, the Presidents were generally re-elected for a second term. Of the seven first Presidents five were sent back to the White House for a second period of four years. But this has never been done since the days of General Jackson; nor will it be done, unless a stronger conservative reaction takes place than the country even as yet seems to promise. As things have lately ordered themselves, it may almost be said that no man in the Union would be so improbable a candidate for the Presidency as the outgoing President. And it has been only natural that it should be so. Looking at the men themselves who have lately been chosen, the fault has not consisted in their non-reelection, but in their original selection. There has been no desire for great men; no search after a man of such a nature, that when tried the people should be anxious to keep him. "It will not be in my time," says the expiring President. And so, without dismay, he sees the empire of his country slide away from him.

A President, with the possibility of re-election before him, would be as a minister who goes out, knowing that he may possibly come in again before the session is over, — and perhaps believing that the chances of his doing so are in his favour. Under the existing political phase of things in the United States, no President has any such prospect; — but the ministers of the President have that chance. It is no uncommon thing at present for a minister under one President to reappear as a minister under another; but a statesman has no assurance that he will do so because he has shown ministerial capacity. We know intimately the names of all our possible ministers, — too intimately as some of us think, — and would be taken much by surprise if a gentleman without an official reputation were placed at the head of a high office. If something of this feeling prevailed as to the President's cabinet, if there were some assurance that competent statesmen would be appointed as Secretaries of State, a certain amount of national responsibility would by degrees attach itself to them, and the President's shoulders would, to that amount, be lightened. As it is, the President pretends to bear a burden which, if really borne, would indicate the possession of Herculean shoulders. But, in fact, the burden at present is borne by no one. The government of the United States is not in truth responsible either to the people or to Congress.

But these ministers, if it be desired that they shall have weight in the country, should sit in Congress either as senators or as representatives. That they cannot so sit without an amendment of the constitution I have explained in the previous chapter; and any such amendment cannot be very readily made. Without such seats they cannot really share the responsibility of the President, or be in any degree amenable to public opinion for the advice which they give in their public functions. It will be said that the constitution has expressly intended that they should not be responsible, and such, no doubt, has been the case. But the constitution, good as it is, cannot be taken as perfect. The government has become greater than seems to have been contemplated when that code was drawn up. It has spread itself as it were over a wider surface, and has extended to matters which it was not then necessary to touch. That theory of governing by the means of little men was very well while the government itself was small. A President and his clerks may have sufficed when there were from thirteen to eighteen States; while there were no territories, or none at least that required government; while the population was still below five millions; while a standing army was an evil not known and not feared; while foreign politics was a troublesome embroglio in which it was quite unnecessary that the United States should take a part. Now there are thirty-four States. The territories populated by American citizens stretch from the States on the Atlantic to those on the Pacific. There is a population of thirty million souls. At the present moment the United States are employing more soldiers than any other nation, and have acknowledged the necessity of maintaining a large army even when the present troubles shall be over. In addition to this the United States have occasion for the use of statecraft with all the great kingdoms of Europe. That theory of ruling by little men will not do much longer. It will be well that they should bring forth their big men and put them in the place of rulers.

The President has at present seven ministers. They are the Secretary of State, who is supposed to have the direction of Foreign Affairs; the Secretary of the Treasury, who answers to our Chancellor of the Exchequer; the Secretaries of the Army and of the Navy; the Minister of the Interior; the Attorney-General; and the Postmaster-General. If these officers were allowed to hold seats in one House or in the other, — or rather if the President were enjoined to place in these offices men who were known as members of Congress, not only would the position of the President's ministers be enhanced and their weight increased, but the position also of Congress would be enhanced and the weight of Congress would be increased. I may, perhaps, best exemplify this by suggesting what would be the effect on our Parliament by withdrawing from it the men who at the present moment, — or at any moment, — form the Queen's cabinet. I will not say that by adding to Congress the men who usually form the President's cabinet, a weight would be given equal to that which the withdrawal of the British cabinet would take from the British Parliament. I cannot pay that compliment to the President's choice of servants. But the relationship between Congress and the President's ministers would gradually come to resemble that which exists between Parliament and the Queen's ministers. The Secretaries of State and of the Treasury would after a while obtain that honour of leading the Houses which is exercised by our high political officers, and the dignity added to the positions would make the places worthy of the acceptance of great men. It is hardly so at present. The career of one of the President's ministers is not a very high career as things now stand; nor is the man supposed to have achieved much who has achieved that position. I think it would be otherwise if the ministers were the leaders of the legislative Houses. To Congress itself would be given the power of questioning and ultimately of controlling these ministers. The power of the President would no doubt be diminished as that of Congress would be increased. But an alteration in that direction is in itself desirable. It is the fault of the present system of government in the United States that the President has too much of power and weight, while the Congress of the nation lacks power and weight. As matters now stand, Congress has not that dignity of position which it should hold; and it is without it because it is not endowed with that control over the officers of the government which our Parliament is enabled to exercise.

The want of this close connection with Congress and the President's ministers has been so much felt, that it has been found necessary to create a medium of communication. This has been done by a system which has now become a recognized part of the machinery of the government, but which is, I believe, founded on no regularly organized authority. At any rate no provision is made for it in the constitution; nor, as far as I am aware, has it been established by any special enactment or written rule. Nevertheless, I believe I am justified in saying that it has become a recognized link in the system of government adopted by the United States. In each House standing committees are named, to which are delegated the special consideration of certain affairs of state. There are, for instance, committees of foreign affairs, of finance, the judiciary committee, and others of a similar nature. To these committees are referred all questions which come before the House bearing on the special subject to which each is devoted. Questions of taxation are referred to the finance committee before they are discussed in the House; and the House, when it goes into such discussion, has before it the report of the committee. In this way very much of the work of the legislature is done by branches of each House, and by selected men whose time and intellects are devoted to special subjects. It is easy to see that much time and useless debate may be thus saved, and I am disposed to believe that this system of committees has worked efficiently and beneficially. The mode of selection of the members has been so contrived as to give to each political party that amount of preponderance in each committee which such party holds in the House. If the democrats have in the Senate a majority, it would be within their power to vote none but democrats into the committee on finance; but this would be manifestly unjust to the republican party, and the injustice would itself frustrate the object of the party in power; therefore the democrats simply vote to themselves a majority in each committee, keeping to themselves as great a preponderance in the committee as they have in the whole House, and arranging also that the chairman of the committee shall belong to their own party. By these committees the chief legislative measures of the country are originated and inaugurated,—as they are with us by the ministers of the Crown, and the chairman of each committee is supposed to have a certain amicable relation with that minister who presides over the office with which his committee is connected. Mr. Sumner is at present chairman of the committee on foreign affairs, and he is presumed to be in connection with Mr. Seward, who, as Secretary of State, has the management of the foreign relations of the Government.

But it seems to me that this supposed connection between the committees and the ministers is only a makeshift, showing by its existence the absolute necessity of close communication between the executive and the legislative, but showing also by its imperfections the great want of some better method of communication. In the first place the chairman of the committee is in no way bound to hold any communication with the minister. He is simply a senator, and as such has no ministerial duties, and can have none. He holds no appointment under the President, and has no palpable connection with the executive. And then it is quite as likely that he may be opposed in politics to the minister as that he may agree with him. If the two be opposed to each other on general politics, it may be presumed that they cannot act together in union on one special subject. Nor, whether they act in union or do not so act, can either have any authority over the other. The minister is not responsible to Congress, nor is the chairman of the committee in any way bound to support the minister. It is presumed that the chairman must know the minister's secrets, but the chairman may be bound by party considerations to use those secrets against the minister.

The system of committees appears to me to be good as regards the work of legislation. It seems well adapted to effect economy of time and the application of special men to special services. But I am driven to think that that connection between the chairmen of the committees and the ministers, which I have attempted to describe, is an arrangement very imperfect in itself, but plainly indicating the necessity of some such close relation between the executive and the legislature of the United States as does exist in the political system of Great Britain. With us the Queen's minister has a greater weight in Parliament than the President's minister could hold in Congress, because the Queen is bound to employ a minister in whom the Parliament has confidence. As soon as such confidence ceases, the minister ceases to be minister. As the Crown has no politics of its own, it is simply necessary that the minister of the day should hold the politics of the people as testified by their representatives. The machinery of the President's Government cannot be made to work after this fashion. The President himself is a political officer, and the country is bound to bear with his politics for four years, whatever those politics may be. The ministry which he selects on coming to his seat will probably represent a majority in Congress, seeing that the same suffrages which have elected the President will also have elected the Congress. But there exists no necessity on the part of the President to employ ministers who shall carry with them the support of Congress. If, however, the ministers sat in Congress, — if it were required of each minister that he should have a seat either in one House or in the other, — the President would, I think, find himself constrained to change a ministry in which Congress should decline to confide. It might not be so at first, but there would be a tendency in that direction.

The governing powers do not rest exclusively with the President, or with the President and his ministers; they are shared in a certain degree with the Senate, which sits from time to time in executive Session, laying aside at such periods its legislative character. It is this executive authority which lends so great a dignity to the Senate, gives it the privilege of preponderating over the other House, and makes it the political safeguard of the nation. The questions of government as to which the Senate is empowered to interfere are soon told. All treaties made by the President must be sanctioned by the Senate; and all appointments made by the President must be confirmed by the Senate. The list is short, and one is disposed to think, when first hearing it, that the thing itself does not amount to much. But it does amount to very much; it enables the Senate to fetter the President, if the Senate should be so inclined, both as regards foreign politics and home politics. A Secretary for Foreign Affairs at Washington may write what despatches he pleases without reference to the Senate; but the Senate interferes before those despatches can have resulted in any fact which may be detrimental to the nation. It is not only that the Senate is responsible for such treaties as are made, but that the President is deterred from the making of treaties for which the Senate would decline to make itself responsible. Even though no treaty should ever be refused its sanction by the Senate, the protecting power of the Senate in that matter would not on that account have been less necessary or less efficacious. Though the bars with which we protect our house may never have been tried by a thief, we do not therefore believe that our house would have been safe if such bars had been known to be wanting. And then, as to that matter of state appointments, is it not the fact that all governing powers consist in the selection of the agents by whom the action of Government shall be carried on? It must come to this, I imagine, when the argument is pushed home. The power of the most powerful man depends only on the extent of his authority over his agents. According to the constitution of the United States, the President can select no agent either at home or abroad, for purposes either of peace or war, or to the employment of whom the Senate does not agree with him. Such a rule as this should save the nation from the use of disreputable agents as public servants. It might, perhaps, have done more towards such salvation than it has as yet effected;—and it may well be hoped that it will do more in future.

Such are the executive powers of the Senate; and it is, I think, remarkable that the Senate has always used these powers with extreme moderation. It has never shown a factious inclination to hinder Government by unnecessary interference, or a disposition to clip the President's wings by putting itself altogether at variance with him. I am not quite sure whether some fault may not have lain on the other side; whether the Senate may not have been somewhat slack in exercising the protective privileges given to it by the constitution. And here I cannot but remark how great is the deference paid to all governors and edicts of Government throughout the United States. One would have been disposed to think that such a feeling would be stronger in an old country such as Great Britain than in a young country such as the States. But I think that it is not so. There is less disposition to question the action of government either at Washington or at New York, than there is in London. Men in America seem to be content when they have voted in their governors, and to feel that for them all political action is over until the time shall come for voting for others. And this feeling, which seems to prevail among the people, prevails also in both Houses of Congress. Bitter denunciations against the President's policy or the President's ministers are seldom heard. Speeches are not often made with the object of impeding the action of Government. That so small and so grave a body as the Senate should abstain from factious opposition to the Government when employed on executive functions was perhaps to be expected. It is of course well that it should be so. I confess, however, that it has appeared to me that the Senate has not used the power placed in its hands as freely as the constitution has intended. But I look at the matter as an Englishman, and as an Englishman I can endure no government action which is not immediately subject to Parliamentary control.

Such are the governing powers of the United States. I think it will be seen that they are much more limited in their scope of action than with us; but within that scope of action much more independent and self-sufficient. And, in addition to this, those who exercise power in the United States are not only free from immediate responsibility, but are not made subject to the hope or fear of future judgment. Success will bring no award, and failure no punishment. I am not aware that any political delinquency has ever yet brought down retribution on the head of the offender in the United States, or that any great deed has been held as entitling the doer of it to his country's gratitude. Titles of nobility they have none; pensions they never give; and political disgrace is unknown. The line of politics would seem to be cold and unalluring. It is cold;—and would be unalluring, were it not that as a profession it is profitable. In much of this I expect that a change will gradually take place. The theory has been that public affairs should be in the hands of little men. The theory was intelligible while the public affairs were small; but they are small no longer, and that theory, I fancy, will have to alter itself. Great men are needed for the government, and in order to produce great men a career of greatness must be opened to them. I can see no reason why the career and the men should not be forthcoming.

CHAPTER XI
THE LAW COURTS AND LAWYERS
OF THE UNITED STATES

I do not propose to make any attempt to explain in detail the practices and rules of the American Courts of Law. No one but a lawyer should trust himself with such a task, and no lawyer would be enabled to do so in the few pages which I shall here devote to the subject. My present object is to explain, as far as I may be able to do so, the existing political position of the country. As this must depend more or less upon the power vested in the hands of the judges, and upon the tenure by which those judges hold their offices, I shall endeavour to describe the circumstances of the position in which the American judges are placed; the mode in which they are appointed; the difference which exists between the national judges and the State judges; and the extent to which they are or are not held in high esteem by the general public whom they serve.

It will, I think, be acknowledged that this last matter is one of almost paramount importance to the welfare of a country. At home in England we do not realize the importance to us in a political as well as social view of the dignity and purity of our judges, because we take from them all that dignity and purity can give as a matter of course. The honesty of our bench is to us almost as the honesty of heaven. No one dreams that it can be questioned or become questionable, and therefore there are but few who are thankful for its blessings. Few Englishmen care to know much about their own courts of law, or are even aware that the judges are the protectors of their liberties and property. There are the men, honoured on all sides, trusted by every one, removed above temptation, holding positions which are coveted by all lawyers. That it is so is enough for us; and as the good thence derived comes to us so easily, we forget to remember that we might possibly be without it. The law courts of the States have much in their simplicity and the general intelligence of their arrangements to recommend them. In all ordinary causes justice is done with economy, with expedition, and I believe with precision. But they strike an Englishman at once as being deficient in splendour and dignity, as wanting that reverence which we think should be paid to words falling from the bench, and as being in danger as to that purity, without which a judge becomes a curse among a people, a chief of thieves, and an arch-minister of the Evil One. I say as being in danger;—not that I mean to hint that such want of purity has been shown, or that I wish it to be believed that judges with itching palms do sit upon the American bench; but because the present political tendency of the State arrangements threatens to produce such danger. We in England trust implicitly in our judges,—not because they are Englishmen, but because they are Englishmen carefully selected for their high positions. We should soon distrust them if they were elected by universal suffrage from all the barristers and attorneys practising in the different courts; and so elected only for a period of years, as is the case with reference to many of the State judges in America. Such a mode of appointment would, in our estimation, at once rob them of their prestige. And our distrust would not be diminished if the pay accorded to the work were so small that no lawyer in good practice could afford to accept the situation. When we look at a judge in court, venerable beneath his wig and adorned with his ermine, we do not admit to ourselves that that high officer is honest because he is placed above temptation by the magnitude of his salary. We do not suspect that he, as an individual, would accept bribes and favour suitors if he were in want of money. But, still, we know as a fact that an honest man, like any other good article, must be paid for at a high price. Judges and bishops expect those rewards which all men win who rise to the highest steps on the ladder of their profession. And the better they are paid, within measure, the better they will be as judges and bishops. Now, the judges in America are not well paid, and the best lawyers cannot afford to sit upon the bench.

With us the practice of the law and the judicature of our law courts are divided. We have Chancery barristers and Common Law barristers; and we have Chancery Courts and Courts of Common Law. In the States there is no such division. It prevails neither in the national or federal courts of the United States, nor in the courts of any of the separate States. The code of laws used by the Americans is taken almost entirely from our English laws,—or rather, I should say, the federal code used by the nation is so taken, and also the various codes of the different States,—as each State takes whatever laws it may think fit to adopt. Even the precedents of our courts are held as precedents in the American courts, unless they chance to jar against other decisions given specially in their own courts with reference to cases of their own. In this respect the founders of the American law proceedings have shown a conservation bias and a predilection for English written and traditional law, which are much at variance with that general democratic passion for change by which we generally presume the Americans to have been actuated at their revolution. But though they have kept our laws, and still respect our reading of those laws, they have greatly altered and simplified our practice. Whether a double set of courts for Law and Equity are or are not expedient, either in the one country or in the other, I do not pretend to know. It is, however, the fact that there is no such division in the States.

Moreover there is no division in the legal profession. With us we have barristers and attorneys. In the States the same man is both barrister and attorney; and, which is perhaps in effect more startling, every lawyer is presumed to undertake law cases of every description. The same man makes your will, sells your property, brings an action for you of trespass against your neighbour, defends you when you are accused of murder, recovers for you two-and-sixpence, and pleads for you in an argument of three days' length when you claim to be the sole heir to your grandfather's enormous property. I need not describe how terribly distinct with us is the difference between an attorney and a barrister, or how much further than the poles asunder is the future Lord Chancellor, pleading before the Lords Justices at Lincoln's Inn, from the gentleman who at the Old Bailey is endeavouring to secure the personal liberty of the ruffian who a week or two since walked off with all your silver spoons. In the States no such differences are known. A lawyer there is a lawyer, and is supposed to do for any client any work that a lawyer may be called on to perform. But though this is the theory, and as regards any difference between attorney and barrister is altogether the fact, the assumed practice is not, and cannot be maintained as regards the various branches of a lawyer's work. When the population was smaller, and the law cases were less complicated, the theory and the practice were no doubt alike. As great cities have grown up, and properties large in amount have come under litigation, certain lawyers have found it expedient and practicable to devote themselves to special branches of their profession. But this, even up to the present time, has not been done openly as it were, or with any declaration made by a man as to his own branch of his calling. I believe that no such declaration on his part would be in accordance with the rules of the profession. He takes a partner, however, and thus attains his object;—or more than one partner, and then the business of the house is divided among them according to their individual specialities. One will plead in court, another will give chamber-counsel, and a third will take that lower business which must be done, but which first-rate men hardly like to do.

It will easily be perceived that law in this way will be made cheaper to the litigant. Whether or no that may be an unadulterated advantage, I have my doubts. I fancy that the united professional incomes of all the lawyers in the States would exceed in amount those made in England. In America every man of note seems to be a lawyer, and I am told that any lawyer who will work may make a sure income. If it be so, it would seem that Americans per head pay as much or more for their law as men do in England. It may be answered that they get more law for their money. That may be possible, and even yet they may not be gainers. I have been inclined to think that there is an unnecessarily slow and expensive ceremonial among us in the employment of barristers through a third party; it has seemed that the man of learning, on whose efforts the litigant really depends, is divided off from his client and employer by an unfair barrier, used only to enhance his own dignity and give an unnecessary grandeur to his position. I still think that the fault with us lies in this direction. But I feel that I am less inclined to demand an immediate alteration in our practice than I was before I had seen any of the American courts of law.

It should be generally understood that lawyers are the leading men in the States, and that the governance of the country has been almost entirely in their hands ever since the political life of the nation became full and strong. All public business of importance falls naturally into their hands, as with us it falls into the hands of men of settled wealth and landed property. Indeed, the fact on which I insist is much more clear and defined in the States than it is with us. In England the lawyers also obtain no inconsiderable share of political and municipal power. The latter is perhaps more in the hands of merchants and men in trade than of any other class; and even the highest seats of political greatness are more open with us to the world at large than they seem to be in the States to any that are not lawyers. Since the days of Washington every President of the United States has, I think, been a lawyer, excepting General Taylor. Other Presidents have been generals, but then they have also been lawyers. General Jackson was a successful lawyer. Almost all the leading politicians of the present day are lawyers. Seward, Cameron, Welles, Stanton, Chase, Sumner, Crittenden, Harris, Fessenden, are all lawyers. Webster, Clay, Calhoun, and Cass were lawyers. Hamilton and Jay were lawyers. Any man with an ambition to enter upon public life becomes a lawyer as a matter of course. It seems as though a study and practice of the law were necessary ingredients in a man's preparation for political life. I have no doubt that a very large proportion of both Houses of legislature would be found to consist of lawyers. I do not remember that I know of the circumstance of more than one senator who is not a lawyer. Lawyers form the ruling class in America as the landowners do with us. With us that ruling class is the wealthiest class; but this is not so in the States. It might be wished that it were so.

The great and ever-present difference between the national or federal affairs of the United States government, and the affairs of the government of each individual State should be borne in mind at all times by those who desire to understand the political position of the States. Till this be realized no one can have any correct idea of the bearings of politics in that country. As a matter of course we in England have been inclined to regard the Government and Congress of Washington as paramount throughout the States, in the same way that the Government of Downing Street and the Parliament of Westminster are paramount through the British isles. Such a mistake is natural; but not the less would it be a fatal bar to any correct understanding of the constitution of the United States. The national and State governments are independent of each other, and so also are the national and State tribunals. Each of these separate tribunals has its own judicature, its own judges, its own courts, and its own functions. Nor can the supreme tribunal at Washington exercise any authority over the proceedings of the Courts in the different States, or influence the decisions of their judges. For not only are the national judges and the State judges independent of each other; but the laws in accordance with which they are bound to act, may be essentially different. The two tribunals, those of the nation and of the State, are independent and final in their several spheres. On a matter of State jurisprudence no appeal lies from the supreme tribunal of New York or Massachusetts to the supreme tribunal of the nation at Washington.

The national tribunals are of two classes. First, there is the Supreme Court specially ordained by the constitution. And then there are such inferior courts as Congress may from time to time see fit to establish. Congress has no power to abolish the Supreme Court, or to erect another tribunal superior to it. This court sits at Washington, and is a final court of appeal from the inferior national courts of the federal empire. A system of inferior courts, inaugurated by Congress, has existed for about sixty years. Each State for purposes of national jurisprudence is constituted as a district; some few large States, such as New York, Pennsylvania, and Illinois, being divided into two districts. Each district has one district court presided over by one judge. National causes in general, both civil and criminal, are commenced in these district courts, and those involving only small amounts are ended there. Above these district courts are the national circuit courts, the districts or States having been grouped into circuits as the counties are grouped with us. To each of these circuits is assigned one of the judges of the Supreme Court of Washington, who is the ex-officio judge of that circuit, and who therefore travels as do our Common Law judges. In each district he sits with the judge of that district, and they two together form the circuit court. Appeals from the district court lie to the circuit court in cases over a certain amount, and also in certain criminal cases. It follows therefore that appeals lie from one judge to the same judge when sitting with another,—an arrangement which would seem to be fraught with some inconvenience. Certain causes, both civil and criminal, are commenced in the circuit courts. From the circuit courts the appeal lies to the Supreme Court at Washington; but such appeal beyond the circuit court is not allowed in cases which are of small magnitude or which do not involve principles of importance. If there be a division of opinion in the circuit court the case goes to the Supreme Court;—from whence it might be inferred that all cases brought from the district court to the circuit court would be sent on to the Supreme Court, unless the circuit judge agreed with the district judge; for the district judge having given his judgment in the inferior court, would probably adhere to it in the superior court. No appeal lies to the Supreme Court at Washington in criminal cases.

All questions that concern more than one State, or that are litigated between citizens of different States, or which are international in their bearing, come before the national judges. All cases in which foreigners are concerned, or the rights of foreigners, are brought or may be brought into the national courts. So also are all causes affecting the Union itself, or which are governed by the laws of Congress and not by the laws of any individual State. All questions of Admiralty law and maritime jurisdiction, and cases affecting ambassadors or consuls, are there tried. Matters relating to the Post-office, to the Customs, the collection of national taxes, to patents, to the army and navy, and to the mint, are tried in the national courts. The theory is that the national tribunals shall expound and administer the national laws and treaties, protect national offices and national rights; and that foreigners and citizens of other States shall not be required to submit to the decisions of the State tribunals;—in fact, that national tribunals shall take cognizance of all matters as to which the general government of the nation is responsible. In most of such cases the national tribunals have exclusive jurisdiction. In others it is optional with the plaintiff to select his tribunal. It is then optional with the defendant, if brought into a State court, to remain there or to remove his cause into the national tribunal. The principle is, that either at the beginning, or ultimately, such questions shall or may be decided by the national tribunals. If in any suit properly cognizable in a State court the decision should turn on a clause in the constitution, or on a law of the United States, or on the act of a national offence, or on the validity of a national act, an appeal lies to the Supreme Court of the United States and to its officers. The object has been to give to the national tribunals of the nation full cognizance of its own laws, treaties, and congressional acts.

The judges of all the national tribunals, of whatever grade or rank, hold their offices for life, and are removable only on impeachment. They are not even removable on an address of Congress; thus holding on a firmer tenure even than our own judges, who may, I believe, be moved on an address by Parliament. The judges in America are not entitled to any pension or retiring allowances; and as there is not, as regards the judges of the national courts, any proviso that they shall cease to sit after a certain age, they are, in fact, immoveable whatever may be their infirmities. Their position in this respect is not good, seeing that their salaries will hardly admit of their making adequate provision for the evening of life. The salary of the Chief Justice of the United States is only £1300 per annum. All judges of the national courts of whatever rank are appointed by the President, but their appointments must be confirmed by the Senate. This proviso, however, gives to the Senate practically but little power, and is rarely used in opposition to the will of the President. If the President name one candidate, who on political grounds is distasteful to a majority of the Senate, it is not probable that a second nomination made by him will be more satisfactory. This seems now to be understood, and the nomination of the cabinet ministers and of the judges, as made by the President, are seldom set aside or interfered with by the Senate, unless on grounds of purely personal objection.

The position of the national judges as to their appointments and mode of tenure is very different from that of the State judges, to whom in a few lines I shall more specially allude. This should, I think, be specially noticed by Englishmen when criticising the doings of the American courts. I have observed statements made to the effect that decisions given by American judges as to international or maritime affairs affecting English interests could not be trusted, because the judges so giving them would have been elected by popular vote, and would be dependent on the popular voice for reappointment. This is not so. Judges are appointed by popular vote in very many of the States. But all matters affecting shipping, and all questions touching foreigners are tried in the national courts before judges who have been appointed for life. I should not myself have had any fear with reference to the ultimate decision in the affair of Slidell and Mason had the "Trent" been carried into New York. I would, however, by no means say so much had the cause been one for trial before the tribunals of the State of New York.

I have been told that we in England have occasionally fallen into the error of attributing to the Supreme Court at Washington a quasi political power which it does not possess. This court can give no opinion to any department of the Government, nor can it decide upon or influence any subject that has not come before it as a regularly litigated case in law. Though especially founded by the constitution, it has no peculiar power under the constitution, and stands in no peculiar relation either to that or to Acts of Congress. It has no other power to decide on the constitutional legality of an act of Congress or an act of a State legislature or of a public officer than every court, State and national, high and low, possesses and is bound to exercise. It is simply the national court of last appeal.

In the different States such tribunals have been established as each State by its constitution and legislation has seen fit to adopt. The States are entirely free on this point. The usual course is to have one Supreme Court, sometimes called by that name, sometimes the Court of Appeals, and sometimes the Court of Errors. Then they have such especial courts as their convenience may dictate. The State jurisprudence includes all causes not expressly or by necessary implication secured to the national courts. The tribunals of the States have exclusive control over domestic relations, religion, education, the tenure and descent of land, the inheritance of property, police regulations, municipal economy, and all matters of internal trade. In this category of course come the relations of husband and wife, parent and child, master and servant, owner and slave, guardian and ward, tradesman and apprentice. So also do all police and criminal regulations not external in their character,—highways, railroads, canals, schools, colleges, the relief of paupers, and those thousand other affairs of the world by which men are daily surrounded in their own homes and their own districts. As to such subjects Congress can make no law, and over them Congress and the national tribunals have no jurisdiction. Congress cannot say that a man shall be hung for murder in New York; nor if a man be condemned to be hung in New York can the President pardon him. The legislature of New York must say whether or no hanging shall be the punishment adjudged to murder in that State; and the Governor of the State of New York must pronounce the man's pardon,—if it be that he is to be pardoned. But Congress must decide whether or no a man shall be hung for murder committed on the high seas, or in the national forts or arsenals; and in such a case it is for the President to give or to refuse the pardon.

The judges of the States are appointed as the constitution or the laws of each State may direct in that matter. The appointments, I think, in all the old States were formerly vested in the Governor. In some States such is still the case. In some, if I am not mistaken, the nomination is now made, directly, by the legislature. But in most of the States the power of appointing has been claimed by the people, and the judges are voted in by popular election, just as the President of the Union and the Governors of the different States are voted in. There has for some years been a growing tendency in this direction, and the people in most of the States have claimed the power;—or rather the power has been given to the people by politicians who have wished to get into their hands in this way the patronage of the courts. But now, at the present moment, there is arising a strong feeling of the inexpediency of appointing judges in such a manner. An antidemocratic bias is taking possession of men's minds, causing a reaction against that tendency to universal suffrage in everything which prevailed before the war began. As to this matter of the mode of appointing judges, I have heard but one opinion expressed; and I am inclined to think that a change will be made in one State after another, as the constitutions of the different States are revised. Such revisions take place generally at periods of about twenty-five years' duration. If, therefore, it be acknowledged that the system be bad, the error can be soon corrected.

Nor is this mode of appointment the only evil that has been adopted in the State judicatures. The judges in most of the States are not appointed for life, nor even during good behaviour. They enter their places for a certain term of years, varying from fifteen down, I believe, to seven. I do not know whether any are appointed for a term of less than seven years. When they go out they have no pensions; and as a lawyer who has been on the bench for seven years can hardly recall his practice, and find himself at once in receipt of his old professional income, it may easily be imagined how great will be the judge's anxiety to retain his position on the bench. This he can do only by the universal suffrages of the people, by political popularity, and a general standing of that nature which enables a man to come forth as the favourite candidate of the lower orders. This may or may not be well when the place sought for is one of political power,—when the duties required are political in all their bearings. But no one can think it well when the place sought for is a judge's seat on the bench;—when the duties required are solely judicial. Whatever hitherto may have been the conduct of the judges in the courts of the different States, whether or no impurity has yet crept in, and the sanctity of justice has yet been outraged, no one can doubt the tendency of such an arrangement. At present even a few visits to the courts constituted in this manner will convince an observer that the judges on the bench are rather inferior than superior to the lawyers who practise before them. The manner of address, the tone of voice, the lack of dignity in the judge, and the assumption by the lawyer before him of a higher authority than his, all tell this tale. And then the judges in these courts are not paid at a rate which will secure the services of the best men. They vary in the different States, running from about £600 to about £1000 per annum. But a successful lawyer practising in the courts in which these judges sit, not unfrequently earns £3000 a year. A professional income of £2000 a year is not considered very high. When the different conditions of the bench are considered, when it is remembered that the judge may lose his place after a short term of years, and that during that short term of years he receives a payment much less than that earned by his successful professional brethren, it can hardly be expected that first-rate judges should be found. The result is seen daily in society. You meet Judge This and Judge That, not knowing whether they are ex-judges or in-judges; but you soon learn that your friends do not hold any very high social position on account of their forensic dignity.

It is, perhaps, but just to add that in Massachusetts, which I cannot but regard as in many respects the noblest of the States, the judges are appointed by the Governor, and are appointed for life.

CHAPTER XII
THE FINANCIAL POSITION

The Americans are proud of much that they have done in this war, and indeed much has been done which may justify pride; but of nothing are they so proud as of the noble dimensions and quick growth of their Government debt. That Mr. Secretary Chase, the American Chancellor of the Exchequer, participates in this feeling I will not venture to say; but if he do not, he is well nigh the only man in the States who does not do so. The amount of expenditure has been a subject of almost national pride, and the two million of dollars a day which has been roughly put down as the average cost of the war, has always been mentioned by northern men in a tone of triumph. This feeling is, I think, intelligible; and although we cannot allude to it without a certain amount of inward sarcasm,—a little gentle laughing in the sleeve, at the nature of this national joy, I am not prepared to say that it is altogether ridiculous. If the country be found able and willing to pay the bill, this triumph in the amount of the cost will hereafter be regarded as having been anything but ridiculous. In private life an individual will occasionally be known to lavish his whole fortune on the accomplishment of an object which he conceives to be necessary to his honour. If the object be in itself good, and if the money be really paid, we do not laugh at such a man for the sacrifices which he makes.

For myself, I think that the object of the northern States in this war has been good. I think that they could not have avoided the war without dishonour, and that it was incumbent on them to make themselves the arbiters of the future position of the South, whether that future position shall or shall not be one of secession. This they could only do by fighting. Had they acceded to secession without a civil war, they would have been regarded throughout Europe as having shown themselves inferior to the South, and would for many years to come have lost that prestige which their spirit and energy had undoubtedly won for them; and in their own country such submission on their part would have practically given to the South the power of drawing the line of division between the two new countries. That line, so drawn, would have given Virginia, Maryland, Kentucky, and Missouri to the southern Republic. The great effect of the war to the North will be, that the northern men will draw the line of secession, if any such line be drawn. I still think that such line will ultimately be drawn, and that the southern States will be allowed to secede. But if it be so, Virginia, Maryland, Kentucky, and Missouri will not be found among these seceding States; and the line may not improbably be driven south of North Carolina and Tennessee. If this can be so, the object of the war will, I think, hereafter be admitted to have been good. Whatever may be the cost in money of joining the States which I have named to a free-soil northern people, instead of allowing them to be buried in that dismal swamp, which a confederacy of southern slave States will produce, that cost can hardly be too much. At the present moment there exists in England a strong sympathy with the South, produced partly by the unreasonable vituperation with which the North treated our Government at the beginning of the war, and by the capture of Mason and Slidell; partly also by that feeling of good-will which a looker-on at a combat always has for the weaker side. But, although this sympathy does undoubtedly exist, I do not imagine that many Englishmen are of opinion that a confederacy of southern slave States will ever offer to the general civilization of the world very many attractions. It cannot be thought that the South will equal the North in riches, in energy, in education, or general well-being. Such has not been our experience of any slave country; such has not been our experience of any tropical country; and such especially has not been our experience of the southern States of the North American Union. I am no abolitionist; but to me it seems impossible that any Englishman should really advocate the cause of slavery against the cause of free soil. There are the slaves, and I know that they cannot be abolished,—neither they nor their chains; but, for myself, I will not willingly join my lot with theirs. I do not wish to have dealings with the African negro either as a free man or as a slave, if I can avoid them, believing that his employment by me in either capacity would lead to my own degradation. * Such, I think, are the feelings of Englishmen generally on this matter. And if such be the case, will it not be acknowledged that the northern men have done well to fight for a line which shall add five or six States to that Union which will in truth be a union of free men, rather than to that Confederacy which, even if successful, must owe its success to slavery?

> *In saying this I fear that I shall be misunderstood, let me use what foot-note or other mode of protestation I may to guard myself. In thus speaking of the African negro, I do not venture to despise the work of God's hands. That He has made the negro, for His own good purposes, as He has the Esquimaux, I am aware. And I am aware that it is my duty, as it is the duty of us all, to see that no injury be done

to him, and, if possible, to assist him in his condition. When I declare that I desire no dealings with the negro, I speak of him in the position in which I now find him, either as a free servant or a slave. In either position he impedes the civilization and the progress of the white man.

In considering this matter it must be remembered that the five or six States of which we are speaking are at present slave States, but that, with the exception of Virginia,—of part only of Virginia,—they are not wedded to slavery. But even in Virginia, great as has been the gain which has accrued to that unhappy State from the breeding of slaves for the southern market,—even in Virginia slavery would soon die out if she were divided from the South, and joined to the North. In those other States, in Maryland, in Kentucky, and in Missouri there is no desire to perpetuate the institution. They have been slave States, and as such have resented the rabid abolition of certain northern orators. Had it not been for those orators, and their oratory, the soil of Kentucky would now have been free. Those five or six States are now slave States; but a line of secession drawn south of them will be the line which cuts off slavery from the North. If those States belong to the North when secession shall be accomplished, they will belong to it as free States; but if they belong to the South, they will belong to the South as slave States. If they belong to the North, they will become rich as the North is, and will share in the education of the North. If they belong to the South they will become poor as the South is, and will share in the ignorance of the South. If we presume that secession will be accomplished,—and I for one am of that opinion,—has it not been well that a war should be waged with such an object as this? If those five or six States can be gained, stretching east and west from the Atlantic to the centre of the continent, hundreds of miles beyond the Mississippi, and north and south over four degrees of latitude,—if that extent of continent can be added to the free soil of the northern territory, will not the contest that has done this have been worth any money that can have been spent on it?

So much as to the object to be gained by the money spent on the war! And I think that in estimating the nature of the financial position which the war has produced, it was necessary that we should consider the value of the object which has been in dispute. The object I maintain has been good. Then comes the question whether or no the bill will be fairly paid;—whether they who have spent the money will set about that disagreeable task of settling the account with a true purpose and an honest energy. And this question splits itself into two parts. Will the Americans honestly wish to pay the bill; and if they do so wish, will they have the power to pay it? Again that last question must be once more divided. Will they have the power to pay, as regards the actual possession of the means, and if possessing them, will they have the power of access to those means?

The nation has obtained for itself an evil name for repudiation. We all know that Pennsylvania behaved badly about her money affairs, although she did at last pay her debts. We all know that Mississippi has behaved very badly about her money affairs, and has never paid her debts, nor does she intend to pay them. And, which is worse than this, for it applies to the nation generally and not to individual States, we all know that it was made a matter of boast in the States that in the event of a war with England the enormous amount of property held by Englishmen in the States should be confiscated. That boast was especially made in the mercantile city of New York; and when the matter was discussed it seemed as though no American realized the iniquity of such a threat. It was not apparently understood that such a confiscation on account of a war would be an act of national robbery justified simply by the fact that the power of committing it would be in the hands of the robbers. Confiscation of so large an amount of wealth would be a smart thing, and men did not seem to perceive that any disgrace would attach to it in the eyes of the world at large. I am very anxious not to speak harsh words of the Americans; but when questions arise as to pecuniary arrangements I find myself forced to acknowledge that great precaution is at any rate necessary.

But, nevertheless, I am not sure that we shall be fair if we allow ourselves to argue as to the national purpose in this matter from such individual instances of dishonesty as those which I have mentioned. I do not think it is to be presumed that the United States as a nation will repudiate its debts because two separate States may have been guilty of repudiation. Nor am I disposed to judge of the honesty of the people generally from the dishonest threatenings of New York, made at a moment in which a war with England was considered imminent. I do believe that the nation, as a nation, will be as ready to pay for the war as it has been ready to carry on the war. That "ignorant impatience of taxation," to which it is supposed that we Britons are very subject, has not been a complaint rife among the Americans generally. We, in England, are inclined to believe that hitherto they have known nothing of the merits and demerits of taxation, and have felt none of its annoyances, because their entire national expenditure has been defrayed by light Custom duties; but the levies made in the separate States for State purposes, or chiefly for municipal purposes, have been very heavy. They are, however, collected easily, and, as far as I am aware, without any display of ignorant impatience. Indeed, an American is rarely impatient of any ordained law. Whether he be told to do this, or to pay for that, or to abstain from the other, he does do and pay and abstain without grumbling, provided that he has had a hand in voting for those who made the law and for those who carry out the law. The people generally have, I think, recognized the fact that they will have to put their necks beneath the yoke, as the peoples of other nations have put theirs, and support the weight of a great national debt. When the time comes for the struggle,—for the first uphill heaving against the terrible load which they will henceforth have to drag with them in their career, I think it will be found that they are not ill-inclined to put their shoulders to the work.

Then as to their power of paying the bill! We are told that the wealth of a nation consists in its labour, and that that nation is the most wealthy which can turn out of hand the greatest amount of work. If this be so the American States must form a very wealthy nation, and as such be able to support a very heavy burden. No one, I presume, doubts that that nation which works the most, or works rather to the best effect, is the richest. On this account England is richer than other countries, and is able to bear, almost without the sign of an effort, a burden which would crush any other land. But of this wealth the States own almost as much as Great Britain owns. The population of the northern States is industrious, ambitious of wealth, and capable of work as is our population. It possesses, or is possessed by, that restless longing for labour which creates wealth almost unconsciously. Whether this man be rich or be a bankrupt, whether the bankers of that city fail or make their millions, the creative energies of the American people will not become dull. Idleness is impossible to them, and therefore poverty is impossible. Industry and intellect together will always produce wealth; and neither industry nor intellect is ever wanting to an American. They are the two gifts with which the fairy has endowed him. When she shall have added honesty as a third, the tax-gatherer can desire no better country in which to exercise his calling.

I cannot myself think that all the millions that are being spent would weigh upon the country with much oppression, if the weight were once properly placed upon the muscles that will have to bear it. The difficulty will be in the placing of the weight. It has, I know, been argued that the circumstances under which our national debt has extended itself to its present magnificent dimensions cannot be quoted as parallel to those of the present American debt, because we, while we were creating the debt, were taxing ourselves very heavily, whereas the Americans have gone a-head with the creation of their debt before they have levied a shilling on themselves towards the payment of those expenses for which the debt has been encountered. But this argument, even if it were true in its gist, goes no way towards proving that the Americans will be unable to pay.

The population of the present free-soil States is above eighteen millions; that of the States which will probably belong to the Union if secession be accomplished is about twenty-two millions. At a time when our debt had amounted to six hundred millions sterling, we had no population such as that to bear the burden. It may be said that we had more amassed wealth than they have. But I take it that the amassed wealth of any country can go but a very little way in defraying the wants or in paying the debts of a people. We again come back to the old maxim, that the labour of a country is its wealth; and that a country will be rich or poor in accordance with the intellectual industry of its people.

But the argument drawn from that comparison between our own conduct when we were creating our debt, and the conduct of the Americans while they have been creating their debt, — during the twelve months from April 1, 1861, to March 31, 1862, let us say, — is hardly a fair argument. We, at any rate, knew how to tax ourselves, — if only the taxes might be forthcoming. We were already well used to the work; and a minister with a willing House of Commons had all his material ready to his hand. It has not been so in the United States. The difficulty has not been with the people who should pay the taxes, but with the minister and the Congress which did not know how to levy them. Certainly not as yet have those who are now criticising the doings on the other side of the water, a right to say that the American people are unwilling to make personal sacrifices for the carrying out of this war. No sign has as yet been shown of an unwillingness on the part of the people to be taxed. But wherever a sign could be given, it has been given on the other side. The separate States have taxed themselves very heavily for the support of the families of the absent soldiers. The extra allowances made to maimed men, amounting generally to twenty-four shillings a month, have been paid by the States themselves, and have been paid almost with too much alacrity.

I am of opinion that the Americans will show no unwillingness to pay the amount of taxation which must be exacted from them; and I also think that as regards their actual means they will have the power to pay it. But as regards their power of obtaining access to those means, I must confess that I see many difficulties in their way. In the first place they have no financier, — no man who by natural aptitude and by long continued contact with great questions of finance, has enabled himself to handle the money affairs of a nation with a master's hand. In saying this I do not intend to impute any blame to Mr. Chase, the present Secretary at the Treasury. Of his ability to do the work properly, had he received the proper training, I am not able to judge. It is not that Mr. Chase is incapable. He may be capable or incapable. But it is that he has not had the education of a national financier, and that he has no one at his elbow to help him who has had that advantage.

And here we are again brought to that general absence of state craft which has been the result of the American system of government. I am not aware that our Chancellors of the Exchequer have in late years always been great masters of finance; but they have at any rate been among money men and money matters, and have had financiers at their elbows if they have not deserved the name themselves. The very fact that a Chancellor of the Exchequer sits in the House of Commons and is forced in that House to answer all questions on the subject of finance, renders it impossible that he should be ignorant of the rudiments of the science. If you put a white cap on a man's head and place him in a kitchen, he will soon learn to be a cook. But he will never be made a cook by standing in the dining-room and seeing the dishes as they are brought up. The Chancellor of the Exchequer is our cook; and the House of Commons, not the Treasury chambers, is his kitchen. Let the Secretary of the United States Treasury sit in the House of Representatives. He would learn more there by contest with opposing members than he can do by any amount of study in his own chamber.

But the House of Representatives itself has not as yet learned its own lesson with reference to taxation. When I say that the United States are in want of a financier, I do not mean that the deficiency rests entirely with Mr. Chase. This necessity for taxation, and for taxation at so tremendous a rate, has come suddenly, and has found the representatives of the people unprepared for such work. To us, as I conceive, the science of taxation, in which we certainly ought to be great, has come gradually. We have learned by slow lessons what taxes will be productive, under what circumstances they will be most productive, and at what point they will be made unproductive by their own weight. We have learned what taxes may be levied so as to afford funds themselves, without injuring the proceeds of other taxes, and we know what taxes should be eschewed as being specially oppressive to the general industry and injurious to the well-being of the nation. This has come of much practice, and even we, with all our experience, have even got something to learn. But the public men in the States who are now devoting themselves to this matter of taxing the people have, as yet, no such experience. That they have inclination enough for the work is, I think, sufficiently demonstrated by the national tax bill, the wording of which is now before me, and which will have been passed into law before this volume can be published. It contains a list of every taxable article on the earth or under the earth. A more sweeping catalogue of taxation was probably never put forth. The Americans, it has been said by some of us, have shown no disposition to tax themselves for this war; but before the war has as yet been well twelve months in operation, a bill has come out with a list of taxation so oppressive, that it must, as regards many of its items, act against itself and cut its own throat. It will produce terrible fraud in its evasion, and create an army of excise officers who will be as locusts over the face of the country. Taxes are to be laid on articles which I should have said that universal consent had declared to be unfit for taxation. Salt, soap, candles, oil, and other burning fluids, gas, pins, paper, ink, and leather, are to be taxed. It was at first proposed that wheat-flour should be taxed, but that item has, I believe, been struck out of the bill in its passage through the House. All articles manufactured of cotton, wool, silk, worsted, flax, hemp, jute, india-rubber, gutta percha, wood (?), glass, pottery wares, leather, paper, iron, steel, lead, tin, copper, zinc, brass, gold and silver, horn, ivory, bone, bristles, wholly or in part, or of other materials, are to be taxed;—provided always that books, magazines, pamphlets, newspapers, and reviews shall not be regarded as manufactures. It will be said that the amount of taxation to be levied on the immense number of manufactured articles which must be included in this list will be light,—the tax itself being only 3 per cent. ad valorem. But with reference to every article, there will be the necessity of collecting this 3 per cent.! As regards each article that is manufactured, some government official must interfere to appraise its value and to levy the tax. Who shall declare the value of a barrel of wooden nutmegs; or how shall the Excise-officer get his tax from every cobbler's stall in the country? And then tradesmen are to pay licences for their trades,—a confectioner £2, a tallow-chandler £2, a horsedealer £2. Every man whose business it is to sell horses shall be a horsedealer. True. But who shall say whether or no it be a man's business to sell horses? An apothecary £2, a photographer £2, a pedlar £4, £3, £2, or £1, according to his mode of travelling. But if the gross receipts of any of the confectioners, tallow-chandlers, horsedealers, apothecaries, photographers, pedlars, or the like do not exceed £200 a year, then such tradesmen shall not be required to pay for any licence at all. Surely such a proviso can only have been inserted with the express view of creating fraud and ill blood! But the greatest audacity has, I think, been shown in the levying of personal taxes,—such taxes as have been held to be peculiarly disagreeable among us, and have specially brought down upon us the contempt of lightly-taxed people, who, like the Americans, have known nothing of domestic interference. Carriages are to be taxed,—as they are with us. Pianos also are to be taxed, and plate. It is not signified by this clause that such articles shall pay a tax, once for all, while in the maker's hands, which tax would no doubt fall on the future owner of such piano or plate; in such case the owner would pay, but would pay without any personal contact with the tax-gatherer. But every owner of a piano or of plate is to pay annually according to the value of the articles he owns. But perhaps the most audacious of all the proposed taxes is that on watches. Every owner of a watch is to pay 4s. a year for a gold watch and

2s. a year for a silver watch! The American tax-gatherers will not like to be cheated. They will be very keen in searching for watches. But who can say whether they or the carriers of watches will have the best of it in such a hunt. The tax-gatherers will be as hounds ever at work on a cold scent. They will now be hot and angry, and then dull and disheartened. But the carriers of watches who do not choose to pay will generally, one may predict, be able to make their points good.

With such a tax bill,—which I believe came into action on the 1st of May, 1862,—the Americans are not fairly open to the charge of being unwilling to tax themselves. They have avoided none of the irritating annoyances of taxation, as also they have not avoided, or attempted to lighten for themselves, the dead weight of the burden. The dead weight they are right to endure without flinching; but their mode of laying it on their own backs justifies me, I think, in saying that they do not yet know how to obtain access to their own means. But this bill applies simply to matters of excise. As I have said before, Congress, which has hitherto supported the government by custom duties, has also the power of levying excise duties, and now, in its first session since the commencement of the war, has begun to use that power without much hesitation or bashfulness. As regards their taxes levied at the Custom House, the government of the United States has always been inclined to high duties, with the view of protecting the internal trade and manufactures of the country. The amount required for national expenses was easily obtained, and these duties were not regulated, as I think, so much with a view to the amount which might be collected, as to that of the effect which the tax might have in fostering native industry. That, if I understand it, was the meaning of Mr. Morrill's bill, which was passed immediately on the secession of the southern members of Congress, and which instantly enhanced the price of all foreign manufactured goods in the States. But now the desire for protection, simply as protection, has been swallowed up in the acknowledged necessity for revenue; and the only object to be recognized in the arrangement of the custom duties is the collection of the greatest number of dollars. This is fair enough. If the country can at such a crisis raise a better revenue by claiming a shilling a pound on coffee than it can by claiming sixpence, the shilling may be wisely claimed, even though many may thus be prohibited from the use of coffee. But then comes the great question, What duty will really give the greatest product? At what rate shall we tax coffee so as to get at the people's money? If it be so taxed that people won't use it, the tax cuts its own throat. There is some point at which the tax will be most productive; and also there is a point up to which the tax will not operate to the serious injury of the trade. Without the knowledge which should indicate these points, a Chancellor of the Exchequer, with his myrmidons, would be groping in the dark. As far as we can yet see, there is not much of such knowledge either in the Treasury Chambers or the House of Representatives at Washington.

But the greatest difficulty which the States will feel in obtaining access to their own means of taxation, is that which is created by the constitution itself, and to which I alluded when speaking of the taxing powers which the constitution had given to Congress, and those which it had denied to Congress. As to custom duties and excise duties, Congress can do what it pleases, as can the House of Commons. But Congress cannot levy direct taxation according to its own judgment. In those matters of customs and excise, Congress and the Secretary of the Treasury will probably make many blunders; but having the power they will blunder through, and the money will be collected. But direct taxation, in an available shape, is beyond the power of Congress under the existing rule of the constitution. No income-tax, for instance, can be laid on the general incomes of the United States, that shall be universal throughout the States. An income-tax can be levied, but it must be levied in proportion to the representation. It is as though our Chancellor of the Exchequer, in collecting an income-tax, were obliged to demand the same amount of contribution from the town of Chester as from the town of Liverpool, because both Chester and Liverpool return two Members to Parliament. In fitting his tax to the capacity of Chester, he would be forced to allow Liverpool to escape unscathed. No skill in money matters on the part of the Treasury Secretary, and no aptness for finance on the part of the Committee on Ways and Means, can avail here. The constitution must apparently be altered before any serviceable resort can be had to direct taxation. And yet, at such an emergency as that now existing, direct taxation would probably give more ready assistance than can be afforded either by the Customs or the Excise.

It has been stated to me that this difficulty in the way of direct taxation can be overcome without any change in the constitution. Congress could only levy from Rhode Island the same amount of income-tax that it might levy from Iowa; but it will be competent to the legislature of Rhode Island itself to levy what income-tax it may please on itself; and to devote the proceeds to national or federal purposes. Rhode Island may do so; and so may Massachusetts, New York, Connecticut, and the other rich Atlantic States. They may tax themselves according to their riches, while Iowa, Illinois, Wisconsin, and such-like States are taxing themselves according to their poverty. I cannot myself think that it would be well to trust to the generosity of the separate States for the finances needed by the national Government. We should not willingly trust to Yorkshire or Sussex to give us their contributions to the national income, especially if Yorkshire and Sussex had small Houses of Commons of their own, in which that question of giving might be debated. It may be very well for Rhode Island or New York to be patriotic! But what shall be done with any State that declines to evince such patriotism? The legislatures of the different States may be invited to impose a tax of 5 per cent. on all incomes in each State; but what will be done if Pennsylvania, for instance, should decline, or Illinois should hesitate? What if the legislature of Massachusetts should offer 6 per cent., or that of New Jersey decide that 4 per cent. was sufficient? For a while the arrangement might possibly be made to answer the desired purpose. During the first ebullition of high feeling, the different States concerned might possibly vote the amount of taxes required for federal purposes. I fear it would not be so, but we may allow that the chance is on the card. But it is not conceivable that such an arrangement should be continued when, after a year or two, men came to talk over the war with calmer feelings and a more critical judgment. The State legislatures would become inquisitive, opinionative, and probably factious. They would be unwilling to act in so great a matter under the dictation of the federal Congress; and by degrees one, and then another, would decline to give its aid to the central government. However broadly the acknowledgment may have been made, that the levying of direct taxes was necessary for the nation, each State would be tempted to argue that a wrong mode and a wrong rate of levying had been adopted, and words would be forthcoming instead of money. A resort to such a mode of taxation would be a bad security for government Stock.

All matters of taxation, moreover, should be free from any taint of generosity. A man who should attempt to lessen the burdens of his country by gifts of money to its Exchequer would be laying his country under an obligation, for which his country would not thank him. The gifts here would be from States, and not from individuals; but the principle would be the same. I cannot imagine that the United States' Government would be willing to owe its revenue to the good will of different States, or its want of revenue to their caprice. If under such an arrangement the western States were to decline to vote the quota of income-tax or property-tax to which the eastern States had agreed, — and in all probability they would decline, — they would in fact be seceding. They would thus secede from the burdens of their general country; but in such event no one could accuse such States of unconstitutional secession.

It is not easy to ascertain with precision what is the present amount of debt due by the United States; nor probably has any tolerably accurate guess been yet given of the amount to which it may be extended during the present war. A statement made in the House of Representatives, by Mr. Spaulding, a member of the Committee of Ways and Means, on the 29th of

January last, may perhaps be taken as giving as trustworthy information as any that can be obtained. I have changed Mr. Spaulding's figures from dollars into pounds, that they may be more readily understood by English readers.

There was	Due up to July 1,1861	£18,173,566
"	Added in July and August	5,379,357
"	Borrowed in August	10,000,000
"	Borrowed in October	10,000,000
"	Borrowed in November	10,000,000
"	Amount of Treasury Demand Notes issued	7,800,000
		£61,352,923

This was the amount of the debt due up to January 15th, 1862. Mr. Spaulding then calculates that the sum required to carry on the Government up to July 1st, 1862, will be £68,647,077. And that a further sum of £110,000,000 will be wanted on or before the 1st of July, 1863. Thus the debt at that latter date would stand as follows:—

Amount of Debt up to January, 1862	£61,352,923
Added by July 1st, 1862	68,647,077
Again added by July 1st, 1863	110,000,000
	£240,000,000

The first of these items may no doubt be taken as accurate. The second has probably been founded on facts which leave little doubt as to its substantial truth. The third, which professes to give the proposed expense of the war for the forthcoming year, viz. from 1st July, 1862, to 30th June, 1863, must necessarily have been obtained by a very loose estimate. No one can say what may be the condition of the country during the next year,— whether the war may then be raging throughout the southern States, or whether the war may not have ceased altogether. The North knows little or nothing of the capacity of the South. How little it knows may be surmised from the fact that the whole southern army of Virginia retreated from their position at Manassas before the northern generals knew that they were moving; and that when they were gone no word whatever was left of their numbers. I do not believe that the northern Government is even yet able to make any probable conjecture as to the number of troops which the southern confederacy is maintaining, and if this be so, they can certainly make no trustworthy estimates as to their own expenses for the ensuing year.

Two hundred and forty millions is, however, the sum named by a gentleman presumed to be conversant with the matter, as the amount of debt which may be expected by midsummer, 1863; and if the war be continued till then, it will probably be found that he has not exceeded the mark. It is right, however, to state that Mr. Chase in his estimate does not rate the figures so high. He has given it as his opinion that the debt will be about one hundred and four millions in July, 1862, and one hundred and eighty millions in July, 1863. As to the first amount, with reference to which a tolerably accurate calculation may probably be made, I am inclined to prefer the estimate as given by the member of the committee; and as to the other, which hardly, as I think, admits of any calculation, his calculation is at any rate as good as that made in the Treasury.

But it is the immediate want of funds, and not the prospective debt of the country, which is now doing the damage. In this opinion Mr. Chase will probably agree with me; but readers on this side of the water will receive what I say with a smile. Such a state of affairs is certainly one that has not uncommonly been reached by financiers; it has also often been experienced by gentlemen in the management of their private affairs. It has been common in Ireland, and in London has created the wealth of the pawnbrokers. In the States at the present time the government is very much in this condition. The prospective wealth of the country is almost unbounded, but there is great difficulty in persuading any pawnbroker to advance money on the pledge. In February last Mr. Chase was driven to obtain the sanction of the legislature for paying the national creditors by bills drawn at twelve months' date, and bearing 6 per cent. interest. It is the old story of the tailor who calls with his little account, and draws on his insolvent debtor at ninety days. If the insolvent debtor be not utterly gone as regards solvency he will take up the bill when due, even though he may not be able to pay a simple debt. But then, if he be utterly insolvent, he can do neither the one nor the other! The Secretary of the Treasury, when he asked for permission to accept these bills,—or to issue these certificates, as he calls them,—acknowledged to pressing debts of over five millions sterling which he could not pay; and to further debts of eight millions which he could not pay, but which he termed floating;—debts, if I understand him, which were not as yet quite pressing. Now I imagine that to be a lamentable condition for any Chancellor of an Exchequer,—especially as a confession is at the same time made that no advantageous borrowing is to be done under the existing circumstances. When a Chancellor of the Exchequer confesses that he cannot borrow on advantageous terms, the terms within his reach must be very bad indeed. This position is indeed a sad one, and at any rate justifies me in stating that the immediate want of funds is severely felt.

But the very arguments which have been used to prove that the country will be ultimately crushed by the debt, are those which I should use to prove that it will not be crushed. A comparison has more than once been made between the manner in which our debt was made, and that in which the debt of the United States is now being created; and the great point raised in our favour is, that while we were borrowing money we were also taxing ourselves, and that we raised as much by taxes as we did by loans. But it is too early in the day to deny to the Americans the credit which we thus take to ourselves. We were a tax-paying nation when we commenced those wars which made our great loans necessary, and only went on in that practice which was habitual to us. I do not think that the Americans could have taxed themselves with greater alacrity than they have shown. Let us wait, at any rate, till they shall have had time for the operation, before we blame them for not making it. It is then argued that we in England did not borrow nearly so fast as they have borrowed in the States. That is true. But it must be remembered that the dimensions and proportions of wars now are infinitely greater than they were when we began to borrow. Does any one imagine that we would not have borrowed faster, if by faster borrowing we could have closed the war more speedily? Things go faster now than they did then. Borrowing for the sake of a war may be a bad thing to do, — as also it may be a good thing; but if it be done at all, it should be so done as to bring the war to the end with what greatest despatch may be possible.

The only fair comparison, as it seems to me, which can be drawn between the two countries with reference to their debts, and the condition of each under its debt, should be made to depend on the amount of the debt and probable ability of the country to bear that burden. The amount of the debt must be calculated by the interest payable on it, rather than by the figures representing the actual sum due. If we debit the United States Government with seven per cent. on all the money borrowed by them, and presume that amount to have reached in July, 1863, the sum named by Mr. Spaulding, they will then have loaded themselves with an annual charge of £16,800,000 sterling. It will have been an immense achievement to have accomplished in so short a time, but it will by no means equal the annual sum with which we are charged. And, moreover, the comparison will have been made in a manner that is hardly fair to the Americans. We pay our creditors three per cent. now that we have arranged our affairs, and have settled down into the respectable position of an old gentleman whose estates, though deeply mortgaged, are not over-mortgaged. But we did not get our money at three per cent. while our wars were on hand, and there yet existed some doubt as to the manner in which they might be terminated.

This attempt, however, at guessing what may be the probable amount of the debt at the close of the war is absolutely futile. No one can as yet conjecture when the war may be over, or what collateral expenses may attend its close. It may be the case that the government in fixing some boundary between the future United States and the future southern Confederacy, will be called on to advance a very large sum of money as compensation for slaves who shall have been liberated in the border States, or have been swept down south into the cotton regions with the retreating hordes of the southern army. The total of the bill cannot be reckoned up while the work is still unfinished. But, after all, that question as to the amount of the bill is not to us the question of the greatest interest. Whether the debt shall amount to two, or three, or even to four hundred millions sterling,—whether it remain fixed at its present modest dimensions, or swell itself out to the magnificent proportions of our British debt,—will the resources of the country enable it to bear such a burden? Will it be found that the Americans share with us that elastic power of endurance which has enabled us to bear a weight that would have ruined any other people of the same number? Have they the thews and muscles, the energy and endurance, the power of carrying which we possess? They have got our blood in their veins, and have these qualities gone with the blood? It is of little avail either to us or to the truth that we can show some difference between our position and their position which may seem to be in our favour. They, doubtless, could show other points of difference on the other side. With us, in the early years of this century, it was a contest for life and death, in which we could not stop to count the cost,—in which we believed that we were fighting for all that we cared to call our own, and in which we were resolved that we would not be beaten, as long as we had a man to fight and a guinea to spend. Fighting in this mind we won. Had we fought in any other mind, I think I may say that we should not have won. To the Americans of the northern States this also is a contest for life and death. I will not here stay to argue whether this need have been so. I think they are right; but this at least must be accorded to them—that having gone into this matter of civil war, it behoves them to finish it with credit to themselves. There are many Englishmen who think that we were wrong to undertake the French war; but there is, I take it, no Englishman who thinks that we ought to have allowed ourselves to be beaten when we had undertaken it. To the Americans it is now a contest of life and death. They also cannot stop to count the cost. They also will go on as long as they have a dollar to spend or a man to fight.

It appears that we were paying fourteen millions a year interest on our national debt in the year 1796. I take this statement from an article in "The Times," in which the question of the finances of the United States is handled. But our population in 1796 was only sixteen millions. I estimate the population of the northern section of the United States, as the States will be after the war, at twenty-two millions. In the article alluded to these northern Americans are now stated to be twenty millions. If then we, in 1796, could pay fourteen millions a year with a population of sixteen millions, the United States, with a population of twenty or twenty-two millions, will be able to pay the sixteen or seventeen millions sterling of interest which will become due from them,—if their circumstances of payment are as good as were ours. They can do that and more than that if they have the same means per man as we had. And as the means per man resolves itself at last into the labour per man, it may be said that they can pay what we could pay, if they can and will work as hard as we could and did work. That which did not crush us will not crush them, if their future energy be equal to our past energy.

And on this question of energy I think that there is no need for doubt. Taking man for man and million for million, the Americans are equal to the English in intellect and industry. They create wealth at any rate as fast as we have done. They develop their resources, and open out the currents of trade, with an energy equal to our own. They are always at work, improving, utilizing, and creating. Austria, as I take it, is succumbing to monetary difficulties, not because she has been extravagant, but because she has been slow at progress;—because it has been the work of her rulers to repress rather than encourage the energies of her people; because she does not improve, utilize, and create. England has mastered her monetary difficulties because the genius of her government and her people has been exactly opposite to the genius of Austria. And the States of America will master their money difficulties, because they are born of England, and are not born of Austria. What! Shall our eldest child become bankrupt in its first trade difficulty; be utterly ruined by its first little commercial embarrassment? The child bears much too strong a resemblance to its parent for me to think so.

CHAPTER XIII
THE POST-OFFICE

Any Englishman or Frenchman residing in the American States cannot fail to be struck with the inferiority of the Post-office arrangements in that country to those by which they are accommodated in their own country. I have not been a resident in the States, and as a traveller might probably have passed the subject without special remark, were it not that the service of the Post-office has been my own profession for many years. I could therefore hardly fail to observe things which to another man would have been of no material moment. At first I was inclined to lean heavily in my judgment upon the deficiencies of a department which must be of primary importance to a commercial nation. It seemed that among a people so intelligent, and so quick in all enterprises of trade, a well arranged Post-office would have been held to be absolutely necessary, and that all difficulties would have been made to succumb in their efforts to put that establishment, if no other, upon a proper footing. But as I looked into the matter, and in becoming acquainted with the circumstances of the Post-office learned the extent of the difficulties absolutely existing, I began to think that a very great deal had been done, and that the fault, as to that which had been left undone, rested, not with the Post-office officials, but was attributable partly to political causes altogether outside the Post-office, and partly,—perhaps chiefly,—to the nature of the country itself.

It is, I think, undoubtedly true that the amount of accommodation given by the Post-office of the States is small,—as compared with that afforded in some other countries, and that that accommodation is lessened by delays and uncertainty. The point which first struck me was the inconvenient hours at which mails were brought in and despatched. Here, in England, it is the object of our Post-office to carry the bulk of our letters at night; to deliver them as early as possible in the morning, and to collect them and take them away for despatch as late as may be in the day;—so that the merchant may receive his letters before the beginning of his day's business, and despatch them after its close. The bulk of our letters is handled in this manner, and the advantage of such an arrangement is manifest. But it seemed that in the States no such practice prevailed. Letters arrived at any hour in the day miscellaneously, and were despatched at any hour, and I found that the postmaster at one town could never tell me with certainty when letters would arrive at another. If the towns were distant, I would be told that the conveyance might take about two or three days; if they were near, that my letter would get to hand "some time to-morrow." I ascertained, moreover, by painful experience that the whole of a mail would not always go forward by the first despatch. As regarded myself this had reference chiefly to English letters and newspapers.—"Only a part of the mail has come," the clerk would tell me. With us the owners of that part which did not "come," would consider themselves greatly aggrieved and make loud complaint. But, in the States, complaints made against official departments are held to be of little moment.

Letters also in the States are subject to great delays by irregularities on railways. One train does not hit the town of its destination before another train, to which it is nominally fitted, has been started on its journey. The mail trains are not bound to wait; and thus, in the large cities, far distant from New York, great irregularity prevails. It is, I think, owing to this,— at any rate partly to this,—that the system of telegraphing has become so prevalent. It is natural that this should be so between towns which are in the due course of post perhaps forty-eight hours asunder; but the uncertainty of the post increases the habit, to the profit, of course, of the companies which own the wires,—but to the manifest loss of the Post-office.

But the deficiency which struck me most forcibly in the American Post-office, was the absence of any recognized official delivery of letters. The United States Post-office does not assume to itself the duty of taking letters to the houses of those for whom they are intended, but holds itself as having completed the work for which the original postage has been paid, when it has brought them to the window of the Post-office of the town to which they are addressed. It is true that in most large towns,—though by no means in all,—a separate arrangement is made by which a delivery is afforded to those who are willing to pay a further sum for that further service; but the recognized official mode of delivery is from the office window. The merchants and persons in trade have boxes at the windows, for which they pay. Other old-established inhabitants in towns, and persons in receipt of a considerable correspondence, receive their letters by the subsidiary carriers and pay for them separately. But the poorer classes of the community, those persons among which it is of such paramount importance to increase the blessing of letter writing, obtain their letters from the Post-office windows.

In each of these cases the practice acts to the prejudice of the department. In order to escape the tax on delivery, which varies from two cents to one cent a letter, all men in trade, and many who are not in trade, hold office boxes; consequently immense space is required. The space given at Chicago, both to the public without and to the officials within, for such delivery, is more than four times that required at Liverpool for the same purpose. But Liverpool is three times the size of Chicago. The corps of clerks required for the window delivery is very great, and the whole affair is cumbrous in the extreme. The letters at most offices are given out through little windows, to which the inquirer is obliged to stoop. There he finds himself opposite to a pane of glass with a little hole; and when the clerk within shakes his head at him, he rarely believes but what his letters are there if he could only reach them. But in the second case, the tax on the delivery, which is intended simply to pay the wages of the men who take them out, is paid with a bad grace; it robs the letter of its charm, and forces it to present itself in the guise of a burden. It makes that disagreeable which for its own sake the Post-office should strive in every way to make agreeable. This practice, moreover, operates as a direct prevention to a class of correspondence, which furnishes in England a large proportion of the revenue of the Post-office. Mercantile houses in our large cities send out thousands of trade circulars, paying postage on them; but such circulars would not be received, either in England or elsewhere, if a demand for postage were made on their delivery. Who does not receive these circulars in our country by the dozen, consigning them generally to the waste-paper basket, after a most cursory inspection? As regards the sender, the transaction seems to us often to be very vain; but the Post-office gets its penny. So also would the American Post-office get its three cents.

But the main objection in my eyes to the American Post-office system is this,—that it is not brought nearer to the poorer classes. Everybody writes or can write in America, and therefore the correspondence of their millions should be, million for million, at any rate equal to ours. But it is not so: and this, I think, comes from the fact that communication by Post-office is not made easy to the people generally. Such communication is not found to be easy by a man who has to attend at a Post-office window on the chance of receiving a letter. When no arrangement more comfortable than that is provided, the Post-office will be used for the necessities of letter-writing, but will not be esteemed as a luxury. And thus not only do the people lose a comfort which they might enjoy, but the Post-office also loses that revenue which it might make.

I have said that the correspondence circulating in the United States is less than that of the United Kingdom. In making any comparison between them I am obliged to arrive at facts, or rather at the probabilities of facts, in a somewhat circuitous mode, as the Americans have kept no account of the number of letters which pass through their post-offices in a year. We can, however, make an estimate which, if incorrect, shall not at any rate be incorrect against them. The gross postal revenue of the United States, for the year ended 30th June, 1861, was in round figures £1,700,000. This was the amount actually earned, exclusive of a sum of £140,000 paid to the Post-office by the government for the carriage of what is called in that country free mail matter; otherwise, books, letters, and parcels franked by members of Congress. The gross postal revenue of the United Kingdom was in the last year, in round figures, £3,358,000, exclusive of a sum of £179,000 claimed as earned for carrying official postage, and also exclusive of £127,866, that being the amount of money order commission which in this country is considered a part of the Post-office revenue. In the United States there is at present no money order office. In the United Kingdom the sum of £3,358,000 was earned by the conveyance and delivery of

593   millions of letters,
73   millions of newspapers,
12   millions of books.

What number of each was conveyed through the post in the United States we have no means of knowing; but presuming the average rate of postage on each letter in the States to be the same as it is in England, and presuming also that letters, newspapers, and books circulated in the same proportion there as they do with us, the sum above named of £1,700,000 will have been earned by carrying about 300 millions of letters. But the average rate of postage in the States is, in fact, higher than it is in England. The ordinary single rate of postage there is three cents or three half-pence, whereas with us it is a penny; and if three half-pence might be taken as the average rate in the United States, the number of letters would be reduced from 300 to 200 millions a year. There is however a class of letters which in the States are passed through the Post-office at the rate of one halfpenny a letter, whereas there is no rate of postage with us less than a penny. Taking these halfpenny letters into consideration, I am disposed to regard the average rate of American postage at about five farthings, which would give the number of letters at 250 millions. We shall at any rate be safe in saying that the number is considerably less than 300 millions, and that it does not amount to half the number circulated with us. But the difference between our population and their population is not great. The population of the States during the year in question was about 27 millions, exclusive of slaves, and that of the British isles was about 29 millions. No doubt, in the year named, the correspondence of the States had been somewhat disturbed by the rebellion; but that disturbance, up to the end of June, 1861, had been very trifling. The division of the southern from the northern States, as far as the Post-office was concerned, did not take place till the end of May, 1861; and therefore but one month in the year was affected by the actual secession of the South. The gross postal revenue of the States which have seceded was, for the year prior to secession, twelve hundred thousand five hundred dollars, and for that one month of June it would therefore have been a little over one hundred thousand dollars, or £20,000. That sum may therefore be presumed to have been abstracted by secession from the gross annual revenue of the Post-office. Trade, also, was no doubt injured by the disturbance in the country, and the circulation of letters was, as a matter of course, to some degree affected by this injury; but it seems that the gross revenue of 1861 was less than that of 1860 by only one thirty-sixth. I think, therefore, that we may say, making all allowance that can be fairly made, that the number of letters circulating in the United Kingdom is more than double that which circulates, or ever has circulated, in the United States.

That this is so, I attribute not to any difference in the people of the two countries,—not to an aptitude for letter writing among us which is wanting with the Americans,—but to the greater convenience and wider accommodation of our own Post-office. As I have before stated, and will presently endeavour to show, this wider accommodation is not altogether the result of better management on our part. Our circumstances as regards the Post-office have had in them less of difficulties than theirs. But it has arisen in great part from better management; and in nothing is their deficiency so conspicuous as in the absence of a free delivery for their letters.

In order that the advantages of the Post-office should reach all persons, the delivery of letters should extend not only to towns, but to the country also. In France all letters are delivered free. However remote may be the position of a house or cottage, it is not too remote for the postman. With us all letters are not delivered; but the exceptions refer to distant solitary houses and to localities which are almost without correspondence. But in the United States there is no free delivery, and there is no delivery at all except in the large cities. In small towns, in villages, even in the suburbs of the largest cities, no such accommodation is given. Whatever may be the distance, people expecting letters must send for them to the Post-office;— and they who do not expect them, leave their letters uncalled for. Brother Jonathan goes out to fish in these especial waters with a very large net. The little fish, which are profitable, slip through; but the big fish, which are by no means profitable, are caught,—often at an expense greater than their value.

There are other smaller sins upon which I could put my finger,— and would do so were I writing an official report upon the subject of the American Post-office. In lieu of doing so, I will endeavour to explain how much the States' office has done in this matter of affording Post-office accommodation,—and how great have been the difficulties in the way of Post-office reformers in that country.

In the first place, when we compare ourselves to them, we must remember that we live in a tea-cup, and they in a washing-tub. As compared with them we inhabit towns which are close to each other. Our distances, as compared with theirs, are nothing. From London to Liverpool the line of railway traverses about two hundred miles, but the mail train which conveys the bags for Liverpool, carries the correspondence of probably four or five millions of persons. The mail train from New York to Buffalo passes over about four hundred miles, and on its route serves not one million. A comparison of this kind might be made with the same effect between any of our great internal mail routes and any of theirs. Consequently, the expense of conveyance to them is, per letter, very much greater than with us, and the American Post-office is as a matter of necessity driven to an economy in the use of railways for the Post-office service, which we are not called on to practise. From New York to Chicago is nearly 1000 miles. From New York to St. Louis is over 1600. I need not say that in England we know nothing of such distances, and that therefore our task has been comparatively easy. Nevertheless the States have followed in our track, and have taken advantage of Sir Rowland Hill's wise audacity in the reduction of postage with greater quickness than any other nation but our own. Through all the States letters pass for three cents over a distance less than 3000 miles. For distances above 3000 miles the rate is ten cents or five-pence. This increased rate has special reference to the mails for California, which are carried daily across the whole continent at a cost to the States Government of two hundred thousand pounds a year.

With us the chief mail trains are legally under the management of the Postmaster-General. He fixes the hours at which they shall start and arrive, being of course bound by certain stipulations as to pace. He can demand trains to run over any line at any hour, and can in this way secure the punctuality of mail transportation. Of course such interference on the part of a government official in the working of a railway is attended with a very heavy expense to the Government. Though the British Post-office can demand the use of trains at any hour, and as regards those trains can make the despatch of mails paramount to all other matters, the British Post-office cannot fix the price to be paid for such work. This is generally done by arbitration, and of course for such services the payment is very high. No such practice prevails in the States. The Government has no power of using the mail lines as they are used by our Post-office, nor could the expense of such a practice be borne or nearly borne by the proceeds of letters in the

States. Consequently the Post-office is put on a par with ordinary customers, and such trains are used for mail matter as the directors of each line may see fit to use for other matter. Hence it occurs that no offence against the Post-office is committed when the connection between different mail trains is broken. The Post-office takes the best it can get, paying as other customers pay, and grumbling as other customers grumble when the service rendered falls short of that which has been promised.

It may, I think, easily be seen that any system such as ours, carried across so large a country, would go on increasing in cost at an enormous ratio. The greater the distance, the greater is the difficulty in securing the proper fitting of fast-running trains. And moreover, it must be remembered that the American lines have been got up on a very different footing from ours, at an expense per mile of probably less than a fifth of that laid out on our railways. Single lines of rail are common, even between great towns with large traffic. At the present moment—May, 1862—the only railway running into Washington, that namely from Baltimore, is a single line over the greater distance. The whole thing is necessarily worked at a cheaper rate than with us; not because the people are poorer, but because the distances are greater. As this is the case throughout the whole railway system of the country, it cannot be expected that such despatch and punctuality should be achieved in America as are achieved here, in England, or in France. As population and wealth increase, it will come. In the mean time that which has been already done over the extent of the vast North American continent is very wonderful. I think, therefore, that complaint should not be made against the Washington Post-office, either on account of the inconvenience of the hours, or on the head of occasional irregularity. So much has been done in reducing the rate to three cents, and in giving a daily mail throughout the States, that the department should be praised for energy, and not blamed for apathy.

In the year ended 30th June, 1861, the gross revenue of the Post-office of the States was, as I have stated, £1,700,000. In the same year its expenditure was in round figures £2,720,000. Consequently there was an actual loss, to be made up out of general taxation, amounting to £1,020,000. In the accounts of the American officers this is lessened by £140,000, that sum having been arbitrarily fixed by the Government as the amount earned by the Post-office in carrying free mail matter. We have a similar system in computing the value of the service rendered by our Post-office to the Government in carrying government despatches; but with us the amount named as the compensation depends on the actual weight carried. If the matter so carried be carried solely on the Government service, as is I believe the case with us, any such claim on behalf of the Post-office is apparently unnecessary.

The Crown works for the Crown, as the right hand works for the left. The Post-office pays no rates or taxes, contributes nothing to the poor, runs its mails on turnpike roads free of toll, and gives receipts on unstamped paper. With us no payment is in truth made, though the Post-office in its accounts presumes itself to have received the money. But in the States the sum named is handed over by the State Treasury to the Post-office Treasury. Any such statement of credit does not in effect alter the real fact, that over a million sterling is required as a subsidy by the American Post-office, in order that it may be enabled to pay its way. In estimating the expenditure of the office the department at Washington debits itself with the sums paid for the ocean transit of its mails, amounting to something over £150,000. We also now do the same, with the much greater sum paid by us for such service, which now amounts to £949,228, or nearly a million sterling. Till lately this was not paid out of the Post-office moneys, and the Post-office revenue was not debited with the amount.

Our gross Post-office revenue is, as I have said, £3,358,250. As before explained, this is exclusive of the amount earned by the money order department, which, though managed by the authorities of the Post-office, cannot be called a part of the Post-office; and exclusive also of the official postage, which is, in fact, never received. The expenditure of our British Post-office, inclusive of the sum paid for the ocean mail service, is £3,064,527. We therefore make a net profit of £293,723 out of the Post-office, as compared with a loss of £1,020,000, on the part of the United States.

But perhaps the greatest difficulty with which the American Post-office is burdened, is that "free mail matter" to which I have alluded, for carrying which, the Post-office claims to earn £140,000, and for the carriage of which, it might as fairly claim to earn £1,350,000, or half the amount of its total expenditure, for I was informed by a gentleman whose knowledge on the subject could not be doubted, that the free mail matter so carried, equalled in bulk and weight all that other matter which was not carried free. To such an extent has the privilege of franking been carried in the States! All members of both Houses frank what they please, — for in effect the privilege is stretched to that extent. All Presidents of the Union, past and present, can frank, as, also, all Vice-Presidents, past and present; and there is a special act, enabling the widow of President Polk to frank! Why it is that widows of other Presidents do not agitate on the matter, I cannot understand. And all the Secretaries of State can frank; and ever so many other public officers. There is no limit in number to the letters so franked, and the nuisance has extended itself to so huge a size, that members of Congress in giving franks, cannot write the franks themselves. It is illegal for them to depute to others the privilege of signing their names for this purpose, but it is known at the

Post-office that it is done. But even this is not the worst of it. Members of the House of Representatives have the power of sending through the post all those huge books which, with them as with us, grow out of Parliamentary debates and workings of Committees. This, under certain stipulations, is the case also in England; but in England, luckily, no one values them. In America, however, it is not so. A voter considers himself to be noticed if he gets a book. He likes to have the book bound, and the bigger the book may be, the more the compliment is relished. Hence it comes to pass that an enormous quantity of useless matter is printed and bound, only that it may be sent down to constituents and make a show on the parlour shelves of constituents' wives. The Post-office groans and becomes insolvent, and the country pays for the paper, the printing, and the binding. While the public expenses of the nation were very small, there was, perhaps, no reason why voters should not thus be indulged; but now the matter is different, and it would be well that the conveyance by post of these Congressional libraries should be brought to an end. I was also assured that members very frequently obtain permission for the printing of a speech which has never been delivered,—and which never will be delivered,—in order that copies may be circulated among their constituents. There is in such an arrangement an ingenuity which is peculiarly American in its nature. Everybody concerned is no doubt cheated by the system. The constituents are cheated; the public, which pays, is cheated; and the Post-office is cheated. But the House is spared the hearing of the speech, and the result on the whole is perhaps beneficial.

We also, within the memory of many of us, had a franking privilege, which was peculiarly objectionable inasmuch as it operated towards giving a free transmission of their letters by post to the rich, while no such privilege was within reach of the poor. But with us it never stretched itself to such an extent as it has now achieved in the States. The number of letters for members was limited. The whole address was written by the franking member himself, and not much was sent in this way that was bulky. I am disposed to think that all government and Congressional jobs in the States bear the same proportion to government and Parliamentary jobs which have been in vogue among us. There has been an unblushing audacity in the public dishonesty,—what I may perhaps call the State dishonesty,—at Washington, which I think was hardly ever equalled in London. Bribery, I know, was disgracefully current in the days of Walpole, of Newcastle, and even of Castlereagh;—so current, that no Englishman has a right to hold up his own past government as a model of purity. But the corruption with us did blush and endeavour to hide itself. It was disgraceful to be bribed, if not so to offer bribes. But at Washington corruption has been so common that

I can hardly understand how any honest man can have held up his head in the vicinity of the Capitol, or of the State office.

But the country has, I think, become tired of this. Hitherto it has been too busy about its more important concerns, in extending commerce, in making railways, in providing education for its youth, to think very much of what was being done at Washington. While the taxes were light and property was secure, while increasing population gave daily increasing strength to the nation, the people as a body were content with that theory of being governed by their little men. They gave a bad name to politicians, and allowed politics, as they say, "to slide." But all this will be altered now. The tremendous expenditure of the last twelve months has allowed dishonesty of so vast a grasp to make its ravages in the public pockets, that the evil will work its own cure. Taxes will be very high, and the people will recognize the necessity of having honest men to look after them. The nation can no longer afford to be indifferent about its Government, and will require to know where its money goes, and why it goes. This franking privilege is already doomed, if not already dead. When I was in Washington a Bill was passed through the Lower House by which it would be abolished altogether. When I left America its fate in the Senate was still doubtful, and I was told by many that that Bill would not be allowed to become law without sundry alterations. But, nevertheless, I regard the franking privilege as doomed, and offer to the Washington Post-office officials my best congratulations on their coming deliverance.

The Post-office in the States is also burdened by another terrible political evil, which in itself is so heavy, that one would at first sight declare it to be enough to prevent anything like efficiency. The whole of its staff is removeable every fourth year,—that is to say, on the election of every new President. And a very large proportion of its staff is thus removed periodically to make way for those for whom a new President is bound to provide, by reason of their services in sending him to the White House. They have served him and he thus repays them by this use of his patronage in their favour. At four hundred and thirty-four Post-offices in the States,— those being the offices to which the highest salaries are attached,—the President has this power, and exercises it as a matter of course. He has the same power with reference, I believe, to all the appointments held in the Post-office at Washington. This practice applies by no means to the Post-office only. All the government clerks,—clerks employed by the central government at Washington,—are subject to the same rule. And the rule has also been adopted in the various States with reference to State offices.

To a stranger this practice seems so manifestly absurd, that he can hardly conceive it possible that a government service should be conducted on such terms. He cannot, in the first place, believe that men of sufficient standing before the world could be found to accept office under such circumstances; and is led to surmise that men of insufficient standing must be employed, and that there are other allurements to the office beyond the very moderate salaries which are allowed. He cannot, moreover, understand how the duties can be conducted, seeing that men must be called on to resign their places as soon as they have learned to make themselves useful. And, finally, he is lost in amazement as he contemplates this barefaced prostitution of the public employ to the vilest purposes of political manœuvring. With us also patronage has been used for political purposes, and to some small extent is still so used. We have not yet sufficiently recognized the fact, that in selecting a public servant nothing should be regarded but the advantage of the service in which he is to be employed. But we never, in the lowest times of our political corruption, ventured to throw over the question of service altogether, and to declare publicly, that the one and only result to be obtained by Government employment was political support. In the States political corruption has become so much a matter of course, that no American seems to be struck with the fact that the whole system is a system of robbery.

From sheer necessity some of the old hands are kept on when these changes are made. Were this not done the work would come absolutely to a dead lock. But it may be imagined how difficult it must be for men to carry through any improvements in a great department, when they have entered an office under such a system, and are liable to be expelled under the same. It is greatly to the praise of those who have been allowed to grow old in the service that so much has been done. No men, however, are more apt at such work than Americans, or more able to exert themselves at their posts. They are not idle. Independently of any question of remuneration, they are not indifferent to the well-being of the work they have in hand. They are good public servants, unless corruption come in their way.

While speaking on the subject of patronage, I cannot but allude to two appointments which had been made by political interest, and with the circumstances of which I became acquainted. In both instances a good place had been given to a gentleman by the incoming President,—not in return for political support, but from motives of private friendship,—either his own friendship or that of some mutual friend. In both instances I heard the selection spoken of with the warmest praise, as though a noble act had been done in the nomination of a private friend instead of a political partisan. And yet in each case a man was appointed who knew nothing of his work; who, from age and circumstances, was not likely to become acquainted with his work; who, by his appointment, kept out of the place those who did understand the work, and had earned a right to promotion by so understanding it. Two worthy gentlemen,—for they were both worthy,— were pensioned on the government for a term of years under a false pretence. That this should have been done is not perhaps remarkable; but it did seem remarkable to me that everybody regarded such appointments as a good deed—as a deed so exceptionably good as to be worthy of great praise. I do not allude to these selections on account of the political vice shown by the Presidents in making them, but on account of the political virtue;—in order that the nature of political virtue in the States may be understood. It had never occurred to any one to whom I spoke on the subject, that a President in bestowing such places was bound to look for efficient work in return for the public money which was to be paid.

Before I end this chapter I must insert a few details respecting the Post-office of the States, which, though they may not be specially interesting to the general reader, will give some idea of the extent of the department. The total number of post-offices in the States on 30th June, 1861, was 28,586. With us the number in England, Scotland, and Ireland, at the same period was about 11,400. The population served may be regarded as nearly the same. Our lowest salary is £3 per annum. In the States the remuneration is often much lower. It consists of a commission on the letters, and is sometimes less than ten shillings a year. The difficulty of obtaining persons to hold these offices, and the amount of work which must thereby be thrown on what is called the "appointment branch," may be judged by the fact that 9235 of these offices were filled up by new nominations during the last year. When the patronage is of such a nature it is difficult to say which give most trouble, the places which nobody wishes to have, or those which everybody wishes to have.

The total amount of postage on European letters, *i.e.*, letters passing between the States and Europe, in the last year as to which accounts were kept between Washington and the European post-offices, was £275,000. Of this over £150,000 was on letters for the United Kingdom; and £130,000 was on letters carried by the Cunard packets.

According to the accounts kept by the Washington office, the letters passing from the States to Europe and from Europe to the States are very nearly equal in number, about 101 going to Europe for every 100 received from Europe. But the number of newspapers sent from the States is more than double the number received in the States from Europe.

On 30th June, 1861, mails were carried through the then loyal States of the Union over 140,400 miles daily. Up to 31st May preceding, at which time the

Government mails were running all through the United States, 96,000 miles were covered in those States which had then virtually seceded, and which in the following month were taken out from the Post-office accounts,—making a total of 236,400 miles daily. Of this mileage something less than one third is effected by railways, at an average cost of about sixpence a mile. Our total mileage per day is 151,000 miles, of which 43,823 are done by railway, at a cost of about sevenpence-halfpenny per mile.

As far as I could learn the servants of the Post-office are less liberally paid in the States than with us,—excepting as regards two classes. The first of these is that class which is paid by weekly wages,—such as letter-carriers and porters. Their remuneration is of course ruled by the rate of ordinary wages in the country; and as ordinary wages are higher in the States than with us, such men are paid accordingly. The other class is that of postmasters at second-rate towns. They receive the same compensation as those at the largest towns;—unless indeed there be other compensation than those written in the books at Washington. A postmaster is paid a certain commission on letters, till it amounts to £400 per annum: all above that going back to the Government. So also out of the fees paid for boxes at the window he receives any amount forthcoming, not exceeding £400 a year; making in all a maximum of £800. The postmaster of New York can get no more. But any moderately large town will give as much, and in this way an amount of patronage is provided which in a political view is really valuable.

But with all this the people have made their way, because they have been intelligent, industrious, and in earnest. And as the people have made their way, so has the Post-office. The number of its offices, the mileage it covers, its extraordinary cheapness, the rapidity with which it has been developed, are all proofs of great things done; and it is by no means standing still even in these evil days of war. Improvements are even now on foot, copied in a great measure from ourselves. Hitherto the American office has not taken upon itself the task of returning to their writers undelivered and undeliverable letters. This it is now going to do. It is, as I have said, shaking off from itself that terrible incubus the franking privilege. And the expediency of introducing a money-order office into the States, connected with the Post-office as it is with us, is even now under consideration. Such an accommodation is much needed in the country; but I doubt whether the present moment, looking at the fiscal state of the country, is well adapted for establishing it.

I was much struck by the great extravagance in small things manifested by the Post-office through the States, and have reason to believe that the same remark would be equally true with regard to other public establishments. They use needless forms without end,—making millions of entries which no one is ever expected to regard. Their expenditure in stationery might, I think, be reduced by one half, and the labour might be saved which is now wasted in the abuse of that useless stationery. Their mail-bags are made in a costly manner, and are often large beyond all proportion or necessity. I could greatly lengthen this list if I were addressing myself solely to Post-office people; but as I am not doing so, I will close these semi-official remarks with an assurance to my colleagues in Post-office work on the other side of the water that I greatly respect what they have done, and trust that before long they may have renewed opportunities for the prosecution of their good work.

CHAPTER XIV
AMERICAN HOTELS

I find it impossible to resist the subject of inns. As I have gone on with my journey, I have gone on with my book, and have spoken here and there of American hotels as I have encountered them. But in the States the hotels are so large an institution, having so much closer and wider a bearing on social life than they do in any other country, that I feel myself bound to treat them in a separate chapter as a great national feature in themselves. They are quite as much thought of in the nation as the legislature, or judicature, or literature of the country; and any falling off in them, or any improvement in the accommodation given, would strike the community as forcibly as a change in the constitution, or an alteration in the franchise.

Moreover I consider myself as qualified to write a chapter on hotels;— not only on the hotels of America but on hotels generally. I have myself been much too frequently a sojourner at hotels. I think I know what an hotel should be, and what it should not be; and am almost inclined to believe, in my pride, that I could myself fill the position of a landlord with some chance of social success, though probably with none of satisfactory pecuniary results.

Of all hotels known to me, I am inclined to think that the Swiss are the best. The things wanted at an hotel are, I fancy, mainly as follows:—a clean bedroom with a good and clean bed,—and with it also plenty of water. Good food, well dressed and served at convenient hours, which hours should on occasions be allowed to stretch themselves. Wines that shall be drinkable. Quick attendance. Bills that shall not be absolutely extortionate, smiling faces, and an absence of foul smells. There are many who desire more than this;—who expect exquisite cookery, choice wines, subservient domestics, distinguished consideration, and the strictest economy. But they are uneducated travellers who are going through the apprenticeship of their hotel lives;—who may probably never become free of the travellers' guild, or learn to distinguish that which they may fairly hope to attain from that which they can never accomplish.

Taking them as a whole I think that the Swiss hotels are the best. They are perhaps a little close in the matter of cold water, but even as to this, they generally give way to pressure. The pressure, however, must not be violent, but gentle rather, and well continued. Their bedrooms are excellent. Their cookery is good, and to the outward senses is cleanly. The people are civil. The whole work of the house is carried on upon fixed rules which tend to the comfort of the establishment. They are not cheap, and not always quite honest. But the exorbitance or dishonesty of their charges rarely exceeds a certain reasonable scale, and hardly ever demands the bitter misery of a remonstrance.

The inns of the Tyrol are, I think, the cheapest I have known, affording the traveller what he requires for half the price, or less than half, that demanded in Switzerland. But the other half is taken out in stench and nastiness. As tourists scatter themselves more profusely, the prices of the Tyrol will no doubt rise. Let us hope that increased prices will bring with them besoms, scrubbing-brushes, and other much needed articles of cleanliness.

The inns of the north of Italy are very good, and indeed, the Italian inns throughout, as far as I know them, are much better than the name they bear. The Italians are a civil, kindly people, and do for you, at any rate, the best they can. Perhaps the unwary traveller may be cheated. Ignorant of the language, he may be called on to pay more than the man who speaks it, and who can bargain in the Italian fashion as to price. It has often been my lot, I doubt not, to be so cheated. But then I have been cheated with a grace that has been worth all the money. The ordinary prices of Italian inns are by no means high.

I have seldom thoroughly liked the inns of Germany which I have known. They are not clean, and water is very scarce. Smiles too are generally wanting, and I have usually fancied myself to be regarded as a piece of goods out of which so much profit was to be made.

The dearest hotels I know are the French;—and certainly not the best. In the provinces they are by no means so cleanly as those of Italy. Their wines are generally abominable, and their cookery often disgusting. In Paris grand dinners may no doubt be had, and luxuries of every description,— except the luxury of comfort. Cotton-velvet sofas and ormolu clocks stand in the place of convenient furniture, and logs of wood, at a franc a log, fail to impart to you the heat which the freezing cold of a Paris winter demands. They used to make good coffee in Paris, but even that is a thing of the past. I fancy that they import their brandy from England, and manufacture their own cigars. French wines you may get good at a Paris hotel; but you would drink them as good and much cheaper if you bought them in London and took them with you.

The worst hotels I know are in the Havana. Of course I do not speak here of chance mountain huts, or small far-off roadside hostels in which the traveller may find himself from time to time. All such are to be counted apart, and must be judged on their merits, by the circumstances which surround them. But with reference to places of wide resort, nothing can beat the hotels of the Havana in filth, discomfort, habits of abomination, and absence of everything which the traveller desires. All the world does not go to the Havana, and the subject is not, therefore, one of general interest. But in speaking of hotels at large, so much I find myself bound to say.

In all the countries to which I have alluded the guests of the house are expected to sit down together at one table. Conversation is at any rate possible, and there is the show if not the reality of society.

And now one word as to English inns. I do not think that we Englishmen have any great right to be proud of them. The worst about them is that they deteriorate from year to year instead of becoming better. We used to hear much of the comfort of the old English wayside inn, but the old English wayside inn has gone. The railway hotel has taken its place, and the railway hotel is too frequently gloomy, desolate, comfortless, and almost suicidal. In England too, since the old days are gone, there are wanting the landlord's bow, and the kindly smile of his stout wife. Who now knows the landlord of an inn, or cares to inquire whether or no there be a landlady? The old welcome is wanting, and the cheery warm air which used to atone for the bad port and tough beef has passed away;—while the port is still bad and the beef too often tough.

In England, and only in England, as I believe, is maintained in hotel life the theory of solitary existence. The sojourner at an English inn,—unless he be a commercial traveller, and, as such, a member of a universal, peripatetic tradesman's club,—lives alone. He has his breakfast alone, his dinner alone, his pint of wine alone, and his cup of tea alone. It is not considered practicable that two strangers should sit at the same table, or cut from the same dish. Consequently his dinner is cooked for him separately, and the hotel keeper can hardly afford to give him a good dinner. He has two modes of life from which to choose. He either lives in a public room,—called a coffee-room,—and there occupies during his comfortless meal a separate small table too frequently removed from fire and light, though generally exposed to draughts; or else he indulges in the luxury of a private sitting-room, and endeavours to find solace on an old horse-hair sofa, at the cost of seven shillings a day. His bedroom is not so arranged that he can use it as a sitting-room. Under either phase of life he can rarely find himself comfortable, and therefore he lives as little at an hotel as the circumstances of his business or of his pleasure will allow. I do not think that any of the requisites of a good inn are habitually to be found in perfection at our Kings' Heads and White Horses, though the falling-off is not so lamentably distressing as it sometimes is in other countries. The bedrooms are dingy rather than dirty. Extra payment to servants will generally produce a tub of cold water. The food is never good, but it is usually eatable, and you may have it when you please. The wines are almost always bad, but the traveller can fall back upon beer. The attendance is good, provided always that the payment for it is liberal. The cost is generally too high, and unfortunately grows larger and larger from year to year. Smiling faces are out of the question unless specially paid for; and as to that matter of foul smells there is often room for improvement. An English inn to a solitary traveller without employment is an embodiment of dreary desolation. The excuse to be made for this is that English men and women do not live much at inns in their own country.

The American inn differs from all those of which I have made mention, and is altogether an institution apart, and a thing of itself. Hotels in America are very much larger and more numerous than in other countries. They are to be found in all towns, and I may almost say in all villages. In England and on the Continent we find them on the recognized routes of travel and in towns of commercial or social importance. On unfrequented roads and in villages there is usually some small house of public entertainment in which the unexpected traveller may obtain food and shelter, and in which the expected boon companions of the neighbourhood smoke their nightly pipes, and drink their nightly tipple. But in the States of America the first sign of an incipient settlement is an hotel five stories high, with an office, a bar, a cloak-room, three gentlemen's parlours, two ladies' parlours, a ladies' entrance, and two hundred bedrooms.

These, of course, are all built with a view to profit, and it may be presumed that in each case the originators of the speculation enter into some calculation as to their expected guests. Whence are to come the sleepers in those two hundred bedrooms, and who is to pay for the gaudy sofas and numerous lounging chairs of the ladies' parlours? In all other countries the expectation would extend itself simply to travellers;—to travellers or to strangers sojourning in the land. But this is by no means the case as to these speculations in America. When the new hotel rises up in the wilderness, it is presumed that people will come there with the express object of inhabiting it. The hotel itself will create a population,—as the railways do. With us railways run to the towns; but in the States the towns run to the railways. It is the same thing with the hotels.

Housekeeping is not popular with young married people in America, and there are various reasons why this should be so. Men there are not fixed in their employment as they are with us. If a young Benedict cannot get along as a lawyer at Salem, perhaps he may thrive as a shoemaker at Thermopylæ. Jefferson B. Johnson fails in the lumber line at Eleutheria, but hearing of an opening for a Baptist preacher at Big Mud Creek moves himself off with his wife and three children at a week's notice. Aminadab Wiggs takes an engagement as a clerk at a steam-boat office on the Pongowonga river, but he goes to his employment with an inward conviction that six months will see him earning his bread elsewhere. Under such circumstances even a large wardrobe is a nuisance, and a collection of furniture would be as appropriate as a drove of elephants. Then, again, young men and women marry without any means already collected on which to commence their life. They are content to look forward and to hope that such means will come. In so doing they are guilty of no imprudence. It is the way of the country; and, if the man be useful for anything, employment will certainly come to him. But he must live on the fruits of that employment, and can only pay his way from week to week and from day to day. And as a third reason I think I may allege that the mode of life found in these hotels is liked by the people who frequent them. It is to their taste. They are happy, or at any rate contented, at these hotels, and do not wish for household cares. As to the two first reasons which I have given I can agree as to the necessity of the case, and quite concur as to the expediency of marriage under such circumstances. But as to that matter of taste, I cannot concur at all. Anything more forlorn than a young married woman at an American hotel, it is impossible to conceive.

Such are the guests expected for those two hundred bedrooms. The chance travellers are but chance additions to these, and are not generally the main stay of the house. As a matter of course the accommodation for travellers which these hotels afford increases and creates travelling. Men come because they know they will be fed and bedded at a moderate cost, and in an easy way, suited to their tastes. With us, and throughout Europe, inquiry is made before an unaccustomed journey is commenced, on that serious question of wayside food and shelter. But in the States no such question is needed. A big hotel is a matter of course, and therefore men travel. Everybody travels in the States. The railways and the hotels have between them so churned up the people that an untravelled man or woman is a rare animal. We are apt to suppose that travellers make roads, and that guests create hotels; but the cause and effect run exactly in the other way. I am almost disposed to think that we should become cannibals if gentlemen's legs and ladies' arms were hung up for sale in purveyors' shops.

After this fashion and with these intentions hotels are built. Size and an imposing exterior are the first requisitions. Everything about them must be on a large scale. A commanding exterior, and a certain interior dignity of demeanour is more essential than comfort or civility. Whatever an hotel may be it must not be "mean." In the American vernacular the word "mean" is very significant. A mean white in the South is a man who owns no slaves. Men are often mean, but actions are seldom so called. A man feels mean when the bluster is taken out of him. A mean hotel, conducted in a quiet unostentatious manner, in which the only endeavour made had reference to the comfort of a few guests, would find no favour in the States. These hotels are not called by the name of any sign, as with us in our provinces. There are no "Presidents' Heads" or "General Scotts." Nor by the name of the landlord, or of some former landlord, as with us in London, and in many cities of the Continent. Nor are they called from some country or city which may have been presumed at some time to have had special patronage for the establishment. In the nomenclature of American hotels the speciality of American hero-worship is shown, as in the nomenclature of their children. Every inn is a house, and these houses are generally named after some hero, little known probably in the world at large, but highly estimated in that locality at the moment of the christening.

They are always built on a plan which to a European seems to be most unnecessarily extravagant in space. It is not unfrequently the case that the greater portion of the ground-floor is occupied by rooms and halls which make no return to the house whatever. The visitor enters a great hall by the front door, and almost invariably finds it full of men who are idling about, sitting round on stationary seats, talking in a listless manner, and getting through their time as though the place were a public lounging room. And so it is. The chances are that not half the crowd are guests at the hotel. I will now follow the visitor as he makes his way up to the office. Every hotel has an office. To call this place the bar, as I have done too frequently, is a lamentable error. The bar is held in a separate room appropriated solely to drinking. To the office, which is in fact a long open counter, the guest walks up, and there inscribes his name in a book. This inscription was to me a moment of misery which I could never go through with equanimity. As the name is written, and as the request for accommodation is made, half a dozen loungers look over your name and listen to what you say. They listen attentively, and spell your name carefully, but the great man behind the bar does not seem to listen or to heed you. Your destiny is never imparted to you on the instant. If your wife or any other woman be with you, (the word "lady" is made so absolutely distasteful in American hotels that I cannot bring myself to use it in writing of them) she has been carried off to a lady's waiting room, and there remains in august wretchedness till the great man at the bar shall have decided on her fate. I have never been quite able to fathom the mystery of these delays. I think they must have originated in the necessity of waiting to see what might be the influx of travellers at the moment, and then have become exaggerated and brought to their present normal state by the gratified feeling of almost divine power with which for the time it invests that despotic arbiter. I have found it always the same, though arriving with no crowd, by a conveyance of my own, when no other expectant guests were following me. The great man has listened to my request in silence, with an imperturbable face, and has usually continued his conversation with some loafing friend, who at the time is probably scrutinizing my name in the book. I have often suffered in patience; but patience is not specially the badge of my tribe, and I have sometimes spoken out rather freely. If I may presume to give advice to my travelling countrymen how to act under such circumstances I should recommend to them freedom of speech rather than patience. The great man when freely addressed generally opens his eyes, and selects the key of your room without further delay. I am inclined to think that the selection will not be made in any way to your detriment by reason of that freedom of speech. The lady in the ballad who spoke out her own mind to Lord Bateman was sent to her home honourably in a coach and three. Had she held her tongue we are justified in presuming that she would have been returned on a pillion behind a servant.

I have been greatly annoyed by that silence on the part of the hotel clerk. I have repeatedly asked for room, and received no syllable in return. I have persisted in my request, and the clerk has nodded his head at me. Until a traveller is known, these gentlemen are singularly sparing of speech,— especially in the West. The same economy of words runs down from the great man at the office all through the servants of the establishment. It arises, I believe, entirely from that want of courtesy which democratic institutions create. The man whom you address has to make a battle against the state of subservience, presumed to be indicated by his position, and he does so by declaring his indifference to the person on whose wants he is paid to attend. I have been honoured on one or two occasions by the subsequent intimacy of these great men at the hotel offices, and have then found them ready enough at conversation.

That necessity of making your request for rooms before a public audience is not in itself agreeable, and sometimes entails a conversation which might be more comfortably made in private. "What do you mean by a dressing-room, and why do you want one?" Now that is a question which an Englishman feels awkward at answering before five-and-twenty Americans, with open mouths and eager eyes; but it has to be answered. When I left England, I was assured that I should not find any need for a separate sitting-room, seeing that drawing-rooms more or less sumptuous were prepared for the accommodation of "ladies." At first we attempted to follow the advice given to us, but we broke down. A man and his wife travelling from town to town, and making no sojourn on his way, may eat and sleep at an hotel without a private parlour. But an Englishwoman cannot live in comfort for a week, or even, in comfort, for a day, at any of these houses, without a sitting-room for herself. The ladies' drawing-room is a desolate wilderness. The American women themselves do not use it. It is generally empty, or occupied by some forlorn spinster, eliciting harsh sounds from the wretched piano which it contains.

The price at these hotels throughout the Union is nearly always the same, viz., two and a half dollars a day, for which a bedroom is given, and as many meals as the guest can contrive to eat. This is the price for chance guests. The cost to monthly boarders is, I believe, not more than the half of this. Ten shillings a day, therefore, covers everything that is absolutely necessary, servants included. And this must be said in praise of these inns: that the traveller can compute his expenses accurately, and can absolutely bring them within that daily sum of ten shillings. This includes a great deal of eating, a great deal of attendance, the use of reading-rooms and smoking-rooms—which, however, always seem to be open to the public as well as to the guests,—and a bedroom with accommodation which is at any rate as good as the average accommodation of hotels in Europe. In the large Eastern towns baths are attached to many of the rooms. I always carry my own, and have never failed in getting water. It must be acknowledged that the price is very low. It is so low that I believe it affords, as a rule, no profit whatsoever. The profit is made upon extra charges, and they are higher than in any other country that I have visited. They are so high that I consider travelling in America, for an Englishman with his wife or family, to be more expensive than travelling in any part of Europe. First in the list of extras comes that matter of the sitting-room, and by that for a man and his wife the whole first expense is at once doubled. The ordinary charge is five dollars, or one pound a day! A guest intending to stay for two or three weeks at an hotel, or perhaps for one week, may, by agreement, have this charge reduced. At one inn I stayed a fortnight, and having made no such agreement was charged the full sum. I felt myself stirred up to complain, and did in that case remonstrate. I was asked how much I wished to have returned,—for the bill had been paid,—and the sum I suggested was at once handed to me. But even with such reduction the price is very high, and at once makes the American hotel expensive. Wine also at these houses is very costly, and very bad. The usual price is two dollars, or eight shillings, a bottle. The people of the country rarely drink wine at dinner in the hotels. When they do so, they drink champagne; but their normal drinking is done separately, at the bar, chiefly before dinner, and at a cheap rate. "A drink," let it be what it may, invariably costs a dime, or fivepence. But if you must have a glass of sherry with your dinner, it costs two dollars; for sherry does not grow into pint bottles in the States. But the guest who remains for two days can have his wine kept for him. Washing also is an expensive luxury. The price of this is invariable, being always fourpence for everything washed. A cambric handkerchief or muslin dress all come out at the same price. For those who are cunning in the matter this may do very well; but for men and women whose cuffs and collars are numerous it becomes expensive. The craft of those who are cunning is shown, I think, in little internal washings, by which the cambric handkerchiefs are kept out of the list, while the muslin dresses are placed upon it. I am led to this surmise by the energetic measures taken by the hotel keepers to prevent such domestic washings, and by the denunciations which in every hotel are pasted up in every room against the practice. I could not at first understand why I was always warned against washing my own clothes in my own bedroom, and told that no foreign laundress could on any account be admitted into the house. The injunctions given on this head are almost frantic in their energy, and therefore I conceive that hotel keepers find themselves exposed to much suffering in the matter. At these hotels they wash with great rapidity, sending you back your clothes in four or five hours if you desire it.

Another very stringent order is placed before the face of all visitors at American hotels, desiring them on no account to leave valuable property in their rooms. I presume that there must have been some difficulty in this matter in bygone years, for in every State a law has been passed declaring that hotel keepers shall not be held responsible for money or jewels stolen out of rooms in their houses, provided that they are furnished with safes for keeping such money, and give due caution to their guests on the subject. The due caution is always given, but I have seldom myself taken any notice of it. I have always left my portmanteau open, and have kept my money usually in a travelling desk in my room. But I never to my knowledge lost anything. The world, I think, gives itself credit for more thieves than it possesses. As to the female servants at American inns, they are generally all that is disagreeable. They are uncivil, impudent, dirty, slow,—provoking to a degree. But I believe that they keep their hands from picking and stealing.

I never yet made a single comfortable meal at an American hotel, or rose from my breakfast or dinner with that feeling of satisfaction which should, I think, be felt at such moments in a civilized land in which cookery prevails as an art. I have had enough, and have been healthy and am thankful. But that thankfulness is altogether a matter apart, and does not bear upon the question. If need be I can eat food that is disagreeable to my palate, and make no complaint. But I hold it to be compatible with the principles of an advanced Christianity to prefer food that is palatable. I never could get any of that kind at an American hotel. All meal-times at such houses were to me periods of disagreeable duty; and at this moment, as I write these lines at the hotel in which I am still staying, I pine for an English leg of mutton. But I do not wish it to be supposed that the fault of which I complain,—for it is a grievous fault,—is incidental to America as a nation. I have stayed in private houses, and have daily sat down to dinners quite as good as any my own kitchen could afford me. Their dinner parties are generally well done, and as a people they are by no means indifferent to the nature of their comestibles. It is of the hotels that I speak, and of them I again say that eating in them is a disagreeable task,—a painful labour. It is as a schoolboy's lesson, or the six hours' confinement of a clerk at his desk.

The mode of eating is as follows. Certain feeding hours are named, which generally include nearly all the day. Breakfast from six till ten. Dinner from one till five. Tea from six till nine. Supper from nine till twelve. When the guest presents himself at any of these hours he is marshalled to a seat, and a bill is put into his hand containing the names of all the eatables then offered for his choice. The list is incredibly and most unnecessarily long. Then it is that you will see care written on the face of the American hotel liver, as he studies the programme of the coming performance. With men this passes off unnoticed, but with young girls the appearance of the thing is not attractive. The anxious study, the elaborate reading of the daily book, and then the choice proclaimed with clear articulation. "Boiled mutton and caper sauce, roast duck, hashed venison, mashed potatoes, poached eggs and spinach, stewed tomatoes. Yes; and waiter,—some squash." There is no false delicacy in the voice by which this order is given, no desire for a gentle whisper. The dinner is ordered with the firm determination of an American heroine, and in some five minutes' time all the little dishes appear at once, and the lady is surrounded by her banquet.

How I did learn to hate those little dishes and their greasy contents! At a London eating-house things are often not very nice, but your meat is put on a plate and comes before you in an edible shape. At these hotels it is brought to you in horrid little oval dishes, and swims in grease. Gravy is not an institution at American hotels, but grease has taken its place. It is palpable, undisguised grease, floating in rivers,—not grease caused by accidental bad cookery, but grease on purpose. A beef-steak is not a beef-steak unless a quarter of a pound of butter be added to it. Those horrid little dishes! If one thinks of it how could they have been made to contain Christian food? Every article in that long list is liable to the call of any number of guests for four hours. Under such circumstances how can food be made eatable? Your roast mutton is brought to you raw;—if you object to that you are supplied with meat that has been four times brought before the public. At hotels on the continent of Europe different dinners are cooked at different hours, but here the same dinner is kept always going. The house breakfast is maintained on a similar footing. Huge boilers of tea and coffee are stewed down and kept hot. To me those meals were odious. It is of course open to any one to have separate dinners and separate breakfasts in his own room; but by this little is gained and much is lost. He or she who is so exclusive pays twice over for such meals,—as they are charged as extras on the bill; and, after all, receives the advantage of no exclusive cooking. Particles from the public dinners are brought to the private room, and the same odious little dishes make their appearance.

But the most striking peculiarity of the American hotels is in their public rooms. Of the ladies' drawing-room I have spoken. There are two and sometimes three in one hotel, and they are generally furnished at any rate expensively. It seems to me that the space and the furniture are almost thrown away. At watering places, and sea-side summer hotels they are, I presume, used; but at ordinary hotels they are empty deserts. The intention is good, for they are established with the view of giving to ladies at hotels the comforts of ordinary domestic life; but they fail in their effect. Ladies will not make themselves happy in any room, or with ever so much gilded furniture, unless some means of happiness be provided for them. Into these rooms no book is ever brought, no needle-work is introduced; from them no clatter of many tongues is ever heard. On a marble table in the middle of the room always stands a large pitcher of iced water, and from this a cold, damp, uninviting air is spread through the atmosphere of the ladies' drawing-room.

Below, on the ground floor, there is, in the first place, the huge entrance hall, at the back of which, behind a bar, the great man of the place keeps the keys and holds his court. There are generally seats around it, in which smokers sit,—or men not smoking but ruminating. Opening off from this are reading rooms, smoking rooms, shaving rooms, drinking rooms, parlours for gentlemen in which smoking is prohibited, and which are generally as desolate as the ladies' sitting-rooms above. In those other more congenial chambers is always gathered together a crowd, apparently belonging in no way to the hotel. It would seem that a great portion of an American inn is as open to the public as an Exchange, or as the wayside of the street. In the West, during the early months of this war, the traveller would always see many soldiers among the crowd,—not only officers, but privates. They sit in public seats, silent but apparently contented, sometimes for an hour together. All Americans are given to gatherings such as these. It is the much-loved institution to which the name of "loafing" has been given.

I do not like the mode of life which prevails in the American hotels. I have come across exceptions, and know one or two that are comfortable, — always excepting that matter of eating and drinking. But taking them as a whole I do not like their mode of life. I feel, however, bound to add that the hotels of Canada, which are kept, I think, always after the same fashion, are infinitely worse than those of the United States. I do not like the American hotels; but I must say in their favour that they afford an immense amount of accommodation. The traveller is rarely told that an hotel is full, so that travelling in America is without one of those great perils to which it is subject in Europe. It must also be acknowledged that for the ordinary purposes of a traveller they are very cheap.

CHAPTER XV
LITERATURE

In speaking of the literature of any country we are, I think, too much inclined to regard the question as one appertaining exclusively to the writers of books,—not acknowledging, as we should do, that the literary character of a people will depend much more upon what it reads than what it writes. If we can suppose any people to have an intimate acquaintance with the best literary efforts of other countries, we should hardly be correct in saying that such a people had no literary history of their own because it had itself produced nothing in literature. And, with reference to those countries which have been most fertile in the production of good books, I doubt whether their literary histories would not have more to tell of those ages in which much has been read than of those in which much has been written.

The United States have been by no means barren in the production of literature. The truth is so far from this that their literary triumphs are perhaps those which of all their triumphs are the most honourable to them, and which, considering their position as a young nation, are the most permanently satisfactory. But though they have done much in writing, they have done much more in reading. As producers they are more than respectable, but as consumers they are the most conspicuous people on the earth. It is impossible to speak of the subject of literature in America without thinking of the readers rather than of the writers. In this matter their position is different from that of any other great people, seeing that they share the advantages of our language. An American will perhaps consider himself to be as little like an Englishman as he is like a Frenchman. But he reads Shakespeare through the medium of his own vernacular, and has to undergo the penance of a foreign tongue before he can understand Molière. He separates himself from England in politics and perhaps in affection; but he cannot separate himself from England in mental culture. It may be suggested that an Englishman has the same advantages as regards America; and it is true that he is obtaining much of such advantage. Irving, Prescott, and Longfellow are the same to England as though she herself had produced them. But the balance of advantage must be greatly in favour of America. We have given her the work of four hundred years, and have received back in return the work of fifty.

And of this advantage the Americans have not been slow to avail themselves. As consumers of literature they are certainly the most conspicuous people on the earth. Where an English publisher contents himself with thousands of copies an American publisher deals with ten thousands. The sale of a new book, which in numbers would amount to a considerable success with us, would with them be a lamentable failure. This of course is accounted for, as regards the author and the publisher, by the difference of price at which the book is produced. One thousand in England will give perhaps as good a return as the ten thousand in America. But as regards the readers there can be no such equalization. The thousand copies cannot spread themselves as do the ten thousand. The one book at a guinea cannot multiply itself, let Mr. Mudie do what he will, as do the ten books at a dollar. Ultimately there remain the ten books against the one; and if there be not the ten readers against the one, there are five, or four, or three. Everybody in the States has books about his house. "And so has everybody in England," will say my English reader, mindful of the libraries, or book-rooms, or book-crowded drawing-rooms of his friends and acquaintances. But has my English reader who so replies examined the libraries of many English cabmen, of ticket porters, of warehousemen, and of agricultural labourers? I cannot take upon myself to say that I have done so with any close search in the States. But when it has been in my power I have done so, and I have always found books in such houses as I have entered. The amount of printed matter which is poured forth in streams from the printing-presses of the great American publishers is, however, a better proof of the truth of what I say than anything that I can have seen myself.

But of what class are the books that are so read? There are many who think that reading in itself is not good unless the matter read be excellent. I do not myself quite agree with this, thinking that almost any reading is better than none; but I will of course admit that good matter is better than bad matter. The bulk of the literature consumed in the States is no doubt composed of novels,—as it is also, now-a-days, in this country. Whether or no an unlimited supply of novels for young people is or is not advantageous, I will not here pretend to say. The general opinion with ourselves I take it is, that novels are bad reading if they be bad of their kind. Novels that are not bad are now-a-days accepted generally as indispensable to our households. Whatever may be the weakness of the American literary taste in this respect, it is, I think, a weakness which we share. There are more novel readers among them than with us, but only, I think, in the proportion that there are more readers.

I have no hesitation in saying, that works by English authors are more popular in the States than those written by themselves; and, among English authors of the present day, they by no means confine themselves to the novelists. The English names of whom I heard most during my sojourn in the States were perhaps those of Dickens, Tennyson, Buckle, Tom Hughes, Martin Tupper, and Thackeray. As the owners of all these names are still living, I am not going to take upon myself the delicate task of criticising the American taste. I may not perhaps coincide with them in every respect. But if I be right as to the names which I have given, such a selection shows that they do get beyond novels. I have little doubt but that many more copies of Dickens's novels have been sold during the last three years, than of the works either of Tennyson or of Buckle; but such also has been the case in England. It will probably be admitted that one copy of the "Civilization" should be held as being equal to five-and-twenty of "Nicholas Nickleby," and that a single "In Memoriam" may fairly weigh down half-a-dozen "Pickwicks." Men and women after their day's work are not always up to the "Civilization." As a rule they are generally up to "Proverbial Philosophy," and this, perhaps, may have had something to do with the great popularity of that very popular work.

I would not have it supposed that American readers despise their own authors. The Americans are very proud of having a literature of their own. Among the literary names which they honour, there are none, I think, more honourable than those of Cooper and Irving. They like to know that their modern historians are acknowledged as great authors, and as regards their own poets will sometimes demand your admiration for strains with which you hardly find yourself to be familiar. But English books are, I think, the better loved;—even the English books of the present day. And even beyond this,—with those who choose to indulge in the costly luxuries of literature,— books printed in England are more popular than those which are printed in their own country; and yet the manner in which the American publishers put out their work is very good. The book sold there at a dollar, or a dollar and a quarter, quite equals our ordinary five shilling volume. Nevertheless English books are preferred,—almost as strongly as are French bonnets. Of books absolutely printed and produced in England the supply in the States is of course small. They must necessarily be costly, and as regards new books, are always subjected to the rivalry of a cheaper American copy. But of the reprinted works of English authors the supply is unlimited, and the sale very great. Almost everything is reprinted; certainly everything which can be said to attain any home popularity. I do not know how far English authors may be aware of the fact; but it is undoubtedly a fact that their influence as authors is greater on the other side of the Atlantic than on this. It is there that they have their most numerous school of pupils. It is there that they are recognized as teachers by hundreds of thousands. It is of those thirty millions that they should think, at any rate in part, when they discuss within their own hearts that question which all authors do discuss, whether that which they write shall in itself be good or bad,—be true or false. A writer in England may not, perhaps, think very much of this with reference to some trifle of which his English publisher proposes to sell some seven or eight hundred copies. But he begins to feel that he should have thought of it when he learns that twenty or thirty thousand copies of the same have been scattered through the length and breadth of the United States. The English author should feel that he writes for the widest circle of readers ever yet obtained by the literature of any country. He provides not only for his own country and for the States, but for the readers who are rising by millions in the British colonies. Canada is supplied chiefly from the presses of Boston, New York, and Philadelphia, but she is supplied with the works of the mother country. India, as I take it, gets all her books direct from London, as do the West Indies. Whether or no the Australian colonies have as yet learned to reprint our books I do not know, but I presume that they cannot do so as cheaply as they can import them. London with us, and the three cities which I have named on the other side of the Atlantic, are the places at which this literature is manufactured; but the demand in the western hemisphere is becoming more brisk than that which the old world creates. There is, I have no doubt, more literary matter printed in London than in all America put together. A greater extent of letter-press is put up in London than in the three publishing cities of the States. But the number of copies issued by the American publishers is so much greater than those which ours put forth, that the greater bulk of literature is with them. If this be so, the demand with them is of course greater than it is with us.

I have spoken here of the privilege which an English author enjoys by reason of the ever widening circle of readers to whom he writes. I speak of the privilege of an English author as distinguished from that of an American author. I profess my belief that in the United States an English author has an advantage over one of that country merely in the fact of his being English, as a French milliner has undoubtedly an advantage in her nationality let her merits or demerits as a milliner be what they may. I think that English books are better liked because they are English. But I do not know that there is any feeling with us either for or against an author because he is American. I believe that Longfellow stands in our judgment exactly where he would have stood had he been a tutor at a college in Oxford instead of a Professor at Cambridge in Massachusetts. Prescott is read among us as an historian without any reference as to his nationality, and by many, as I take it, in absolute ignorance of his nationality. Hawthorne, the novelist, is quite as well known in England as he is in his own country. But I do not know that to either of these three is awarded any favour or is denied any justice because he is an American. Washington Irving published many of his works in this country, receiving very large sums for them from Mr. Murray, and I fancy that in dealing with his publisher he found neither advantage nor disadvantage in his nationality;—that is, of course, advantage or disadvantage in reference to the light in which his works would be regarded. It must be admitted that there is no jealousy in the States against English authors. I think that there is a feeling in their favour, but no one can at any rate allege that there is a feeling against them. I think I may also assert on the part of my own country that there is no jealousy here against American authors. As regards the tastes of the people, the works of each country flow freely through the other. That is as it should be. But when we come to the mode of supply, things are not exactly as they should be; and I do not believe that any one will contradict me when I say that the fault is with the Americans.

I presume that all my readers know the meaning of the word copyright. A man's copyright, or right in his copy, is that amount of legal possession in the production of his brains which has been secured to him by the laws of his own country and by the laws of others. Unless an author were secured by such laws, his writings would be of but little pecuniary value to him, as the right of printing and selling them would be open to all the world. In England and in America, and as I conceive in all countries possessing a literature, there is such a law securing to authors and to their heirs for a term of years the exclusive right over their own productions. That this should be so in England as regards English authors is so much a matter of course, that the copyright of an author would seem to be as naturally his own as a gentleman's deposit at his bank or his little investment in the three per cents. The right of an author to the value of his own productions in other countries than his own is not so much a matter of course; but nevertheless, if such productions have any value in other countries, that value should belong to him. This has been felt to be the case between England and France, and treaties have been made securing his own property to the author in each country. The fact that the languages of England and France are different makes the matter one of comparatively small moment. But it has been found to be for the honour and profit of the two countries, that there should be such a law, and an international copyright does exist. But if such an arrangement be needed between two such countries as France and England,—between two countries which do not speak the same language or share the same literature,—how much more necessary must it be between England and the United States? The literature of the one country is the literature of the other. The poem that is popular in London will certainly be popular in New York. The novel that is effective among American ladies will be equally so with those of England. There can be no doubt as to the importance of having a law of copyright between the two countries. The only question can be as to the expediency and the justice. At present there is no international copyright between England and the United States, and there is none because the States have declined to sanction any such law. It is known by all who are concerned in the matter on either side of the water that as far as Great Britain is concerned such a law would meet with no impediment.

Therefore it is to be presumed that the legislators of the States think it expedient and just to dispense with any such law. I have said that there can be no doubt as to the importance of the question, seeing that the price of English literature in the States must be most materially affected by it. Without such a law the Americans are enabled to import English literature without paying for it. It is open to any American publisher to reprint any work from an English copy, and to sell his reprints without any permission obtained from the English author or from the English publisher. The absolute material which the American publisher sells, he takes, or can take, for nothing. The paper, ink, and composition he supplies in the ordinary way of business; but of the very matter which he professes to sell,—of the book which is the object of his trade, he is enabled to possess himself for nothing. If you, my reader, be a popular author, an American publisher will take the choicest work of your brain and make dollars out of it, selling thousands of copies of it in his country, whereas you can, perhaps, only sell hundreds of it in your own; and will either give you nothing for that he takes,—or else will explain to you that he need give you nothing, and that in paying you anything he subjects himself to the danger of seeing the property which he has bought taken again from him by other persons. If this be so that question whether or no there shall be a law of international copyright between the two countries cannot be unimportant.

But it may be inexpedient that there shall be such a law. It may be considered well, that as the influx of English books into America is much greater than the out-flux of American books back to England, the right of obtaining such books for nothing should be reserved, although the country in doing so robs its own authors of the advantage which should accrue to them from the English market. It might perhaps be thought anything but smart to surrender such an advantage by the passing of an international copyright bill. There are not many trades in which the tradesman can get the chief of his goods for nothing; and it may be thought, that the advantage arising to the States from such an arrangement of circumstances should not be abandoned. But how then about the justice? It would seem that the less said upon that subject the better. I have heard no one say that an author's property in his own works should not, in accordance with justice, be insured to him in the one country as well as in the other. I have seen no defence of the present position of affairs, on the score of justice. The price of books would be enhanced by an international copyright law, and it is well that books should be cheap. That is the only argument used. So would mutton be cheap, if it could be taken out of a butcher's shop for nothing!

But I absolutely deny the expediency of the present position of the matter, looking simply to the material advantage of the American people in the matter, and throwing aside altogether that question of justice. I must here, however, explain that I bring no charge whatsoever against the American publishers. The English author is a victim in their hands, but it is by no means their fault that he is so. As a rule, they are willing to pay for the works of popular English writers, but in arranging as to what payments they can make, they must of course bear in mind the fact that they have no exclusive right whatsoever in the things which they purchase. It is natural, also, that they should bear in mind when making their purchases, and arranging their prices, that they can have the very thing they are buying without any payment at all, if the price asked do not suit them. It is not of the publishers that I complain, or of any advantage which they take; but of the legislators of the country, and of the advantage which accrues, or is thought by them to accrue to the American people from the absence of an international copyright law. It is mean on their part to take such advantage if it existed; and it is foolish in them to suppose that any such advantage can accrue. The absence of any law of copyright no doubt gives to the American publisher the power of reprinting the works of English authors without paying for them,—seeing that the English author is undefended. But the American publisher who brings out such a reprint is equally undefended in his property. When he shall have produced his book, his rival in the next street may immediately reprint it from him, and destroy the value of his property by underselling him. It is probable that the first American publisher will have made some payment to the English author for the privilege of publishing the book honestly,—of publishing it without recurrence to piracy,—and in arranging his price with his customers he will be, of course, obliged to debit the book with the amount so paid. If the author receive ten cents a copy on every copy sold, the publisher must add that ten cents to the price he charges for it. But he cannot do this with security, because the book can be immediately reprinted, and sold without any such addition to the price. The only security which the American publisher has against the injury which may be so done to him, is the power of doing other injury in return. The men who stand high in the trade, and who are powerful because of the largeness of their dealings, can in a certain measure secure themselves in this way. Such a firm would have the power of crushing a small tradesman who should interfere with him. But if the large firm commits any such act of injustice, the little men in the trade have no power of setting themselves right by counter injustice. I need hardly point out what must be the effect of such a state of things upon the whole publishing trade; nor need I say more to prove that some law which shall regulate property in foreign copyrights would be as expedient with reference to America, as it would be just towards England. But the wrong done by America to herself does not rest here. It is true that more English books are read in the States than American books in England, but it is equally true that the literature of America is daily gaining readers among us. That injury to which English authors are subjected from the want of protection in the States, American authors suffer from the want of protection here. One can hardly believe that the legislators of the States would willingly place the brightest of their own fellow countrymen in this position, because in the event of a copyright bill being passed, the balance of advantage would seem to accrue to England!

Of the literature of the United States, speaking of literature in its ordinary sense, I do not know that I need say much more. I regard the literature of a country as its highest produce, believing it to be more powerful in its general effect, and more beneficial in its results, than either statesmanship, professional ability, religious teaching, or commerce. And in no part of its national career have the United States been so successful as in this. I need hardly explain that I should commit a monstrous injustice were I to make a comparison in this matter between England and America. Literature is the child of leisure and wealth. It is the produce of minds which by a happy combination of circumstances have been enabled to dispense with the ordinary cares of the world. It can hardly be expected to come from a young country, or from a new and still struggling people. Looking around at our own magnificent colonies I hardly remember a considerable name which they have produced, except that of my excellent old friend, Sam Slick. Nothing, therefore, I think, shows the settled greatness of the people of the States more significantly than their firm establishment of a national literature. This literature runs over all subjects. American authors have excelled in poetry, in science, in history, in metaphysics, in law, in theology, and in fiction. They have attempted all, and failed in none. What Englishman has devoted a room to books, and devoted no portion of that room to the productions of America?

But I must say a word of literature in which I shall not speak of it in its ordinary sense, and shall yet speak of it in that sense which of all perhaps, in the present day, should be considered the most ordinary. I mean the every-day periodical literature of the press. Most of those who can read, it is to be hoped, read books; but all who can read do read newspapers. Newspapers in this country are so general that men cannot well live without them; but to men, and to women also, in the United States they may be said to be the one chief necessary of life. And yet in the whole length and breadth of the United States there is not published a single newspaper which seems to me to be worthy of praise.

A really good newspaper,—one excellent at all points,—would indeed be a triumph of honesty and of art! Not only is such a publication much to be desired in America, but it is still to be desired in Great Britain also. I used, in my younger days, to think of such a newspaper as a possible publication, and in a certain degree I then looked for it. Now I expect it only in my dreams. It should be powerful without tyranny, popular without triumph, political without party passion, critical without personal feeling, right in its statements and just in its judgments, but right and just without pride. It should be all but omniscient, but not conscious of its omniscience; it should be moral, but not strait-laced; it should be well-assured, but yet modest; though never humble, it should be free from boasting. Above all these things it should be readable; and above that again it should be true. I used to think that such a newspaper might be produced, but I now sadly acknowledge to myself the fact that humanity is not capable of any work so divine.

The newspapers of the States generally may not only be said to have reached none of the virtues here named, but to have fallen into all the opposite vices. In the first place they are never true. In requiring truth from a newspaper the public should not be anxious to strain at gnats. A statement setting forth that a certain gooseberry was five inches in circumference, whereas in truth its girth was only two and a half, would give me no offence. Nor would I be offended at being told that Lord Derby was appointed to the premiership, while in truth the Queen had only sent for his lordship, having as yet come to no definite arrangement. The demand for truth which may reasonably be made upon a newspaper amounts to this,—that nothing should be stated not believed to be true, and that nothing should be stated as to which the truth is important, without adequate ground for such belief.

If a newspaper accuse me of swindling, it is not sufficient that the writer believe me to be a swindler. He should have ample and sufficient ground for such belief;—otherwise in making such a statement he will write falsely. In our private life we all recognize the fact that this is so. It is understood that a man is not a whit the less a slanderer because he believes the slander which he promulgates. But it seems to me that this is not sufficiently recognized by many who write for the public press. Evil things are said, and are probably believed by the writers; they are said with that special skill for which newspaper writers have in our days become so conspicuous, defying alike redress by law or redress by argument; but they are too often said falsely. The words are not measured when they are written, and they are allowed to go forth without any sufficient inquiry into their truth. But if there be any ground for such complaint here in England, that ground is multiplied ten times—twenty times—in the States. This is not only shown in the abuse of individuals, in abuse which is as violent as it is perpetual, but in the treatment of every subject which is handled. All idea of truth has been thrown overboard. It seems to be admitted that the only object is to produce a sensation, and that it is admitted by both writer and reader that sensation and veracity are incompatible. Falsehood has become so much a matter of course with American newspapers that it has almost ceased to be falsehood. Nobody thinks me a liar because I deny that I am at home when I am in my study. The nature of the arrangement is generally understood. So also is it with the American newspapers.

But American newspapers are also unreadable. It is very bad that they should be false, but it is very surprising that they should be dull. Looking at the general intelligence of the people, one would have thought that a readable newspaper, put out with all pleasant appurtenances of clear type, good paper, and good internal arrangement, would have been a thing specially within their reach. But they have failed in every detail. Though their papers are always loaded with sensation headings, there are seldom sensation paragraphs to follow. The paragraphs do not fit the headings. Either they cannot be found, or if found they seem to have escaped from their proper column to some distant and remote portion of the sheet. One is led to presume that no American editor has any plan in the composition of his newspaper. I never know whether I have as yet got to the very heart's core of the daily journal, or whether I am still to go on searching for that heart's core. Alas, it too often happens that there is no heart's core! The whole thing seems to have been put out at hap-hazard. And then the very writing is in itself below mediocrity;—as though a power of expression in properly arranged language was not required by a newspaper editor, either as regards himself or as regards his subordinates. One is driven to suppose that the writers for the daily press are not chosen with any view to such capability. A man ambitious of being on the staff of an American newspaper should be capable of much work, should be satisfied with small pay, should be indifferent to the world's good usage, should be rough, ready, and of long sufferance; but, above all, he should be smart. The type of almost all American newspapers is wretched—I think I may say of all;—so wretched that that alone forbids one to hope for pleasure in reading them. They are ill-written, ill-printed, ill-arranged, and in fact are not readable. They are bought, glanced at, and thrown away.

They are full of boastings,—not boastings simply as to their country, their town, or their party,—but of boastings as to themselves. And yet they possess no self-assurance. It is always evident that they neither trust themselves, nor expect to be trusted. They have made no approach to that omniscience which constitutes the great marvel of our own daily press; but finding it necessary to write as though they possessed it, they fall into blunders which are almost as marvellous. Justice and right judgment are out of the question with them. A political party end is always in view, and political party warfare in America admits of any weapons. No newspaper in America is really powerful or popular; and yet they are tyrannical and overbearing. The "New York Herald" has, I believe, the largest sale of any daily newspaper; but it is absolutely without political power, and in these times of war has truckled to the Government more basely than any other paper. It has an enormous sale, but so far is it from having achieved popularity, that no man on any side ever speaks a good word for it. All American newspapers deal in politics as a matter of course; but their politics have ever regard to men and never to measures. Vituperation is their natural political weapon; but since the President's ministers have assumed the power of stopping newspapers which are offensive to them, they have shown that they can descend to a course of eulogy which is even below vituperation.

I shall be accused of using very strong language against the newspaper press of America. I can only say that I do not know how to make that language too strong. Of course there are newspapers as to which the editors and writers may justly feel that my remarks, if applied to them, are unmerited. In writing on such a subject, I can only deal with the whole as a whole. During my stay in the country, I did my best to make myself acquainted with the nature of its newspapers, knowing in how great a degree its population depends on them for its daily store of information. Newspapers in the States of America have a much wider, or rather closer circulation, than they do with us. Every man and almost every woman sees a newspaper daily. They are very cheap, and are brought to every man's hand without trouble to himself, at every turn that he takes in his day's work. It would be much for the advantage of the country, that they should be good of their kind; but, if I am able to form a correct judgment on the matter, they are not good.

CHAPTER XVI
CONCLUSION

In one of the earlier chapters of this volume,—now some seven or eight chapters past,—I brought myself on my travels back to Boston. It was not that my way homewards lay by that route, seeing that my fate required me to sail from New York; but I could not leave the country without revisiting my friends in Massachusetts. I have told how I was there in the sleighing time, and how pleasant were the mingled slush and frost of the snowy winter. In the morning the streets would be hard and crisp, and the stranger would surely fall if he were not prepared to walk on glaciers. In the afternoon he would be wading through rivers,—and if properly armed at all points with india-rubber, would enjoy the rivers as he waded. But the air would be always kindly, and the east wind there, if it was east as I was told, had none of that power of dominion which makes us all so submissive to its behests in London. For myself, I believe that the real east wind blows only in London.

And when the snow went in Boston I went with it. The evening before I left I watched them as they carted away the dirty uncouth blocks which had been broken up with pickaxes in Washington Street, and was melancholy as I reflected that I too should no longer be known in the streets. My weeks in Boston had not been very many, but nevertheless there were haunts there which I knew as though my feet had trodden them for years. There were houses to which I could have gone with my eyes blindfold; doors of which the latches were familiar to my hands; faces which I knew so well that they had ceased to put on for me the fictitious smiles of courtesy. Faces, houses, doors, and haunts, where are they now? For me they are as though they had never been. They are among the things which one would fain remember as one remembers a dream. Look back on it as a vision and it is all pleasant. But if you realize your vision and believe your dream to be a fact, all your pleasure is obliterated by regret.

I know that I shall never again be at Boston, and that I have said that about the Americans which would make me unwelcome as a guest if I were there. It is in this that my regret consists;—for this reason that I would wish to remember so many social hours as though they had been passed in sleep.

They who will expect blessings from me, will say among themselves that I have cursed them. As I read the pages which I have written I feel that words which I intended for blessings when I prepared to utter them have gone nigh to turn themselves into curses.

I have ever admired the United States as a nation. I have loved their liberty, their prowess, their intelligence, and their progress. I have sympathized with a people who themselves have had no sympathy with passive security and inaction. I have felt confidence in them, and have known, as it were, that their industry must enable them to succeed as a people, while their freedom would insure to them success as a nation. With these convictions I went among them wishing to write of them good words,—words which might be pleasant for them to read, while they might assist perhaps in producing a true impression of them here at home. But among my good words there are so many which are bitter, that I fear I shall have failed in my object as regards them. And it seems to me, as I read once more my own pages, that in saying evil things of my friends, I have used language stronger than I intended; whereas I have omitted to express myself with emphasis when I have attempted to say good things. Why need I have told of the mud of Washington, or have exposed the nakedness of Cairo? Why did I speak with such eager enmity of those poor women in the New York cars, who never injured me, now that I think of it? Ladies of New York, as I write this, the words which were written among you, are printed and cannot be expunged; but I tender to you my apologies from my home in England. And as to that Van Wyck committee! Might I not have left those contractors to be dealt with by their own Congress, seeing that that Congress committee was by no means inclined to spare them? I might have kept my pages free from gall, and have sent my sheets to the press unhurt by the conviction that I was hurting those who had dealt kindly by me! But what then? Was any people ever truly served by eulogy; or an honest cause furthered by undue praise?

O my friends with thin skins,—and here I protest that a thick skin is a fault not to be forgiven in a man or a nation, whereas a thin skin is in itself a merit, if only the wearer of it will be the master and not the slave of his skin,—O, my friends with thin skins, ye whom I call my cousins and love as brethren, will ye not forgive me these harsh words that I have spoken? They have been spoken in love,—with a true love, a brotherly love, a love that has never been absent from the heart while the brain was coining them. I had my task to do, and I could not take the pleasant and ignore the painful. It may perhaps be that as a friend I had better not have written either good or bad. But no! To say that would indeed be to speak calumny of your country. A man may write of you truly, and yet write that which you would read with pleasure;—only that your skins are so thin! The streets of Washington are muddy and her ways are desolate. The nakedness of Cairo is very naked. And those ladies of New York—is it not to be confessed that they are somewhat imperious in their demands? As for the Van Wyck committee, have I not repeated the tale which you have told yourselves? And is it not well that such tales should be told?

And yet ye will not forgive me; because your skins are thin, and because the praise of others is the breath of your nostrils.

I do not know that an American as an individual is more thin-skinned than an Englishman; but as the representative of a nation it may almost be said of him that he has no skin at all. Any touch comes at once upon the net-work of his nerves and puts in operation all his organs of feeling with the violence of a blow. And for this peculiarity he has been made the mark of much ridicule. It shows itself in two ways; either by extreme displeasure when anything is said disrespectful of his country; or by the strong eulogy with which he is accustomed to speak of his own institutions and of those of his countrymen whom at the moment he may chance to hold in high esteem. The manner in which this is done is often ridiculous. "Sir, what do you think of our Mr. Jefferson Brick? Mr. Jefferson Brick, sir, is one of our most remarkable men." And again. "Do you like our institutions, sir? Do you find that philanthropy, religion, philosophy, and the social virtues are cultivated on a scale commensurate with the unequalled liberty and political advancement of the nation?" There is something absurd in such a mode of address when it is repeated often. But hero-worship and love of country are not absurd; and do not these addresses show capacity for hero-worship and an aptitude for the love of country? Jefferson Brick may not be a hero; but a capacity for such worship is something. Indeed the capacity is everything, for the need of a hero will at last produce the hero needed. And it is the same with that love of country. A people that are proud of their country will see that there is something in their country to justify their pride. Do we not all of us feel assured by the intense nationality of an American that he will not desert his nation in the hour of her need? I feel that assurance respecting them; and at those moments in which I am moved to laughter by the absurdities of their addresses, I feel it the strongest.

I left Boston with the snow, and returning to New York found that the streets there were dry and that the winter was nearly over. As I had passed through New York to Boston the streets had been by no means dry. The snow had lain in small mountains over which the omnibuses made their way down Broadway, till at the bottom of that thoroughfare, between Trinity Church and Bowling Green, alp became piled upon alp, and all traffic was full of danger. The accursed love of gain still took men to Wall

Street, but they had to fight their way thither through physical difficulties which must have made even the state of the money market a matter almost of indifference to them. They do not seem to me to manage the winter in New York so well as they do in Boston. But now, on my last return thither, the alps were gone, the roads were clear, and one could travel through the city with no other impediment than those of treading on women's dresses if one walked, or having to look after women's band-boxes and pay their fares and take their change, if one used the omnibuses.

And now had come the end of my adventures, and as I set my foot once more upon the deck of the Cunard steamer I felt that my work was done. Whether it were done ill or well, or whether indeed any approach to the doing of it had been attained, all had been done that I could accomplish. No further opportunity remained to me of seeing, hearing, or of speaking. I had come out thither, having resolved to learn a little that I might if possible teach that little to others; and now the lesson was learned, or must remain unlearned. But in carrying out my resolution I had gradually risen in my ambition, and had mounted from one stage of inquiry to another, till at last I had found myself burdened with the task of ascertaining whether or no the Americans were doing their work as a nation well or ill; and now, if ever, I must be prepared to put forth the result of my inquiry. As I walked up and down the deck of the steamboat I confess I felt that I had been somewhat arrogant.

I had been a few days over six months in the States, and I was engaged in writing a book of such a nature that a man might well engage himself for six years, or perhaps for sixty, in obtaining the materials for it. There was nothing in the form of government, or legislature, or manners of the people, as to which I had not taken upon myself to say something. I was professing to understand their strength and their weakness; and was daring to censure their faults and to eulogize their virtues. "Who is he," an American would say, "that he comes and judges us? His judgment is nothing." "Who is he," an Englishman would say, "that he comes and teaches us? His teaching is of no value."

In answer to this I have but a small plea to make. I have done my best. I have nothing "extenuated, and have set down nought in malice." I do feel that my volumes have blown themselves out into proportions greater than I had intended;—greater not in mass of pages, but in the matter handled. I am frequently addressing my own muse, who I am well aware is not Clio, and asking her whither she is wending. "Cease, thou wrong-headed one, to meddle with these mysteries." I appeal to her frequently, but ever in vain. One cannot drive one's muse, nor yet always lead her. Of the various women with which a man is blessed, his muse is by no means the least difficult to manage.

But again I put in my slight plea. In doing as I have done, I have at least done my best. I have endeavoured to judge without prejudice, and to hear with honest ears, and to see with honest eyes. The subject, moreover, on which I have written, is one which, though great, is so universal in its bearings, that it may be said to admit of being handled without impropriety by the unlearned as well as the learned;—by those who have grown gray in the study of constitutional lore, and by those who have simply looked on at the government of men as we all look on at those matters which daily surround us. There are matters as to which a man should never take a pen in hand unless he has given to them much labour. The botanist must have learned to trace the herbs and flowers before he can presume to tell us how God has formed them. But the death of Hector is a fit subject for a boy's verses though Homer also sang of it. I feel that there is scope for a book on the United States' form of government as it was founded, and as it has since framed itself, which might do honour to the life-long studies of some one of those great constitutional pundits whom we have among us; but, nevertheless, the plain words of a man who is no pundit need not disgrace the subject, if they be honestly written, and if he who writes them has in his heart an honest love of liberty. Such were my thoughts as I walked the deck of the Cunard steamer. Then I descended to my cabin, settled my luggage, and prepared for the continuance of my work. It was fourteen days from that time before I reached London, but the fourteen days to me were not unpleasant. The demon of sea-sickness usually spares me, and if I can find on board one or two who are equally fortunate—who can eat with me, drink with me, and talk with me—I do not know that a passage across the Atlantic is by any means a terrible evil.

In finishing these volumes after the fashion in which they have been written throughout, I feel that I am bound to express a final opinion on two or three points, and that if I have not enabled myself to do so, I have travelled through the country in vain. I am bound by the very nature of my undertaking to say whether, according to such view as I have enabled myself to take of them, the Americans have succeeded as a nation politically and socially; and in doing this I ought to be able to explain how far slavery has interfered with such success. I am bound also, writing at the present moment, to express some opinion as to the result of this war, and to declare whether the North or the South may be expected to be victorious,— explaining in some rough way what may be the results of such victory, and how such results will affect the question of slavery. And I shall leave my task unfinished if I do not say what may be the possible chances of future quarrel between England and the States. That there has been and is much hot blood and angry feeling no man doubts; but such angry feeling has existed among many nations without any probability of war. In this case, with reference to this ill-will that has certainly established itself between us and that other people, is there any need that it should be satisfied by war and allayed by blood?

No one, I think, can doubt that the founders of the great American Commonwealth made an error in omitting to provide some means for the gradual extinction of slavery throughout the States. That error did not consist in any liking for slavery. There was no feeling in favour of slavery on the part of those who made themselves prominent at the political birth of the nation. I think I shall be justified in saying that at that time the opinion that slavery is itself a good thing, that it is an institution of divine origin and fit to be perpetuated among men as in itself excellent, had not found that favour in the southern States in which it is now held. Jefferson, who has been regarded as the leader of the southern or democratic party, has left ample testimony that he regarded slavery as an evil. It is, I think, true that he gave such testimony much more freely when he was speaking or writing as a private individual than he ever allowed himself to do when his words were armed with the weight of public authority. But it is clear that, on the whole, he was opposed to slavery, and I think there can be little doubt that he and his party looked forward to a natural death for that evil. Calculation was made that slavery when not recruited afresh from Africa could not maintain its numbers, and that gradually the negro population would become extinct. This was the error made. It was easier to look forward to such a result and hope for such an end of the difficulty, than to extinguish slavery by a great political movement, which must doubtless have been difficult and costly. The northern States got rid of slavery by the operation of their separate legislatures, some at one date and some at others. The slaves were less numerous in the North than in the South, and the feeling adverse to slaves was stronger in the North than in the South. Mason and Dixon's line, which now separates slave soil from free soil, merely indicates the position in the country at which the balance turned. Maryland and Virginia were not inclined to make great immediate sacrifices for the manumission of their slaves; but the gentlemen of those States did not think that slavery was a divine institution, destined to flourish for ever as a blessing in their land.

The maintenance of slavery was, I think, a political mistake;—a political mistake, not because slavery is politically wrong, but because the politicians of the day made erroneous calculations as to the probability of its termination. So the income tax may be a political blunder with us;—not because it is in itself a bad tax, but because those who imposed it conceived that they were imposing it for a year or two, whereas, now, men do not expect to see the end of it. The maintenance of slavery was a political mistake; and I cannot think that the Americans in any way lessen the weight of their own error by protesting, as they occasionally do, that slavery was a legacy made over to them from England. They might as well say, that travelling in carts without springs, at the rate of three miles an hour, was a legacy made over to them by England. On that matter of travelling they have not been contented with the old habits left to them, but have gone ahead and made railroads. In creating those railways the merit is due to them; and so also is the demerit of maintaining those slaves.

That demerit and that mistake have doubtless brought upon the Americans the grievances of their present position; and will, as I think, so far be accompanied by ultimate punishment that they will be the immediate means of causing the first disintegration of their nation. I will leave it to the Americans themselves to say, whether such disintegration must necessarily imply that they have failed in their political undertaking. The most loyal citizens of the northern States would have declared a month or two since, — and for aught I know would declare now, — that any disintegration of the States implied absolute failure. One stripe erased from the banner, one star lost from the firmament, would entail upon them all the disgrace of national defeat! It had been their boast that they would always advance, never retreat. They had looked forward to add ever State upon State, and territory to territory, till the whole continent should be bound together in the same union. To go back from that now, to fall into pieces and be divided, to become smaller in the eyes of the nations, — to be absolutely halfed, as some would say of such division, would be national disgrace, and would amount to political failure. "Let us fight for the whole," such men said, and probably do say. "To lose anything is to lose all!"

But the citizens of the States who speak and think thus, though they may be the most loyal, are perhaps not politically the most wise. And I am inclined to think that that defiant claim of every star, that resolve to possess every stripe upon the banner, had become somewhat less general when I was leaving the country than I had found it to be at the time of my arrival there. While things were going badly with the North, — while there was no tale of any battle to be told except of those at Bull's Run and Springfield, no northern man would admit a hint that secession might ultimately prevail in Georgia or Alabama. But the rebels had been driven out of Missouri when I was leaving the States, they had retreated altogether from Kentucky, having been beaten in one engagement there, and from a great portion of Tennessee, having been twice beaten in that State. The coast of North Carolina, and many points of the southern coast, were in the hands of the northern army, while the army of the South was retreating from all points into the centre of their country. Whatever may have been the strategetical merits or demerits of the northern generals, it is at any rate certain that their apparent successes were greedily welcomed by the people, and created an idea that things were going well with the cause. And, as all this took place, it seemed to me that I heard less about the necessary integrity of the old flag. While as yet they were altogether unsuccessful, they were minded to make no surrender.

But with their successes came the feeling, that in taking much they might perhaps allow themselves to yield something. This was clearly indicated by the message sent to Congress by the President in February, 1862, in which he suggested that Congress should make arrangements for the purchase of the slaves in the border States; so that in the event of secession—accomplished secession—in the gulf States, the course of those border States might be made clear for them. They might hesitate as to going willingly with the North, while possessing slaves,—as to setting themselves peaceably down as a small slave adjunct to a vast free soil nation, seeing that their property would always be in peril. Under such circumstances a slave adjunct to the free soil nation would not long be possible. But if it could be shown to them that in the event of their adhering to the North, compensation would be forthcoming, then, indeed, the difficulty in arranging an advantageous line between the two future nations might be considerably modified. This message of the President's was intended to signify, that secession on favourable terms might be regarded by the North as not undesirable. Moderate men were beginning to whisper that, after all, the gulf States were no source either of national wealth or of national honour. Had there not been enough at Washington of cotton lords and cotton laws? When I have suggested that no senator from Georgia would ever again sit in the United States senate, American gentlemen have received my remark with a slight demur, and have then proceeded to argue the case. Six months before they would have declaimed against me and not have argued.

I will leave it to Americans themselves to say whether that disintegration of the States, should it ever be realized, will imply that they have failed in their political undertaking. If they do not protest that it argues failure, their feelings will not be hurt by any such protestations on the part of others. I have said that the blunder made by the founders of the nation with regard to slavery has brought with it this secession as its punishment. But such punishments come generally upon nations as great mercies. Ireland's famine was the punishment of her imprudence and idleness, but it has given to her prosperity and progress. And indeed, to speak with more logical correctness, the famine was no punishment to Ireland, nor will secession be a punishment to the northern States. In the long result step will have gone on after step, and effect will have followed cause, till the American people will at last acknowledge, that all these matters have been arranged for their advantage and promotion. It may be that a nation now and then goes to the wall, and that things go from bad to worse with a large people. It has been so with various nations and with many people since history was first written. But when it has been so, the people thus punished have been idle and bad. They have not only done evil in their generation, but have done more evil than good, and have contributed their power to the injury rather than to the improvement of mankind. It may be that this or that national fault may produce or seem to produce some consequent calamity. But the balance of good or evil things which fall to a people's share will indicate with certainty their average conduct as a nation. The one will be the certain consequence of the other. If it be that the Americans of the northern States have done well in their time, that they have assisted in the progress of the world, and made things better for mankind rather than worse, then they will come out of this trouble without eventual injury. That which came in the guise of punishment for a special fault, will be a part of the reward resulting from good conduct in the general. And as to this matter of slavery, in which I think that they have blundered both politically and morally,— has it not been found impossible hitherto for them to cleanse their hands of that taint? But that which they could not do for themselves the course of events is doing for them. If secession establish herself, though it be only secession of the gulf States, the people of the United States will soon be free from slavery.

In judging of the success or want of success of any political institutions or of any form of government, we should be guided, I think, by the general results, and not by any abstract rules as to the right or wrong of those institutions or of that form. It might be easy for a German lawyer to show that our system of trial by jury is open to the gravest objections, and that it sins against common sense. But if that system gives us substantial justice, and protects us from the tyranny of men in office, the German lawyer will not succeed in making us believe that it is a bad system. When looking into the matter of the schools at Boston, I observed to one of the committee of management that the statements with which I was supplied, though they told me how many of the children went to school, did not tell me how long they remained at school. The gentleman replied that that information was to be obtained from the result of the schooling of the population generally. Every boy and girl around us could read and write, and could enjoy reading and writing. There was therefore evidence to show that they remained at school sufficiently long for the required purposes. It was fair that I should judge of the system from the results. Here in England, we generally object to much that the Americans have adopted into their form of government, and think that many of their political theories are wrong. We do not like universal suffrage. We do not like a periodical change in the first magistrate; and we like quite as little a periodical permanence in the political officers immediately under the chief magistrate. We are, in short, wedded to our own forms and therefore opposed by judgment to forms differing from our own. But I think we all acknowledge that the United States, burdened as they are with these political evils,—as we think them, have grown in strength and material prosperity with a celerity of growth hitherto unknown among nations. We may dislike Americans personally, we may find ourselves uncomfortable when there, and unable to sympathize with them when away; we may believe them to be ambitious, unjust, self-idolatrous, or irreligious. But, unless we throw our judgment altogether overboard, we cannot believe them to be a weak people, a poor people, a people with low spirits or a people with idle hands. To what is it that the government of a country should chiefly look? What special advantages do we expect from our own government? Is it not that we should be safe at home and respected abroad;—that laws should be maintained, but that they should be so maintained that they should not be oppressive? There are, doubtless, countries in which the government professes to do much more than this for its people,—countries in which the government is paternal; in which it regulates the religion of the people, and professes to enforce on all the national children respect for the governors, teachers, spiritual pastors, and masters. But that is not our idea of a government. That is not what we desire to see established among ourselves or established among others. Safety from foreign foes, respect from foreign foes and friends, security under the law and security from the law,—this is what we expect from our government; and if I add to this that we expect to have these good things provided at a fairly moderate cost, I think I have exhausted the list of our requirements.

And if the Americans with their form of government have done for themselves all that we expect our government to do for us; if they have with some fair approach to general excellence obtained respect abroad and security at home from foreign foes; if they have made life, liberty, and property safe under their laws, and have also so written and executed their laws as to secure their people from legal oppression,—I maintain that they are entitled to a verdict in their favour, let us object as we may to universal suffrage, to four years' Presidents, and four years' presidential cabinets. What, after all, matters the theory or the system, whether it be King or President, universal suffrage or ten-pound voter, so long as the people be free and prosperous? King and President, suffrage by poll and suffrage by property, are but the means. If the end be there, if the thing has been done, King and President, open suffrage and close suffrage may alike be declared to have been successful. The Americans have been in existence as a nation for seventy-five years, and have achieved an amount of foreign respect during that period greater than any other nation ever obtained in double the time. And this has been given to them, not in deference to the statesman-like craft of their diplomatic and other officers, but on grounds the very opposite of those. It has been given to them because they form a numerous, wealthy, brave, and self-asserting nation. It is, I think, unnecessary to prove that such foreign respect has been given to them: but were it necessary, nothing would prove it more strongly than the regard which has been universally paid by European governments to the blockade placed during this war on the southern ports by the government of the United States. Had the United States been placed by general consent in any class of nations below the first,

England, France, and perhaps Russia would have taken the matter into their own hands, and have settled for the States, either united or disunited, at any rate that question of the blockade. And the Americans have been safe at home from foreign foes; so safe, that no other strong people but ourselves have enjoyed anything approaching to their security since their foundation. Nor has our security been equal to theirs if we are to count our nationality as extending beyond the British Isles. Then as to security under their laws and from their laws! Those laws and the system of their management have been taken almost entirely from us, and have so been administered that life and property have been safe, and the subject also has been free from oppression. I think that this may be taken for granted, seeing that they who have been most opposed to American forms of government, have never asserted the reverse. I may be told of a man being lynched in one State, or tarred and feathered in another, or of a duel in a third being "fought at sight." So I may be told also of men garotted in London, and of tithe proctors buried in a bog without their ears in Ireland. Neither will seventy years of continuance nor will seven hundred secure such an observance of laws as will prevent temporary ebullition of popular feeling, or save a people from the chance disgrace of occasional outrage. Taking the general, life and limb and property have been as safe in the States as in other civilized countries with which we are acquainted.

As to their personal liberty under their laws, I know it will be said that they have surrendered all claim to any such precious possession by the facility with which they have now surrendered the privilege of the writ of habeas corpus. It has been taken from them, as I have endeavoured to show, illegally, and they have submitted to the loss and to the illegality without a murmur! But in such a matter I do not think it fair to judge them by their conduct in such a moment as the present. That this is the very moment in which to judge of the efficiency of their institutions generally, of the aptitude of those institutions for the security of the nation, I readily acknowledge. But when a ship is at sea in a storm, riding out all that the winds and waves can do to her, one does not condemn her because a yard-arm gives way, nor even though the mainmast should go by the board. If she can make her port, saving life and cargo, she is a good ship, let her losses in spars and rigging be what they may. In this affair of the habeas corpus we will wait a while before we come to any final judgment. If it be that the people, when the war is over, shall consent to live under a military or other dictatorship,—that they shall quietly continue their course as a nation without recovery of their rights of freedom, then we shall have to say that their institutions were not founded in a soil of sufficient depth, and that they gave way before the first high wind that blew on them. I myself do not expect such a result.

I think we must admit that the Americans have received from their government, or rather from their system of policy, that aid and furtherance which they required from it; and, moreover, such aid and furtherance as we expect from our system of government. We must admit that they have been great, and free, and prosperous, as we also have become. And we must admit, also, that in some matters they have gone forward in advance of us. They have educated their people, as we have not educated ours. They have given to their millions a personal respect, and a standing above the abjectness of poverty, which with us are much less general than with them. These things, I grant, have not come of their government, and have not been produced by their written constitution. They are the happy results of their happy circumstances. But so, also, those evil attributes which we sometimes assign to them are not the creatures of their government, or of their constitution. We acknowledge them to be well educated, intelligent, philanthropic, and industrious; but we say that they are ambitious, unjust, self-idolatrous, and irreligious. If so, let us at any rate balance the virtues against the vices. As to their ambition, it is a vice that leans so to virtue's side, that it hardly needs an apology. As to their injustice, or rather dishonesty, I have said what I have to say on that matter. I am not going to flinch from the accusation I have brought, though I am aware that in bringing it I have thrown away any hope that I might have had of carrying with me the good will of the Americans for my book. The love of money, — or rather of making money, — carried to an extreme, has lessened that instinctive respect for the rights of meum and tuum which all men feel more or less, and which, when encouraged within the human breast, finds its result in perfect honesty. Other nations, of which I will not now stop to name even one, have had their periods of natural dishonesty. It may be that others are even now to be placed in the same category. But it is a fault which industry and intelligence combined will after a while serve to lessen and to banish. The industrious man desires to keep the fruit of his own industry, and the intelligent man will ultimately be able to do so. That the Americans are self-idolaters is perhaps true, — with a difference. An American desires you to worship his country, or his brother; but he does not often, by any of the usual signs of conceit, call upon you to worship himself. As an American, treating of America, he is self-idolatrous; but that is a self-idolatry which I can endure. Then, as to his want of religion — and it is a very sad want — I can only say of him, that I, as an Englishman, do not feel myself justified in flinging the first stone at him. In that matter of religion, as in the matter of education, the American, I think, stands on a level higher than ours. There is not in the States so absolute an ignorance of religion as is to be found in some of our manufacturing and mining districts, and also, alas! in some of our agricultural districts; but also, I think, there is less of respect and veneration for God's word among their educated classes, than there is with us; and, perhaps, also less knowledge as to God's word. The general religious level is, I think, higher with them;

but there is with us, if I am right in my supposition, a higher eminence in religion, as there is also a deeper depth of ungodliness.

I think then that we are bound to acknowledge that the Americans have succeeded as a nation, politically and socially. When I speak of social success, I do not mean to say that their manners are correct according to this or that standard. I will not say that they are correct, or are not correct. In that matter of manners I have found that those, with whom it seemed to me natural that I should associate, were very pleasant according to my standard. I do not know that I am a good critic on such a subject, or that I have ever thought much of it with the view of criticising. I have been happy and comfortable with them, and for me that has been sufficient. In speaking of social success I allude to their success in private life as distinguished from that which they have achieved in public life;—to their successes in commerce, in mechanics, in the comforts and luxuries of life, in medicine and all that leads to the solace of affliction, in literature, and I may add also, considering the youth of the nation, in the arts. We are, I think, bound to acknowledge that they have succeeded. And if they have succeeded, it is vain for us to say that a system is wrong which has, at any rate, admitted of such success. That which was wanted from some form of government, has been obtained with much more than average excellence; and therefore the form adopted has approved itself as good. You may explain to a farmer's wife with indisputable logic, that her churn is a bad churn; but as long as she turns out butter in greater quantity, in better quality, and with more profit than her neighbours, you will hardly induce her to change it. It may be that with some other churn she might have done even better; but, under such circumstances, she will have a right to think well of the churn she uses.

The American constitution is now, I think, at the crisis of its severest trial. I conceive it to be by no means perfect, even for the wants of the people who use it; and I have already endeavoured to explain what changes it seems to need. And it has had this defect,—that it has permitted a falling away from its intended modes of action, while its letter has been kept sacred. As I have endeavoured to show, universal suffrage and democratic action in the Senate were not intended by the framers of the constitution. In this respect, the constitution has, as it were, fallen through, and it is needed that its very beams should be re-strengthened. There are also other matters as to which it seems that some change is indispensable. So much I have admitted. But, not the less, judging of it by the entirety of the work that it has done, I think that we are bound to own that it has been successful.

And now, with regard to this tedious war, of which from day to day we are still, in this month of May, 1862, hearing details which teach us to think that it can hardly as yet be near its end;—to what may we rationally look as its result? Of one thing I myself feel tolerably certain,—that its result will not be nothing, as some among us have seemed to suppose may be probable. I cannot believe that all this energy on the part of the North will be of no avail, more than I suppose that southern perseverance will be of no avail. There are those among us who say that as secession will at last be accomplished, the North should have yielded to the South at once, and that nothing will be gained by their great expenditure of life and treasure. I can by no means bring myself to agree with these. I also look to the establishment of secession. Seeing how essential and thorough are the points of variance between the North and the South, how unlike the one people is to the other, and how necessary it is that their policies should be different; seeing how deep are their antipathies, and how fixed is each side in the belief of its own rectitude and in the belief also of the other's political baseness, I cannot believe that the really southern States will ever again be joined in amicable union with those of the North. They, the States of the Gulf, may be utterly subjugated, and the North may hold over them military power. Georgia and her sisters may for a while belong to the Union, as one conquered country belongs to another. But I do not think that they will ever act with the Union;—and, as I imagine, the Union before long will agree to a separation. I do not mean to prophesy that the result will be thus accomplished. It may be that the South will effect their own independence before they lay down their arms. I think, however, that we may look forward to such independence, whether it be achieved in that way, or in this, or in some other.

But not on that account will the war have been of no avail to the North. I think it must be already evident to all those who have looked into the matter that had the North yielded to the first call made by the South for secession all the slave States must have gone. Maryland would have gone, carrying Delaware in its arms; and if Maryland, all south of Maryland. If Maryland had gone, the capital would have gone. If the Government had resolved to yield, Virginia to the east would assuredly have gone, and I think there can be no doubt that Missouri, to the west, would have gone also. The feeling for the Union in Kentucky was very strong, but I do not think that even Kentucky could have saved itself. To have yielded to the southern demands would have been to have yielded everything. But no man now believes, let the contest go as it will, that Maryland and Delaware will go with the South. The secessionists of Baltimore do not think so, nor the gentlemen and ladies of Washington, whose whole hearts are in the southern cause. No man thinks that Maryland will go; and few, I believe, imagine that either Missouri or Kentucky will be divided from the North. I will not pretend what may be the exact line, but I myself feel confident that it will run south both of Virginia and of Kentucky.

If the North do conquer the South, and so arrange their matters that the southern States shall again become members of the Union, it will be admitted that they have done all that they sought to do. If they do not do this;—if instead of doing this, which would be all that they desire, they were in truth to do nothing;—to win finally not one foot of ground from the South,—a supposition which I regard as impossible;—I think that we should still admit after a while that they had done their duty in endeavouring to maintain the integrity of the empire. But if, as a third and more probable alternative, they succeed in rescuing from the South and from slavery four or five of the finest States of the old Union,—a vast portion of the continent, to be beaten by none other in salubrity, fertility, beauty, and political importance,—will it not then be admitted that the war has done some good, and that the life and treasure have not been spent in vain?

That is the termination of the contest to which I look forward. I think that there will be secession, but that the terms of secession will be dictated by the North, not by the South; and among these terms I expect to see an escape from slavery for those border States to which I have alluded. In that proposition which, in February last (1862), was made by the President, and which has since been sanctioned by the Senate, I think we may see the first step towards this measure. It may probably be the case that many of the slaves will be driven south; that as the owners of those slaves are driven from their holdings in Virginia they will take their slaves with them, or send them before them. The manumission, when it reaches Virginia, will not probably enfranchise the half million of slaves who, in 1860, were counted among its population. But as to that I confess myself to be comparatively careless. It is not the concern which I have now at heart. For myself, I shall feel satisfied if that manumission shall reach the million of whites by whom Virginia is populated; or if not that million in its integrity then that other million by which its rich soil would soon be tenanted. There are now about four millions of white men and women inhabiting the slave States which I have described, and I think it will be acknowledged that the northern States will have done something with their armies if they succeed in rescuing those four millions from the stain and evil of slavery.

There is a third question which I have asked myself, and to which I have undertaken to give some answer. When this war be over between the northern and southern States will there come upon us Englishmen a necessity of fighting with the Americans? If there do come such necessity, arising out of our conduct to the States during the period of their civil war, it will indeed be hard upon us, as a nation, seeing the struggle that we have made to be just in our dealings towards the States generally, whether they be North or South. To be just in such a period, and under such circumstances, is very difficult. In that contest between Sardinia and Austria it was all but impossible to be just to the Italians without being unjust to the Emperor of Austria. To have been strictly just at the moment one should have begun by confessing the injustice of so much that had gone before! But in this American contest such justice, though difficult, was easier. Affairs of trade rather than of treaties chiefly interfered; and these affairs, by a total disregard of our own pecuniary interests, could be so managed that justice might be done. This I think was effected. It may be, of course, that I am prejudiced on the side of my own nation; but striving to judge of the matter as best I may without prejudice, I cannot see that we, as a nation, have in aught offended against the strictest justice in our dealings with America during this contest. But justice has not sufficed. I do not know that our bitterest foes in the northern States have accused us of acting unjustly. It is not justice which they have looked for at our hands, and looked for in vain;—not justice, but generosity! We have not, as they say, sympathized with them in their trouble! It seems to me that such a complaint is unworthy of them as a nation, as a people, or as individuals. In such a matter generosity is another name for injustice,—as it too often is in all matters. A generous sympathy with the North would have been an ostensible and crashing enmity to the South. We could not have sympathized with the North without condemning the South, and telling to the world that the South were our enemies. In ordering his own household a man should not want generosity or sympathy from the outside; and if not a man, then certainly not a nation. Generosity between nations must in its very nature be wrong. One nation may be just to another, courteous to another, even considerate to another with propriety. But no nation can be generous to another without injustice either to some third nation, or to itself.

But though no accusation of unfairness has, as far as I am aware, ever been made by the government of Washington against the government of London, there can be no doubt that a very strong feeling of antipathy to England has sprung up in America during this war, and that it is even yet so intense in its bitterness, that were the North to become speedily victorious in their present contest very many Americans would be anxious to turn their arms at once against Canada. And I fear that that fight between the Monitor and the Merrimac has strengthened this wish by giving to the Americans an unwarranted confidence in their capability of defending themselves against any injury from British shipping. It may be said by them, and probably would be said by many of them, that this feeling of enmity had not been engendered by any idea of national injustice on our side;—that it might reasonably exist, though no suspicion of such injustice had arisen in the minds of any. They would argue that the hatred on their part had been engendered by scorn on ours,—by scorn and ill words heaped upon them in their distress.

They would say that slander, scorn, and uncharitable judgments create deeper feuds than do robbery and violence, and produce deeper enmity and worse rancour. "It is because we have been scorned by England, that we hate England. We have been told from week to week, and from day to day, that we were fools, cowards, knaves, and madmen. We have been treated with disrespect, and that disrespect we will avenge." It is thus that they speak of England, and there can be no doubt that the opinion so expressed is very general. It is not my purpose here to say whether in this respect England has given cause of offence to the States, or whether either country has given cause of offence to the other. On both sides have many hard words been spoken, and on both sides also have good words been spoken. It is unfortunately the case that hard words are pregnant, and as such they are read, digested, and remembered; while good words are generally so dull that nobody reads them willingly, and when read they are forgotten. For many years there have been hard words bandied backwards and forwards between England and the United States, showing mutual jealousies and a disposition on the part of each nation to spare no fault committed by the other. This has grown of rivalry between the two, and in fact proves the respect which each has for the other's power and wealth. I will not now pretend to say with which side has been the chiefest blame, if there has been chiefest blame on either side. But I do say that it is monstrous in any people or in any person to suppose that such bickerings can afford a proper ground for war. I am not about to dilate on the horrors of war. Horrid as war may be, and full of evil, it is not so horrid to a nation, nor so full of evil, as national insult unavenged, or as national injury unredressed. A blow taken by a nation and taken without atonement is an acknowledgment of national inferiority than which any war is preferable. Neither England nor the States are inclined to take such blows. But such a blow, before it can be regarded as a national insult, as a wrong done by one nation on another, must be inflicted by the political entity of the one on the political entity of the other. No angry clamours of the press, no declamations of orators, no voices from the people, no studied criticisms from the learned few or unstudied censures from society at large, can have any fair weight on such a question or do aught towards justifying a national quarrel. They cannot form a casus belli. Those two Latin words, which we all understand, explain this with the utmost accuracy. Were it not so, the peace of the world would indeed rest upon sand. Causes of national difference will arise,—for governments will be unjust as are individuals. And causes of difference will arise because governments are too blind to distinguish the just from the unjust. But in such cases the government acts on some ground which it declares. It either shows or pretends to show some casus belli. But in this matter of threatened war between the States and England it is declared openly that such war is to take place because the English have abused the Americans, and because, consequently, the Americans hate the English. There seems to exist an impression that no other ostensible ground for fighting need be shown, although such an event as that of war between the two nations would, as all men acknowledge, be terrible in its results. "Your newspapers insulted us when we were in our difficulties. Your writers said evil things of us. Your legislators spoke of us with scorn. You exacted from us a disagreeable duty of retribution just when the performance of such a duty was most odious to us. You have shown symptoms of joy at our sorrow. And, therefore, as soon as our hands are at liberty, we will fight you." I have known schoolboys to argue in that way, and the arguments have been intelligible. But I cannot understand that any government should admit such an argument.

Nor will the American government willingly admit it. According to existing theories of government the armies of nations are but the tools of the governing powers. If at the close of the present civil war the American government,—the old civil government consisting of the President with such checks as Congress constitutionally has over him,—shall really hold the power to which it pretends, I do not fear that there will be any war. No President, and I think no Congress, will desire such a war. Nor will the people clamour for it, even should the idea of such a war be popular. The people of America are not clamorous against their government. If there be such a war it will be because the army shall have then become more powerful than the Government. If the President can hold his own the people will support him in his desire for peace. But if the President do not hold his own;—if some General with two or three hundred thousand men at his back shall then have the upper hand in the nation,—it is too probable that the people may back him. The old game will be played again that has so often been played in the history of nations, and some wretched military aspirant will go forth to flood Canada with blood, in order that the feathers of his cap may flaunt in men's eyes and that he may be talked of for some years to come as one of the great curses let loose by the Almighty on mankind.

I must confess that there is danger of this. To us the danger is very great. It cannot be good for us to send ships laden outside with iron shields instead of inside with soft goods and hardware to those thickly thronged American ports. It cannot be good for us to have to throw millions into those harbours instead of taking millions out from them. It cannot be good for us to export thousands upon thousands of soldiers to Canada of whom only hundreds would return. The whole turmoil, cost, and paraphernalia of such a course would be injurious to us in the extreme, and the loss of our commerce would be nearly ruinous. But the injury of such a war to us would be as nothing to the injury which it would inflict upon the States. To them for many years it would be absolutely ruinous. It would entail not only all those losses which such a war must bring with it; but that greater loss which would arise to the nation from the fact of its having been powerless to prevent it. Such a war would prove that it had lost the freedom for which it had struggled, and which for so many years it has enjoyed. For the sake of that people as well as for our own,—and for their sakes rather than for our own,—let us, as far as may be, abstain from words which are needlessly injurious. They have done much that is great and noble, even since this war has begun, and we have been slow to acknowledge it. They have made sacrifices for the sake of their country which we have ridiculed. They have struggled to maintain a good cause, and we have disbelieved in their earnestness. They have been anxious to abide by their constitution, which to them has been as it were a second gospel, and we have spoken of that constitution as though it had been a thing of mere words in which life had never existed. This has been done while their hands were very full and their back heavily laden. Such words coming from us, or from parties among us, cannot justify those threats of war which we hear spoken; but that they should make the hearts of men sore and their thoughts bitter against us can hardly be matter of surprise.

As to the result of any such war between us and them, it would depend mainly, I think, on the feelings of the Canadians. Neither could they annex Canada without the good-will of the Canadians, nor could we keep Canada without that good-will. At present the feeling in Canada against the northern States is so strong and so universal that England has little to fear on that head.

I have now done my task, and may take leave of my readers on either side of the water with a hearty hope that the existing war between the North and South may soon be over, and that none other may follow on its heels to exercise that new-fledged military skill which the existing quarrel will have produced on the other side of the Atlantic. I have written my book in obscure language if I have not shown that to me social successes and commercial prosperity are much dearer than any greatness that can be won by arms. The Americans had fondly thought that they were to be exempt from the curse of war,—at any rate from the bitterness of the curse. But the days for such exemption have not come as yet. While we are hurrying on to make twelve-inch shield-plates for our men-of-war, we can hardly dare to think of the days when the sword shall be turned into the ploughshare. May it not be thought well for us if, with such work on our hands, any scraps of iron shall be left to us with which to pursue the purposes of peace? But at least let us not have war with these children of our own. If we must fight, let us fight the French, "for King George upon the throne." The doing so will be disagreeable, but it will not be antipathetic to the nature of an Englishman. For my part, when an American tells me that he wants to fight with me, I regard his offence as compared with that of a Frenchman under the same circumstances, as I would compare the offence of a parricide or a fratricide with that of a mere common-place murderer. Such a war would be plus quam civile bellum. Which of us two could take a thrashing from the other and afterwards go about our business with contentment?

On our return to Liverpool, we stayed for a few hours at Queenstown, taking in coal, and the passengers landed that they might stretch their legs and look about them. I also went ashore at the dear old place which I had known well in other days, when the people were not too grand to call it Cove, and were contented to run down from Cork in river steamers, before the Passage railway was built. I spent a pleasant summer there once in those times;—God be with the good old days! And now I went ashore at Queenstown, happy to feel that I should be again in a British isle, and happy also to know that I was once more in Ireland. And when the people came around me as they did, I seemed to know every face and to be familiar with every voice. It has been my fate to have so close an intimacy with Ireland, that when I meet an Irishman abroad, I always recognize in him more of a kinsman than I do in an Englishman. I never ask an Englishman from what county he comes, or what was his town. To Irishmen I usually put such questions, and I am generally familiar with the old haunts which they name. I was happy therefore to feel myself again in Ireland, and to walk round from Queenstown to the river at Passage by the old way that had once been familiar to my feet.

Or rather I should have been happy if I had not found myself instantly disgraced by the importunities of my friends! A legion of women surrounded me, imploring alms, begging my honour to bestow my charity on them for the love of the Virgin, using the most holy names in their adjurations for halfpence, clinging to me with that half joking, half lachrymose air of importunity which an Irish beggar has assumed as peculiarly her own. There were men too, who begged as well as women. And the women were sturdy and fat, and, not knowing me as well as I knew them, seemed resolved that their importunities should be successful. After all, I had an old world liking for them in their rags. They were endeared to me by certain memories and associations which I cannot define. But then what would those Americans think of them;—of them and of the country which produced them? That was the reflection which troubled me. A legion of women in rags clamorous for bread, protesting to heaven that they are starving, importunate with voices and with hands, surrounding the stranger when he puts his foot on the soil so that he cannot escape, does not afford to the cynical American who then first visits us,—and they all are cynical when they visit us,—a bad opportunity for his sarcasm. He can at any rate boast that he sees nothing of that at home. I myself am fond of Irish beggars. It is an acquired taste,—which comes upon one as does that for smoked whisky, or Limerick tobacco. But I certainly did wish that there were not so many of them at Queenstown.

I tell all this here not to the disgrace of Ireland;—not for the triumph of America. The Irishman or American who thinks rightly on the subject will know that the state of each country has arisen from its opportunities. Beggary does not prevail in new countries, and but few old countries have managed to exist without it. As to Ireland we may rejoice to say that there is less of it now than there was twenty years since. Things are mending there. But though such excuses may be truly made,—although an Englishman when he sees this squalor and poverty on the quays at Queenstown, consoles himself with reflecting that the evil has been unavoidable, but will perhaps soon be avoided,—nevertheless he cannot but remember that there is no such squalor and no such poverty in the land from which he has returned. I claim no credit for the new country. I impute no blame to the old country. But there is the fact. The Irishman when he expatriates himself to one of those American States loses much of that affectionate, confiding, master-worshipping nature which makes him so good a fellow when at home. But he becomes more of a man. He assumes a dignity which he never has known before. He learns to regard his labour as his own property. That which he earns he takes without thanks, but he desires to take no more than he earns. To me personally he has perhaps become less pleasant than he was. But to himself—! It seems to me that such a man must feel himself half a god, if he has the power of comparing what he is with what he was.

It is right that all this should be acknowledged by us. When we speak of America and of her institutions we should remember that she has given to our increasing population rights and privileges which we could not give;—which as an old country we probably can never give. That self-asserting, obtrusive independence which so often wounds us, is, if viewed aright, but an outward sign of those good things which a new country has produced for its people. Men and women do not beg in the States;—they do not offend you with tattered rags; they do not complain to heaven of starvation; they do not crouch to the ground for halfpence. If poor, they are not abject in their poverty. They read and write. They walk like human beings made in God's form. They know that they are men and women, owing it to themselves and to the world that they should earn their bread by their labour, but feeling that when earned it is their own. If this be so,—if it be acknowledged that it is so,—should not such knowledge in itself be sufficient testimony of the success of the country and of her institutions?

APPENDIX A
DECLARATION OF INDEPENDENCE

When, in the course of human events, it becomes necessary for one people to dissolve the political bands which have connected them with another, and to assume, among the powers of the earth, the separate and equal station to which the laws of nature and of nature's God entitle them, a decent respect to the opinions of mankind requires that they should declare the causes which impel them to the separation.

We hold these truths to be self-evident: that all men are created equal; that they are endowed by their Creator with certain inalienable rights; that among these are life, liberty, and the pursuit of happiness. That, to secure these rights, governments are instituted among men, deriving their just powers from the consent of the governed; and that, whenever any form of government becomes destructive of these ends, it is the right of the people to alter or abolish it, and to institute new government, laying its foundations on such principles, and organizing its powers in such form, as to them shall seem most likely to effect their safety and happiness. Prudence, indeed, will dictate that governments, long established, should not be changed for light and transient causes; and, accordingly, all experience hath shown, that mankind are more disposed to suffer, while evils are sufferable, than to right themselves by abolishing the forms to which they are accustomed. But, when a long train of abuses and usurpations, pursuing invariably the same object, evinces a design to reduce them under absolute despotism, it is their right, it is their duty, to throw off such government, and to provide new guards for their future security. Such has been the patient sufferance of the colonies, and such is now the necessity which constrains them to alter their former systems of government. The history of the present king of Great Britain is a history of repeated injuries and usurpations, all having, in direct object, the establishment of an absolute tyranny over these States. To prove this, let facts be submitted to a candid world.

He has refused his assent to laws the most wholesome and necessary for the public good.

He has forbidden his governors to pass laws of immediate and pressing importance, unless suspended in their operations till his assent should be obtained; and, when so suspended, he has utterly neglected to attend to them.

He has refused to pass other laws for the accommodation of large districts of people, unless those people would relinquish the right of representation in the legislature—a right inestimable to them, and formidable to tyrants only.

He has called together legislative bodies at places unusual, uncomfortable, and distant from the repository of their public records, for the sole purpose of fatiguing them into compliance with his measures.

He has dissolved representative houses repeatedly, for opposing with manly firmness his invasions on the rights of the people.

He has refused, for a long time after such dissolutions, to cause others to be elected; whereby the legislative powers, incapable of annihilation, have returned to the people at large for their exercise; the State remaining, in the meantime, exposed to all the dangers of invasion from without, and convulsions within.

He has endeavoured to prevent the population of these States; for that purpose, obstructing the laws of naturalization of foreigners, refusing to pass others to encourage their migration thither, and raising the conditions of new appropriations of lands.

He has obstructed the administration of justice, by refusing his assent to laws for establishing judiciary powers.

He has made judges dependent on his will alone for the tenure of their offices, and the amount and payment of their salaries.

He has erected a multitude of new offices, and sent hither swarms of officers to harass our people, and eat out their substance.

He has kept among us, in time of peace, standing armies, without the consent of our legislatures.

He has affected to render the military independent of, and superior to, the civil power.

He has combined, with others, to subject us to a jurisdiction foreign to our constitution, and unacknowledged by our laws; giving his assent to their acts of pretended legislation.

For quartering large bodies of armed troops among us.

For protecting them, by a mock trial, from punishment for any murders which they should commit on the inhabitants of these States.

For cutting off our trade with all parts of the world.

For imposing taxes on us without our consent

For depriving us, in many cases, of the benefit of trial by jury.

For transporting us beyond seas, to be tried for pretended offences.

For abolishing the free system of English laws in a neighbouring province, establishing therein an arbitrary government, and enlarging its boundaries, so as to render it at once an example and fit instrument for introducing the same absolute rule into these colonies.

For taking away our charters, abolishing our most valuable laws, and altering, fundamentally, the forms of our governments.

For suspending our own legislatures, and declaring themselves invested with power to legislate for us in all cases whatsoever.

He has abdicated government here, by declaring us out of his protection and waging war against us.

He has plundered our seas, ravaged our coasts, burnt our towns, and destroyed the lives of our people.

He is, at this time, transporting large armies of foreign mercenaries to complete the works of death, desolation, and tyranny, already begun, with circumstances of cruelty and perfidy scarcely paralleled in the most barbarous ages, and totally unworthy the head of a civilized nation.

He has constrained our fellow-citizens, taken captive on the high seas, to bear arms against their country, to become the executioners of their friends and brethren, or to fall themselves by their hands.

He has excited domestic insurrections amongst us, and has endeavoured to bring on the inhabitants of our frontiers the merciless Indian savages, whose known rule of warfare is an undistinguished destruction of all ages, sexes, and conditions.

In every stage of these oppressions, we have petitioned for redress in the most humble terms. Our repeated petitions have been answered only by repeated injuries. A prince, whose character is thus marked by every act which may define a tyrant, is unfit to be the ruler of a free people.

Nor have we been wanting in attention to our British brethren. We have warned them, from time to time, of the attempts by their legislature, to extend an unwarrantable jurisdiction over us. We have reminded them of the circumstances of our emigration and settlement here. We have appealed to their native justice and magnanimity, and we have conjured them, by the ties of our common kindred, to disavow these usurpations, which would inevitably interrupt our connections and correspondence. They, too, have been deaf to the voice of justice and of consanguinity. We must, therefore, acquiesce in the necessity which denounces our separation, and hold them, as we hold the rest of mankind, enemies in war, in peace, friends.

We, therefore, the Representatives of the United States of America, in General Congress assembled, appealing to the Supreme Judge of the world for the rectitude of our intentions, do, in the name and by the authority of the good people of these colonies, solemnly publish and declare that these United Colonies are, and of right ought to be, free and independent States; that they are absolved from all allegiance to the British crown, and that all political connection between them and the state of Great Britain is, and ought to be, totally dissolved; and that, as free and independent States, they have full power to levy war, conclude peace, contract alliances, establish commerce, and to do all other acts and things which independent States may of right do. And, for the support of this declaration, with a firm reliance on the protection of Divine Providence, we mutually pledge to each other our lives, our fortunes, and our sacred honour.

The foregoing declaration was, by order of Congress, engrossed, and signed by the following members:

JOHN HANCOCK.

New Hampshire.

Josiah Bartlett,
William Whipple,
Matthew Thornton.

Massachusetts Bay.

Samuel Adams,
John Adams,
Robert Treat Paine,
Elbridge Gerry.

Rhode Island.

Stephen Hopkins,
William Ellery.

Delaware.

Cæsar Rodney,
George Read,
Thomas M'Kean.

Maryland.

Samuel Chase,
William Paca,
Thomas Stone,
Charles Carroll,
of Carrollton.

Virginia.

George Wythie,
Richard Henry Lee,
Thomas Jefferson,
Benjamin Harrison,
Thomas Nelson, Jr.
Francis Lightfoot Lee,
Carter Braxton.

Connecticut.
Roger Sherman,
Samuel Huntington,
William Williams,
Oliver Wolcott.

New York.
William Floyd,
Philip Livingston,
Francis Lewis,
Lewis Morris.

Pennsylvania.
Robert Morris,
Benjamin Rush,
Benjamin Franklin,
John Morton,
George Clymer,
James Smith,
George Taylor,
James Wilson,
George Ross.

New Jersey.
Richard Stockton,
John Witherspoon,
Francis Hopkinson,
John Hart,
Abraham Clark.

North Carolina.
William Hooper,
Joseph Hewes,
John Penn.

South Carolina.
Edward Rutledge,
Thomas Heyward, Jr.
Thomas Lynch, Jr.
Arthur Middleton.

Georgia.
Button Gwinnett,
Lyman Hall,
George Walton.

4 *July*, 1776.

APPENDIX B
ARTICLES OF CONFEDERATION, ETC

TO ALL TO WHOM THESE PRESENTS SHALL COME

We, the undersigned, delegates of the States,
affixed to our names, send greeting:

Whereas, the delegates of the United States of America, in Congress assembled did, on the fifteenth day of November, in the year of our Lord one thousand seven hundred and seventy-seven, and in the second year of the independence of America, agree to certain articles of confederation and perpetual union between the States of New Hampshire, Massachusetts Bay, Rhode Island and Providence Plantations, Connecticut, New York, New Jersey, Pennsylvania, Delaware, Maryland, Virginia, North Carolina, South Carolina, and Georgia, in the words following, viz:

> Articles of confederation and perpetual union between the States of New Hampshire, Massachusetts Bay, Rhode Island and Providence Plantations, Connecticut, New York, New Jersey, Pennsylvania, Delaware, Maryland, Virginia, North Carolina, South Carolina, and Georgia.

Article 1. The style of this confederacy shall be, "The United States of America."

Art. 2. Each State retains its sovereignty, freedom, and independence, and every power, jurisdiction, and right, which is not by this confederation expressly delegated to the United States in Congress assembled.

Art. 3. The said States hereby severally enter into a firm league of friendship with each other for their common defence, the security of their liberties, and their mutual and general welfare; binding themselves to assist each other against all force offered to, or attacks made upon them, or any of them, on account of religion, sovereignty, trade, or any other pretext whatever.

Art. 4. The better to secure and perpetuate mutual friendship and intercourse among the people of the different States in this union, the free inhabitants of each of these States, paupers, vagabonds, and fugitives from justice excepted, shall be entitled to all privileges and immunities of free citizens in the several States; and the people of each State shall have free ingress and regress to and from any other State, and shall enjoy therein all the privileges of trade and commerce, subject to the same duties, impositions, and restrictions, as the inhabitants thereof respectively, provided that such restrictions shall not extend so far as to prevent the removal of property imported into any State to any other State, of which the owner is an inhabitant; provided, also, that no imposition, duties, or restriction, shall be laid by any State on the property of the United States, or either of them.

If any person guilty of or charged with treason, felony, or other high misdemeanor, in any State, shall flee from justice, and be found in any of the United States, he shall upon demand of the Governor, or executive power of the State from which he fled, be delivered up, and removed to the State having jurisdiction of his offence.

Full faith and credit shall be given in each of these States to the records, acts, and judicial proceedings of the courts and magistrates of every other State.

Art. 5. For the more convenient management of the general interests of the United States, delegates shall be annually appointed in such manner as the legislature of each State shall direct, to meet in Congress on the first Monday in November, in every year, with a power reserved to each State to recall its delegates or any of them, at any time within the year, and to send others in their stead for the remainder of the year.

No State shall be represented in Congress by less than two nor more than seven members; and no person shall be capable of being a delegate for more than three years in any term of six years; nor shall any person, being a delegate, be capable of holding an office under the United States, for which he, or another for his benefit, receives any salary, fees, or emolument of any kind.

Each State shall maintain its own delegates in a meeting of the States, and while they act as members of the committee of the States.

In determining questions in the United States in Congress assembled, each State shall have one vote.

Freedom of speech and debate in Congress shall not be impeached or questioned in any court or place out of Congress; and the members of

Congress shall be protected in their persons from arrests and imprisonments, during the time of their going to and from and attendance on Congress, except for treason, felony, or breach of the peace.

Art. 6. No State, without the consent of the United States in Congress assembled, shall send an embassy to, or receive any embassy from, or enter into any conference, agreement, alliance, or treaty, with any king, prince, or State; nor shall any person holding any office of profit or trust under the United States or any of them, accept of any present, emolument, office, or title of any kind whatever, from any king, prince, or foreign State; nor shall the United States in Congress assembled, or any of them, grant any title of nobility.

No two or more States shall enter into any treaty, confederation, or alliance whatever between them, without the consent of the United States in Congress assembled, specifying accurately the purpose for which the same is to be entered into, and how long it shall continue.

No State shall lay any imposts or duties, which may interfere with any stipulations in treaties entered into by the United States in Congress assembled, with any king, prince, or State, in pursuance of any treaties already proposed by Congress to the courts of France and Spain.

No vessels of war shall be kept up in time of peace, by any State, except such number as shall be deemed necessary by the United States in Congress assembled, for the defence of such State or its trade; nor shall any body of forces be kept up by any State in time of peace, except such number only as, in the judgment of the United States in Congress assembled, shall be deemed requisite to garrison the forts necessary for the defence of such State; but every State shall always keep up a well-regulated and disciplined militia, sufficiently armed and accoutred, and shall provide and have constantly ready for use, in public stores, a number of field pieces and tents, and a proper quantity of arms, ammunition, and camp equipage.

No State shall engage in any war without the consent of the United States in Congress assembled, unless such State be actually invaded by enemies, or shall, have received certain advice of a resolution being formed by some nation of Indians to invade such State, and the danger is so imminent as not to admit of a delay till the United States in Congress assembled can be consulted; nor shall any State grant commissions to any ships or vessels of war, or letters of marque or reprisal, except it be after a declaration of war by the United States in Congress assembled, and then only against the Kingdom or State, and the subjects thereof, against which war has been so declared, and under such regulations as shall be established by the United States in Congress assembled, unless such State be infested by pirates, in which case vessels of war may be fitted out for that occasion, and kept so long as the danger shall continue, or until the United States in Congress assembled shall determine otherwise.

Art. 7. When land forces are raised by any State for the common defence, all officers of or under the rank of colonel, shall be appointed by the legislature of each State respectively, by whom such forces shall be raised, or in such manner as such State shall direct; and all vacancies shall be filled up by the State which first made the appointment.

Art. 8. All charges of war, and all other expenses that shall be incurred for the common defence or general welfare, and allowed by the United States in Congress assembled, shall be defrayed out of a common treasury, which shall be supplied by the several States in proportion to the value of all land within each State granted to or surveyed for any person, as such land and the buildings and improvements thereon shall be estimated, according to such mode as the United States in Congress assembled shall from time to time direct and appoint.

The taxes for paying that proportion shall be laid and levied by the authority and direction of the legislatures of the several States, within the time agreed upon by the United States in Congress assembled.

Art. 9. The United States in Congress assembled shall have the sole and exclusive right and power of determining on peace and war, except in the cases mentioned in the sixth Article: of sending and receiving ambassadors: entering into treaties and alliances; provided that no treaty of commerce shall be made whereby the legislative power of the respective States shall be restrained from imposing such imposts and duties on foreigners as their own people are subjected to, or from prohibiting the exportation or importation of any species of goods or commodities whatsoever: of establishing rules for deciding in all cases, what captures on land or water shall be legal, and in what manner prizes taken by land or naval forces in the service of the United States shall be divided or appropriated: of granting letters of marque and reprisal, in times of peace: appointing courts for the trial of piracies and felonies committed on the high seas, and establishing courts for receiving and determining finally appeals in all cases of captures; provided, that no member of Congress shall be appointed a judge of any of the said courts.

The United States in Congress assembled shall also be the last resort on appeal in all disputes and differences now subsisting, or that hereafter may arise between two or more States concerning boundary, jurisdiction, or any other cause whatever; which authority shall always be exercised in the manner following: whenever the legislative or executive authority or lawful agent of any State in controversy with another shall present a petition to

Congress, stating the matter in question, and praying for a hearing, notice thereof shall be given by order of Congress to the legislative or executive authority of the other State in controversy, and a day assigned for the appearance of the parties, by their lawful agents, who shall then be directed to appoint by joint consent commissioners or judges to constitute a court for hearing and determining the matter in question; but if they cannot agree, Congress shall name three persons out of each of the United States, and from the list of such persons each party shall alternately strike out one, the petitioners beginning, until the number shall be reduced to thirteen; and from that number not less than seven nor more than nine names, as Congress shall direct, shall, in the presence of Congress, be drawn out by lot; and the persons whose names shall be so drawn, or any five of them, shall be commissioners or judges, to hear and finally determine the controversy, so always as a major part of the judges, who shall hear the cause, shall agree in the determination; and if either party shall neglect to attend at the day appointed, without showing reasons which Congress shall judge sufficient, or being present shall refuse to strike, the Congress shall proceed to nominate three persons out of each State, and the Secretary of Congress shall strike in behalf of such party absent or refusing; and the judgment and sentence of the court to be appointed in the manner before prescribed, shall be final and conclusive; and if any of the parties shall refuse to submit to the authority of such court, or to appear, or defend their claim or cause, the court shall nevertheless proceed to pronounce sentence or judgment, which shall in like manner be final and decisive, the judgment or sentence, and other proceedings, being in either case transmitted to Congress, and lodged among the acts of Congress for the security of the parties concerned: provided, that every commissioner, before he sits in judgment, shall take an oath, to be administered by one of the judges of the supreme or superior court of the State, where the cause shall be tried, "well and truly to hear and determine the matter in question, according to the best of his judgment, without favour, affection, or hope of reward;" provided also, that no State shall be deprived of territory for the benefit of the United States.

All controversies concerning the private right of soil, claimed under different grants of two or more States, whose jurisdiction as they may respect such lands and the States which passed such grants are adjusted, the said grants or either of them being at the same time claimed to have originated antecedent to such settlement of jurisdiction, shall, on the petition of either party to the Congress of the United States, be finally determined, as near as may be, in the same manner as is before prescribed for deciding disputes respecting territorial jurisdiction between different States.

The United States in Congress assembled shall also have the sole and exclusive right and power of regulating the alloy and value of coin struck by their own authority, or by that of the respective States; fixing the standard of weights and measures throughout the United States: regulating the trade and managing all affairs with Indians not members of any of the States; provided, that the legislative right of any State within its own limits be not infringed or violated: establishing and regulating post-offices from one State to another, throughout all the United States, and exacting such postage on the papers passing through the same as may be requisite to defray the expenses of the said office: appointing all officers of the land forces in the service of the United States, excepting regimental officers: appointing all the officers of the naval forces, and commissioning all officers whatever in the service of the United States: making rules for the government and regulation of the said land and naval forces, and directing their operations.

The United States in Congress assembled shall have authority to appoint a committee to sit in the recess of Congress, to be denominated "a Committee of the States;" and to consist of one delegate from each State, and to appoint such other committees and civil officers as may be necessary for managing the general affairs of the United States, under their direction: to appoint one of their number to preside, provided that no person be allowed to serve in the office of President more than one year in any term of three years: to ascertain the necessary sums of money to be raised for the service of the United States, and to appropriate and apply the same for defraying the public expenses: to borrow money or emit bills on the credit of the United States, transmitting every half year to the respective States an account of the sums of money so borrowed or emitted: to build and equip a navy: to agree upon the number of land forces, and to make requisitions from each State for its quota, in proportion to the number of white inhabitants in each State; which requisition shall be binding, and thereupon the legislature of each State shall appoint the regimental officers, raise the men, and clothe, arm, and equip them in a soldier-like manner, at the expense of the United States; and the officers and men so clothed, armed, and equipped, shall march to the place appointed, and within the time agreed on by the United States in Congress assembled: but if the United States in Congress assembled, shall, on consideration of circumstances, judge proper that any State should not raise men, or should raise a smaller number than its quota, and that any other State should raise a greater number of men than the quota thereof, such extra number shall be raised, officered, clothed, armed, and equipped, in the same manner as the quota of such State, unless the legislature of such State shall judge that such extra number cannot safely be spared out of the same; in which case they shall raise, officer, clothe, arm, and equip, as many of such extra number as they judge can safely be spared. And the officers and men so clothed, armed, and equipped, shall march to the place appointed, and within the time agreed on by the United States in Congress assembled.

The United States in Congress assembled shall never engage in a war, nor grant letters of marque and reprisal in time of peace, nor enter into any treaties or alliances, nor coin money, nor regulate the value thereof, nor ascertain the sums and expenses necessary for the defence and welfare of the United States or any of them, nor emit bills, nor borrow money on the credit of the United States, nor appropriate money, nor agree upon the number of vessels of war to be built or purchased, or the number of land or sea forces to be raised, nor appoint a commander in chief of the army or navy, unless nine States assent to the same; nor shall a question on any other point, except for adjourning from day to day, be determined, unless by the votes of a majority of the United States in Congress assembled.

The Congress of the United States shall have power to adjourn to any time within the year, and to any place within the United States, so that no period of adjournment be for a longer duration than the space of six months; and shall publish the journal of their proceedings monthly, except such parts thereof relating to treaties, alliances, or military operations, as in their judgment require secresy; and the yeas and nays of the delegates of each State on any question shall be entered on the journal when it is desired by any delegate; and the delegates of a State, or any of them, at his or their request, shall be furnished with a transcript of the said journal, except such parts as are above excepted, to lay before the legislatures of the several States.

Art. 10. The Committee of the States, or any nine of them, shall be authorized to execute in the recess of Congress, such of the powers of Congress as the United States in Congress assembled, by the consent of nine States, shall, from time to time, think expedient to vest them with; provided that no power be delegated to the said committee, for the exercise of which, by the articles of confederation, the voice of nine States in the Congress of the United States assembled is requisite.

Art. 11. Canada, acceding to this confederation, and joining in the measures of the United States, shall be admitted into, and entitled to, all the advantages of this union: but no other colony shall be admitted into the same unless such admission be agreed to by nine States.

Art. 12. All bills of credit emitted, moneys borrowed, debts contracted, by or under the authority of Congress, before the assembling of the United States, in pursuance of the present confederation, shall be deemed and considered as a charge against the United States, for payment and satisfaction whereof the said United States and the public faith are hereby solemnly pledged.

Art. 13. Every State shall abide by the determination of the United States in Congress assembled, on all questions which, by this confederation, are submitted to them. And the Articles of this confederation shall be inviolably observed by every State, and the union shall be perpetual; nor shall any alteration at any time hereafter be made in any of them, unless such alteration be agreed to in a Congress of the United States, and be afterwards confirmed by the legislature of every State.

And whereas it has pleased the Great Governor of the world to incline the hearts of the legislatures we respectively represent in Congress, to approve of and to authorize us to ratify the said Articles of confederation and perpetual union: Know ye, That we, the undersigned delegates, by virtue of the power and authority to us given for that purpose, do, by these presents, in the name and in behalf of our respective constituents, fully and entirely ratify and confirm each and every of the said Articles of confederation and perpetual union, and all and singular the matters and things therein contained; and we do further solemnly plight and engage the faith of our respective constituents, that they shall abide by the determinations of the United States in Congress assembled, on all questions which, by the said confederation, are submitted to them; and that the Articles thereof shall be inviolably observed by the States we respectively represent; and that the union shall be perpetual.

In witness whereof, we have hereunto set our hands, in Congress. Done at Philadelphia, in the State of Pennsylvania, the ninth day of July, in the year of our Lord one thousand seven hundred and seventy-eight, and in the third year of the independence of America.

On the part and behalf of the State of New Hampshire.

Josiah Bartlet,	John Wentworth, jun.,
	August 8, 1778.

On the part and behalf of the State of Massachusetts Bay.

John Hancock,	Francis Dana,
Samuel Adams,	James Lovell,
Elbridge Gerry,	Samuel Holten.

On the part and in behalf of the State of Rhode
Island and Providence Plantations.

William Ellery,   John Collins.
Henry Marchant,

On the part and behalf of the State of Connecticut.

Roger Sherman,   Titus Hosmer,
Samuel Huntington,   Andrew Adams.
Oliver Wolcott,

On the part and behalf of the State of New York.

Jas. Duane,   Wm. Duer,
Fra. Lewis,   Gouv. Morris.

On the part and in behalf of the State of New Jersey.

Jno. Witherspoon,   Nath. Scudder,
                                               Nov. 26, 1778.

On the part and behalf of the State of Pennsylvania.

Robt. Morris,   William Clingan,
Daniel Roberdeau,   Joseph Reed,
Jona. Bayard Smith,   22d July, 1778.

On the part and behalf of the State of Delaware.

Tho. M'Kean,   Nicholas Van Dyke.
Feb. 13, 1779,
John Dickinson,
May 5th, 1779,

On the part and behalf of the State of Maryland.

John Hanson,   Daniel Carroll,
March 1,1781,   March 1, 1781.

On the part and behalf of the State of Virginia.

Richard Henry Lee,   Jno. Harvie,
John Banister,   Francis Lightfoot Lee.
Thomas Adams,

On the part and behalf of the State of North Carolina.

John Penn,   Jno. Williams.
July 21,1778,
Corns. Harnett,

On the part and behalf of the State of South Carolina.

Henry Laurens,   Richard Hutson,
William Henry Drayton,   Thos. Heywood, jun.
Jno. Mathews,

On the part and behalf of the State of Georgia.

Jno. Walton,   Edwd. Langworthy.
24th July, 1778,
Edwd. Telfair,

Note.—From the circumstance of delegates from the same State having signed the Articles of confederation at different times, as appears by the dates, it is probable they affixed their names as they happened to be present in Congress, after they had been authorized by their constituents.

The above Articles of confederation continued in force until the 4th day of March, 1789, when the constitution of the United States took effect.

APPENDIX C
CONSTITUTION OF THE UNITED STATES

PREAMBLE

We, the people of the United States, in order to form a more perfect union, establish justice, insure domestic tranquillity, provide for the common defence, promote the general welfare, and secure the blessings of liberty to ourselves and our posterity, do ordain and establish this Constitution for the United States of America.

ARTICLE I

Of the Legislature.

SECTION I

1. All legislative powers herein granted, shall be vested in a Congress of the United States, which shall consist of a Senate and House of Representatives.

SECTION II

1. The House of Representatives shall be composed of members chosen every second year by the people of the several States; and the electors in each State shall have the qualifications requisite for electors of the most numerous branch of the State legislature.

2. No person shall be a representative who shall not have attained to the age of twenty-five years, and been seven years a citizen of the United States, and who shall not, when elected, be an inhabitant of that State in which he shall be chosen.

3. Representatives and direct taxes shall be apportioned among the several States which may be included within this union, according to their respective numbers, which shall be determined by adding to the whole number of free persons, including those bound to service for a term of years, and excluding Indians not taxed, three-fifths of all other persons. The actual enumeration shall be made within three years after the first meeting of the Congress of the United States, and within every subsequent term of ten years,

in such manner as they shall by law direct. The number of representatives shall not exceed one for every thirty thousand, but each State shall have at least one representative; and until such enumeration shall be made, the State of *New Hampshire* shall be entitled to choose three; *Massachusetts*, eight; *Rhode Island*, and *Providence Plantations*, one; *Connecticut*, five; *New York*, six; *New Jersey*, four; *Pennsylvania*, eight; *Delaware*, one; *Maryland*, six; *Virginia*, ten; *North Carolina*, five; *South Carolina*, five; and *Georgia*, three.

4. When vacancies happen in the representation from any State, the executive authority thereof shall issue writs of election to fill up such vacancies.

5. The House of Representatives shall choose their speaker and other officers, and shall have the sole power of impeachment.

SECTION III

1. The Senate of the United States shall be composed of two senators from each State, chosen by the legislature thereof, for six years, and each senator shall have one vote.

2. Immediately after they shall be assembled in consequence of the first election, they shall be divided, as equally as may be, into three classes. The seats of the senators of the first class shall be vacated at the expiration of the second year, of the second class at the expiration of the fourth, and of the third class at the expiration of the sixth year, so that one-third may be chosen every second year; and if vacancies happen, by resignation or otherwise, during the recess of the legislature of any State, the executive thereof may make temporary appointments until the next meeting of the legislature, which shall then fill such vacancies.

3. No person shall be a senator who shall not have attained to the age of thirty years, and been nine years a citizen of the United States, and who shall not, when elected, be an inhabitant of that State for which he shall be chosen.

4. The Vice-President of the United States shall be President of the Senate, but shall have no vote, unless they be equally divided.

5. The Senate shall choose their other officers, and also a president pro tempore, in the absence of the Vice-President, or when he shall exercise the office of President of the United States.

6. The Senate shall have the sole power to try all impeachments. When sitting for that purpose, they shall be on oath or affirmation. When the President of the United States is tried, the chief justice shall preside; and no person shall be convicted without the concurrence of two-thirds of the members present.

7. Judgment in case of impeachment shall not extend further than to removal from office, and disqualification to hold and enjoy any office of honour, trust, or profit, under the United States; but the party convicted shall, nevertheless, be liable and subject to indictment, trial, judgment, and punishment according to law.

SECTION IV

1. The times, places, and manner of holding elections for senators and representatives, shall be prescribed in each State by the legislature thereof; but the Congress may at any time, by law, make or alter such regulations, except as to the place of choosing senators.

2. The Congress shall assemble at least once in every year, and such meeting shall be on the first Monday in December, unless they shall by law appoint a different day.

SECTION V

1. Each House shall be the judge of the elections, returns, and qualifications of its own members; and a majority of each shall constitute a quorum to do business; but a smaller number may adjourn from day to day, and may be authorized to compel the attendance of absent members, in such manner and under such penalties as each House may provide.

2. Each House may determine the rule of its proceedings, punish its members for disorderly behaviour, and, with the concurrence of two-thirds, expel a member.

3. Each House shall keep a journal of its proceedings, and from time to time publish the same, excepting such parts as may in their judgment require secrecy; and the yeas and nays of the members of either House, on any question, shall, at the desire of one-fifth of those present, be entered on the journal.

4. Neither House during the Session of Congress shall, without the consent of the other, adjourn for more than three days, nor to any other place than that in which the two Houses shall be sitting.

SECTION VI

1. The senators and representatives shall receive a compensation for their services, to be ascertained by law, and paid out of the treasury of the United States. They shall in all cases, except treason, felony, and breach of the peace, be privileged from arrest during their attendance at the session of their respective Houses, and in going to or returning from the same; and for any speech or debate in either House, they shall not be questioned in any other place.

2. No senator or representative shall, during the time for which he was elected, be appointed to any civil office under the authority of the United States, which shall have been created, or the emoluments whereof shall have been increased, during such time; and no person holding any office under the United States shall be a member of either House during his continuance in office.

SECTION VII

1. All Bills for raising revenue shall originate in the House of Representatives; but the Senate may propose or concur with amendments, as on other Bills.

2. Every Bill which shall have passed the House of Representatives and the Senate shall, before it become a law, be presented to the President of the United States; if he approve, he shall sign it; but if not, he shall return it, with his objections, to that House in which it shall have originated, who shall enter the objection at large on their journal, and proceed to reconsider it. If, after such reconsideration, two-thirds of that House shall agree to pass the Bill, it shall be sent, together with the objections, to the other House, by which it shall likewise be reconsidered, and if approved by two-thirds of that House, it shall become a law. But in all such cases the votes of both Houses shall be determined by yeas and nays, and the names of the persons voting for and against the Bill shall be entered on the journal of each House respectively. If any Bill shall not be returned by the President within ten days (Sundays excepted) after it shall have been presented to him, the same shall be a law in like manner as if he had signed it, unless the Congress by their adjournment prevent its return, in which case it shall not be a law.

3. Every order, resolution, or vote to which the concurrence of the Senate and House of Representatives may be necessary, (except a question of adjournment), shall be presented to the President of the United States; and before the same shall take effect, shall be approved by him, or being disapproved by him, shall be repassed by two-thirds of the Senate and House of Representatives, according to the rules and limitations prescribed in the case of a Bill.

SECTION VIII

The Congress shall have power—

1. To lay and collect taxes, duties, imposts, and excises, to pay the debts and provide for the common defence and general welfare of the United States; but all duties, imposts, and excises shall be uniform throughout the United States:

2. To borrow money on the credit of the United States:

3. To regulate commerce with foreign nations, and among the several States, and with the Indian tribes:

4. To establish a uniform rule of naturalization, and uniform laws on the subject of bankruptcies, throughout the United States:

5. To coin money, regulate the value thereof, and of foreign coin, and fix the standard of weights and measures:

6. To provide for the punishment of counterfeiting the securities and current coin of the United States:

7. To establish post offices and post roads:

8. To promote the progress of science and useful arts, by securing for limited times to authors and inventors the exclusive right to their respective writings and discoveries:

9. To constitute tribunals inferior to the Supreme Court:

10. To define and punish piracies and felonies committed on the high seas, and offences against the law of nations:

11. To declare war, grant letters of marque and reprisal, and make rules concerning captures on land and water:

12. To raise and support armies; but no appropriation of money to that use shall be for a longer term than two years:

13. To provide and maintain a navy:

14. To make rules for the government and regulation of the land and naval forces:

15. To provide for calling forth the militia to execute the laws of the Union, suppress insurrections, and repel invasions:

16. To provide for organizing, arming, and disciplining the militia, and for governing such part of them as may be employed in the service of the United States, reserving to the States respectively the appointment of the officers and the authority of training the militia according to the discipline prescribed by Congress:

17. To exercise exclusive legislation, in all cases whatsoever, over such district (not exceeding ten miles square) as may, by cession of particular States and the acceptance of Congress, become the seat of government of the United States, and to exercise like authority over all places purchased, by the consent of the legislature of the State in which the same shall be, for the erection of forts, magazines, arsenals, dock-yards, and other needful buildings: and,

18. To make all laws which shall be necessary and proper for carrying into execution the foregoing powers, and all other powers vested by this Constitution in the government of the United States, or any department or officer thereof.

SECTION IX

1. The migration or importation of such persons as any of the States now existing shall think proper to admit, shall not be prohibited by the Congress prior to the year one thousand eight hundred and eight, but a tax or duty may be imposed on such importation, not exceeding ten dollars for each person.

2. The privilege of the writ of *habeas corpus* shall not be suspended unless when, in case of rebellion or invasion, the public safety may require it.

3. No Bill of attainder, or ex-post-facto law, shall be passed.

4. No capitation or other direct tax shall be laid; unless in proportion to the census or enumeration hereinbefore directed to be taken.

5. No tax or duty shall be laid on articles exported from any State. No preference shall be given by any regulation of commerce or revenue to the ports of one State over those of another; nor shall vessels bound to or from one State be obliged to enter, clear, or pay duties in another.

6. No money shall be drawn from the treasury but in consequence of appropriations made by law; and a regular statement and account of the receipts and expenditures of all public money shall be published from time to time.

7. No title of nobility shall be granted by the United States, and no person holding any office of profit or trust under them shall, without the consent of Congress, accept of any present, emolument, office, or title of any kind whatever, from any king, prince, or foreign State.

SECTION X

1. No State shall enter into any treaty, alliance, or confederation; grant letters of marque and reprisal; coin money; emit bills of credit; make anything but gold and silver coin a tender in payment of debts; pass any Bill of attainder, ex-post-facto law, or law impairing the obligation of contracts; or grant any title of nobility.

2. No State shall, without the consent of Congress, lay any imposts or duties on imports or exports, except what may be absolutely necessary for executing its inspection laws; and the net produce of all duties and imposts

laid by any State on imports or exports shall be for the use of the treasury of the United States, and all such laws shall be subject to the revision and control of Congress. No State shall, without the consent of Congress, lay any duty on tonnage, keep troops or ships of war in time of peace, enter into any agreement or compact with another State, or with a foreign power, or engage in war, unless actually invaded, or in such imminent danger as will not admit of delay.

ARTICLE II

Of the Executive.

SECTION I

1. The executive power shall be vested in a President of the United States of America. He shall hold his office during the term of four years, and, together with the Vice-President, chosen for the same term, be elected as follows:—

2. Each State shall appoint, in such manner as the legislature thereof may direct, a number of electors, equal to the whole number of senators and representatives to which the State may be entitled in Congress; but no senator or representative, or person holding any office of trust or profit under the United States, shall be appointed an elector.

3. The electors shall meet in their respective States, and vote by ballot for two persons, of whom one at least shall not be an inhabitant of the same State with themselves. And they shall make a list of all the persons voted for, and of the number of votes for each; which list they shall sign and certify, and transmit sealed to the seat of the government of the United States, directed to the President of the Senate. The President of the Senate shall, in the presence of the Senate and House of Representatives, open all the certificates, and the votes shall then be counted. The person having the greatest number of votes shall be the President, if such number be a majority of the whole number of electors appointed; and if there be more than one who have such a majority, and have an equal number of votes, then the House of Representatives shall immediately choose by ballot one of them for President; and if no person have a majority, then, from the five highest on the list, the said House shall in like manner choose the President. But in choosing the President, the votes shall be taken by States; the representation from each State having one vote; a quorum for this purpose shall consist of a member or members from two-thirds of the States, and a majority of all the States shall be necessary to a choice. In every case, after the choice of the President, the person having the greatest number of votes of the electors

shall be Vice-President. But if there should remain two or more who have equal votes, the Senate shall choose from them by ballot the Vice-President.

4. The Congress may determine the time of choosing the electors and the day on which they shall give their votes, which day shall be the same throughout the United States.

5. No person except a natural-born citizen, or a citizen of the United States at the time of the adoption of this Constitution, shall be eligible to the office of President; neither shall any person be eligible to that office who shall not have attained to the age of thirty-five years, and been fourteen years a resident within the United States.

6. In case of the removal of the President from office, or of his death, resignation, or inability to discharge the powers and duties of the said office, the same shall devolve on the Vice-President; and the Congress may by law provide for the case of removal, death, resignation, or inability, both of the President and Vice-President, declaring what officer shall then act as President: and such officer shall act accordingly, until the disability be removed or a President shall be elected.

7. The President shall, at stated times, receive for his services a compensation, which shall neither be increased nor diminished during the period for which he shall have been elected, and he shall not receive within that period any other emolument from the United States, or any of them.

8. Before he enter on the execution of his office, he shall take the following oath or affirmation:

"I do solemnly swear (or affirm) that I will faithfully execute the office of President of the United States, and will, to the best of my ability, preserve, protect, and defend the Constitution of the United States."

SECTION II

1. The President shall be commander-in-chief of the army and navy of the United States and of the militia of the several States, when called into the actual service of the United States; he may require the opinion in writing of the principal officer in each of the executive departments, upon any subject relating to the duties of their respective offices; and he shall have power to grant reprieves and pardons for offences against the United States, except in cases of impeachment.

2. He shall have power, by and with the advice and consent of the Senate, to make treaties, provided two-thirds of the senators present concur: and he shall nominate, and by and with the advice and consent of the Senate, shall appoint ambassadors, other public ministers and consuls, judges of the Supreme Court, and all other officers of the United States, whose appointments are not herein otherwise provided for, and which shall be established by law. But the Congress may by law vest the appointment of such inferior officers as they think proper in the President alone, in the courts of law, or in the heads of departments.

3. The President shall have power to fill up all vacancies that may happen during the recess of the Senate, by granting commissions, which shall expire at the end of their next session.

SECTION III

1. He shall, from time to time, give to Congress information of the state of the Union, and recommend to their consideration such measures as he shall judge necessary and expedient; he may, on extraordinary occasions, convene both Houses, or either of them; and in case of disagreement between them, with respect to the time of adjournment, he may adjourn them to such time as he shall think proper; he shall receive ambassadors and other public ministers; he shall take care that the laws be faithfully executed; and shall commission all the officers of the United States.

SECTION IV

1. The President, Vice-President, and all civil officers of the United States, shall be removed from office on impeachment for and conviction of treason, bribery, or other high crimes and misdemeanors.

ARTICLE III

Of the Judiciary.

SECTION I

1. The judicial power of the United States shall be vested in one Supreme Court, and in such inferior courts as Congress may, from time to time, order and establish. The judges, both of the Supreme and inferior courts, shall hold their offices during good behaviour; and shall, at stated times, receive for their services a compensation, which shall not be diminished during their continuance in office.

SECTION II

1. The judicial power shall extend to all cases in law and equity arising under this Constitution, the laws of the United States, and treaties made, or which shall be made, under their authority; to all cases affecting ambassadors, other public ministers, and consuls; to all cases of admiralty and maritime jurisdiction; to controversies to which the United States shall be a party; to controversies between two or more states; between a State and citizens of another State; between citizens of different States; between citizens of the same State claiming lands under grants of different States; and between a State, or the citizens thereof and foreign States, citizens or subjects.

2. In all cases affecting ambassadors, other public ministers, and consuls, and those in which a State shall be a party, the Supreme Court shall have original jurisdiction. In all the other cases before mentioned, the Supreme Court shall have appellate jurisdiction, both as to law and fact, with such exceptions, and under such regulations as Congress shall make.

3. The trial of all crimes, except in cases of impeachment, shall be by jury, and such trial shall be held in the State where the said crimes shall have been committed; but when not committed within any State, the trial shall be at such place or places as Congress may by law have directed.

SECTION III

1. Treason against the United States shall consist only in levying war against them, or in adhering to their enemies, giving them aid and comfort. No person shall be convicted of treason, unless on the testimony of two witnesses to the same overt act, or confession in open court.

2. Congress shall have power to declare the punishment of treason; but no attainder of treason shall work corruption of blood, or forfeiture, except during the life of the person attainted.

ARTICLE IV

Miscellaneous.

SECTION I

1. Full faith and credit shall be given in each State to the public acts, records, and judicial proceedings of every other State. And Congress may, by general laws, prescribe the manner in which such acts, records, and proceedings shall be proved, and the effect thereof.

SECTION II

1. The citizens of each State shall be entitled to all the privileges and immunities of citizens in the several States.

2. A person charged in any State with treason, felony, or other crime, who shall flee from justice and be found in another State, shall, on demand of the executive authority of the State from which he fled, be delivered up, to be removed to the State having jurisdiction of the crime.

3. No person held to service or labour in one State, under the laws thereof, escaping into another, shall, in consequence of any law or regulation therein, be discharged from such service or labour; but shall be delivered up on claim of the party to whom such service or labour may be due.

SECTION III

1. New States may be admitted by Congress into this Union; but no new State shall be formed or erected within the jurisdiction of any other State, nor any State be formed by the junction of two or more States, or parts of States, without the consent of the legislatures of the States concerned, as well as of Congress.

2. Congress shall have power to dispose of, and make all needful rules and regulations respecting the territory, or other property belonging to the United States; and nothing in this Constitution shall be so construed as to prejudice any claims of the United States or of any particular State.

SECTION IV

1. The United States shall guarantee to every State in this union a republican form of government, and shall protect each of them against invasion; and, on application of the legislature, or of the executive (when the legislature cannot be convened), against domestic violence.

ARTICLE V

Of Amendments.

1. Congress, whenever two-thirds of both Houses shall deem it necessary, shall propose amendments to this Constitution; or, on the application of the legislatures of two-thirds of the several States, shall call a convention for proposing amendments, which, in either case, shall be valid to all intents and purposes, as part of this Constitution, when ratified by the legislatures of three-fourths of the several States, or by conventions in three-

fourths thereof, as the one or the other mode of ratification may be proposed by Congress; provided, that no amendment which may be made prior to the year one thousand eight hundred and eight, shall in any manner affect the first and fourth clauses in the ninth section of the first Article; and that no State, without its consent, shall be deprived of its equal suffrage in the Senate.

ARTICLE VI

Miscellaneous.

1. All debts contracted and engagements entered into, before the adoption of this Constitution, shall be as valid against the United States under this Constitution, as under the confederation.

2. This Constitution, and the laws of the United States which shall be made in pursuance thereof, and all treaties made, or which shall be made, under the authority of the United States, shall be the supreme law of the land; and the judges in every State shall be bound thereby, anything in the constitution or laws of any State to the contrary notwithstanding.

3. The senators and representatives before mentioned, and the members of the several State legislatures, and all executive and judicial officers, both of the United States, and of the several States, shall be bound by oath or affirmation to support this Constitution; but no religious test shall ever be required as a qualification to any office, or public trust, under the United States.

ARTICLE VII

Of the Ratification.

1. The ratification of the conventions of nine States shall be sufficient for the establishment of this Constitution between the States so ratifying the same.

> Done in Convention, by the unanimous consent of the States present, the seventeenth day of September, in the year of our Lord one thousand seven hundred and eighty-seven, and of the Independence of the United States of America the twelfth. In witness whereof, we have hereunto subscribed our names.

GEORGE WASHINGTON,
President, and Deputy from Virginia.

New Hampshire.
John Langdon,
Nicholas Gilman.

Massachusetts.
Nathaniel Gorman,
Rufus King.

Connecticut.
William Samuel Johnson,
Roger Sherman.

New York.
Alexander Hamilton.

New Jersey.
William Livingston,
David Brearly,
William Patterson,
Jonathan Dayton.

Pennsylvania.
Benjamin Franklin,
Thomas Mifflin,
Robert Morris,
George Clymer,
Thomas Fitzsimons,
Jared Ingersoll,
James Wilson,
Governeur Morris.

Delaware.
George Read,
Gunning Bedford, jun.,
John Dickinson,
Richard Bassett,
Jacob Broom.

Maryland.
James M'Henry,
Daniel of St. Tho. Jenifer,
Daniel Carroll.

Virginia.
John Blair,
James Madison, jr.

North Carolina.
William Blount,
Richard Dobbs Spaight,
Hugh Williamson.

South Carolina.
John Rutledge,
Chas. Cotesworth Pinckney,
Charles Pinckney,
Pierce Butler.

Georgia.
William Few,
Abraham Baldwin.

Attest.,   WILLIAM JACKSON, *Secretary.*

AMENDMENTS TO THE CONSTITUTION

Art. 1. Congress shall make no law respecting an establishment of religion, or prohibiting the free exercise thereof; or abridging the freedom of speech, or of the press; or the right of the people peaceably to assemble, and to petition the government for a redress of grievances.

Art. 2. A well-regulated militia being necessary to the security of a free State, the right of the people to keep and bear arms shall not be infringed.

Art. 3. No soldier shall, in time of peace, be quartered in any house without the consent of the owner; nor in time of war, but in a manner to be prescribed by law.

Art. 4. The right of the people to be secure in their persons, houses, papers, and effects, against unreasonable searches and seizures, shall not be violated; and no warrants shall issue but upon probable cause, supported by oath or affirmation, and particularly describing the place to be searched, and the persons or things to be seized.

Art. 5. No person shall be held to answer for a capital or otherwise infamous crime, unless on a presentment or indictment of a grand jury, except in cases arising in the land or naval forces, or in the militia when in actual service in time of war, or public danger; nor shall any person be subject for the same offence, to be put twice in jeopardy of life or limb; nor shall be compelled, in any criminal case, to be witness against himself; nor be deprived of life, liberty, or property, without due process of law; nor shall private property be taken for public use without just compensation.

Art. 6. In all criminal prosecutions, the accused shall enjoy the right to a speedy and public trial, by an impartial jury of the State and district wherein the crime shall have been committed, which district shall have been previously ascertained by law, and to be informed of the nature and cause of the accusation; to be confronted with the witnesses against him; to have compulsory process for obtaining witnesses in his favour; and to have the assistance of counsel for his defence.

Art. 7. In suits at common law, where the value in controversy shall exceed twenty dollars, the right of trial by jury shall be preserved; and no fact tried by jury shall be otherwise re-examined in any court of the United States than according to the rules of the common law.

Art. 8. Excessive bail shall not be required, nor excessive fines imposed, nor cruel and unusual punishments inflicted.

Art. 9. The enumeration in the Constitution of certain rights, shall not be construed to deny or disparage others retained by the people.

Art. 10. The powers not delegated to the United States by the Constitution, nor prohibited by it to the States, are reserved to the States respectively, or to the people.

Art. 11. The judicial power of the United States shall not be construed to extend to any suit in law or equity commenced or prosecuted against one of the United States by citizens of another State, or by citizens or subjects of another State, or by citizens or subjects of any foreign State.

Art. 12. § 1. The electors shall meet in their respective States, and vote by ballot for President and Vice-President, one of whom, at least, shall not be an inhabitant of the same State as themselves; they shall name in their ballots the person voted for as President, and in distinct ballots the person voted for with Vice-President; and they shall make distinct lists of all persons voted for as President, and of all persons voted for as Vice-President, and of the number of votes for each, which list they shall sign and certify, and transmit sealed to the seat of government of the United States, directed to the President of the Senate: the President of the Senate shall in the presence of the Senate and House of Representatives, open all the certificates, and the votes shall then be counted; the person having the greatest number of votes for President shall be the President, if such number be a majority of the whole number of electors appointed; and if no person have such a majority, then from the persons having the highest numbers, not exceeding three, on the list of those voted for as President, the House of Representatives shall choose immediately by ballot the President. But in choosing the President, the votes shall be taken by States, the representation from each State having one vote; a quorum for this purpose shall consist of a member or members from two-thirds of the States, and a majority of all the States shall be necessary to a choice. And if the House of Representatives shall not choose a President whenever the right of choice shall devolve upon them, before the fourth day of March next following, then the Vice-President shall act as President, as in the case of the death or other constitutional disability of the President.

2. The person having the greatest number of votes as Vice-President, shall be the Vice-President, if such number be a majority of the whole number of electors appointed; and if no person have a majority, then from the two highest numbers on the list, the Senate shall choose the Vice-President: a quorum for the purpose shall consist of two-thirds of the whole number of senators, and a majority of the whole number shall be necessary to a choice.

3. But no person constitutionally ineligible to the office of President shall be eligible to that of Vice-President of the United States.

Note.—At the fourth presidential election, Thomas Jefferson and Aaron Burr were the democratic candidates for President and Vice-President. By the electoral returns they had an even number of votes. In the House of Representatives, Burr, by intrigue, got up a party to vote for him for President; and the House was so divided that there was a tie. A contest was carried on for several days, and so warmly, that even sick members were brought to the House on their beds. Finally one of Burr's adherents withdrew, and Jefferson was elected by one majority—which was the occasion of this twelfth article.